Health Issues among Incarcerated Women

Health Issues among Incarcerated Women

EDITED BY

RONALD L. BRAITHWAITE

KIMBERLY JACOB ARRIOLA

CASSANDRA NEWKIRK

RUTGERS UNIVERSITY PRESS

NEW BRUNSWICK, NEW JERSEY, AND LONDON

Library of Congress Cataloging-in-Publication Data

Health issues among incarcerated women / edited by Ronald L. Braithwaite, Kimberly Jacob Arriola, and
Cassandra Newkirk.
    p. ; cm.
  Includes bibliographical references and index.
  ISBN-13: 978-0-8135-3690-3 (hardcover : alk. paper)
  ISBN-13: 978-0-8135-3691-0 (pbk. : alk. paper)
  1. Women prisoners–Medical care–United States. 2. Women prisoners–Health and hygiene–United
States. I. Braithwaite, Ronald L., 1945- II. Arriola, Kimberly Jacob, 1972- III. Newkirk, Cassandra.
  HV8843.H43   2006

  A British Cataloging-in-Publication record for this book is available from the British Library

Manufactured in the United States of America

This book is dedicated to all of the women behind the walls who are struggling to survive.

CONTENTS

PART ONE
Toward Understanding the Need

PART TWO
Mental Health and Addictive Behaviors

PART THREE
Sexual and Reproductive Health

PART FOUR
Infectious Diseases

PART FIVE
Chronic Conditions

PART SIX
Social, Political and Environmental Issues

LIST OF TABLES

LIST OF FIGURES

ACKNOWLEDGMENTS

This book is the result of many dedicated persons believing in the need to draw attention to the health needs and issues among incarcerated women. A debt of gratitude is due to our families, who provided encouragement and support during the various stages of this project. We are especially thankful to our many graduate students at the Rollins School of Public Health of Emory University, who provided research assistance during the final stages of this effort. They include Tracy Louden, Nancy Sprauve, Margaret Farrow, Temituoyo Louis, and Lashawnda Lindsey. We are also grateful for the technical support provided by Richard Gooden during the conceptual stages of the project and Vanessa Braithwaite's efforts during the final editing stage. This project would not have come to fruition without the clerical support provided by Keisha Marshall and Betty Stevens. Lastly, we express sincere appreciation to Audra Wolfe at Rutgers University Press. Without her untiring efforts, this book would not have seen the light.

Health Issues
among Incarcerated Women

DAVID SATCHER

One of the two goals of *Healthy People 2010* is the elimination of disparities in health among different racial, ethnic, and socioeconomic groups. It is clear that if we are to be successful in eliminating disparities in health, we must better understand the needs of incarcerated women. These women represent a group who is highly disenfranchised; marginalized; and ill-prepared to survive, lead healthy lives, and serve as good parents and citizens.

Men tend to be significantly more represented in the incarcerated population than women in our society. However, for more than a decade now, the rate of increase of women among the incarcerated has been much greater than that among men. Women who are incarcerated tend to reflect significant failure on the part of society in that they are most likely to have been victims of physical and sexual abuse as children and to have been in abusive relationships as adults. They have the greatest risk for mental health and substance abuse problems, infectious diseases such as hepatitis C and HIV/AIDS, and of being left out of the health care system in this country.

If incarcerated women reflect the failure of our society to provide a group of our citizens the kind of opportunities and protection that they deserve, then the question becomes whether the experience of incarceration is one that contributes to improving their lives. We want incarceration not only to protect society from offenders, where this is felt to be needed, but to rehabilitate them such that once they leave jail or prison, they are better prepared to function as good citizens, good parents, and generally good people.

The answer to this question is mixed as seen throughout this book dealing with the health needs of incarcerated women. It is certainly true that women in jail or prison are more likely to receive health care and even quality health care for substance abuse, mental health problems, infectious diseases, and chronic diseases than women from this same group in the general population. And therefore incarceration provides a potential opportunity for women in this group to receive access to the kind of care that was denied them in the general population. However, there are many women who are not able to take advantage of this opportunity because correctional facilities vary widely in terms of the services that they offer and the quality of these services. And almost invariably, when women are discharged or released from jail or prison, they are not likely to receive the continuity of care or involvement in protection of their health that they received in prison. This is a problem not only for formerly incarcerated women but for the communities to which they return.

Incarcerated women are also members of families. In fact, more than two-thirds of women in prison have minor children, and 80 percent of them have children of some age. When women are incarcerated, most of the time, their children do not receive continuity of parenting. Many women are not able to receive visits from their children and many of them lose custody of their children. So incarceration often leads to the breakup of family; it often leads to children either staying with grandparents or becoming dependent on foster care. There are many indications that the experience that children have when their mothers are in prison is one that increases the risk that they will also be the victims of the kinds of circumstances that led to the imprisonment of their mothers, and therefore, the incarceration of women increases the risk that society will also have to incarcerate their children. Thus incarcerated women have experiences that negatively impact not only themselves but their families and the communities from which they come.

There are certainly examples of meritorious programs, and it should be pointed out that states and correctional facilities vary widely in the kind of experiences that they provide for incarcerated women. Some states provide opportunities for women with substance abuse problems to enter drug courts and to receive the kind of attention and care that they would not have otherwise received, benefiting not only the women but their families and their communities. Some states provide opportunities for family courts, in which special efforts are made to make sure that the family remains together and that incarcerated women in fact improve their parenting skills and their relationships with their children and other family members. Some correctional facilities make sure that women receive quality health care and treatment for mental health, substance abuse, and other health problems that these women disproportionately experience.

But what happens to women when they are released from jail or prison—even from facilities that have the best services available? Unfortunately, all too often, there is very little planning for reintegration of women into the communities from which they come. Many women do not receive health screening during their incarceration, so when they return to their communities, they are more likely to be vehicles for the spread of contagious diseases such as HIV/AIDS, hepatitis C, and, in some cases, tuberculosis. In addition, many of the contracted health care providers in correctional facilities do not make the necessary contacts with the public health system in the community to assure that there is continuity of care. This is especially serious when dealing with women who are victims of substance abuse or substance addiction, as well as women who have had their infectious diseases controlled or stabilized during incarceration but are also threats to spread these diseases once they return to their communities. Thus discharge planning and the reintegration of women into society is a major problem.

This book, *Health Issues among Incarcerated Women,* is on the one hand a shocking look into the magnitude of the problems facing these women before, during, and after they leave incarceration. But on the other hand, it provides a tremendous opportunity for us to change the way things are done, identify exemplary models for the incarceration of women in the United States, and to try to raise the level of our engagement with these women to one that would better promote their health and the health of their families, their communities, and our nation in general. This is potentially a major contribution to the future of health care in this country and to the elimination of disparities in health.

DAVID SATCHER
Interim President, Morehouse School of Medicine,
sixteenth U.S. Surgeon General

PART ONE

Toward Understanding
the Need

1

An Overview of Incarcerated Women's Health

KIMBERLY JACOB ARRIOLA
RONALD L. BRAITHWAITE
CASSANDRA F. NEWKIRK

I am an invisible man. No, I am not a spook like those who haunted Edgar Allan Poe; nor am I one of your Hollywood-movie ectoplasms. I am a man of substance, of flesh and bone, fiber and liquids—and I might even be said to possess a mind. I am invisible, understand, simply because people refuse to see me. . . . When they approach me they see only my surroundings, them-selves, or figments of their imagination—indeed, everything and anything except me.

—Ralph Ellison

Although originally written to chronicle the plight of one who was both black and American, Ralph Ellison's *Invisible Man* (1952/1982) also describes the angst that American society feels towards incarcerated populations, particularly incarcerated women. Largely African American, many incarcerated women bear the *quadruple* burden of their race/ethnicity, class, gender, and status as a criminal offender. That membership in these social groups—African American, woman, poor, criminal offender—confers serious health risk is clear. *How* group member-ship is embodied is much less clear. The invisibility of incarcerated women has resulted in little research and policy development that would advance their health status. Thus it is no surprise that in large part, their health is ailing as compared to incarcerated men and women in the general population (Maruschak and Beck 1997).

Incarcerated women face many of the same health concerns that women in the general population face, only with more frequency and greater seriousness of disease, illness, and injury (Maruschak and Beck 1997). The poorer health status of incarcerated women exists for several reasons. First, as previously mentioned, the majority of incarcerated women are poor people of color who were unemployed and lacked access to proper health care prior to arrest. This sociodemographic group perhaps fares worse than any other when considering health disparities in the United States. It is no coincidence that the people who suffer poor health status are also the ones who are disproportionately incarcerated in the United States: the poor health status of incarcerated women reflects the inequalities that exist in the social, political, and economic structures of the larger society. Second, incarceration itself may negatively impact the health of female inmates (Freudenberg 2002; Marquart et al. 1997; Stoller 2003). It has been argued that access to health care in correctional settings is "continually thwarted by rules, custodial priorities, poor health care management, incompetence, and indifference" (Stoller 2003, 2263). Acoca (1998) adds to this list of internal impediments the loss of freedom to engage in basic self-care and the physical environment of correctional facilities (for example, constant loud noise, unsanitary eating and toilet facilities, and so forth). Third, many of the same behaviors that led to women's incarceration also negatively impact their health. For example, illegal drug use and commercial sex work are behaviors that contribute to the increasing number of women being incarcerated and the higher prevalence of HIV/AIDS among incarcerated women as compared to women in the general population (De Groot 2000; Watson, Stimpson, and Hostick 2004). There are multiple causes for incarcerated women being of relatively poor health status, so there must be multiple solutions to this problem.

Sociodemographic Characteristics of Female Inmates

The number of women in U.S. jails and prisons has dramatically increased over the past decade and is increasing at a rate higher than that of men. Jails are locally operated correctional facilities that confine individuals who are awaiting arraignment or trial; those who are being temporarily detained or awaiting transfer to a state, federal, or health facility; and those with a sentence of one year or less (Bonczar and Beck 2003). State and federal prisons house convicted offenders with sentences of more than one year. The male prison population and the number of men sentenced to more than one year has increased by 82 percent from 1990 to 2002, but the female prison population and the number of women sentenced to more than one year has increased by 118 percent and 115 percent, respectively (Beck, Karberg, and Harrison 2002; Harrison and Karberg 2003; see table 1.1). Unfortunately, the growth in the female prison population has not led to an increase in specialized services for women (OJS Special Report 1998). Health services for incarcerated women continue to be subpar, with less availability than the care offered to male offenders (Acoca 1998). It is often argued that because women comprise a much smaller proportion of the correctional population than men, less attention and fewer resources are needed to deliver health services to incar-

TABLE 1.1

Prisoners in state or federal facilities, by gender, 1990, 2000, 2001

	Men	Women
All inmates		
12/31/90	729,840	44,065
12/31/95	1,057,406	68,468
6/30/01	1,311,195	94,336
6/30/02	1,330,019	96,099
Percent change	82.2%	118.1%
Sentenced to more than 1 year		
12/31/90	699,416	40,564
12/31/95	1,021,059	63,963
6/30/01	1,257,246	86,301
6/30/02	1,273,881	87,317
Percent change	82.1%	115.3%
*Incarceration rate**		
12/31/90	572	32
12/31/95	781	47
6/30/01	900	59
6/30/02	902	60
Rate change	330	28

* The total number of prisoners with a sentence of more than one year per 100,000 U.S. residents.

Adapted from Beck, Karberg, and Harrison (2002) and Harrison and Karberg (2003).

cerated women. However, the dramatically increasing female inmate population and the specialized reproductive health needs of women undermine the utility of this argument (Anderson in press).

Aside from the increasing numbers, one may wonder what the typical female inmate looks like. Her profile is quite different than that of many women in the general population. The median age of women incarcerated in federal, state, and local facilities is thirty-six, thirty-three, and thirty-one years old, respectively (Greenfeld and Snell 1999). Approximately half of these women have at least a high school education. Half of the women in prison and almost 75 percent of the women in jail were unemployed upon arrest (Snell and Morton 1994). African Americans are disproportionately represented in correctional facilities (Beck, Karberg, and Harrison 2002). In every age group, black women have a higher

TABLE 1.2

Number of female inmates in state or federal prisons and local jails per 100,000 residents, by race, Hispanic origin, and age, 2002

Number of female inmates per 100,000 residents

Age	Total*	White†	Black†	Hispanic
Total	113	68	349	137
18–19	100	67	233	133
20–24	230	158	520	287
25–29	282	170	752	314
30–34	348	213	1,024	366
35–39	297	183	924	302
40–44	187	107	650	193
45–54	83	50	281	120
55 or older	9	7	25	17

* Includes American Indians, Alaska Natives, Asians, Native Hawaiians, and other Pacific Islanders

† Excludes Hispanics.

Adapted from Harrison and Karberg (2003).

incarceration rate than whites and Hispanics (see table 1.2). Specifically, African American women are seven times more likely to be incarcerated in their lifetime than white women and two times more likely to be incarcerated than Hispanic women (see table 1.3). In 1998, although women of color comprised only 26 percent of women in the United States, they represented between 64 percent and 71 percent of the inmates in jails and state and federal prisons (Greenfeld and Snell 1999).

Incarcerated women are more likely than women in the general population to have grown up with only one parent and to have had at least one immediate family member who had been incarcerated (Beck, Karberg, and Harrison 2002). Women tend to be incarcerated for nonviolent drug or property offenses (Beck, Karberg, and Harrison 2002; Greenfeld and Snell 1999; National Women's Law Center 1995; OJP Special Report 1998). One-third of incarcerated women reported having been abused by an intimate partner in the past (Beck, Karberg, and Harrison 2002). Between 44 percent and 60 percent report having been physically or sexually assaulted at some point in their lives, and nearly 70 percent of incarcerated women were abused before the age of eighteen (see table 1.4; Beck, Karberg, and Harrison 2002; Greenfeld and Snell 1999). Among state prisoners, men and women are equally likely to have used drugs in the past, but women are more likely to have used drugs within one month of their incarceration. However, women in federal

TABLE 1.3

Prevalence (per 100,000) of imprisonment in women, by age and lifetime prevalence

Age	White	Black	Hispanic
20	–	3	1
25	2	11	4
30	3	20	7
35	4	27	9
40	4	31	12
45	5	33	13
50	5	34	14
55	5	35	15
65	5	36	15
Lifetime	5	36	15

Adapted from Greenfeld and Snell (1999).

TABLE 1.4

History of physical and/or sexual abuse in women prisoners

	Probation %	Local jails %	State prisons %
Ever abused			
Physically	15	10	18
Sexually	7	10	11
Both	18	27	28
Ever physically or sexually abused	41	48	57
Before age 18	16	21	12
After age 18	13	11	20
Both periods	13	16	25

Adapted from Greenfeld and Snell (1999).

TABLE 1.5

Drug use in state and federal prisoners, 1997

	Male	*Female*	*Total*
State prisoners			
Total number of prisoners	993,365	66,242	1,059,607
Ever in the past	83%	84%	83%
Used regularly	69%	74%	70%
Used in the month prior to offense	56%	62%	57%
Used at the time of the offense	32%	40%	33%
Federal prisoners			
Total number of prisoners	82,646	6,426	89,072
Ever in the past	74%	63%	73%
Used regularly	58%	47%	57%
Used in the month prior to offense	45%	67%	45%
Used at the time of the offense	23%	19%	22%

Adapted from Mumola (1999).

prisons are less likely than men to report having ever used drugs and are also less likely to report using drugs within one month of incarceration (see table 1.5).

Two-thirds of incarcerated women have children under the age of eighteen while approximately 15 percent have infants less than six weeks old (Greenfeld and Snell 1999; Snell and Morton 1994). Between 5 and 10 percent of women enter correctional facilities pregnant (*Birth and development* 2004; National Women's Law Center 1995). Approximately 1.3 million children in the United States have mothers who are incarcerated (Greenfeld and Snell 1999). Since each state has only a few prisons designated specifically for women, mothers are usually incarcerated farther away from home than fathers (Beck, Karberg, and Harrison 2002). Bloom and Steinhart (1993) estimate that more than 60 percent of children with incarcerated mothers live over 100 miles away from their mother's prison.

Health Concerns of Female Inmates

Incarcerated women face multiple serious health concerns before, during, and after their incarceration. These health concerns generally relate to their mental health and addictive behaviors, sexual and reproductive health, infectious diseases, and chronic diseases. However, some behaviors and health conditions are particularly relevant to the lives of incarcerated women. Mullen, Cummins, Velasquez, von Sternberg, and Carvajal (2003) identified three risk factors that are highly prevalent among incarcerated women: (1) the use of illicit drugs and drug addiction, (2) unprotected sex with multiple and high-risk partners, and (3) mental health problems. Each of these risk factors will be considered in turn.

Illicit Drug Use and Addiction

As previously stated, incarcerated women have experienced high levels of violence and abuse in their lives. It is hypothesized that many individuals who have not recovered from violent trauma use alcohol and drugs as a way to manage the pain, which then puts them at risk for revictimization. Thus, there is an endless cycle of violence, abuse, and drug use in the lives of many incarcerated women. Data clearly show that drug use accounts for a disproportionate number of arrests and convictions among women (Beck, Karberg, and Harrison 2002; Greenfeld and Snell 1999). For example, 18 percent of females arrested in 1998 were arrested for drug offenses (this does not include the large number of individuals who engaged in violent or property offenses to support a drug habit). Of female felony convictions in state courts, 37 percent were convicted of drug felonies in 1996. Moreover, 25 percent of women report committing their offense to support their drug habit, and victim self-reports indicate that about 40 percent of female violent offenders appeared to be under the influence of alcohol and/or drugs at the time of the offense. For the period from 1990 to 1996, drug offenses accounted for 19 percent of women offenders on probation, 30 percent of women in local jails, 34 percent of women in state prisons, and 72 percent of women in federal prisons (Greenfeld and Snell 1999). Thus, it is clear that illicit drug use and abuse plays an important role in the large number of women being incarcerated. Despite these alarming statistics, drug use among female detainees remains largely an untreated problem (Haywood et al. 2000).

Unprotected Sex with Multiple and High-Risk Partners

Women who use drugs are more likely to have multiple and high-risk sexual partners than women who do not use drugs, which puts them at risk for contracting HIV and other sexually transmitted infections (Cotten-Oldenburg et al. 1999). Having sex in exchange for money, drugs, or shelter makes women particularly vulnerable to infection because of the number of partners and the power differential that may prohibit them from insisting on barrier methods of contraception. Sex exchange is particularly detrimental to women's health in the context of substance abuse because it may be the most lucrative way to obtain money or drugs, and contraception is not likely to be a priority. Moreover, women may come in contact with partners who inject drugs or have a sexually transmitted infection (El-Bassel et al. 1996). Unfortunately, it is often the case that substance abuse, sex exchange, and poor health converge in the lives of incarcerated women. In many cases, it is the substance abuse or sex exchange that causes women to be arrested, but ultimately the poor health must be addressed by correctional health care staff and programs (Cotten-Oldenburg et al. 1999).

Mental Health Problems

Surveillance data clearly indicate high rates of psychiatric disorders among incarcerated women as compared to women in the general population. With the deinstitutionalization of the mentally ill in the 1960s and 1970s, many individuals with severe mental illness have entered the criminal justice system instead of the mental health system (Lamb and Weinberger 2001). Research suggests that 19 percent of female pretrial detainees have a lifetime prevalence of severe disorders (including schizophrenia, manic episodes, and major depressive episodes). Moreover, 34 percent have had post-traumatic stress disorder, 14 percent have had antisocial personality disorder, and 10 percent have had dysthymic disorder. Of the women entering jail, 81 percent have had at least one psychiatric disorder over the course of their lives (Teplin, Abram, and McClelland 1996). The prevalence of psychiatric disorders among women convicted of a felony is quite similar; 13 percent have had a major depressive episode, 12 percent have had antisocial personality disorder, 7 percent have had dysthymia, and 64 percent have had at least one psychiatric disorder over the course of their lives (Jordan et al. 1996). According to Kaplan and Sadock (1998), these prevalence estimates are much larger than those for men and women in the general population who both have lifetime prevalence estimates of approximately 33 percent.

Mental illness appears to magnify the negative life circumstances that individuals experienced prior to incarceration (Ditton 1999). For example, inmates with severe mental illness were more likely than other inmates to be homeless and unemployed prior to arrest. They report higher rates of physical and sexual abuse than other inmates and more alcohol and drug use than other inmates. It is well documented that psychiatric disorders and alcohol and drug abuse disorders are highly co-morbid. Research suggests that 72 percent of female jail detainees with a severe mental disorder also have an alcohol or drug use disorder (Abram, Teplin, and McClelland 2003). A survey conducted by the Bureau of Justice Statistics revealed that mentally ill state inmates were more likely than other inmates to be under the influence of alcohol or drugs while committing their current offense (Ditton 1999).

There are three hypothesized pathways through which mental illness is linked to criminal behavior: (1) mentally ill individuals commit misdemeanor offenses that involve survival behaviors; (2) those with character disorders also abuse alcohol and drugs, which leads to criminal behavior; and (3) the severely disordered person engages in violent and nonviolent criminal offenses (Hiday 1999). It is evident that early experiences of abuse, substance abuse, poverty, mental illness, and HIV risk behavior oftentimes work together to impact women's likelihood of engaging in criminal behavior.

Why Should We Care about the Health of Incarcerated Women?

The general public tends to be apathetic regarding the health of correctional inmates. Indeed, many individuals feel that it is unfair that both pretrial and convicted inmates have a constitutional right to medical care since this right is not afforded to members of the general population (Sylla and Thomas 2000). If not for inmates' rights advocates (for example, Prison Activist Resource Center, the Western Prison Project, the American Civil Liberties Union, and the Legislative Action Coalition on Prison Health), correctional administrators would feel little pressure to advance the health of female inmates. With the assistance of inmate advocates, most correctional health care reform has occurred because of litigation that resulted in court mandates for correctional facilities to make improvements.

Court mandates aside, as researchers, health care providers, correctional officials, and policymakers, we *should* care about the health of female inmates. Most importantly, female inmates are still human beings. In fact, they are human beings whose health is poor compared to women in the general population and incarcerated men. Thus, health care and public health professionals have a moral and ethical obligation to help improve their health status despite the fact that they have been charged with or convicted of committing a crime. There are professional organizations and accrediting bodies that help ensure the quality of care that is delivered in correctional facilities. The National Commission on Correctional Health Care offers health services accreditation that correctional facilities may obtain on a voluntary basis and has issued a position statement on women's health care in correctional settings (2005). The American Psychiatric Association, American Public Health Association, and American Correctional Association have guidelines for the delivery of services in correctional settings. Women's firsthand experiences of being incarcerated are chronicled in Galbraith (1998). They express the great need to have health care professionals become more humane. They express the view that it is futile to punish them without treatment because to do so decreases the likelihood of their ability to take some control and responsibility for their lives and futures. Neither they nor society are any better off for having incarcerated them if there is no change in their lives.

It is the case that the majority of incarcerated women will return to society; by and large, they do not serve life sentences. Thus, it is crucial that all efforts are made to prepare these women for reentry into society and not have them return to the circumstances that led them to jail or prison. Without reentry assistance, women are likely to return to the criminal and health risk behavior that led to their incarceration. Whatever health concerns go unaddressed during incarceration will still exist once the former offender has returned to the community. Upon release, any infectious disease that an ex-offender has, for example, may be transmitted to individuals in the general population. It is for this reason that many public health professionals argue that risk reduction policies implemented by correctional policymakers to advance the health and well-being of incarcerated populations will ultimately impact the community at large (Braithwaite and Arriola 2003).

Not only is addressing the medical and mental health needs important from a public health perspective, but it is also important because inadequately trained medical and mental health staff may cause more harm than good to some inmates. Health care professionals that work in a correctional environment often appear inhumane because of ambivalent feelings towards the women. Taylor (2001) states that some health care professionals continue to perpetuate sexist and racist attitudes and practices, which corroborates the stories that incarcerated women tell about the health care they received in jails and prisons. Galbraith (1998) reports that medical exams are often cold and impersonal, often conducted by male physicians that do not explain what they are doing, which serves to further traumatize an already terrified woman. This behavior is perceived as representing yet another uncaring individual in their lives. Galbraith relates that women who have been incarcerated tell of being made to feel less than human by medical professionals who use distancing mechanisms. Medical professionals oftentimes do not realize the consequences of their behavior as there is little understanding of the women's histories and the consequences of such behavior.

Purpose of This Book

Several books (Galbraith 1998; Gonnerman 2004; Lamb 2003; Watterson 1996) have been published that present firsthand accounts of women's experiences from behind the walls. Women who have experienced incarceration also contributed to this book. These accounts all too often relate how difficult it is to access adequate health care in correctional settings. Keamy (1998) acknowledges that although women are most often housed in separate facilities, they are subjected to the same programs, policies, and procedures that govern their male counterparts, including health care. Keamy additionally states that the health services provided to women may fail to address issues related to reproductive function as well as the complex psychosocial issues of these women. This book is an attempt to provide more in-depth information about medical and mental health issues of incarcerated women from a gender-specific perspective.

Women, no matter their ethnic or cultural background, often feel invisible. Galbraith (1998) postulates that societies teach women to recede and that they are not as important as men. Because they are not considered as important, the issues that arise in their lives are often downplayed by all segments of society including health care professionals. According to Taylor (2001), African American women suffer a disproportionate risk of ill health just because of their race, and the penal system is yet another health hazard for these women.

This book is an attempt to dispel some of the misperceptions and misunderstandings about the health issues of incarcerated women. With heightened understanding, it is hoped that health care professionals will be more sensitive with the result being improved health care for women who are incarcerated. It is also our hope that policymakers will be influenced to advocate for the necessary changes that would lead to more appropriate gender-specific care and that researchers will find the information they need to advance current understanding of this topic.

In most settings where women receive health care, correctional settings included, the psychosocial issues are not addressed although these issues may have a major impact on the subjective as well as objective complaints of the woman patient. In the controlled environment of a correctional facility, these psychosocial influences are even greater because the woman has almost no control of anything in her environment. This lack of attention to psychological issues also leads to exacerbation of physical complaints. These complaints may present as nonspecific pain and a sense of uneasiness. The histories of trauma and subsequent substance abuse often lead to the development of disabling mental illnesses. When women present to the medical staff with vague and nonspecific complaints, they are often overlooked because clinicians become desensitized and take on the correctional jargon that "they just want attention." One of the goals of this book is to provide information regarding the intricate and often complex presentations of medical and psychological symptoms in the closed correctional environment. How health care professionals navigate such a system to provide adequate and gender-specific care is explored.

Galbraith (1998) reminds us that it is well known that many women develop psychological symptoms of mental distress at an early age as a way of dealing with the trauma in their lives. Health care professionals seldom take histories that elicit this information, and the authors of this book will explore ways of eliciting this sensitive but necessary information. Suicide attempts and self-injurious behaviors are more common among women who have been traumatized than men. This behavior is often a cry for help rather than a desire to end their lives. Herman (1997) explains that self-injurious behavior is a way for the numbed trauma survivor to jolt herself into feeling something, even if it is pain. Although mental health professionals understand this behavior, most correctional health care professionals become frustrated because their job then becomes to keep the woman from harming herself again. This book will help all health care professionals gain an appreciation for these complex issues that must be dealt with every day when working with incarcerated women who cannot get away from their pain.

This book is a useful tool for health care professionals who currently work with women in a correctional environment or students of criminal justice. Health care professionals who work in correctional settings and researchers who study this population will find the information useful as the chapters on specific disorders have been written with the special needs of incarcerated women in mind.

Overview of the Book

The introductory chapters of the book present a framework from which to begin to understand the special health care needs of incarcerated women. The introduction provides a general overview. Chapter 2 explores the issue of diversity among women who are incarcerated in this country and looks at the culture of the correctional setting. Chapter 3 presents the powerful stories of two women who have been incarcerated and experienced health care delivery in prison firsthand. Violence and abuse play a large role in the lives of incarcerated women and is discussed in chapter 4. All too often, adult women who are incarcerated had at least one arrest as an adolescent and wound up in the juvenile system. Chapter 5 addresses the health and mental health issues of girls in the juvenile justice system.

The next section of the book deals with disorders that arise secondary to psychosocial factors in the lives of women. Women suffer from the same mental illnesses as men, but some are more prevalent among women than men. Schizophrenia is not addressed specifically in this volume, but the prevalence of this disorder is 0.5 percent to 1.5 percent among both men and women according to the American Psychiatric Association's *Diagnostic and Statistical Manual of Mental Disorders* (2000). Bipolar disorder is discussed in chapter 6 on mood disorders. Depression and bipolar disorder will be discussed at length because women offenders suffer depression to a much greater extent than their male counterparts. Chapter 7 addresses the spectrum of anxiety disorders, including post-traumatic stress disorder, which is often underdiagnosed in the correctional setting although many women have histories of abuse. Chapters 8 and 9 deal with important aspects of substance abuse, including drug courts and risky sexual behaviors that are secondary to the illicit drug abuse.

Chapters 10 and 11 present information on prenatal care and reproductive health that are unique to women. Chapter 11 also presents vital information regarding the appropriate intake medical screening and assessments that all women entering a correctional setting should have access to.

Infectious diseases that are prevalent among incarcerated women are presented in chapters 12 through 14. The presentation and treatment of tuberculosis, hepatitis C, and HIV/AIDS in correctional settings among women is explored. Chapter 15 presents pertinent information regarding adherence to antiretroviral therapy among women in this setting as the habits acquired in this environment regarding treatment of HIV/AIDS may mean the difference between life and death.

Cancer, with a special focus on those more prevalent in women, is written about in chapter 16. Asthma is presented in chapter 17 and is included because of the high rates of asthma among women in the United States.

The topic of legal and ethical issues unique to women is presented in chapter 18 as it is an often-overlooked topic. These issues are unique to women as they reenter society and try to resume their parenting roles. Chapter 19 deals with those special issues of reentry that will be different than that of the male offender. Chapter 20 presents information on compassionate release for women suffering from chronic and/or terminal illnesses.

Conclusion

This book does not purport to be an exhaustive treatment on all of the conceivable health issues facing incarcerated female offenders. For example, diabetes and obesity are two of the most common disorders found among this population and must be considered and dealt with in all settings that care for incarcerated women. Neither of these topics was included due to limited resources available to adequately address them. Additionally, there are health issues specific to the needs of lesbian and bisexual women that go unaddressed in this book due to a lack of resources. Finally, outside of several personal accounts, this book has little information about the range of health rights that are violated by correctional facilities. The unique health needs among incarcerated females should not and cannot be underestimated. There is an old adage that directs macro systems to pay now or pay later. This adage seems appropriate here as we recount the number of discrepancies that divide the health status of whites and people of color across the inmate population.

In social marketing, corporate America places a premium on "knowing your customer." If rehabilitation is to ever be realized within the American correctional system, we will need to know more about its correctional population and what makes it tick. This is especially true for female inmates as related to their health status. For some information, one could argue that it is "nice" to know, but for so much of the information related to disease prevention and health promotion, there are mountains of information that one *needs* to know. For example, one might need to know the pre-incarceration mental health status of inmates before releasing them in the general population. Similarly, the medical history taken at intake should be comprehensive enough to identify chronic and/or communicable illness. Consequently, interventions developed must be culturally relevant and tailored for the emphasis population. A big error is made when the female population's wants and needs are built based on male prototypes. We must invest as a nation in the prevention of criminality among all inmates, but this investment may take a different form for female offenders. We know so little about the dynamics of institutional life upon them; and what we do know about the long-term impact of incarceration on their children, family, and communities is not good.

REFERENCES

Abram, K. M., L. A. Teplin, and G. M. McClelland. 2003. Comorbidity of severe psychiatric disorders and substance use disorders among women in jail. *American Journal of Psychiatry* 160: 1007–10.

Acoca, L. 1998. Diffusing the time bomb: Understanding and meeting the growing health care needs of incarcerated women in America. *Crime and Delinquency* 44: 46–69.

American Psychiatric Association. 2000. *Diagnostic and statistical manual of mental disorders,* 4th ed. Washington, DC: American Psychiatric Association.

Anderson, T. L. Forthcoming. Issues in the availability of health care for women prisoners. In *Female prisoners in the United States: Programming needs, availability, and efficacy,* ed. S. Sharp. Newark, NJ: Prentice Hall.

Anderson, T. L., A. B. Rosay, and C. Saum. 2002. The impact of drug use and crime involvement on health problems among female drug offenders. *Prison Journal* 82: 50–68.

Beck, A., J. Karberg, and P. Harrison. 2002. *Prison and jail inmates at midyear 2001* (NCJ 191702). Washington, DC: Bureau of Justice Statistics. http://www.ojp.usdoj.gov/bjs/pub/pdf/pjimo1.pdf (accessed May 11, 2004).

Birth and development of children of incarcerated women in the United States. 2004. Dickinson College. http://www.dickinson.edu/~egica/researchprisons.html (accessed April 30, 2004).

Bloom, B., and D. Steinhart. 1993. *Why punish the children? A reappraisal of the children of incarcerated mothers in America.* San Francisco, CA: National Council on Crime and Delinquency.

Bonczar, T., and A. Beck. 2003. Lifetime likelihood of going to state or federal prison. U.S. Department of Justice, Bureau of Justice Statistics Special Report.

Braithwaite, R. L., and K. J. Arriola. 2003. Male prisoners and HIV prevention: A call for action ignored. *American Journal of Public Health* 93: 759–63.

Cotten-Oldenburg, N. U., B. K. Jordan, S. L. Martin, and L. Kupper. 1999. Women inmates' risky sex and drug behaviors: Are they related? *American Journal of Drug and Alcohol Abuse* 25: 129–49.

De Groot, A. 2000. HIV infection among incarcerated women: Epidemic behind bars. *AIDS Reader* 10: 287–95.

Ditton, P. M. 1999. *Mental health and treatment of inmates and probationers.* NCJ 174463. U.S. Department of Justice, Office of Justice Programs, Bureau of Justice Statistics Special Report.

El-Bassel, N., L. Gilbert, R. F. Schilling, A. Ivanoff, D. Borne, and S. F. Safyer. 1996. Correlates of crack abuse among drug-using incarcerated women: Psychological trauma, social support, and coping behavior. *American Journal of Drug and Alcohol Abuse* 22: 41–56.

Ellison, R. [1952] 1982. *Invisible Man.* New York: Random House.

Freudenberg, N. 2002. Adverse effects of U.S. jail and prison policies on the health and well-being of women of color. *American Journal of Public Health* 92: 1895–99.

Galbraith, S. 1998. *And so I began to listen to their stories . . . Working with women in the criminal justice system.* National GAINS Center for People with Co-Occurring Disorders in the Justice System. Delmar, NY: Policy Research Associates, Inc.

Gonnerman, J. 2004. *Life on the outside: The prison odyssey of Elaine Bartlett.* New York: Farrar, Straus and Giroux.

Greenfeld, A. G., and T. L. Snell. 1999. *Women offenders* (NCJ 175688). Washington, DC: Bureau of Justice Statistics. http://www.ojp.usdoj.gov/bjs/pub/pdf/wo.pdf (accessed April 30, 2004).

Harrison, P., and J. Karberg. 2003. *Prison and jail inmates at midyear 2002.* Washington, DC: Bureau of Justice Statistics. http://www.usdoj.gov/bjs/pub/pdf/pjimo2.pdf (accessed May 3, 2004).

Haywood, T. W., H. M. Kravitz, L. B. Goldman, and A. Freeman. 2000. Characteristics of women in jail and treatment orientations: A review. *Behavior Modification* 24: 307–24.

Herman, J. 1997. *Trauma and recovery.* New York: Basic Books.

Hiday, V. A. 1999. Mental illness and the criminal justice system. In *A handbook for the study of mental health: Social contexts, theories, and systems,* ed. A. V. Horwitz and T. L. Scheid. Cambridge, MA: Cambridge University Press. 508–25.

Jordan, B. K., W. E. Schlenger, J. A. Fairbank, and J. M. Caddell. 1996. Prevalence of psychiatric disorders among incarcerated women: II. Convicted felons entering prison. *Archives of General Psychiatry* 53: 513–19.

Kaplan, H. I., and B. J. Sadock. 1998. *Synopsis of psychiatry*. Philadelphia: Lippincott Williams and Wilkins.

Keamy, L. 1998. Women's health care in the incarcerated setting. In *Clinical practice in correctional medicine,* ed. M. Puisis. St. Louis: Mosby. 188–205.

Lamb, H. R., and L. E. Weinberger. 2001. Persons with severe mental illness in jails and prisons: A review. *New Directions in Mental Health Services* 90: 29–49.

Lamb, W. 2003. *Couldn't keep it to myself.* Women of York Correctional Institution. New York: Harper Collins.

Maruschak, L., and A. Beck. 1997. *Medical problems of inmates, 1997* (NCJ 181644). Washington, DC: Bureau of Justice Statistics. http://www.usdoj.gov/bjs/pub/pdf/mpi97.pdf.

Marquart, J. W., D. E. Merianos, J. L. Hebert, and L. Carroll. 1997. Health condition and prisoners: A review of research and emerging areas of inquiry. *Prison Journal* 77: 184–208.

Mullen, P. D., A. G. Cummins, M. M. Velasquez, K. von Sternberg, and R. Carvajal. 2003. Jails as important but constrained venues for addressing women's health. *Family and Community Health* 26: 157–68.

Mumola, C. J. 1999. *Substance abuse and treatment, state and federal prisoners, 1997* (NCJ 172871). Bureau of Justice Statistics Special Report. U.S. Department of Justice. http://www.ojp.usdoj.gov/bjs/abstract/satsfp97.htm (accessed May 5, 2004).

National Commission on Correctional Health Care. 2005. Position statement on women's health in correctional settings. http://www.ncchc.org/resources/statements/womenshealth.html (accessed February 7, 2005).

National Women's Law Center. 1995. *Women in prison fact sheet*. Washington, DC: The Center.

OJS Special Report. 1998. Women in criminal justice: A twenty year update: Executive summary. Office of Justice Programs Special Report. Office of Justice Programs. U.S. Department of Justice. http://www.ojp.usdoj.gov/reports/98Guides/wcjs98/execsumm.htm (accessed May 5, 2004).

Snell, T., and D. C. Morton. 1994. *Women in Prison* (NCJ 145321). Washington, DC: Bureau of Justice Statistics. http://www.ojp.usdoj.gov/bjs/pub/pdf/wopris.pdf (accessed June 8, 2005).

Stoller, N. 2003. Space, place, and movement as aspects of health care in three women's prisons. *Social Science and Medicine* 56: 2263–75.

Sylla, M., and D. Thomas. 2000. *The rules: Law and AIDS in corrections*. HIV and Hepatitis Education Prison Project. Brown Medical School Office of Continuing Medical Education and the Brown University AIDS Program. http://www.hivcorrections.org/archives/nov00/ (accessed April 30, 2005).

Taylor, S. 2001. The health status of black women. In *Health issues in the black community*, ed. R. Braithwaite and S. Taylor. San Francisco: Jossey-Bass. 44–61.

Teplin, L. A., K. M. Abram, and G. M. McClelland. 1996. Prevalence of psychiatric disorders among incarcerated women: I. Pretrial jail detainees. *Archives of General Psychiatry* 53: 505–12.

Watson, R., A. Stimpson, and T. Hostick. 2004. Prison health care: A review of the literature. *International Journal of Nursing Studies* 41: 119–28.

Watterson, K. 1996. *Women in prison: Inside the concrete womb*. Boston: Northeastern University Press.

2

Understanding How Race, Class, and Gender Impact the Health of Incarcerated Women

RONALD L. BRAITHWAITE

According to a recent Kaiser Family Foundation survey (2001), notable differences in health status exist between white women and women of color in the general U.S. population. Women of color are more likely to report that they are in fair or poor health. One-fifth of African American women, 29 percent of Latinas, and 13 percent of white women assess their health status as fair or poor. African American women are more likely to have a physical condition that limits routine activities such as participating in school or work or conducting daily housework. Despite their reports of poorer health status, Latinas are actually less likely to report that they have a chronic condition in need of ongoing care. Incidence of chronic illnesses also varies for women by race and ethnicity. Over half (57 percent) of African American women ages 45 to 64 have been diagnosed with hypertension, twice the rate for white women (28 percent) of the same age. African American women (40 percent) are also significantly more likely to have arthritis than Latinas (33 percent) and white women (32 percent). African American (16 percent) and Latina (17 percent) women both experience higher prevalence of diabetes compared to white women (9 percent).

While health disparities among women in the general population are well documented; women entering the correctional system represent a population already at high risk for communicable diseases, substance abuse, and mental health problems (Cotton-Oldenburg et al. 1997; Fogel and Martin 1992; Hammett 1998; Martin et al. 1995; Smith and Dillard 1997). Because the number of incarcerated men historically has far exceeded that of incarcerated women (women represented 6.5 percent of prison inmates at the end of 1998), limited attention has been paid to the unique health concerns of this smaller population (Beck and Mumola 1999). With increasing numbers of women entering and exiting the prison system, there is a compelling need to ensure that mechanisms are in place that can adequately address the above-noted health issues.

Medical issues that relate to reproductive health and to the psychosocial issues that surround imprisonment of single female heads of households are often overlooked. Women in prison complain of the lack of regular gynecological and breast exams and argue that their medical concerns are often dismissed as exaggerations. Additionally, many imprisoned women are survivors of physical and sexual abuse and have lacked previous health care in their communities. These two factors put them at even greater risk for having high-risk pregnancies and for developing life-threatening illnesses such as HIV/AIDS, hepatitis C, and HPV/cervical cancer. Moreover, despite being imprisoned and presumably safe from harm, in prisons throughout the United States, women are victims of sexual abuse by prison staff, at times during routine medical examinations.

In regards to mental health, imprisoned women may also have a higher prevalence of depression than imprisoned men. While this may reflect the gender differences in depression seen in the general population, it also may relate to a loss of connection to a woman's outside community. The leading mental illness problems among female prisoners include physical and sexual abuse/trauma, victimization, depression, and substance abuse (Young 1998). Dual substance abuse and mental health problems are very common among male and female prisoners, but more so for females. Women in prison have higher rates of substance abuse, antisocial personality disorder, borderline personality disorder, post-traumatic stress disorder, and histories of sexual and physical abuse than their male counterparts. Women frequently engage in self-mutilating behaviors, are verbally abusive, and report numerous suicide attempts (Henderson 1998).

Historically women have been underrepresented in all levels of the criminal justice system. This underrepresentation of women has resulted in a criminal justice system created by males for males in which the diverse needs of women are forgotten and neglected (Belknap 1996). Prior to the 1980s, when the female prison population was relatively low, this was not a pressing issue that received a significant amount of attention. However, over the past twenty years, the number of females held in state and federal prisons increased sixfold and has outpaced the growth rate of the male prison population (see figure 2.1). In 1980, approximately 13,000 women were incarcerated in federal and state prisons; by 2002, this number had increased to over 96,000 (Harrison and Beck 2003). When examining the racial composition of the growth in female prisoners, statistics show that African American and Hispanic women are the fastest growing portion of the prison population. Two-thirds of the women confined in local jails and state and federal prisons are black, Hispanic, or of other non-white ethnic groups (Richie 2001). Table 2.1 shows the high percentage of minority women under the surveillance of the U.S. criminal justice system.

The large increase in female inmates, especially minority females, over the last twenty years warrants the attention to the diverse needs of women. Covington and Bloom (2003) assert that the steady rise of women in prison is related to forces that shape government policy. These larger forces include increasingly severe

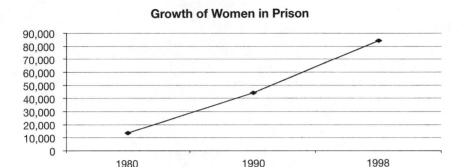

FIGURE 2.1. Number of Women in Prison.

Source: U.S. General Accounting Office, *Women in Prison: Issues and Challenges Confronting U.S. Correctional Systems.* Washington, DC, 1999.

penalties for drug offenses of all kinds, the shift toward a view of lawbreaking as an individual pathology that ignores the structural and social causes of crime, government polices that prescribe simplistic and punitive enforcement response to complex social problems, and federal and state mandatory sentencing laws. All of these trends ignore the complexity of the female offender. In order to address the diverse needs of women, it is important to understand the many factors contributing to the increase of women's incarceration, how incarceration affects their lives, and how the diversity of staff affects women's prison experience.

Factors Contributing to Female Incarceration

Women tend to commit survival crimes to earn money, feed a drug-dependent life, and escape physical conditions and relationships. Belknap (1996) argued that chemical dependency, victimization, and lack of economic resources are factors that consistently land women in jails and prisons. The increase in women's im-

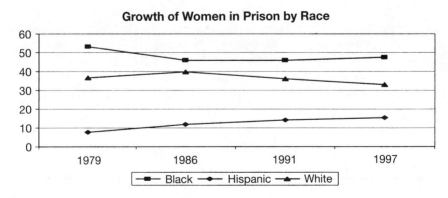

FIGURE 2.2. Number of Women in Prison by Race

Source: U.S. General Accounting Office, *Women in Prison: Issues and Challenges Confronting U.S. Correctionsl Systems.* Washington, DC, 1999.

TABLE 2.1
Percentage of women under criminal justice system by race

Characteristics of women	Probation %	Local jails %	State prisons %	Federal prisons %
African American	27	44	48	35
Hispanic	10	15	15	32
White	62	36	33	29
Other	1	5	4	4

Source: Greenfield and Snell (1999)

prisonment is largely accounted for by an increase in minor property and drug-related crimes. For example, in 1975 women were most likely to be incarcerated for larceny, embezzlement, and prostitution. However, during the 1980s the percentage of women charged with drug offenses skyrocketed when crack cocaine was introduced in urban areas across the United States. This inexpensive drug created addictions in low-income areas, expanded urban drug markets, and brought on associated violence. Individuals with this addiction, especially low-income women of color, sought to satisfy their craving for crack cocaine though prostitution, theft, and serving as distributors of drugs. In 1997, for instance, Hispanic (44 percent) and African American women (39 percent) were more likely to be incarcerated for a drug offense than white women (23 percent). A recent report examining the impact of the "war on drugs" on women's arrests and sentencing showed that in New York, California, and Minnesota, minority women represent a disproportionate share of the women sentenced to prison for a drug offenses (Mauer, Potler, and Richard 1999). In New York from 1986 to 1995, minority women constituted 32 percent of the state population; however, they made up the majority (86 percent) of women arrested for drugs. Fifty-two percent of these drug arrests were black women, 34 percent were Hispanic women, and 14 percent were white. Drug convictions in New York had the greatest impact on Hispanic women, who were 42 percent of these convictions; 77 percent of all felony convictions of Hispanic women were drug related. Mauer, Potler, and Richard (1999) also reported that prison sentences for minority women in New York were significantly impacted by America's war on drugs. In 1995, 156 percent more women received prison sentences than in 1986, with minority women representing 87 percent of all female commitments and 91 percent of female commitments being related to drug offenses. The impact of drug policies in New York on ethnic groups can also be demonstrated in New York's sentencing patterns for minority women. For instance, four of five Hispanic women sentenced to prison in 1995 were convicted of drug charges, as were two out of three black women. Drug convictions also impact the imprisonment of white women, but not to the degree that it has impacted African American and Hispanic women.

California's increase in the female inmate population grew significantly from 1986 to 1995 due to policies that sought to get "tough on crime, " especially drug crimes (Mauer, Potler, and Richard 1999). From 1986 to 1995, California's female inmate population grew by 40 percent. An examination of the racial breakdown of this increased population revealed racial disparities that were less dramatic than in New York. For example, minority women comprised 38 percent of the state population of California, but made up over half the prison sentences for drugs. The overrepresentation of minorities in the prison population in New York and California is even duplicated in Minnesota, where minority women only make up 5 percent of the state population but represent more than a quarter of the state's prison sentences for drugs. African American women in particular have been considerably overrepresented; they constitute 36 percent of all women's drug sentences. Minnesota's drug law mandates different sentences for crack and powdered cocaine users—first-time possessors of crack cocaine automatically receive a four-year sentence and powdered cocaine first-time possessors receive probation—which has significantly contributed to the overrepresentation of African American females in prison.

Mandatory minimum sentencing statutes for drug offenses have significantly increased the number of women in state and federal prisons. During the 1980s, state and federal legislators passed a series of hard mandatory sentencing laws as a part of the "war on drugs." In 1986 and 1988, laws passed by Congress directed that a mandatory five-year sentence be instituted for the possession or sale of crack cocaine. This mode of declaring war on drugs increased the number of women who get arrested or serve time for drug offenses from one out of every eight to one in three. This pattern of harsh sentencing continued well into the 1990s when women were primarily incarcerated for drug-related offenses, and where one-third of the incarcerated females were imprisoned for drug offenses (Mauer, Potler, and Richard 1999). Mandatory sentencing laws have been severely criticized for harsh sentencing rules that are based on male characteristics and male criminality, which has been generalized to women without taking into account women's characteristics, responsibilities, and roles in crime (Covington and Bloom 2003). For example, a young African American female received a sixteen-year prison sentence for her role in arranging the sale of a dozen cars that were used to transport cocaine. Although this female inmate was unaware of the drug activity, she received the maximum sentence for supposedly playing a role in trafficking while the two drug dealers who transported the cocaine and cash up to $500,000 only served six months. Although—or perhaps because—women typically hold small roles in drug rings, they receive longer prison sentences than men: they are not able to negotiate deals as they do not have enough knowledge of the larger drug operation they are a part of (Biddy 1999). Women involved in drug rings are also unable to negotiate sentencing because they receive violent threats from their drug bosses. By remaining silent, they subject themselves to the maximum amount of prison time.

Economic Hardships

Female prisoners generally report experiencing significant economic difficulties prior to entering the criminal justice system. National statistics report that approximately 60 percent of female prisoners were unemployed at the time of arrest and 70 percent of female prisoners have children under the age eighteen to care for and support (Greenfeld and Snell 1999; Snell and Morton 1994). This reality is further exacerbated for Hispanic and African American women, who are likely to have more children than their white counterparts, which makes them more likely to turn to criminal activity to "make ends meet." Financial disparities suggest a partial explanation of overrepresentation of minority women in prison: these women don't have the financial resources to support themselves and their children. In order to provide for their families, these women resort to criminal activity. This is evidenced by statistics that report minority women being more likely to be imprisoned for property offenses (that is, burglary, larceny, motor vehicle theft) and drug-related offenses (Greenfeld and Snell 1999). Several studies have shown that women are initially lured into the illegal drug economy as a means to earn money, and many end up with serious debilitating substance abuse problems (Henderson 1998). These criminal activities provide monetary rewards for supporting their children and drug habits.

Economically, incarcerated women suffer because they are uneducated and have low-paying jobs when they enter into the criminal justice system and, once they are released, have an even harder time becoming financially stable. Women who are financially unstable, especially minority women, receive the longest sentences in part because they cannot afford good lawyers and are dependent on the criminal justice system treating them fairly.

Victimization

Belknap (1996) suggests that incarcerated women are most often the survivors of male violence such as incest, rape, and battering. In 1999, eight in every ten female prisoners reported an extensive history of physical, sexual, and/or emotional abuse (Greenfeld and Snell 1999). Singer, Bussey, Song, and Lunghofer (1995) examined psychosocial issues of women in jail and found that 75.1 percent of the incarcerated women (who were primarily African American and Hispanic) experienced incidents of violence from their male partners. These attackers were often men who were involved in illegal activities such as drug dealing or prostitution and led their partners into criminal activity. In 1993, a Michigan woman was sentenced to life without parole for conspiracy with intent to deliver over 650 grams of cocaine. This conviction was based on two phone calls she allegedly made to collect money for her abusive boyfriend and two receipts she signed for a cash exchange. There was a substantial amount of evidence that showed that this woman had been repeatedly threatened, verbally abused, and brutally beaten for seventeen years by her boyfriend, but the courts refused to admit this evidence of abuse to be considered as cause for her criminal activity. An expert on battered women's syndrome, who after extensive examination of the defendant concluded that her long history of abuse rendered her incapable of exercising "free will," was not permitted to testify on this woman's behalf ("Not part of my sentence" 1999). This case shows how the U.S. criminal justice system fails to consider women's victimization as directly related to their criminal behavior.

Women prisoners are more likely to drink or use illegal drugs for self-medication than male offenders (*Female Offenders* 1999). Drug use offers them psychological comfort and a way to escape from pain that stems from extensive histories of sexual and physical victimization. Recently the Bureau of Justice Statistics studied violence committed against women involved in criminal activity (Harlow 1999). The study indicated that over half of all women in jails and prisons were physically or sexually abused before their imprisonment. This study also reported significant traces of drug and alcohol use among abused women in state prisons. Approximately 70 percent of abused women serving time in correctional facilities said they used illegal drugs during the month before their current offense. One in three women serving time in state prison reports having committed an offense in order to obtain money to support a drug habit (Covington and Bloom 2003). Female inmates are more likely to abuse cocaine and opiates than males. Women are also more likely to be under the influence at the time of arrest. Since women are more likely to be under the influence of cocaine at the time of arrest, they are more likely to receive long sentences because possession of cocaine is subject to long prison sentences.

Ethnic/Cultural Diversity of Prison Staff

Prior to the prison riot at Attica in 1971, diversity of the prison staff had not been addressed. This riot grew out of the male inmates' complaints about their staff's failure to understand and respect their diverse cultures, ethnic backgrounds, and religious needs (Booker 1999; Camp, Saylor, and Wright 2001). After this riot, policies and procedures were developed to address these concerns. Diverse prison staff was recruited to work in prisons, and diversity training was provided for prison staffers to help them establish better relationships with prisoners. Although female inmates have largely not resorted to violence to make their concerns heard, they also feel that prison guards and staff do not respect them or seek to meet their physical, psychological, and social needs (Galbraith 1998).

Male Guards in Women's Prisons

Men have historically worked in U.S. women's prisons as corrections officers although, in deference to the potential for sexual misconduct, their role has at times been restricted to no-contact jobs. However, with the passage of Title VII of the Civil Rights Act of 1964 and the introduction of equal employment rights for women, many of the restrictions on male corrections officers working in women's prisons were eliminated to facilitate the ability of female corrections officers to work in men's prisons. Consequently, men now constitute the majority of corrections officers working in women's prisons, at times outnumbering their female counterparts by two or three to one.

The introduction into U.S. prisons of cross-gender guarding was met with a flurry of lawsuits, filed primarily by male prisoners contesting the invasion of their privacy by female officers. Female prisoners, traditionally less litigious and outspoken, have contested the role of male officers to a lesser extent. Corrections officers of both genders also have sued with some success to contest sexually discriminatory hiring practices and restrictions imposed by prison administrators. In *Torres v. Wisconsin Department of Health and Social Services,* the Seventh Circuit Court permitted the superintendent of a women's prison to restrict male corrections officers from working in the housing units because, considering the women's histories of physical and sexual abuse, rehabilitation could not be achieved with male officers in the units. The Seventh Circuit found that, "given the very special responsibilities of these male correctional officers and the obvious lack of guideposts for them to follow," a certain measure of discretion in restricting their employment was permissible *(Torres v. Wisconsin).*

Female inmates are frequently characterized as being hard to manage, impulsive, unreasonable, and unwilling to be disciplined (Banks 2003). Correctional officers and other staff members perceive women to be more difficult to supervise than men (Van Voorhis and Presser 2001). Banks (2003) reports that both male and female staff consistently prefer working with male inmates rather than female inmates but have different reasons for preferring to work with the male inmates. Male officers typically expressed concern over perceived difficulties in supervising women and the fear of being accused of rape. Supervising female inmates causes male officers to need to modify their behavior, such as being careful of their language and using physical force (Banks 2003). Female officers felt that female inmates were less likely than male inmates to show respect or appreciation for prison staff. Prison administrators of female prisoners also recognize that female offenders need to feel a sense of connectedness while in prison, and suggested this quality makes female offenders more difficult to manage than males. Management of female offenders involves a capacity to respond to expressions of emotion and a willingness and ability to communicate openly with offenders. Interactions with female offenders require prison staff to be active listeners, patient, aware of emotional dynamics, and to possess the ability to respond firmly, fairly, and consistently to female inmates (Morash, Bynum, and Koons 1998).

Prison staff's negative views of female inmates are evident in their interactions with female inmates. For example, Banks (2003) highlights the view of one female inmate:

There's a few here that I do respect, and will always respect, and I show them respect. The other ones I just kind of stay away from because the way I see it, respect is something that's mutual. If you want it, you give it. And I don't care if I'm an inmate or not. I'm still a human being. I'm a woman just like they are. Yeah, I may have committed a crime, but I'm paying for it. I've been paying for it almost a decade of my life. You don't have to talk to me like I'm a dog, 'cause I'm not. If I do something wrong, you write me up for it. Don't stand there and you talk to me like I'm dirt on your shoe just because you get off on it.

Male vs. Female Prisoners: Disparate Treatment

Historically, incarcerated women have been treated less well than men while their gender-specific needs have been ignored. Until recently, most states maintained only one prison facility for women, often located a significant distance from the state's largest metropolitan area. Consequently, many female prisoners were geographically isolated from their children, as well as from legal and community resources.

Because of their small numbers, women are more likely to be incarcerated in a maximum security facility, where women of all security levels are either commingled or separated by internal housing classifications. Men, in contrast, generally are assigned to prisons based on a variety of factors, including their criminal offense, prior criminal history, and psychological profile. Also, because of the greater number of male institutions, men stand a much better chance of being housed near their place of residence, thus making it easier for family, friends, and attorneys to visit.

In comparison to prisons for men, rules within women's prisons tend to be greater in number and pettier in nature. Women prisoners are commonly cited for disciplinary offenses that are typically ignored within male institutions, and while they are less violent than their male counterparts, they appear to receive a greater number of disciplinary citations for less serious infractions.

Challenges to disparate educational and vocational programming have met with mixed success. The absence of equal education and programming opportunities in women's prisons is an issue that cuts across state lines. When suits have been settled out of court, states have generally agreed to augment and improve prison programming for women. But when a department of corrections declines to settle a suit and the case goes to trial, incarcerated women have fared less well. Many courts reviewing such suits have permitted states a degree of discretion to supply "parity of treatment" for women rather than equal treatment to that of male prisoners. This test requires prison officials "to provide women inmates with treatment facilities that are substantially equivalent to those provided for men." In 1997, in *Klinger v. Department of Corrections,* the Eighth Circuit Court of Appeals reversed a district court decision directing the state of Nebraska to provide programs and services "substantially equivalent" to those offered men. In that case, the circuit court determined that inferior programming could be justified because women prisoners in that state were not "similarly situated" to incarcerated men.

Until recently, vocational, educational, and social programs that have been developed for male offenders have been used for female offenders. However, these programs were unsuccessful because they did not address the female offenders' history of abuse, drug addiction, and parental responsibilities. These programs also failed to take into account the female offenders' desire for emotional and social support. The inability to meet the needs of female inmates has had devastating consequences. Numerous reports have stressed the need for more effective programs for female offenders; however, very few effective programs have been identified in the prison literature. Most of the focus has been on modifying the prison and the prison staff's attitudes and behaviors toward female offenders. In order to minimize the impact of negative stereotypes about female inmates in prison staff, gender-responsive training has been implemented in Florida's Department of Corrections. This training program for prison staff who work with female offenders covers gender and cultural diversity, stereotyping, communication, dependency, abuse impact, effects of the incarceration experience, coping behaviors of female offenders, professional interaction stratifies, modestly, privacy, and the significance of inmate's extended family.

Case Examples

In an attempt to develop a greater understanding of how race and gender intersect in the lives of the female prison population, several interviews were conducted with former female inmates. Each former inmate shared her own prison experience and maintained that female inmates are indeed the forgotten and neglected offenders. Aliases have been used in the real stories presented in this section.

Former inmate #1 ("Jane") was an African American woman who served time for offenses related to her drug addiction. The interview with Jane centered on forces in the larger society that lead to the increased rates of imprisoning women. Jane provided her own theory about imprisonment of women, particular minority women, which was based on her personal experiences and the experiences of other women who have been incarcerated. She thinks that race, gender economics, and politics have significantly impacted the imprisonment of women. Jane also noted that gender and race influences the judge's view of the defendant because it is the first thing the judge sees when women enter the courtroom. For women, this has negative implication because women are supposed to "know better" and are not expected to commit crimes. Jane maintained the judges' biases regarding gender and race negatively affect women's court cases, and recent studies have confirmed Jane's view. For example, the Maryland Special Joint Committee on Gender Bias in the Courts asked judges and attorneys if the gender of the parties affected the litigation process or outcomes of court cases. Forty-two percent of the attorneys and 78 percent of the judges who responded reported that they were aware of such cases. Gender was also found to affect the acceptance of women's testimony in court cases (Caplan 1989).

Jane also viewed America's "war on drugs" as a political war zone in which incarcerated women are prisoners of war, children of incarcerated mothers are war orphans, and the casualties are victims of violence in the community. This political war zone has the greatest effect on minority communities because this is where the war on drugs is fought the hardest. Jane views incarcerated women as the prisoners of war because they are held "captive" although they are not directly involved in the war. Imprisoned women are typically convicted for minor drug offenses, but they receive equal or longer sentences than those men who play major roles in drug trafficking. War orphans (children of incarcerated mothers) are placed with extended family members or they are entered into the foster care system. The placement of children of incarcerated women with other family members burdens the family members financially and the children psychologically. Casualties are individuals who experience grievances or hardships due to the war on drugs. These casualties are family members, victims of drug-related violence, and persons suffering from drug addiction.

Brown (2003) reported that many female offenders report that they are treated with contempt by judges, lawyers, and other criminal justice professionals, often being viewed as "anti-mothers" for getting in trouble with the law and deviating from society's norm of family matriarch and primary caregiver. Belknap (1996) asserts that one of the greatest stressors for women prisoners is the separation from their children. This stressor has been shown to have a profound effect on how they function while incarcerated. During an interview with a biracial former female inmate, "Mary," who served eighteen months as a first-time offender for a drug-related offense, shared the trials and tribulations she faced as a mother and prisoner while in prison and after being released. Mary described her prison experience as being hard, with the greatest challenge being separated from her twenty-eight-day-old daughter and her other children. Although her children were placed with her mother, Mary still felt a great deal of anguish from this separation. While dealing with the emotional hardships of her imprisonment and separation from children, Mary decided to make a conscious effort to use her prison time wisely by taking parenting, drug abuse, and fork-lift operator classes to gain the skills she needed to cope on the outside once she was released. To Mary, participating in these activities and staying out of trouble would prove to the parole board and society that she was a mother who loved her children and desired to take an active role in her children's lives. However, after being released from prison, Mary found out that regaining custody of her children would not be an easy task. After serving eighteen months, Mary was granted an early release due to the death of her father. For six months, she lived in a halfway house and sought to regain control over her life by finding steady employment, but she was unable to find a job because of her felony conviction. Mary wrote letters to her governor requesting a pardon, which would restore all her rights as a U.S. citizen, and she received one.

After overcoming this trial, for the next four years Mary faced the greatest challenge of her life, trying to reestablish her family. These challenges included being arrested for warrants that she did not know existed (she had cleared up the ones she knew about while she was trying to visit her children) and having her parental rights violated. For instance, Mary's mother had custody of her children and was trying to adopt them. However, the only way she could adopt them was if Mary had had no contact with her children for a year. Upon this realization, Mary hired a lawyer to help fight her case. However, Mary lost custody of her children when her lawyer saw her white mother and allowed the judge to sign over full custody with no hearing. Mary felt that her rights were violated because she was an African American recovering addict who was on probation. Later, she fired her lawyer and found a new lawyer who fought for visitation rights and a new hearing. Until her hearing, Mary travels over ten hours every weekend to visit her children in Indiana. Although Mary has faced many trials since her release from prison, and knows that many more lie ahead, she maintains that she will persist through these trials to "prove herself to society and get her family back."

Women prisoners are more likely to drink or use illegal drugs for self-medication than men, but few institutional programs are geared toward the female addict (Brown 2003). In another interview with an African American woman, "Alice," who spent two years in prison for a drug-related offense, she voiced her concerns about the lack of gender-responsive programs to help female prisoners to deal with substance abuse and psychological issues. Alice was arrested twice for drug possession. Her first arrest for possession with intent to sell resulted in probation, but her second arrest in which the drugs were found in her system landed her in prison for two years. At the time of her second arrest, Alice was pregnant and suffering from depression and a crack cocaine addiction. She asserted that using drugs allowed her to cope with her depression because it gave her psychological comfort. However, once she was incarcerated she received no treatment for depression or drug abuse problems. Now that she has been released, she still has not been offered any help to reclaim her life, "stay clean," or regain custody of her children. Alice argued that solutions to these problems need to be developed and implemented in women's prisons to provide inmates with the coping skills "to make it on the outside."

Conclusion

Incarceration affects the physical, psychological, and social well-being of women and their families. For poor women of color, their race, class, and gender make this environment particularly harsh. Incarceration also causes families to be dismantled, and children are forced into foster care, which leaves them vulnerable to psychological, educational, and social problems (Freudenberg 2002). Prison eliminates current income and reduces future earnings by diminishing women's prospects for post-release employment, which leads to homelessness. Although the women's prison population is steadily increasing and poses a threat to women and their families, few programs have been instituted to meet the skills development, psychological, and educational needs of this population. Women prisoners of color have unique needs that require responsive correctional programs that address trauma and abuse, vocational skills, medical care, mental health, parenting and childcare, and relationships (Van Voorhis and Presser 2001).

REFERENCES

Banks, C. 2003. *Women in prison.* Santa Barbara, CA: ABC-CLIO, Inc.

Beck, A. J., and C. J. Mumola. 1999. Prisoners in 1998. Bureau of Justice Statistics Bulletin (NCJ 175687). Office of Justice Programs, U.S. Department of Justice. http://www.ojp.usdoj.gov/bjs/.

Belknap, J. 1996. Access to programs and health care for incarcerated women. *Federal Probation* 60, no. 4: 34–40.

Biddy, E. 1999. *Women behind bars: Hard time, getting harder.* http://www.diversityatwork.com/news/feb00/news_usa3.html (accessed June 1, 2004).

Booker, J. W. 1999. Staff equality: A welcome addition to the correctional workplace. *Corrections Today* 61: 94–95.

Brown, J. W. 2003. The female inmate. In *International encyclopedia of justice studies.* http://www.iejs.com/Corrections/female_inmate.htm (accessed June 2003).

Camp, S. D., W. G. Saylor, and K. N. Wright. 2001. Racial diversity of correctional workers and inmates: Organization commitment, teamwork, and worker efficacy in prisons. *Justice Quarterly* 18, no. 2: 1–36.

Caplan, H. D., ed. 1989. *Gender bias in the courts.* Rockville, MD: National Criminal Justice Reference Service.

Cotton-Oldenburg, N. U., S. L. Martin, B. K. Jordan, L. S. Sadowski, and L. Kupper. 1997. Preincarceration risky behaviors among women inmates: Opportunities for prevention. *Prison Journal* 77, no. 3: 281–94.

Covington, S. S., and B. E. Bloom. 2003. Gendered justice: Women in the criminal justice system. In *Gendered justice: Addressing female offenders,* ed. B. E. Bloom. Durham, NC: Carolina Academic Press.

Female Offenders. 1999. Florida Corrections Commissions.

Fogel, C. I., and S. L. Martin. 1992. The mental health of incarcerated women. *Western Journal of Nursing Research* 14, no. 1: 30–47.

Freudenberg, N. 2002. Adverse effects of U.S. jail and prison policies on the health and well-being of women of color. *American Journal of Public Health* 92, no. 12: 1895–99.

Galbraith, S. 1998. *And so I began to listen to their stories . . . Working with women in the criminal justice system.* National GAINS Center for People with Co-Occurring Disorders in the Justice System.

Greenfeld, A. G., and T. L. Snell. 1999. *Women offenders* (NCJ 175688). Washington, DC: Bureau of Justice Statistics. http://www.ojp.usdoj.gov/bjs/pub/pdf/wo.pdf (accessed April 30, 2004).

Hammett, T. M. 1998. Public health/corrections collaborations: Prevention and treatment of HIV/AIDS, STDs, and TB. U.S. Department of Justice. Office of Justice Programs, National Institute of Justice. http://www.ojp.usdoj.gov/nij/corrdocs.htm.

Harlow, C. W. 1999. *Prior abuse reported by inmates and probationers* (NCJ 172879). Washington, DC: U.S. Department of Justice.

Harrison, P. M., and A. J. Beck. 2003. *Prisoners in 2002.* Washington, DC: Bureau of Justice Statistics.

Kaiser Family Foundation. 2001. Kaiser Women's Health Survey

Klinger v. Department of Corrections. 1997. 107F. 3d 609 (8th Cir.).

Martin et al. 1995.

Mauer, M., C. Potler, and W. Richard. 1999. *Gender and justice: Women, drugs, and sentencing policy.* Washington, DC: The Sentencing Project.

Morash, M., T. S. Bynum, and B. A. Koons. 1998. *Women offenders: Programming needs and promising approaches.* Washington, DC: National Institute of Justice.

"Not part of my sentence." 1999. In *Violation of Human Rights of Women in Custody.* Report issued by Amnesty International USA. http://www.amnestyusa.org/rightsforall/women/report/women–061.html (accessed July 1, 2001).

Singer, M. I., J. Bussey, L.-Y. Song, and L. Lunghofer. 1995. The psychosocial issues of women serving time in jail. *Social Work* 40, no. 1: 103–11.

Smith and Dillard 1997.

Snell, T., and D. C. Morton. 1994. *Women in Prison* (NCJ 145321). Washington, DC: Bureau of Justice Statistics. http://www.ojp.usdoj.gov/bjs/pub/pdf/wopris.pdf (accessed June 8, 2005).

Torres v. Wisconsin Department of Health and Social Services. 1988. 859F, 2d 1523 (7th Cir.).

Van Voorhis, P., and L. Presser. 2001. *Classification of women offenders: A national assessment of current practices.* Cincinnati: University of Cincinnati Division of Criminal Justice.

3

Voices of Incarcerated and Formerly Incarcerated Women

SALLIE GLOVER WEBB
DONNA L. HUBBARD

This chapter explores firsthand the stresses and strains experienced by two female inmates sentenced to the Georgia State Corrections System. Sallie Glover Webb, currently incarcerated in Pulaski State Prison for Women, has served sixteen years of a thirty-year prison sentence. Prior to her incarceration, Webb was employed as a nurse. As a health care provider, her perceptions and experiences related herein draw attention to the medical treatment issues that uniquely affect incarcerated women. Donna Hubbard was paroled from the prison system in 1992. She recounts her experiences related to the failure of the mental health and social service system in encouraging rehabilitation among offenders. Throughout her story, which is also told in her book (Hubbard, in press), it becomes evident how the macro systems in our society fail to divert at-risk youth and young adults from the evils that exist on those mean streets of our society.

–Ronald L. Braithwaite

The Voice of Sallie Glover Webb

September 10, 2003

Prison health care is definitely an issue that requires internal investigation and evaluation by the senior prison administrators affiliated with the Georgia State Prison System. From personal experiences as a health care professional before incarceration and my firsthand observation as an inmate during the last sixteen years of my life, I can attest to the lack of appropriate, timely, and sufficient medical care in the women's prison system. The delivery of medical treatment, access to medical evaluation, and proper treatment are barriers we face. Errors in diagnosis, administration of the wrong medications, and lack of medications are just a few problems that I know of. The process we have to go through to see a licensed medical doctor is often slow and tiresome. Prior to receiving any type of medical intervention, the first thing you are required to do is fill out a medical request form. This form asks for general information and the nature of your illness. It is also required when an inmate requests medication refills or treatment from the dentist or optometrist. The medical department receives hundreds of requests daily and their staff is limited. Therefore, not everyone who requests treatment and access to care is actually seen by health care staff: they triage the inmate forms and schedule the patients accordingly.

Because of the overwhelming need for medical treatment among women inmates, I think that Georgia should provide adequate staff to accommodate the needs of the inmates. Sometimes an inmate will be examined by a nurse practitioner or a registered nurse instead of a licensed physician. Motrin and generic antacids are administered as miracle drugs for any illness in prison because that is what is usually prescribed in sick call.

Additionally, a large number of the women in prison are assigned to a mental health caseload that in most cases requires the use of psychiatric medications for patient management. Limited mental health screening is performed before meds are prescribed, and almost no monitoring of drug levels is done once a woman is placed on the psychiatric medication. Routine blood lab work is not collected or monitored to see if the inmate is overmedicated. It is not uncommon to observe women who are overmedicated, walking around like zombies. It makes you wonder if the medications that are prescribed to inmates are helping them or harming them.

There have been several attempted, and some successful, suicides since my incarceration that could have been prevented if adequate medical staff had been available during emergency situations. Lack of after-hours care and medical staff concern has contributed to inmates being pushed beyond their limits to deal with everyday life. I have witnessed a member of the medical staff order lab tests that took months to be administered to the patient, if they were ever done at all.

Continuity of inmate care and coordination with external outside health care providers is another area that should be examined. The state spends thousands of dollars to send an inmate out to a specialist, only for the visit to be in vain because the correctional facility fails to fill an order that was prescribed or to have the specific test done so that the proper diagnosis can be made, be it an MRI or physical therapy.

It is hard to get medical attention if you have a medical emergency anywhere other than medical clinic. If you get sick in the dorm and need to see someone right away, it is almost impossible to get to the medical clinic and to be seen at that time. Regardless of what kind of medical problem an inmate has, the security officer is instructed to give the inmate Tylenol and/or antacid. Emergency care is practically nonexistent; an inmate must collapse for the medical staff to come to the dorm and do an assessment.

Some of my fellow inmates are intimidated by the prison health care system's barriers to treatment. Because of my background in the medical field, I usually get what I need done as far as my health is concerned. I do not mind writing a grievance until my voice is heard, and I get the medical treatment I need. I also assist the other inmates who need help to receive proper medical care. There is a need for inmate advocacy programs within and outside the prison environment.

In 1995, I had an attack of PSVT (ventricular tachycardia—extremely fast heart rate). I checked my pulse and found that it was 130. I passed out twice while sitting in Bible study. One of the sisters woke me after the second time and when I answered her incoherently, I knew I needed to seek medical attention. I went to the security guard and had her contact medical. The nurse whom the security guard spoke to apparently asked, "How does she know that her pulse is 130?"

I shouted, "Because I can count." The medical cart came and got me but by the time they got there, my heart rate was so fast that it could not be counted. I had difficulty breathing. I was administered oxygen at five liters via my nasal canal. The emergency medical technicians (EMT) and fire department were called to the scene. I was still having difficulty breathing with oxygen in my nose. The EMT was going to administer more oxygen only to discover the tank was empty. The EMT got an oxygen tank from the ambulance. I was supposed to be taken to Georgia Baptist Hospital (now Atlanta Medical). En route, I had to be deferred because the facility was full. The security guard instructed the EMT to take me back to the institution until they could find out what to do with me. During my transport, I passed out in the back of the ambulance and became incontinent. The EMT said, "I have called my supervisor, and I am taking her to the nearest hospital because I will not lose a patient in my ambulance." I was taken to Grady Memorial Hospital in Atlanta where I was given adenosine to convert my heart rate. I was admitted and hospitalized for more than a week. I was forced to take an antinausea medication when it wasn't needed because the institution does not have a PRN system, which would allow me to take the medication on an as-needed basis. Thus, even though the doctor ordered a medication PRN, I had to take it on a routine schedule (such as 9 a.m., 1 p.m., 5 p.m. or 9 p.m.) regardless of whether it was needed.

Disregard of inmate-initiated requests for treatment is very common. The medical staff consistently reminds you that you are an inmate, implying that you do not deserve good medical care. Does being in prison mean that I am not entitled to adequate, proper, and timely medical care? One physician stated, "I was sent here to save the state some money by cutting medication and treatment costs." I replied, "Am I to believe that you are the only competent doctor the state has ever hired?" I was made to feel that I was not worthy of proper medical attention, and that is unfair. Officials seem to be more concerned about saving money instead of providing medical treatment and medication that is correct.

A couple of women that I spoke to wanted to share their own concerns about the medical treatment that they have received since being incarcerated. Lynette fell and was told by medical staff that there was nothing wrong with her foot. After days of immense pain, she went to sick call and was charged another $5 for the visit. Medical staff finally took an x-ray, and after waiting five days for the results, it showed that Lynette indeed had a broken foot. She had another incident where she slipped on some chemicals while cleaning the shower as part of her work detail. She was sent to medical and was told there was nothing wrong with her. After going through tremendous pain and after noticing swelling in her leg and foot, she returned to medical to seek care only to be told, again, that there was nothing wrong with her. Years later, she found out that she had torn ligaments due to the fall she took in the shower. She eventually had to receive surgery to correct the problem. Lynette received outside medical treatment from a specialist who performed surgery. After the surgery, Lynette's bandages consisted of a medicated strip and an ace bandage on her knee when she returned to the institution. After the surgery, no follow-up treatment was given, infection set in, and her knee burst. Neither antibiotics nor pain medications were prescribed by the medical staff for her injury. Although the specialist ordered physical therapy, the follow-up treatment was not provided. Lynette was told she would receive physical therapy when it became available. It never became available.

Another woman, GS, has ongoing medical problems that the medical staff seem to take lightly. She has been trying for years to get proper medical treatment for her condition to no avail.

Issues related to improper nutrition and dietary standards inside prisons is another common problem. A lot of our health problems come from improper diets and limited time to eat. The majority of the time, we are only allowed five to seven minutes to eat during meals. This has caused digestive and severe stomach problems. When we have digestive problems, we must go to medical to try and get something to help us. Time and time again, we find ourselves in a no-win situation. These are just a few examples of the improper medical care that inmates receive. It is clear that something has to be done to assist female inmates in the Georgia prison system. As an inmate, I am a voice from the inside, but we need an ear on the outside to listen to our cry for help. We are isolated in prison and have limited resources to help us reach people who are in a place to assist us. I sincerely hope that by writing this chapter, someone out there will hear the voices from the inside and extend their hand to help us. Being sick and in prison is like being buried alive. Formal inmate advocacy programs to ensure proper medical care and treatment reform through state legislation are badly needed.

The Voice of Donna Hubbard

July 13, 2004

I suppose that this chapter of my life will never finish unfolding. In fact, I believe that I will continue to find revelations about the period of my life that I call the "restoration" that will help me become the great woman of God that I am destined to be. I do not say that to boast because there was a price to pay for the anointing of my life. The first price was paid by my Savior, Jesus Christ, and the second was as a result of the choices I made in my life. Nevertheless, let me begin by saying that I feel overwhelmed when I think of how the things that could have destroyed me came together to "make" me who I am today. It was nothing short of a miracle that I survived, and I am sure it was God's grace that allowed me to be here to tell my story today in hopes that it will help someone else to find their way, and to shine some light on the travesty of a system that determines punishment based on one's inability to help oneself.

There are as many stories about incarcerated women as there are women in prison. And there are even more stories that shed light on the journey through self-destruction, addiction, incarceration, and injustice than there are women impacted by the criminal justice system. The victims include the nation, which bears the burden of supporting a system that continues growing in spite of its obvious inefficiency in producing a positive outcome. The incarceration of women has increased almost 700 percent since 1985, and recidivism has not decreased as a result of strict drug laws. More importantly, the concealed victims include the communities that suffer the devastation of drug trafficking, drug infestation, homelessness, unemployment, economic decline, and child endangerment. Most of these communities are inner city, poverty ridden, and underserved. These inner-city communities populated by mostly minorities and women with children are often the most publicized when it comes to the crimes, but the truth is that that's just where the battles are fought. We must also mention the obvious victims that continue to be recognized but overlooked in government policy and services: the families.

The first component is the extended family members who witness firsthand the self-destruction of the mother, and who replace her as a caregiver of the "abandoned" children. The second is the children of these women, who number over 2 million to date. In every war, there are prisoners of war, war orphans, and casualties. Since the "war on drugs" began, the inner-city communities have produced mass numbers in each of these categories. I contend that the children of incarcerated women, who were railroaded as a result of this war, are "war orphans." Many of these same children have followed their parents into prison or have become the casualties. Still, they are the most devastated and helpless victims. I want to tell you a story about these women, their families, children, and communities. Let me begin with myself.

I never thought I would end up in prison. I come from a fairly good family; every family has issues and my family was no exception. But by most standards, I had a good upbringing. In spite of the domestic violence and abuse I witnessed as a child, I had the full expectation that life was going to be great for me. My mother decided to follow a radical lifestyle, at least by average standards. There is nothing "average" about me or my family. My mother gave me a wonderful foundation of culture and diversity, which was radical during the civil rights movement. I knew who I was and the value of my heritage when it was not politically correct. She made me proud to be African American. Indeed, I was saying loud, "I'm black and I'm proud" at the risk of being subjected to ridicule, harassment, and discrimination. Being radical was a way of life for me. And today, I stand in the path of those same arrows as an advocate for women impacted by the criminal justice system—I won't go away and be quiet! But I made foolish choices for which I, my children, and my family paid a price; not to mention the nation and my community. Still, going to prison was not an option I thought was possible.

By the time I was twenty-two years old, I was a divorced mother of three children with only a high school diploma and great expectations. I had been married at a young age, albeit with good intentions; it was through unwise, insincere counsel. After being abused physically and emotionally, and feeling abandoned socially myself, there was nowhere to go but up. Or so I thought. I felt desperate, and desperate women make destructive decisions. I was no exception. I made numerous efforts to improve the quality of my life so as not to end up a statistic. I still strive toward excellence harder than most and am my own staunchest critic. I entered college thinking this would be the answer to all problems: a good education. I found women in prison with every level of certification and degree. It did not keep them from going to prison. It may have made it easier after they got out to get a job, if they got out. But my endeavor to gain footing by education and employment did not pay off the way I thought it would. I could always get a job. But when I faced the challenge of parenting at a young age, finding my own identity after being abused, and healing the wounds I suffered (some I did not know were bleeding), I still found myself lacking the self-love I needed to survive my circumstances. I say self-love because if I had learned how to love myself, I would not have put myself and my children in the conditions I did. Not loving oneself can lead to the inability to determine danger.

I felt I had few options, although I had remarkable opportunities. My mother, a truly phenomenal woman, could only give me her best, and I was a uniquely demanding child. Her efforts to teach me to love where I came from did not teach me to love myself. Society's permission to degrade women as property manipulates our destiny by limiting our choices and condemning us to be little more than adornments, and helped teach me to think little of myself. Let me stop here and clarify this. I am a saved and sanctified anointed woman of God. I am not a feminist in the respect of current political clichés. I do, however, believe God has ordained and predestined women to usher in a new paradigm of leadership. These women will be and are radical by all standards. They have not lived pristine lives, nor have they been spared the scrutiny of society or the church. On the contrary, we must strive to accept ourselves as "tried by the fire." In case you don't understand, that means we accept the fact that we have been "singed" around the edges to become who we are. My fire included going to prison.

I began using drugs to fit in. I was a single mother who was pretty enough to win a beauty pageant but challenged by societal standards. I wanted to be part of the "in" crowd, but didn't know how to get in, and I thought I could get in the back door. I have found today that it is better to be approved by God than accepted by man. Drugs were the elite privilege of those who had figured out how to beat the system. Once they were a part of the party scene, they became leverage as to how accepted or elite you could be. I was exposed to social drugs like marijuana and cocaine as a result of my association and my relationships with athletes and entertainment "stars." When my circumstances could not support that lifestyle, I had to make up reasons to be with the "in" crowd. I ran out of lies soon, so I allowed myself to be used to support my addiction to drugs and attention. During this time, I was primarily guilty of neglecting the most important aspect of my life, my children. Drugs were not the only reason that I neglected my babies. But the drugs helped me to further create a fantasy that evolved into a nightmare. Using drugs is not the greatest problem women in prison face. It is the pattern of thinking that we are not worth the effort to do better, be better, or have better that sends us into a spiral of self-destruction. It is the ignorance of the consequences of being unaccountable, inconsistent, and uncommitted that permits us to continue to abort our destiny. Why are we ignorant of the consequences? Too many really guilty parties get away with more critical crimes than cocaine addiction and child neglect. I have found this one thing to be most true: "hurt people hurt people." I was hurting my children by my neglect and humiliating behavior and I did not realize it. I thought I was only hurting myself.

Drug addiction most often renders the addicted individual unable to translate actions into consequences. We live for the moment and for the euphoria of the next high, a high that is never enough. We look for a way to placate the feelings of unworthiness only to find ourselves feeling more unworthy after our indulgence. You really want to die, but if you don't have the courage to change, you don't have the courage to give up and you simply become a zombie. We appear living in the flesh but are dead in the spirit. It takes someone else who can believe in who you are and not where you are to encourage you to get help. It takes systems that can treat people and their problems without condemning them for their symptoms. It takes communities that are willing to become our sisters' keepers. It takes churches willing to create ministries that are out of the box, and that challenge people to come out of their comfort zones to creatively address these problems. Guess what? Most of the victims are church folk who are faithful enough to pray and believe in God for a solution, but lack the willingness to put their faith into action if it will jeopardize their reputation or inconvenience them. I'm not church bashing, I am a radical woman of God. I believe drugs are simply a cancer that can be treated and cured when addressed and cut out at the root. Being an addict and a prisoner is what I did, not who I am.

I was raped and abused as a result of the lifestyle I assimilated into. As a flight attendant, I led a fast-paced life. I was introduced to people who wanted no more than to count the number of women they could seduce. As an addict, I was vulnerable to physical abuse, domestic violence, and assault. I became promiscuous when I was seeped into the drug world. Once I was raped, beaten with a hammer, and left for dead. When they captured the assailants, I was so ashamed and ridden with guilt that I did not show up in court to testify against them. That left me feeling even more insignificant. Prostitution was the only option I felt safe to choose. I could hide who I was in the dark of night and still function in the day, or so I thought. This left me open to other forms of negligent treatment. Arrested more than twenty times, drug treatment was never once recommended. I was sentenced or detained until they lost me in the system or let me out. When I finally reached what I describe as my first plateau of restoration, I was in California. I gave birth to a baby eight weeks premature as a result of my addiction and was detained for two months before I was released by a compassionate judge and told never to return. I left the state and moved to Minnesota, looking for some redemption. My mother had recently moved there, and I thought if I could just get close to home I could get close to help. Momma didn't have a clue how to help me. She tried, but first she had to get past my deception and denial, her denial, and then the bureaucratic red tape. It happened too late.

Like most women caught in the web of addiction, I was too ashamed to get help and too proud to admit I needed it. The system doesn't do much to help one solicit treatment when it continues to lock up women whose greatest crime is an addiction to a drug they can't even afford to continue to use. No woman should have to go to prison to change. When we look at the way women are sentenced, it makes it even harder for a woman to reach out for help; all we want to do is to get out. But we find that getting out is easy, staying out is hard. Sentencing policies are weighted against us because the system that punishes us is full of "good ole boys" and macho men who feel women have no business getting caught in these situations; we should have known better, and we are used to make a point. If you don't behave, you are going to get "spanked" with your dress up, with a long switch, on your shiny legs, "do you hear me, girl?" Using drugs helped me to hide behind a façade of images I created that were neither real nor beneficial. And because I made the fantasy large, when it began to crumble I fell hard. After years of dodging a real sentence, in and out of jails, I found my way to the federal prison. My sickness had landed me in the grip of chaos. Facing two to four years in prison, I decided I wanted to live—not just get off drugs—and I wanted my life back.

I was not going to give that much of my life away and get nothing back. On top of the emotional and mental anguish I dealt with, I now had guilt. I had left my children to face the ridicule and the rejection that they had no part in creating. I was sentenced in January 1998 to serve two twelve-year sentences as a result of my association with California gang members and drug trafficking. I escaped the mandatory minimum sentencing guidelines by just nine days. However, I did not escape the overwhelming devastation that incarceration can wreak on a woman's psyche. I was dehumanized, humiliated, and made to feel like I was never going to get out. Prison is set up to do just that. I understand the policies are made to ensure safety and separation from society because I committed a crime. Let me say now, I was guilty of many things, but God's mercy allowed me to be convicted only of those charges and permitted me a sentence that was parole eligible. Not that I think prison saved me, but I can say it afforded me the opportunity to take a long hard look at myself and to recognize the consequences of risky behavior. To get something out of this experience, I was going to have to give more than I had ever imagined. It was going to take more than a good high to get through this. When I decided I wanted to live, it meant giving up old thinking and old habits. When you don't believe in yourself, starting over can be even more frightening than the thought of going to prison. You can hide from others in prison, but you can't hide from yourself. What I was looking for was inside me, and I had to find a way to get to it without destroying what little sanity I had left. Change was going to cost me, and I had to change or I was going to die, I knew that. I realized that if I had been released early on, I would have killed myself or I would have been killed. I had no perception of danger. I had to regain my self-respect, self-confidence, and self-esteem in order for me to regain my dignity.

Prison introduced me to every kind of challenge that a woman could face. It made me face some things about myself I had been in denial about. I was messed up in more ways than one. There was every kind of woman convicted of every kind of crime, and I fit right in. We were all looking for life and had found the garbage can instead. We either did not use wisely the opportunities we had, had no opportunities, or had no faith that we could have anything better than we had. I met phenomenal women in prison. Some of the most brilliant, talented, courageous women on the face of the earth are behind prison walls. We faced unbelievable odds to survive. Some, like me, survived life on the streets; suffering mental, physical, and emotional abuse; addiction, assault, neglect, HIV/AIDS; and on top of that, we had become invisible to people who would rather not deal with what the war on drugs had left behind. In spite of all we faced to survive, we had survived. Our stories need to be told and they need to be taken to heart. I met Annie, Boopie, Jo Ann, and April behind prison bars. These women will forever remain in my heart.

Annie was a thirty-something Caucasian woman who was severely mentally challenged. That was an understatement. This was her second or third time in prison for threatening the president with laser beams. For her state-supported guardian, it was easier to see her behind bars than to provide her with the treatment and supervision she needed to lead a productive life. Annie could read and write at a third-grade level. She suffered very limited comprehension. And I guess I felt infuriated that her only options were being locked up in prison or in segregation. She would remind me that it was better than the hospital, where she could only make macaroni paper plates. While it was evident Annie needed supervision even if she were not in prison, she was a person who deserved a better quality of life than she was getting. On medication, she was coherent enough only to follow directions. If she did not take her medication, she could be violent and irrational. No woman—no woman—should have to go to prison to have a life.

I was locked up in segregation because I had violated prison policies. I was in prison because I committed a crime; okay, a few crimes. But women like Annie serve time because society is ill equipped to deal with all of the facets of social neglect. I was in segregation forty-five days where I got to know Annie. I sang with Annie, tried to teach her to write in cursive lettering, ate sitting outside her door when, as an orderly, I was able to come out to clean the hall. I read the Bible to her, laughed with her, cried with her, prayed for her. She wasn't even allowed to have a pencil because she was a danger to herself. But the world didn't get to see the Annie I did. Sometimes she would ask me if I was ever getting out. "Oh, for sure," I would say. She would just stare at me and smile. I left Annie at Lexington Federal Correctional Institution (FCI Lexington) in 1991. I don't know what happened to her.

In January 1990, 400 men were brought into the compound of Lexington. Here, more than 900 women were housed with nothing more on their hands than time and the instinct to nurture. The women ate together, worked together, exercised together, went to chapel together, and enjoyed movies with popcorn on Saturday nights. The difference was that men occupied only one segregated unit on the compound, and if the officers even thought there was any hanky panky going on, you were going to segregation. Right. It was a prime example of "where there was a will, there was a way." From January 1990 to October 1990, the male inmates created quite a stir at FCI Lexington. And just as suddenly as they appeared, they disappeared. A classic case study if ever I saw one. More than eighty babies were born to women who had been involved with these male inmates. Some of the women were from outside the United States. When their babies were born, state policy demanded that they be picked up within seventy-two hours or they would become wards of the state.

Imagine, then, that you came to prison because you lived in a poor South American country and had barely enough to feed your family. Someone offers you money to take a package across the border to America, land of the free and home of the brave. Guilty as a $2 bill, you are detained, arrested, and convicted of drug possession or money possession or both. Unfortunately, the money they confiscated was the money that you counted on to provide your family a better life. Now the money is gone, you are on your way to prison for a long time, you speak little or no English, and have no way to contact your family when you don't return on time. Did I mention you were possibly in the hospital because the only way you could carry that amount of drugs into the country was to sew it into the lining of your body and the packages leaked? Now you are pregnant, about to give birth, cannot contact anyone to come get the baby, and it would take a miracle for them to arrive within the allotted amount of time. Don't forget you speak little or no English and, when you deliver the baby, you will have to leave him or her in the hospital alone. You lose your ability to deal with this situation rationally. You become hysterical, you have just delivered a baby, and now you are in shackles about to be returned to prison with no idea when or if you will ever see your baby. Postpartum depression sets in, and you do not have your baby to fill your emptiness or soothe your wounded heart.

Right about now someone is saying, "Look, when you do the crime, you have to do the time." I have no rebuttal. Still, I would place this with you to consider. What purpose does it serve to destroy the woman and the family, when her greatest crime was poverty and desperation? As I said in the beginning, desperate women make destructive decisions: we all suffer. Boopie was one of the women I described above; she did not come from South America but another part of the world. She joined the more than twenty women who were scheduled to be deported when they finished their sentence.

I was one of those women who gave birth in prison, and while I did not come from outside of the country, I still faced the dilemma of what would happen to my child. My family already had my other children. How could I ask them to take care of another? Why didn't I use protection, you ask? Well, condoms were available from the officers who were willing to take the risk of selling them to us at $20 each. In hindsight, I would say it would have been worth it. But at that time, I still had a long way to go to change, and the pattern of high-risk behavior was activated when I did not run from myself. Sin is an evil tempter. It will take you farther than you want to go, keep you longer than you want to stay, and cost you more than you want to pay. God's answer to sin is forgiveness with grace; man's answer is incarceration without mercy.

It set precedents within the prison system when this case study backfired. Of the eighty-three women who became pregnant, fifty women gave birth to their babies while in Lexington. Some never saw the fathers again. Some did not retain custody of their children and some, like me, managed to find the courage to ask the hard questions, take the criticism, and are now raising these children in spite of their unique beginnings. I did not receive prenatal treatment until my seventh month because I hid my pregnancy, afraid to come forward and be subjected to transfer to another prison. I wasn't the only one; but I was fortunate, I had no complications. The medical staff at Lexington was limited and scarce. I remember one woman who complained of pain around II p.m. and was examined by a physician's assistant who told her to go back to her unit and come into the clinic the next morning. She delivered her baby on the way to the hospital at 2 a.m. One afternoon I was waiting to be seen and witnessed a woman who had given birth just three days prior bowed over in pain in the waiting room because there was not enough staff to attend to her. Am I critical? No. I'm just talking about what happened.

These stories could go on. But let me shine a bit on the lighter side. As a result of the urgent need for caregivers for these children born in a unique situation, a home in Lexington that previously took in only severely physically challenged children began to take in these children and bring them to visit the mothers on Thursdays. The women had to stay out of any trouble, take parenting classes, and complete their education in order to have regular visits with their babies. Families moved to the city to be a part of the children's lives, and this provoked an even greater opportunity for healing and restoration of broken relationships. The family visits increased and the center where the children and families visited was enlarged.

Jo Ann was the most disturbing situation I encountered; an African American woman in her late twenties who suffered from mental illness of many kinds. I would say she was possessed, but medical experts would diagnose her as paranoid schizophrenic, delusional, and suicidal. She had recurring nightmares and would scream out loud at night. She spent her days in prison being self-destructive to the point that she would put permanent hair relaxer on her face and leave it until the skin burned off from the chemical exposure. When that happened, she would be sent to the clinic until the burns turned to scabs and then released to the general population until she healed or repeated this episode. I imagine her personal emotional torture to be much worse than the physical torture she inflicted upon herself. I never could understand why she was not placed in a more supervised situation where she could receive the psychological care she needed. I saw Jo Ann return to Lexington three times during my stay.

In 1992, I was released and moved to Atlanta, Georgia, where I was born. I had made major changes in my life and was gaining the wisdom and the strength to live a productive life. While I was still in prison, I decided not only would I put into practice the valuable principles of accountability, commitment, and consistency in all aspects of my life in order to put me in the position to realize the full potential of the greatness yet to be released in me, but I wanted to make a difference in the lives of women who were on the same journey I had traveled. I felt if I could help just one woman not go back to prison, to take charge of her life, and to move forward from this experience, it was worth it to tell my story over and over again. My reputation and comfort was not as important as doing what God destined me to do. This experience had to have more meaning than to simply teach me a lesson.‧

I had been clean from drugs since 1988. In and out of prison and jail since 1984, I served just short of ten years through the short sentences I served, and had gained wisdom and courage to take on the challenge of initiating a movement to change the way society sees women impacted by the criminal justice system, beginning with the way we see ourselves. The many problems of prison life are overshadowed by the challenges faced by women once we are released. Getting a job is just one aspect of life after prison. If you find a company to hire you, it usually is not one where you can use the limited education or vocational training you received while incarcerated. There are the stipulations placed upon you by the parole system to monitor how you move about in this new freedom, yet offering you little real assistance in improving the quality of your life. All the while, you have the pressing need to regain custody and position with your children and family. Did I mention you have to learn to adjust to a world that did not stop revolving while you were in prison? When I was released, portable CD players were the newest easy-access luxury. I had no clue what they even looked like. I became petrified when presented with my first real purchase for an amount greater than the price of gum; which I had not chewed for a very long time. When I realized the challenges many women would face and I remembered the women I left behind, I thought about how they would act if I was having a hard time. I knew I had to at least try to do something to help.

Once released, I had only one referral to explore for assistance. Aid to Imprisoned Mothers (AIM), founded by a wonderful woman attorney, Sandra Barnhill (whose work is described in chapter 18), was the only place I could get the help I needed without feeling judged and convicted again. They helped me in so many ways; I can only say that without her encouragement and the help of her agency, I could have given up many a day and just disappeared into the gray shadows of obscurity. But like I said, I won't go away and I will not be quiet. A change has got to come. Aid to Imprisoned Mothers helped me believe I could move forward with the vision I had been given to create a support system for women like myself. I had left my spiritual "mother" figure back in prison with a directive to go out and set up a prison ministry. What ministry meant to me was preaching. I knew these women and I would need more than a good sermon. I had a call on my life to preach the good news, but I had a burden for women in prison that had to include more than how to be saved. It had to encompass their lives in ways that would help them learn how to live once they got out. After Barnhill decided to focus her agency's resources on the children of incarcerated women, I found the opportunity I needed to begin to assist women in prison. She pointed me in the direction of the necessary resources and became a great supporter of my work. To this day, she is one of my most valued mentors, and the one I can always go to for guidance when organizational direction is needed.

With the help of AIM, I went to get my daughters who were by then two and five years old from my aunt in Washington, D.C. I was given the opportunity to begin telling my testimony of survival, deliverance, and restoration to churches and conferences around the country. I had secured a decent job at a major hotel chain, a car, and, with the help of Big Bethel Church, I had a three-bedroom apartment and the counseling I would need to keep me on track. After five years, I was recommended for early termination of my parole and supervision. The judge who sentenced me and the Department of Justice saw fit, based on the recommendation of the parole officers who had handled me, to terminate my stipulations and give me ten years off my time of supervised release. It freed me to further develop the vision of a ministry that would be a trailblazer in the area of policy, treatment, and aftercare. As a part of my healing, I began to put together a support group that would bring together other women like me to strengthen our resolve to be successful while affirming one another. As I was strengthened to stand on my own, I saw the vision take shape. Within two years, we had eleven women coming together to share strategies, encourage change, and develop a movement that could function on its own. In our third year, we invited women from every area of success to speak to our group about money management, starting small businesses, parenting, and personal development. We were able to help women directly after release to obtain employment and clothing, refer them to places that would rent them a decent place to live, and, in general, provide a network of aftercare support that could make a difference in whether they stayed out of prison and stayed off drugs. In our fourth year, we witnessed women return to prison from our group, throwing us into a state of confusion. Why? How could this happen? What we realized was that, without a strong support system and a nurturing nonjudgmental environment when released, most women won't make it past thirty days. In 1998, the Woman at the Well Transition Center was incorporated and filed for 501(c)3 tax status to formally bring some structure to our effort. With a $15,000 grant from the Soros Foundation based on faith in what we believed we could do and were doing without funds, we opened our first residential program. It served as a base for the many on-site projects we were developing for inmates in Georgia, Florida, and Alabama prisons. As of today, our programs have been featured in more than eleven prisons nationwide and continue to be a staple in four prisons. Our housing program now includes two houses, and we pride ourselves in being founded, managed, and guided by formerly incarcerated women.

There are five projects ongoing through the center, and we expect to expand our services to include revenue-building ventures that will ensure jobs for the women who have a more difficult time securing employment. Many are HIV positive and are forced to change their professions. Some are only able to work twenty-four hours a week. Many of our residents haven't worked in over ten years and some have never held a permanent job. We are most proud of our twelve-member advisory council that keeps us abreast of the current policies and obstacles facing incarcerated and formerly incarcerated women. These women have been out of prison more than one year and have remained clean, sober, and employed. Now, that is something to celebrate!

The challenge of reunification is the most pressing repercussion to incarceration to address for former inmates. April came to us four years ago. She had been involved faithfully in our life skills and Narcotics Anonymous meetings at the local prison. Once she was eligible for release, she decided to come to the Woman at the Well Transition Center where she completed her residential program with flying colors; she has remained successfully clean, sober, and working for the same company. Her challenge has been getting her children back. Many times, women face the permanent loss of their children as a result of their sentence length or degree of their crime. But there are the few who simply are faced with family and governmental bureaucracy that entangles the process of reunification with our children for years past the release from prison and into a period that begins to eat away at our spirit of recovery and restoration. The mistakes April made that separated her from her children have not stopped her from trying to improve her life and provide a better one for them now. She has a house, is a member of our board of directors, and makes the seven-hour journey to visit her children every other weekend. Still, she is stopped from regaining custody of her children from her mother and family, who still feel they have to protect the children from her. Has she changed? 100 percent! Have they?

I am grateful for the many resources afforded me to make a difference today. I am in college working on my theology degree. I am an ordained minister and a flight attendant for a major airline. I've been given many awards for my work with this population of women, and our program has been featured on several television programs. I am encouraged that the movement to change policies that impact women like me and our children and families are in the foreground instead of in the shadows. I am happy that women like me don't have to hide anymore. But there is still work to be done. I believe we can make a difference in helping women not go to prison by being more proactive with our efforts in the streets through confronting violence, addiction, and high-risk behavior among young girls and women. We as a nation, a city, and a community must begin to come out of our comfort zones. As the church and the family, we have to begin to touch those areas that we have not ventured into before. We *can* make a difference; one woman at a time, one family at a time.

REFERENCE

Hubbard, D. Forthcoming. *My soul looks back and wonders.* Atlanta: self-published.

4

Criminalizing the Victim

Interpersonal Violence in the
Lives of Incarcerated Women

KIMBERLY JACOB ARRIOLA
L. SHAKIYLA SMITH
MARGARET FARROW

My mother was killed when I was in junior high school. A squabble broke out between her boyfriend and his uncle, and she got caught in the crossfire.

—Donna (Johnson 2003)

The overseer on the farm would try to have sex with us when we were children. He used to come over and try to put his penis into my cousin and me and give us money and other things.

—Bettie (Johnson 2003)

I was beaten with the door molding, like the piece off the door with the nails in it and everything, from 9:00 in the evening till 4:00 in the morning, all because he [her boyfriend] went to jail for stealing tape recorders out of parked cars on a busy street, and I wouldn't go to jail and get him.

—DonAlda (Johnson 2003)

All three of these women have two things in common. They were directly or indirectly victims of violence, and the resulting trauma is likely to have contributed to the criminal behavior that lead to their incarceration as suggested by the respondents themselves and theorists (Browne, Miller, and Maguin 1999). The stories of Donna, Bettie, and DonAlda are all too common among incarcerated women, whose lives are overburdened by violence and abuse. Almost 60 percent of female state prison inmates have experienced some form of physical or sexual abuse over the course of their lives; 48 percent of female jail detainees report some form of physical or sexual abuse (Greenfeld and Snell 1999). Like female victims of inti-mate partner violence, incarcerated women tend to be young, poor, African American, and undereducated (Greenfeld and Snell 1999; Rennison and Welchans 2000). There are inextricable ties between violence, abuse, and incarceration among women in the United States. Undoubtedly, this overexposure to violence has widespread implications for both the mental and physical health of incarcer-ated women. The purpose of this chapter is to explore the prevalence of violence among incarcerated women and the mental and physical health consequences of this violence. In doing so, this chapter will focus on violence experienced by women prior to incarceration (excluding violence that occurs in the correctional setting, which is a notable problem). Finally, we will present one theoretical expla-nation for the link between violence and incarceration among African American women, the gender entrapment theoretical model.

Understanding Violence against Women

The World Health Organization (Krug et al. 2002) published a typology of violence with three dimensions: self-directed (including suicidal behavior and self-abuse), interpersonal (including violence against one's family/partner and one's commu-nity), and collective violence (including social, political, and economic violence). Incarcerated women appear to be most impacted by interpersonal violence, which is the focus of this chapter.

In terms of interpersonal violence, incarcerated women may be the victims or perpetrators of violence towards other family members (for example, a child, part-ner, or elder) or members of their community (for example, an acquaintance or stranger). Data clearly indicate that women are more often the victims of violence than the perpetrators in the United States (for example, 7.7 females and 1.5 males per 1,000 are victims of intimate partner violence; Rennison and Welchans 2000). With the exception of elder violence, incarcerated women are highly victimized by all forms of interpersonal violence: child, partner, acquaintance, stranger. Al-though many incarcerated women have not experienced elder abuse before or during their incarceration, they are certainly at risk for being victimized by this form of violence later in life.

According to Krug et al. (2002), each form of interpersonal violence experi-enced by incarcerated women (child, partner, acquaintance, stranger) may take on a physical, sexual, or psychological nature or it may involve deprivation or ne-glect. Physical violence generally includes slapping, hitting, kicking, and beating but is more specifically defined in terms of the victim-perpetrator relationship. For example, "physical abuse of a child is defined as those acts of commission by a caregiver that cause actual physical harm or have the potential for harm" (Krug et al. 2002, 60). Physical violence includes child physical abuse, physical assault by strangers, and physical assault by an intimate partner, among other forms of physical violence.

However, there is much less agreement in the scientific literature about what constitutes sexual violence. The literature has been criticized for having so many different definitions of sexual violence (Maman et al. 2000). The Centers for Disease Control and Prevention (Basile and Saltzman 2002) have recently issued a call for a uniform definition of sexual violence in order to facilitate surveillance. According to their suggested definition, sexual violence includes:

- A completed sex act without the victim's consent, or involving a victim who is unable to consent or refuse;
- An attempted (noncompleted) sex act without the victim's consent, or involving a victim who is unable to consent or refuse;
- Abusive sexual contact, which includes intentional touching, either directly or through the clothing, of the genitalia, anus, groin, breast, inner thigh, or buttocks of any person without his or her consent, or of a person who is unable to consent or refuse; and
- Noncontact sexual abuse, including voyeurism, intentional exposure of an individual to exhibitionism; pornography; verbal or behavioral sexual harassment; threats of sexual violence; or taking nude photographs of a sexual nature of another person without his or her consent or knowledge, or of a person who is unable to consent or refuse (Basile and Saltzman 2002, 9, 10)

Sexual violence may take the form of rape within marriage or dating relationships, rape by strangers, sexual abuse of children, unwanted sexual advances or sexual harassment, and sexual abuse of mentally or physically disabled people among other forms and contexts (Krug et al. 2002).

Psychological violence is also very difficult to define and has been understudied in the research literature perhaps due to problems in definition. As applied to children, psychological abuse includes acts that have an adverse affect on the psychological and emotional health and development of a child and includes "the failure to provide an emotional and supportive environment" (Krug et al. 2002, 60). In the case of adults, it includes intimidation, constant belittling, and humiliation (Krug et al. 2002). Although psychological violence may occur alone, seldom does physical and sexual violence occur without psychological violence (Jewkes 2000).

Finally, neglect is usually discussed in the context of child abuse, although neglect of correctional inmates who are ill has received increasing national attention (see Webb, this volume). In the context of child abuse, neglect refers "to the failure of a parent to provide for the development of the child—where the parent is in a position to do so—in one or more of the following areas: health, education, emotional development, nutrition, shelter and safe living conditions" (Krug et al. 2002, 60). The term "neglect" is seldom used in the context of intimate partner violence; however, various controlling behaviors, such as isolating a person from friends and family, restricting one's access to monetary resources, and monitoring a person's movements often occurs in the context of intimate partner violence and certainly constitutes deprivation.

Discussions of interpersonal violence tend to focus on violence that occurs within the family. However, community violence is a serious threat to women's health and constitutes an often overlooked aspect of interpersonal violence. Community violence includes violence that occurs outside of the home among people who may or may not know each other but who are unrelated (Krug et al. 2002). Implicit in this definition of community violence are two primary factors that are generally considered when measuring violence: the location in which the violence occurs and the relationship between those involved (Guterman, Cameron, and Staller 2000). With few exceptions, in research examining violence and abuse in the lives of incarcerated women, "community violence" is often not explicitly examined or defined, precluding comparisons across studies (Harris et al. 2003). Furthermore, the violence reported in most studies focuses on violence that is personally experienced by women and does not include witnessed violence, which is typically recognized as a component of exposure to community violence. Additionally, beyond child and intimate partner abuse, these studies often do not explicitly specify the location of other types of victimization or women's relationship to those involved. Instead, violence that would presumably fall under the category of community violence is often lumped under a broad category of "other types of non-intimate partner victimization in adulthood" (Browne, Miller, and Maguin 1999; Sable et al. 1999; Zlotnick 1997). Despite these problems with definition and measurement, there is a need to better understand the strong linkages that exist between drugs, poverty, prostitution, and violence and why many of these linkages converge in the lives of incarcerated women (Browne, Miller, and Maguin 1999; Fickenscher et al. 2001; Fogel and Belyea 1999; Harris et al. 2003).

The Prevalence of Violence in the Lives of Incarcerated Women

In the United States, there has been substantial attention given to women's experience of various types of abuse, such as intimate partner violence and child sexual abuse. However, most of the research focuses on women in the community as opposed to incarcerated women. Yet there is a growing body of literature documenting incarcerated women's extensive personal histories of violence and abuse. It is no coincidence that incarcerated women are exposed to violence at much higher rates than women in the general U.S. population. For example, a national telephone survey found that 25 percent of U.S. women had been raped and/or physically assaulted at some point during their lives as compared to 44 percent of women under correctional authority (including probation, jail, and prison; Greenfeld and Snell 1999; Tjaden and Thoennes 1998). Similarly, it is estimated that 22 percent of women in the general U.S. population experience intimate partner violence; whereas estimates for incarcerated women range from 34 percent to 72 percent (Bond and Semaan 1996; Harris et al. 2003; Krug et al. 2002).

A Bureau of Justice Special Report estimates that roughly 60 percent of women in state prisons have experienced some type of physical or sexual abuse at some point in their lives; however, other studies find much higher rates of abuse among incarcerated women (for example, Fickenscher et al. 2001). Because child physical and sexual abuse and intimate partner violence receive the most research attention, we will now explore these specific forms of violence in the lives of incarcerated women.

Child Physical and Sexual Abuse

As it relates to incarcerated women, researchers are beginning to recognize the high prevalence of childhood sexual and physical abuse histories among this population of women, as well as its relationship to women's subsequent drug use and criminal behavior. For example, Browne, Miller, and Maguin (1999) found that 70 percent of women detained in a maximum security prison reported severe physical violence by a caretaker in their childhood or adolescence. Additionally, more than half of the women (59 percent) reported sexual abuse during childhood and adolescence, with 51 percent indicating that the abuse first occurred between the ages of 0 to 9 years and 42 percent indicating that it lasted more than one year in duration. Even more disturbing, Browne, Miller, and Maguin found that 80 percent of women reporting severe childhood physical violence also later experienced severe physical violence by an intimate partner. Additionally, women who experienced sexual abuse in childhood were significantly more likely to experience sexual assaults by nonintimate partners in adulthood (40 percent vs. 23 percent).

Another study examining post-traumatic stress disorder (PTSD) and child abuse in a population of incarcerated women found that not only did nearly half (48 percent) of the women meet the criteria for current PTSD, but also 40 percent reported childhood sexual abuse, and 55 percent reported childhood physical abuse (Zlotnick 1997). Additionally, the study found that those with past or current PTSD had a significantly higher frequency of history of child sexual or physical abuse than those without PTSD. In their study examining the psychosocial issues and service needs of incarcerated women at a municipal jail, Singer, Bussey, Song, and Lunghofer (1995) found that almost half (48 percent) of the women reported sexual abuse as children. Similarly, 44 percent of women interviewed in a Philadelphia county jail reported being beaten by their parents (Bond and Semaan 1996), and 55 percent and 39 percent of women in a maximum security prison in Virginia reported child sexual and physical abuse, respectively (Warren et al. 2002).

In addition to the overwhelming evidence in support of the high prevalence of childhood physical and sexual abuse among incarcerated women, there is also evidence to suggest that there is a relationship between prior abuse and drug use. Specifically, Richie and Johnsen (1996) examined the abuse histories of women in a New York City jail and their relationship to drug use, homelessness, and suicide. They found that 24 percent of the women had experienced physical abuse and 19 percent had experienced sexual abuse during their childhood and adolescence. Even more striking, they found that women who reported child physical abuse were significantly more likely to report drug use and homelessness (OR = 3.47; OR = 3.36) than women who were not physically abused as children. They were also almost ten times more likely to have attempted suicide (OR = 9.7). Additionally, women who reported experiencing child sexual abuse were almost nine times more likely to use drugs (OR = 8.51).

Intimate Partner Violence

Turning to violence toward adult women, intimate partner violence is one of the most common and recognized forms of violence and abuse in the lives of women. In fact, intimate partners (including current and former legal spouses, current and former common-law spouses, current and former boyfriends/girlfriends[1] that may or may not be cohabiting) are the primary perpetrators of violence: 76 percent of women who were physically or sexually assaulted as adults were assaulted by an intimate partner (Tjaden and Thoennes 1998).

Similar to childhood physical and sexual abuse, there have been numerous studies documenting the extreme prevalence of intimate partner violence among incarcerated women. In one study of women who were county jail inmates, an overwhelming 72 percent of study participants reported having been physically assaulted by an intimate partner (Bond and Semann 1996). Fogel and Belyea (1999) found similar results among women incarcerated in a medium- to maximum-security prison. Specifically, 70 percent of the women in their study reported physical abuse by a partner or close other. Additionally, 49 percent of the women had been forced to have sex by a partner, and 25 percent of women reported being afraid of their current partner. In their study of the prevalence and severity of lifetime physical and sexual abuse among incarcerated women, Browne, Miller, and Maguin (1999) also found startling rates of severe intimate partner violence. Seventy-five percent of the women in their study reported intimate partner violence, including being kicked, bitten, or hit with a fist (60 percent); beaten up (57 percent); hit with an object (50 percent); choked, strangled, or smothered (40 percent); and cut with a knife or shot at (25 percent). Additionally, 35 percent of study participants reported being sexually assaulted or raped by an intimate partner. Finally, 62 percent of women reported being injured by an intimate partner. However, another study found a much smaller prevalence of intimate partner violence. Harris et al. (2003) found that 33 percent of incarcerated women had experienced abuse by their partners and about 18 percent feared their partners.

Community Violence

In contrast to other forms of violence, such as child sexual abuse and intimate partner violence, there is little empirical evidence on the prevalence and impact of exposure to community violence in the lives of adult women—both those in the community and incarcerated women. Yet there is some evidence to suggest that community violence is a significant aspect of women's experience of violence and abuse overall (Jenkins 2002; Sanders-Phillips 1996). For incarcerated women, exposure to and the psychological impact of community violence may be even more pronounced than for women in the community (Browne, Miller, and Maguin 1999; Singer et al. 1995). Following Browne, Miller, and Maguin's argument, exposure to community violence may precipitate or support women's involvement with drug use and crime through psychological distress and/or environmental cues that influence behavior. However, there are few studies that explicitly report incarcerated women's exposure to community violence prior to incarceration, and empirical evidence of this exposure is difficult to assess because of the definitional and measurement problems previously discussed.

Despite these problems, it is evident that exposure to community violence is a significant issue for many incarcerated women. A few researchers have documented incarcerated women's extensive histories of personally experienced community violence either implicitly or explicitly, citing experiences of physical and sexual violence. One of the only known studies that directly examines exposure to community violence among incarcerated women and its connection to drug use and sexual risk behaviors, Harris et al. (2003) found that 69 percent of the women in their sample reported both personally experienced and witnessed community violence following their release. Additionally, 19 percent of study participants reported that they either personally experienced or witnessed community violence. Furthermore, personally experienced violence following release was positively correlated with subsequent incarceration for probation violations ($r = .226$, $p = .003$). In another study assessing the health and rehabilitative intervention needs of women incarcerated in a municipal jail, 68 percent of the women surveyed reported sexual victimization as adults (Singer et al. 1995). While some of these victimizations are presumably the result of intimate partner violence (which was not specifically examined in this study), many of the women reported being assaulted in their neighborhoods by strangers and other neighborhood residents. Additionally, 75 percent of the women in this study reported being threatened with physical violence over the past year, and 69 percent actually experienced physical violence. Again, while these threats and attacks came from a variety of sources, many took place in women's communities from drug dealers, other neighborhood residents, and strangers.

While the specific location of the violence is not stated, Browne, Miller, and Maguin (1999) report on women's experiences of physical and sexual abuse by nonintimate partners or family members. Seventy-seven percent of study participants reported experiencing some form of victimization, ranging from threats with weapons to physical and sexual assaults.

Finally, one of the few studies examining the impact of community violence on the health behaviors of adult nonincarcerated women used data from in-depth interviews with women about their exposure to community violence (Smith 2004). Study findings suggested a direct relationship between exposure to community violence and drug use, which is the predominant reason for incarceration among women (Browne, Miller, and Maguin 1999; Fogel and Belyea 1999). The study participants who were former drug users (54 percent) indicated that the environment in their neighborhoods, which were rampant with violence, drugs, and drug dealers, influenced their initiation of drug use and posed a current threat to their recovery processes. Additionally, while not specifically measured in the study, several of the women reported prior drug-related criminal behavior or incarceration.

Health Consequences of Violence

Although incarcerated women's exposure to violence is well documented, we know much less about how this exposure impacts their health. Women who are victims of violence often find themselves negotiating through a life of danger, pain, and suffering. The repeated experience of extreme physical or sexual trauma, whether at the hands of loved ones or strangers, wreaks havoc on every aspect of abused women's lives. Violence combined with socioeconomic hardship negatively impacts the short- and long-term health condition of women and places them on a life trajectory that often leads to incarceration. Research shows that a history of physical abuse is associated with poor health for female inmates (Fickenscher et al. 2001). Thus, in light of the high rates of abuse that incarcerated women experience over the life course, it may not be surprising that their overall physical health status is poor compared to women in the general population. Notably, because women presumably have improved access to mental and physical health services once incarcerated (although this contention is certainly subject for debate), it is within the walls of prisons and jails that the physical and mental effects of violence become apparent.

Mental Health

One of the most frequent psychological consequences of violence against women is PTSD. This is an anxiety disorder occurring in the lives of people who have experienced extreme trauma, be it a single occurrence or a continuous period in the life of the victim. The *Diagnostic and Statistical Manual of Mental Disorders* describes it as the "development of characteristic symptoms following exposure to an extreme traumatic stressor" (American Psychiatric Association 1994). These symptoms are categorized in three groups: (1) reexperiencing, that is, intrusive thoughts, nightmares, flashbacks, and trigger responses; (2) avoidance/numbing, that is, avoiding situations similar to the traumatic event, amnesia, isolation, and emotional numbness; and (3) increased baseline physiological arousal, that is, insomnia, angry outbursts or irritability, and overall jumpiness (Baker and Alfonso n.d.).

Women prisoners under correctional authority experience higher rates of violence than those who are not incarcerated. Therefore, it is not surprising that the prevalence of PTSD for female inmates is greater than that of the general population. In a study of female pretrial detainees in jail, PTSD was one of the three most common psychiatric disorders reported, second only to alcohol abuse and drug abuse (Teplin, Abram, and McClelland 1996). The study found that 33.5 percent of the women exhibited PTSD at some point in their lives. That is three times the rate for women and six times the rate for men in the general U.S. population (National Center for Post Traumatic Stress Disorder, n.d.). Not only did the female jail detainees have extremely high rates of lifetime PTSD, 22.3 percent exhibited PTSD within six months of being interviewed. For these women, most of them were raped or violently assaulted in some way (Teplin, Abram, and McClelland 1996).

The first large-scale epidemiologic study of U.S. women prisoners reported that 30 percent of the women who experienced a traumatic lifetime event showed six or more PTSD symptoms over a six-month period (Jordan et al. 1996). Zlotnick's case study of a state prison reported 48.2 percent women prisoners had current PTSD and 20 percent had lifetime PTSD. Over 87 percent reported at least one extreme traumatic event. When compared to inmates without PTSD, those with PTSD had greater odds of co-morbidity with major depression, borderline personality disorder, and lifetime substance abuse (Zlotnick 1997).

Aside from PTSD, the impact of violence on women prisoners is also revealed in the high rates of psychiatric morbidity in this population as compared to incarcerated men. Ditton reported that 80 percent of the mentally ill female inmates in state prisons had been physically or sexually abused. Research reveals that mental disorders are more prevalent in the female prison population than the incarcerated male population. For women, 24 percent in state prisons and 22 percent in federal prisons are diagnosed as mentally ill, compared to 16 percent and 15 percent for men. When examining who receives mental health services in prison, over 67 percent of women in state prisons, 77 percent in federal prisons and 57 percent in jails receive psychiatric treatment. The comparable rates for male prisoners are 60 percent, 57 percent and 38 percent (Ditton 1999). In state prisons, 27 percent of women are in therapy or counseling, and 22 percent take psychotropic medicine; 12 percent of men are in therapy/counseling, and 9 percent receive medication (Beck and Maruschak 2001).

Substance abuse is the leading psychiatric disorder among incarcerated women. Drug abuse is associated with physical/sexual abuse, with abused girls having an increased risk of drug use (Browne, Miller, and Maguin 1999). Approximately half of all women state prisoners used drugs, alcohol, or both at the time of their arrest. These women also scored higher on every measure of drug abuse than male state prisoners (Greenfeld and Snell 1999). Teplin and colleagues (1996) assessed the mental condition of 1,272 women jail detainees and determined that 80 percent met the criteria for one or more lifetime psychiatric disorders (see table 4.1). Drug abuse was the most prevalent disorder, followed by alcohol abuse. Other studies show similar rates of drug abuse, alcohol abuse, or both (Bond and

Semaan 1996; Harris et al. 2003; Jordan et al. 1996; Phillips, Nixon, and Pfefferbaum 2002).

Physical Health

In general, incarcerated women have worse physical health than women and men
in the general population as well as incarcerated men. In both state and federal
prisons, women are more likely to report a physical or mental condition than men
(see table 4.2; Maruschak and Beck 2001). Physically and sexually abused women
prisoners are often homeless just prior to incarceration (Bond and Semaan 1996;
Browne, Miller, and Maguin 1999; Fickenscher et al. 2001), and prisoners who were
homeless are more likely to report a physical impairment or medical condition
than those with a more stable housing situation (Maruschak and Beck 2001). Female inmates have higher rates of illness than men for infectious diseases, respiratory and digestive conditions, genitourinary disorders, headaches, ear disease,
and skin and musculoskeletal diseases (Anderson 2003).

A history of physical and sexual abuse is highly correlated with drug abuse,
prostitution, and unsafe sex practices (Bond and Semaan 1996; Fickenscher et al.

TABLE 4.1

Lifetime prevalence of specific psychiatric disorders among women entering jail

Disorder	% Totals
Severe Disorders	18.5
Schizophrenial/schizopheniform	2.4
Manic episode	2.6
Major depressive episode	16.9
Dysthymia	9.6
Substance abuse/dependence	70.2
Alcohol abuse/dependence	32.3
Drug abuse/dependence	63.6
Panic disorder	1.6
Generalized anxiety disorder	2.5
Post-traumatic stress disorder	33.5
Antisocial personality disorder	13.8
Any of the above disorders	80.6

Source: Teplin, Abram, and McClelland (1996)

TABLE 4.2

Percent of inmates who reported a physical impairment or mental condition

Facility Type	Any condition	Hearing	Vision	Physical	Mental
State Prisoners					
Gender					
Male	30.7	5.6	8.2	11.8	9.6
Female	34.4	6.5	8.8	13.5	16.1
Federal Prisoners					
Gender					
Male	22.9	5.5	7.5	10.9	4.4
Female	29.9	5.8	8.6	13.9	9.7

Source: Maruschak and Beck (2001)

2001; Fogel and Belyea 1999; Harris et al. 2003). Such behavior prior to incarceration places women prisoners who have been victimized at high risk for sexually transmitted diseases and HIV/AIDS. In 2001, 3.2 percent of all women in state prison were HIV positive, compared to 2 percent of men. In the same year, the rate of HIV positivity was 5 percent in nine states and 10 percent in three other states (Maruschak 2004).

Intravenous drug use and the use of crack cocaine are associated with increased risk for HIV. Women prisoners report the use and abuse of these drugs at an extremely high rate. Crack cocaine usage rates range from over 61 percent to almost 75 percent (Fogel and Belyea 1999; Bond and Semaan 1996). Intraveneous drug use from one study was about 40 percent, with inmates first experimenting with IV drugs as early as age thirteen (Harris et al. 2003). A jail study reported that 97 percent of the women had had sex while using IV drugs (Fogel and Belyea 1999). In another jail study, Bond and Semaan (1996) reported that more than 75 percent of the women had used crack cocaine, 33 percent had used IV drugs, and 50 percent had had sex with a male who injected drugs.

The sexual behavior of incarcerated women also increases their risk for HIV. The women often reported trading sex for money or drugs; 43 percent in one study and over 50 percent in another (Fickenscher et al. 2001; Bond and Semaan 1996). Fogel and Belyea (1999) found over 70 percent of inmates did not use condoms while engaging in sex; many had multiple partners and never used protection. Harris and colleagues reported less than half of the women in their study used condoms for vaginal intercourse and even fewer (26 percent) used condoms for oral sex. In the same study, the threat of physical violence by a partner was found to be associated with the women's HIV/AIDS high-risk behavior.

Problems with Daily Functioning

Women prisoners who have been abused face tremendous barriers to healing and wholeness. The socioeconomic context in which the extreme trauma occurs often sets the stage for incarceration. Poverty, low levels of education, and community crime are the demographic descriptors for most incarcerated women. When victims live in conditions bound by these realities, health service resources are less accessible due to cost constraints or location. Violent abuse occurring in the least healthy communities severely diminishes the opportunity for their members to have a healthy, safe, and productive life.

Thus far, this chapter has focused on mental and physical health consequences of violence. But how is the ability to function impacted by physical and sexual abuse? The conception of dysfunctionality may occur at the onset of the violence; however, it may have long-standing impact on all aspects of victims' lives, including their relationships.

When children are abused by parents, where is their safe space? Possibly other family members, primary caregivers, or outside help such as teachers are expected to step in. But what if there are multiple abusers, and outside help never comes? When there is no place or person that is a source of protection, what recourse do women and girls have to feel safe? For most incarcerated women who have been abused, they found neither safe space nor assistance with processing the trauma that they experienced over the course of their lives. The lack of safe space for girls and women implies the need for them to always be in a heightened state of awareness of danger. Trauma theory argues that the natural instinct to avoid danger has gone awry and is overly sensitive (Bloom 1997). Instead of a normal physiological response arising during infrequent confrontations with danger, trauma theory argues that abused women are continually in a state of readiness to face danger. Their mental, physical, and emotional responses to fear become maladaptive; in essence, their danger "switch" is always on.

Emotionally and physiologically, women in this state do not function well in everyday situations. The skills and understanding necessary for relationships are stagnated; normal interpersonal actions are foreign. Engaging in high-risk sexual behavior, eating disorders, angry and violent behavior, and suicide attempts are common among victims of violence (Browne, Miller, and Maguin 1999; Fickenscher et al. 2001; Maeve 2000; Scanlon 1993). Reliance on substances to manage the pain is common, as evidenced by high co-morbidity of substance abuse and other stress disorders. Severe abuse distorts right and wrong in the eyes of the victims (Scanlon 1993). Women inmates abused as children are often runaways as adolescents. On the streets, these young traumatized women are often prey to drug dealers and pimps offering "protection." These relationships, clearly dangerous and unhealthy, are often the only ones available to victims of abuse living on the street. Often already engaged in deviant sexual and drug behavior, prostitution, robbery, and drug addiction become a way of life for victims of abuse (Browne, Miller, and Maguin 1999; Fickenscher et al. 2001; Maeve 2000).

That women with early experiences of physical and sexual abuse are at increased risk for subsequent violence is a robust finding that has been substantiated in many different populations of women (Breitenbecher 2001; Browne, Miller, and Maguin 1999; Desai et al. 2002; Muehlenhard et al. 1998; Rich et al. 2004). One of the most reliable aftereffects of physical or sexual abuse is victims getting involved with violent intimate partners (Browne, Miller, and Maguin 1999). Such a relationship increases the risk for incarceration as women find themselves needing to resort to violence to protect themselves or others from the perpetrators of violence and are likely to have information about or connections to criminal activity carried out by their partners (Browne, Miller, and Maguin 1999). Violent intimate partners are associated with unsafe sexual behavior by women because women inmates report being afraid to suggest using condoms during sex with violent partners (Harris et al. 2003). Such relationships perpetuate the cycle of violence as well as the physical and mental consequences of abuse, increasing the pain, brokenness, and suffering of the victims.

Adult women living with violent intimate partners are locked into their situation for many reasons. Intimate partner violence impacts the accessibility of health services. Fear and shame often prevent women from seeking medical help for physical or sexual abuse while in the community, even if they maintain regular health visits for themselves and their children. Furthermore, because of the high rates of drug abuse, ex-offenders often do not seek help out of fear that their habit will be discovered and they will return to jail (Staton, Leukefeld, and Logan 2001). Thus, female inmates, both prior to incarceration and post-incarceration, do not receive medical treatment for either intimate partner violence or drug abuse. Without help, the stress and physical and mental harm continue unabated.

The Gender Entrapment Theoretical Model

The research literature has thoroughly documented that the lives of incarcerated women are overburdened by experiences of physical and sexual violence. Moreover, it is clear that this violence has far-reaching negative consequences for their mental and physical health. However, what is less clear is *how* violence is related to the criminal behavior that causes women to become incarcerated. One theoretical framework considers how gender identity development impacts the relationship between intimate partner violence and illegal behavior, particularly in the lives of incarcerated African American women (Richie 1996).

The gender entrapment theoretical model originates from the legal notion of entrapment, "which implies a circumstance whereby an individual is lured into a compromising act" (Richie 1996, 5). Drawing from a black feminist perspective, the theory of gender entrapment argues that African American battered women oftentimes engage in illegal behavior as a logical extension of their marginalized social positions, culturally expected gender roles, and the violence that surrounds them. In other words, race, class, gender, and violence converge in a socially constructed process that forces or coerces women to engage in illegal behavior. This model does not absolve African American battered women from personal responsibility; instead it acknowledges the social, cultural, financial, and political conditions that set them up for illegal behavior, thus compelling them to crime (Richie 1996).

Richie developed the gender entrapment theoretical model from the analysis of thirty-seven life history interviews (including white battered and nonbattered African American women) of women confined in the Rose M. Singer Center, the women's jail at Rikers Island Correctional Facility. At the foundation of the model is the structure and function of the women's household of origin. Richie observed a pattern in which African American battered women tended to grow up in households that were not organized around hegemonic gender roles. However, many of these women aspired to ideological norms of family structure and gender relations (for example, the traditional nuclear family) due to social and cultural expectations. Additionally, African American battered women tended to grow up experiencing limits on the life options that were available to them due to institutional forces of oppression (for example, through discrimination and sexual harassment).

This pattern of gender identity development sets the stage for violence in intimate relationships. Women tolerate this violence because of pressure to conform to traditional gender ideologies that dictate public and private roles for women. As the violence escalates, women are overcome by disbelief that the violence is occurring and the disorganization that characterizes their lives. It is emotionally draining for women to manage the discrepancy between the reality of their situation and the ideological norm. In part due to the social stigma of being battered, African American battered women tend to become isolated from their friends and families and have few social services available to assist them. Finally, the violence continues to escalate and the abuse increases in severity over time.

Recall that the purpose of this model is to understand how African American battered women come to engage in criminal behavior. Again, the model suggests that criminal behavior is a natural response to the violence that women have been victims of. Many women engage in illegal drug use as a way of dealing with the physical and emotional pain of being battered. Poverty in combination with having a controlling and abusive partner may cause women to engage in economic crimes (for example, stolen property, forged checks, stolen credit cards, commercial sex work). The years of abuse force some women to overreact to subsequent physical threats with assaults and property damage. Additionally, some battered women are so terrorized by their partners that they are not able to protect their children from abuse and neglect, which is itself an illegal activity that directly stems from the violence. Finally, some battered women feel extreme loyalty to their batterers, so much so that they will take responsibility for mutual criminal behavior or unknowingly have illegal substances or weapons planted on them.

This model of gender entrapment is the first known model to integrate multiple forms of oppression and violence in the lives of incarcerated African American women. To our knowledge, the model has not yet been tested. Nevertheless, it provides a strong theoretical foundation on which future studies of this population may develop. Finally, the extent to which the model is applicable to the lives of other oppressed women is unclear (for example, poor white women, African American lesbians, and so forth); however, it is likely that many elements of the model will remain relevant to members of any marginalized social group. Finally, although the model does not explicitly speak to the health of African American battered women, there are clearly widespread health implications of the model. For example, mental health may be compromised by the incongruence between one's ideological norms and the reality of her abusive relationship. Physical and mental health is certainly compromised by the physical abuse. Additionally, the use of illegal drugs and commercial sex work increases women's risk for contracting HIV/AIDS and other sexually transmitted diseases (see De Groot and Maddow, this volume).

Preventing Future Violence

Now that we know that incarcerated women experience high rates of violence and that it is negatively impacting their health, what can be done to prevent additional violence in their lives? It has long been argued that correctional settings are ideal for the delivery of health promotion programs (Braithwaite, Hammett, and Mayberry 1996; Freudenberg 2002; Watson, Stimpson, and Hostick 2004). Inmates have the time to focus on prevention, treatment, and care with few outside distractions; they have a constitutional right to health care during their incarceration that they do not have while residing in the general population; and incarceration oftentimes forces inmates to reevaluate their life decisions, sometimes allowing them to make positive changes in their lives. Although female inmates face the constant threat of institutional violence, at least incarceration affords separation from physical and sexual violence committed by intimate partners (although not necessarily emotional abuse). Thus, implementing primary and secondary violence prevention efforts in correctional settings has the potential to be highly effective.

A public health approach to violence in the lives of incarcerated women emphasizes collective action to prevent the future occurrence of violence as well as mitigating the effects of past exposure to violence (Krug et al. 2002). Specifically, there are three types of prevention that are commonly used in health-related fields:

- Primary prevention includes actions taken to prevent violence in the lives of women who have not yet been exposed to violence;
- Secondary prevention includes screening efforts to identify people who have already experienced some form of violence;
- Tertiary prevention includes providing medical or mental health treatment for an individual who has been victimized by violence.

Given the prominent role that violence plays in the lives of incarcerated women, it would be beneficial for correctional facilities to offer prevention services at all three levels. Primary prevention may be less appropriate because so many incarcerated women have already been victimized by violence, but certainly secondary and tertiary prevention is in order for members of this population. Out of recognition of the need for better coordinated violence prevention services, the National Commission on Correctional Health Care (2005) issued a position statement that provides guidelines on how to incorporate violence prevention, education, and treatment in correctional settings (see table 4.3). Generally, these guidelines involve assessing and treating inmates, training staff, and strengthening relationships with community-based organizations.

Finally, there is a need for more research around this topic. Although certainly not enough, some surveillance data have been collected documenting incarcerated women's overexposure to violence. Population-based surveys of

---

TABLE 4.3

National Commission on Correctional Health Care Position Statement on Correctional Health Care and the Prevention of Violence

- Incorporate violence risk assessment—including child and domestic abuse, sexual abuse, and any personal victimization—into receiving screening undertaken of all inmates upon intake, all inmate health assessments, and mental health evaluations.

- Refer as appropriate all inmates with violent histories (i.e. those with expressive violence), including those who exhibit violent behaviors that place the safety and welfare of themselves or others in jeopardy, to treatment by appropriately trained health care providers. Treatment should not consist of only placing the inmate on medication, but should take a balanced biopsychosocial approach to the treatment of inmate violence.

- Protocols and guidelines for violence prevention, intervention, and follow-up should be developed for use by qualified health professionals treating inmates. In addition, health care providers should receive training in these areas. Training should include information on policies and practices designed to prevent violence, nonphysical methods for preventing and/or controlling disruptive behaviors, appropriate use of medical restraints, and effective techniques for personal safety.

- Correctional officer training should include prevention of expressive violence and nonphysical methods for prevention and/or controlling disruptive behaviors stemming from expressive violence. Correctional officer training should continue to address security issues designed to inhibit instrumental and gang-related violence.

- All correctional facilities should establish contacts with community-based organizations able to assist in the treatment and continuity of care upon the inmate's release from the correctional facility.

incarcerated women are very difficult to conduct because of restricted access to inmates for researchers. The overprotection of inmates is justified by the egregious misuse of inmates in scientific research (see Hornblum 1998); however, it can serve to hinder the collection of data that could be used to improve inmates' lives. We know even less about *why* female inmates lives are plagued with violence. There has been little theory development surrounding health promotion among female inmates who have been victims of violence. The current theoretical models need to be tested on different samples of jail and prison female inmates so that they can be used to develop effective interventions for this population. Once this theory development is underway, we can further the development of effective risk reduction programs that reduce the likelihood of revictimization post-release, evaluate the programs, and ultimately disseminate them in correctional facilities and transitional programs across the country.

Conclusions

The convoluted cycle of violence, poor health, illegal behavior, and incarceration persists in the lives of many women. This chapter has documented that the violence that many incarcerated women are exposed to is chronic, severe, and has had long lasting effects on their mental and physical well-being. It is also notable that virtually all incarcerated women are exposed to nonviolent forms of trauma (including emotional abuse, child maltreatment, family separation, loss of liberty, death of a close family member, and so on) although the focus of this chapter has been on violent trauma.

The literature documents interrelationships among experiences of violence and poor mental health. Specifically, victims of violence are at risk for developing PTSD, substance abuse disorders, and a host of other psychiatric disorders, which certainly shapes their likelihood for engaging in illegal behavior and ultimately being incarcerated. Moreover, the literature suggests that the experience of sexual violence, in particular, is associated with engaging in sexual behavior that puts women at risk for HIV/AIDS and sexually transmitted diseases. Finally, many victims of violence are so severely impacted by their experiences of violence that they remain in a constant state of arousal, thereby impacting their ability to function in everyday situations. However, there has been little theory development to understand the role of violence in incarcerated women's lives. The theory of gender entrapment is one explanatory framework that is relevant to the lives of African American women, and it sheds some light on this topic.

Finally, it is noteworthy that many incarcerated women exhibit great strength and determination in the face of their victimization and incarceration. Not all incarcerated women have passively and helplessly accepted their plight as victims of physical and sexual violence. Many incarcerated women acknowledge the violence in their lives, their role in perpetuating the violence (for example, due to a drug habit or out of fear), and the criminal behavior that they engaged in as a function of the violence (see Johnson 2003). Despite the dehumanization of incarceration, they are still human beings that do not want to be defined in terms of their victimization or criminal charges. Through spirituality, poetry, support systems, personal resilience, friends, and family, many incarcerated women are able to recover from tragic exposures to violent trauma.

NOTE

1. Most of the research literature focuses on physical and sexual violence against women in heterosexual relationships. However, more research attention is being given to the battering of lesbians. See Kaschak (2001) for a review of this literature.

REFERENCES

American Psychiatric Association. 1994. *Diagnostic and statistical manual of mental disorders,* 4th ed. Washington, DC: American Psychiatric Association.

Anderson, T. 2003. Issues in the availability of health care for women prisoners. In *Incarcerated women: Rehabilitative programming in women's prisons,* ed. S. Sharp. Englewood Cliffs, NJ: Prentice Hall.

Baker, C., and C. Alfonso. PTSD and criminal behavior: A national center for PTSD Fact Sheet. Department of Veterans Affairs, National Center for Post-Traumatic Stress Disorder. http://www.ncptsd.org/facts/specific/fs_legal.html?printable=yes (accessed June 1, 2004).

Basile, K. C., and L. E. Saltzman. 2002. *Sexual violence surveillance: Uniform definitions and recommended data elements* (Version 1.0). Atlanta, GA: Centers for Disease Control and Prevention National Center for Injury Prevention and Control.

Beck, A., and L. Maruschak. 2001. Mental health treatment in state prisons, 2000. Washington, DC: U.S. Department of Justice; Office of Justice Programs, Bureau of Justice Statistics.

Bloom, S. 1997. *Creating sanctuary: Toward an evaluation of sane societies.* New York: Guilford Press.

Bond, L., and S. Semaan. 1996. At risk for HIV infection: Incarcerated women in a county jail in Philadelphia. *Women and Health* 24: 27–45.

Braithwaite, R. L., T. M. Hammett, and R. M. Mayberry. 1996. *Prisons and aids: A public health challenge.* San Francisco: Jossey-Bass.

Breitenbecher, K. H. 2001. Sexual revictimization among women. A review of the literature focusing on empirical investigations. *Aggressive and Violent Behavior* 6: 415–32.

Browne, A., B. Miller, and E. Maguin. 1999. Prevalence and severity of lifetime physical and sexual victimization among incarcerated women. *International Journal of Law and Psychiatry* 22: 301–22.

Desai, S., I. Arias, M. P. Thompson, and K. C. Basile. 2002. Childhood victimization and subsequent adult revictimization assessed in a nationally representative sample of women and men. *Violence and Victims* 17: 639–53.

Ditton, P. 1999. Mental health and treatment of inmates and probationers. Washington, DC: U.S. Department of Justice; Office of Justice Programs, Bureau of Justice Statistics.

Fickenscher, A., J. Lapidus, P. Silk-Walker, and T. Becker. 2001. Women behind bars: Health needs of inmates in a county jail. *Public Health Reports* 116: 191–96.

Fogel, C., and M. Belyea. 1999. The lives of incarcerated women: Violence, substance abuse, and at risk for HIV. *Journal of the Association of Nurses in AIDS Care* 10, no. 6: 66–74.

Freudenberg, N. 2002. Adverse effects of U.S. jail and prison policies on the health and well-being of women of color. *American Journal of Public Health* 92: 1895–99.

Greenfeld, L. A., and T. L. Snell. 1999. *Women offenders.* Bureau of Justice Statistics Special Report. NCJ 175688. U.S. Department of Justice Office of Justice Programs.

Guterman, N. B., M. Cameron, and K. Staller. 2000. Definitional measurement issues in the study of community violence among children and youths. *Journal of Community Psychology* 28: 571–87.

Harris, R. M., P. W. Sharps, K. Allen, E. H. Anderson, K. Soeken, and A. Rohatas. 2003. The interrelationship between violence, HIV/AIDS, and drug use in incarcerated women. *Journal of the Association of Nurses in AIDS Care* 14: 27–40.

Hornblum, A. M. 1998. *Acres of skin: Human experiments at Holmesburg Prison: A true story of abuse and exploitation in the name of medical science.* New York: Routledge.

Jenkins, E. J. 2002. Black women and community violence: Trauma, grief, and coping. *Women and Therapy: A Feminist Quarterly* 25: 29–44.

Jewkes, R. 2000. Violence against women: An emerging health problem. *International Clinical Psychopharmacology* 15 (Suppl 3): S37–S45.

Johnson, P. C. 2003. *Inner lives: Voices of African American women in prison.* New York: New York University Press.

Jordan, B., W. Schlenger, J. Fairbank, and J. Caddell. 1996. Prevalence of psychiatric disorders among incarcerated women: II. Convicted felons entering prison. *Archives of General Psychiatry* 53, no. 6: 513–19.

Kaschak, E. 2001. *Intimate betrayal: Domestic violence in lesbian relationships.* Binghampton, NY: Haworth Press.

Krug, E. G., L. L. Dahlberg, J. A. Mercy, A. B. Zwi, and R. Lozano, eds. 2002. *World report on violence and health.* Geneva, Switzerland: World Health Organization.

Maeve, M. 2000. Speaking unavoidable truths: Understanding early childhood sexual and physical violence among women in prison. *Journal of Mental Health Nursing* 21: 473–98.

Maman, S., J. Campbell, M. D. Sweat, and A. C. Gielen. 2000. The intersections of HIV and violence: Directions for future research and interventions. *Social Science and Medicine* 50: 459–78.

Maruschak, L. 2004. HIV in prisons, 2001. Washington, DC: U.S. Department of Justice, Office of Justice Programs, Bureau of Justice Statistics.

Maruschak, L., and A. Beck. 2001. Medical problems of inmates, 1997. Washington, DC: U.S. Department of Justice, Office of Justice Programs, Bureau of Justice Statistics.

Muehlenhard, C. L., B. J. Highby, R. S. Lee, T. S. Bryan, and W. A. Dodrill. 1998. The sexual revictimization of women and men sexually abused as children: A review of the literature. *Annual Review of Sex Research* 9: 177–224.

National Center for Post-Traumatic Stress Disorder. What is posttraumatic stress disorder? A National Center for PTSD Fact Sheet. http://www.ncptsd.org/facts/general/fs_what_is_ptsd.html (accessed June 1, 2004).

National Commission on Correctional Health Care. 2005. Position statement on correctional health care and the prevention of violence. http://www.ncchc.org/resources/statements/prevention.html (accessed February 7, 2005).

Phillips, J., S. Nixon, and B. Pfefferbaum. 2002. A comparison of substance abuse among female offender subtypes. *The Journal of the American Academy of Psychiatry and the Law* 30, no. 4: 13–19.

Rennison, C. M., and S. Welchans. 2000. *Intimate partner violence.* Bureau of Justice Statistics Special Report. NCJ 178247. U.S. Department of Justice Office of Justice Programs.

Rich, C. L., A. M. Combs-Lane, H. S. Resnick, and D. G. Kilpatrick. 2004. Child sexual abuse and adult sexual revictimization. In *From child sexual abuse to adult sexual risk: Trauma, revictimization and intervention,* ed. L. J. Koenig, S. S. Doll, A. O'Leary, and W. Pequegnat. Washington, DC: American Psychological Association. 49–68.

Richie, B. E. 1996. *Compelled to crime: The gender entrapment of battered black women.* New York: Routledge.

Richie, B. E., and C. Johnsen. 1996. Abuse histories among newly incarcerated women in a New York City jail. *Journal of the American Medical Women's Association* 51: 111–14.

Sable, M. R., J. R. Fieberg, S. L. Martin, and L. L. Kupper. 1999. Violence victimization experiences of pregnant prisoners. *American Journal of Orthopsychiatry* 69: 392–97.

Sanders-Phillips, K. 1996. Correlates of health promotion behaviors in low-income black women and Latinas. *American Journal of Preventive Medicine* 12: 450–58.

Scanlon, M. 1993. Women in prison. *Psychology Today*, 44–47, 84–86.

Singer, M., J. Bussey, L. Song, and L. Lunghofer. 1995. The psychosocial issues of women serving time in jail. *Social Work* 40, no. 1: 103–13.

Smith, L. S. 2004. Exposure to community violence: Its impact on health behaviors and coping responses among low-income black women. Masters thesis, Emory University, Atlanta, GA.

Staton, M., C. Leukefeld, and T. Logan. 2001. Health service utilization and victimization among incarcerated female substance users. *Substance Use and Misuse* 36, no. 6, 7: 701–16.

Teplin, L., K. Abram, and M. McClelland. 1996. Prevalence of psychiatric disorders among incarcerated women: I. Pretrial jail detainees. *Archives of General Psychiatry* 53, no. 6: 505–12.

Tjaden, P., and N. Thoennes. 1998. *Prevalence, incidence, and consequences of violence against women: Findings from the National Violence Against Women Survey.* National Institute of Justice Centers for Disease Control and Prevention Research in Brief. NCJ 172837. U.S. Department of Justice, Office of Justice Programs.

Warren, J., M. Burnette, S. South, P. Chauhan, R. Bale, and R. Friend. 2002. *The Journal of the American Academy of Psychiatry and the Law* 30, no. 4: 502–9.

Watson, R., A. Stimpson, and T. Hostick. 2004. Prison health care: A review of the literature. *International Journal of Nursing Studies* 41: 119–28.

Zlotnick, C. 1997. Posttraumatic stress disorder (PTSD), PTSD comorbidity, and childhood abuse among incarcerated women. *Journal of Nervous and Mental Disease* 185, no. 12: 761–63.

5

Sugar and Spice

Understanding the Health of Incarcerated Girls

MICHELLE STAPLES-HORNE

"Why Am I Here?"

Historically, it has been commonly accepted that males commit more offenses than females, even among juvenile populations. Most female offenders were involved in the criminal justice system through status offenses (running away, truancy), property offenses, and other nonviolent crimes. As females approach equality in society, so do they close the gap on the types of offenses as well as on arrest rates. This change may be due to girls' attempts to more closely mimic some boys' violent and aggressive behaviors or to the legal system's response of taking a less paternal role than it has in the past. Public policy, school policy, and greater societal changes in attitude regarding domestic and other forms of violence may also influence these changes. Over the last two decades, girls have increasingly entered the juvenile justice system at younger ages and with greater needs. Girls represent a minority within the juvenile correctional system. As such, their specific needs are often overlooked while the system focuses on the needs of the majority male population. In general, girls that end up in the juvenile system tend to represent the more severe cases of neglect, abuse, and victimization. They experience more serious medical and mental health needs and demonstrate lower self-esteem than their male counterparts. In a traditionally male predominated environment, girls have gender specific needs that the system may be ill equipped to provide.

In most cases, girls were victims themselves before they became offenders (Davis et al. 1997; Girls, Inc. 1996; Prescott 1997). When girls are angry, frightened, or unloved, they are more likely to strike inward than boys. They may hurt their bodies through prostitution, substance abuse, eating disorders, or self-mutilation. Other internalizing disorders may manifest themselves as depression and/or anxiety disorders. In one study, female incarcerated youth showed emotional symptoms of depression (28 percent) or anxiety (28 percent) (Kataoka et al. 2001).

Since girls in crisis may be more likely to threaten their own well-being rather than that of others or society in general, we tend to overlook and undertreat their needs (Chesney-Lind 1988). Girls in trouble have been the afterthought of a juvenile justice system designed to deal primarily with boys (Miller et al. 1995).

Girls are three times as likely to have been sexually abused as boys. In some detention facilities, the incidence of girls who have been abused is closer to 90 percent. Most often, abuse is perpetrated by family members or close family friends who are perceived as trusted adults (Davis et al. 1997). Sexual abuse can have a profound impact on a girl during adolescence, resulting in lessened self-esteem, inability to trust, academic failure, eating disorders, teen pregnancy, and other serious concerns. If sexual abuse is not addressed, girls may run away or turn to alcohol or other drugs to numb their emotional pain (Acoca 1998). A few lash out at their perpetrators violently.

The most significant risk factor relating to early onset of delinquency is poor academic performance (Dryfoos 1990; Greenwood et al. 1996; Yoshikawa 1994). Girls who are juvenile offenders may have reacted to academic challenges in the past by skipping school or dropping out altogether (Hugo and Rutherford 1992). A disproportionate number of female juvenile offenders have learning disabilities. By the time they enter the system, they may be at least a grade level behind their peers. They may have developed a negative attitude about learning and lack self-confidence about their own ability to master academic skills (Girls, Inc. 1996).

"Am I the Only One Here?"

Overall, girls do pose a smaller problem than male delinquents. They commit far fewer crimes than boys. In 1995, girls accounted for about one-fourth of juvenile arrests (25.5 percent of those under eighteen arrested in 1995 were female; Maguire and Pastore 1997). Girls who break the law may not be perceived as a danger to society because, traditionally, they have come into contact with the courts for nonviolent status offenses such as curfew violations, running away, or unruly behavior (Chesney-Lind 1988). Theft cases accounted for nearly one-fourth of girls' arrests (Bergsmann 1994).

These trends appear to be changing. During the decade from 1983 to 1993, arrests of female juveniles increased by 31 percent (compared to a 21 percent increase for boys). Between 1989 and 1993, the relative growth in juvenile arrests involving females was 23 percent, more than double the 11 percent growth for males (Poe-Yamagata and Butts 1996). In 1999, law enforcement agencies reported 67,000 arrests for females less than eighteen years of age representing 20 percent of total arrests in that age group (American Bar Association [2001]).

According to the FBI, between 1990 and 1999, the number of arrests of juvenile females increased more or decreased less than the number of male arrests in most offense categories. In 1980, females represented only 11 percent of all juveniles for violent offenses. By 1999, the proportion of violent offenses had increased to 17 percent. There is controversy over the reason for the increase in violent crimes committed by girls as to whether there is a true increase in number of offenses or whether arresting officers are now more likely to charge a girl with a violent offense now than in the past, especially since many of these offenses with girls involve family or friends.

The increase in arrests of female juvenile offenders affects several levels of the juvenile justice system, from probation services to residential programs and aftercare. Between 1988 and 1997, the number of juvenile court delinquency cases involving males increased 39 percent, while the number of cases involving females increased 85 percent. During this period, the relative change in delinquency cases was greater for females than for males in all major offense categories (Office of Juvenile Justice and Delinquency Prevention [OJJDP] 2001).

In 1997, there were over a million arrests of juvenile girls in the United States. In that year, 26 percent of all juvenile arrests were girls. Over a third of these girls were less than fifteen years of age. Girls represented 58 percent of the arrests for runaways. In 1988, 26 percent of the serious crimes committed by females were committed by girls less than eighteen years; by 1997 this figure increased to 31 percent. Between 1993 and 1997, a disturbing increase in serious crimes occurred among female juvenile offenders. During that period, arrests of boys for violent offenses declined by 9 percent, while those for girls increased by 12 percent. Aggravated assault, the most frequent of the violent offenses committed by juveniles, increased for girls by 15 percent while declining for boys by 10 percent. Arrests of girls for drug abuse violations more than doubled (117 percent increase). Girls arrested for offenses against family and children increased by 82 percent between 1993 and 1997. Between 1993 and 2002, arrest rates for females less than eighteen years old increased by 120 percent for drug abuse violations, 54 percent for offenses against family and children, and 7 percent for aggravated assault (Federal Bureau of Investigation 2003).

These statistics highlight the observation that interpersonal relationships play a significant role in female juvenile delinquency. For example, while homicides in 1993 committed by boys usually occurred in conjunction with another crime (57 percent), homicide by girls tended to be members of the girls' own families (32 percent for girls vs. 8 percent for boys). Twenty-four percent of the girls' victims were under three years old, usually their own infant children. According to the Federal Bureau of Investigation's *1993 Supplemental Homicide Reports,* delinquent girls are more likely than delinquent boys to victimize those with whom they have a relationship, such as a family member, and less likely to target strangers (Loper 2000).

Nationwide, girls are becoming involved with the justice system at a younger age. From 1987 to 1991, the number of thirteen- and fourteen-year-old girls in juvenile court increased by 10 percent (Bergsmann 1994). One in five girls in secure confinement is now aged fourteen or younger (OJJDP 1998) Younger girls are at risk of becoming victims of older girls in the system or being negatively influenced by them. They may not be as emotionally mature and have greater issues of separation anxiety than older juveniles. Programming may need to be adapted to fit their developmental stage and educational level.

Ethnic minorities are disproportionately represented in the female offender population (Bergsmann 1989; Campbell 1995; Community Research Associates 1997). African American girls comprised nearly half of all those in secure detention and Hispanics represented 13 percent (Bergsmann 1994). Although 65 percent of the population is Caucasian, only 34 percent of the girls in detention are Caucasian. Seven of every ten cases involving white girls are dismissed, compared to three of every ten cases dismissed for African American girls (OJJDP 1998).

Although their offenses are typically less violent, girls who break the law are sometimes treated more harshly than boys who offend (Davidson 1982). There are fewer community-based services for girls. As a result, girls are twice as likely to be detained, with detention lasting five times longer for girls than boys (Girls, Inc. 1996). In addition, girls are detained for less serious offenses. In 1987, 9 percent of girls in training schools were committed for status offenses, compared to 1.5 percent of boys (OJJDP 1998).

According to data collected from the Annie E. Casey Foundation's *Juvenile Detention Alternative Initiative* (JDAI 1992), a study of detention in several cities across the United States, more girls than boys were detained for minor offenses such as public disorder, probation violations, and status and traffic offenses. The study also found that girls were more likely to be detained for probation and parole violations than boys. Over the four study sites reviewed, girls comprised only 14 percent of the total detention population; however, 30 percent of them returned to detention within one year. Among those, 53 percent of the girls as compared with 47 percent of the boys who returned to detention within one year did so for probation or technical violations (OJJDP 1998).

Gender equity in juvenile justice programming is an important focus of the Juvenile Justice and Delinquency Prevention Act, reauthorized in 1992. Under the act, states may receive challenge grants for "developing and adopting policies to prohibit gender bias in placement and treatment of young offenders" and for "establishing programs to ensure that female youth have access to the full range of health and mental health services, treatment for physical or sexual assault and abuse, self-defense instruction, education in parenting, education in general, and other training and vocational services." (21st Century Department of Justice Appropriations Authorization Act 1992).

"I Haven't Seen a Doctor"

Female juvenile offenders, an adolescent subgroup that has been understudied and underserved, are at increased risk of adverse health outcomes relative to nonincarcerated adolescent populations. This may be due to their prior criminal activities, physical and sexual abuse, lifestyle, and high-risk behaviors. They may already be medically underserved since they are less likely to have access to or use routine health care than juveniles in the general population. Juvenile offenders seldom seek preventive care or maintain routine medical visits. Immunizations are not kept current; preventive counseling and appropriate screenings are not completed. Most adolescents interfacing with the correctional system will access medical care in the community only in an acute situation and then usually through an emergency room rather than through a primary care provider. Many are uninsured and have parents who lack the financial resources to pay directly for medical care out of pocket.

Despite popular belief, juvenile offenders are not a young healthy group without any medical problems. The public's perception is often that these youths are "well enough to get in trouble." Ironically, it is just that behavior of getting into trouble that places them at greater health risk. Smoking, alcohol and drug use, risky sexual behaviors with multiple sex partners and lack of condom use, weapon use, violence, and other risk-taking behaviors place these youths at increased risk of morbidity and mortality. Detention and other secure juvenile settings offer an opportunity to conduct health assessments, diagnose, and offer treatment to girls who may otherwise not have received health care (Moore 2003).

A classic study conducted by Hein et al. in 1980 that included over 47,000 juvenile offenders remains the largest study of the health status of detainees. The population demographics were 80 percent male, 60 percent African American, and 25 percent Hispanic surnamed. Average age was fifteen with an average length of stay of fourteen days. The most commonly diagnosed conditions were minor trauma (21 percent), psychosomatic states (18 percent), upper respiratory infections (17 percent), and minor dermatological problems (14 percent). The largest unmet health need was identified as dental, with 90 percent of the youth with dental caries, and missing, fractured, or infected teeth.

In 1996, according to the National Adolescent Information Center, at any given time 30 percent of incarcerated youth had a chronic medical disease, 25 percent had a sexually transmitted infection (STI), 19 percent had dental problems, 11 percent had asthma or respiratory problems, and 63 percent were involved in regular drug use (Irwin et al. 1996).

Anderson and Farrow in 1998 described health services provided for incarcerated adolescents in Washington State. For short-term detention centers with a mean daily population of 47.2, the most common reasons for sick-call visits were for substance use (36.6 percent), trauma (30.8 percent), psychiatric (21.8 percent), dermatological (19.2 percent), respiratory (15.5 percent), and sexually transmitted diseases (15.3 percent). For long-term facilities with a mean daily population of 161.7, the most common complaints were for dental care (65.9 percent), psychiatric (44.9 percent), dermatological (44.1 percent), respiratory (35.6 percent), trauma (35.4 percent), and substance use (33.7 percent).

Although trends toward increasing numbers of female juvenile offenders create a challenge to the juvenile justice system, a particularly important priority is to address the health care needs of this population. Evidence suggests that incarcerated female adolescents are likely to have significant medical problems including untreated STIs, pregnancies lacking prenatal care, chronic medical conditions, substance use, and psychiatric disorders. Yet most do not have a regular source of medical care and more than half may not have families who are able or willing to help them seek medical care (Feinstein et al. 1998).

"How Do I Get Health Care?"

A health screening and examination is essential for adequate assessment of the health status of youth entering juvenile correctional facilities. Medical staff members should conduct screenings if at all possible. If medical staff is unavailable at times when youth enter the facility, correctional officers may be trained by medical staff to conduct health screenings. A system should be established for the screening correctional officer to refer youth to medical staff in case of a positive finding of an immediate health need on the medical intake screen and to make an appropriate disposition. If correctional officers are used, licensed medical staff should review the health screening no later than twenty-four hours after intake (National Commission on Correctional Health Care [NCCHC] 2004).

The purpose of medical screening is to determine if any current or past medical, mental, or dental conditions or allergies exist; whether drug intoxication, drug use, or communicable diseases are present; and the need for continued medication or treatment. Mental health questions relating to previous mental health diagnoses, previous hospitalizations, and to determine suicidal intent are essential. Evidence suggests that programs for incarcerated female adolescents should include a mental health evaluation designed to screen for emotional disorders and underlying substance abuse (Kataoka et al. 2001). While these needs are not unique to female offenders, they may be more prominent.

The Society for Adolescent Medicine (SAM) advocates screening of all incarcerated adolescents within twenty-four hours of their admission to a facility. Screening should include tests for contagious diseases and, in subsequent days, sexually transmitted diseases among sexually active adolescents (SAM 2000). Evidence clearly suggests that screening adolescent females for nonviral STDs is feasible and beneficial in detention facilities (CDC 1999). A full health assessment for youth should be conducted within seven days to include the screening information and a review of systems, vital signs, and laboratory and diagnostic tests to meet the community health requirements. Physician recommendations may include a dipstick urinalysis; hemoglobin; STI screen for gonorrhea, chlamydia, and HIV; and urine pregnancy test for all females. Laboratory testing requirements may vary with the needs of the youth and community requirements. A purified protein derivative (PPD) skin test should be placed to determine exposure to tuberculosis. A determination of the adolescent's immunization status should be a part of the health assessment. Vision and hearing screening should be done as many youth have unrecognized and undiagnosed difficulties in these areas. Dental screening and the availability of dental care and treatment is necessary in this population due to the fact that many have never had a single dental visit (NCCHC 2004).

The hands-on physical assessment should be done within seven days, preferably by a physician or midlevel provider such as a physician assistant or nurse practitioner. The examination should be tailored to the adolescent female population and should include age-appropriate screenings such as scoliosis, breast examination, and gynecological assessment (NCCHC 2004). Often girls enter juvenile correctional facilities with medical conditions that have been previously undiagnosed or problems that were identified earlier that did not receive proper follow-up. Sometimes conditions such as congenital heart defects are not followed up until the adolescent reaches a juvenile correctional setting and receives an adequate health assessment.

In order to meet their health care requirements, a sick-call process must be established to ensure unimpeded access to health care for incarcerated females. The process should allow youth to directly request sick-call visits without permission or intervention of security staff. Access to health services via intake screening and assessment and through the use of sick call by these youth will reveal numerous health problems among this population.

The provision of health care to female adolescents in an incarcerated environment presents a challenge to health care providers, as well as to administration and security staff. To begin with, the health care model can be perceived as foreign and often contradictory in a correctional setting. Fulfilling security requirements remains the correctional facility's primary goal. Assuring that the juvenile offender receives unimpeded access to health care is the primary goal of the medical provider. On the surface, it may seem that these two goals are at conflict with one another. But it is indeed possible for both goals to be met simultaneously. In order to do so, it is critical to involve all staff not just medical staff in the development and implementation of any health care program. Administrative meetings should be held at least quarterly, including medical, administrative, and security staff. Issues should be discussed that impact the operation of the medical program in the context of operating a secure facility. The use of health care standards provided for correctional settings by national organizations, such as the NCCHC and the American Correctional Association (ACA), can become common ground for correctional and health care staff in the development of policies and procedures that will meet the goals of both parties.

Providing health services to female juvenile offenders requires an interdisciplinary approach to staffing and program development. Of course, the inclusion of licensed health professionals is important in staffing a juvenile correctional facility, but line staff must also be well trained and receive education about medical needs specific to the population served. A female offender's history of victimization may make compliance with simple medical regimes an issue. Emotional

liability may trigger somatic responses such as a herpes outbreak or gastrointesti-
nal upset. Sometimes this leads to the perception by staff that the offender is being manipulative or feigning illness. All staff should be trained to take all medical
complaints seriously and respond appropriately. Medical staff should be aware of
the health problems more likely to affect girls of color, who are disproportionately
represented in the juvenile justice system. Diabetes, for instance, appears with
greater frequency among African Americans (Acoca 1998). Cultural sensitivity on
the part of medical, administrative, and security staff is mandatory and should go
beyond just creating cultural diversity through staff hiring.

Greater health care expenses should be anticipated in operation of a female
juvenile facility as compared to a male facility. Females in general have a higher
rate of use of medical care while in the community. Staffing patterns and ratios at
female facilities should reflect this increased use. The greater prevalence of
chronic diseases, including mental health diagnoses and the provision for prenatal care and delivery also accelerate expenditures for female juvenile facilities.
Medicaid exclusions for the provision of health care to incarcerated youth, as well
as the fact that most incarcerated youth are uninsured, can create a financial burden on facilities and correctional agencies in the provision of quality health care.
Despite financial constraints, the community standard of care must be maintained if not exceeded in this medically underserved population that has a constitutional right to health care while incarcerated (Moore 2003).

"What's Wrong with Me?"

Some of the most common health-related issues presenting among female juvenile offenders in correctional settings include STIs, pregnancy, substance abuse,
and mental health disorders. This does not preclude other acute and chronic
medical conditions that certainly are represented in this population as well. Mental health diagnoses, obesity, diabetes, hypertension, and asthma show an increasing prevalence among female juvenile offenders.

Sexually Transmitted Infections and Diseases

Among adolescents, those detained for legal offenses represent a highly vulnerable population for the acquisition and transmission of STDs (Eng and Butler
1997). Recent data from the Centers for Disease Control and Prevention (CDC) indicated that rates of gonorrhea among U.S. adolescent detainees were 152 and 42
times greater among males and females, respectively, when compared to adolescents from the general population (CDC 1996). Surveillance surveys have consistently indicated high rates of chlamydia, gonorrhea, and trichomonas infection
among detained adolescents. Recent studies have found that between 7 percent
and 11 percent of detained adolescent males and between 10 percent and 28 percent of detained adolescent females tested positive for chlamydia (Canterbury et
al. 1995; Oh, Cloud, et al. 1994; Oh, Smith, et al. 1998; Pack et al. 2000). Likewise,

studies have found that between 3 percent and 7 percent of detained adolescent males and between 5 percent and 13 percent of detained adolescent females tested positive for gonorrhea (Canterbury et al. 1995; Oh, Cloud et al. 1994; Oh, Smith et al. 1998; Pack et al. 2000; Shafer et al. 1993). Trichomonas may also be a common STD among detained adolescents, particularly females (Oh, Cloud et al. 1994). A recent study also assessed the prevalence of genital herpes in a sample of detained adolescents and found that 15 percent of the males and 20 percent of the females tested positive (Huerta et al. 1996).

Numerous studies have demonstrated that detained youth are more likely than adolescents from the general population to engage in risky behaviors that may lead to infection with the human immunodeficiency virus (HIV). For example, DiClemente, Lanier, Horan, and Lodico found that detained youth were significantly more likely than youth attending schools to be sexually active, initiate sexual activity before age twelve, report having multiple sex partners, and report injection drug use (DiClemente et al. 1991). A study of detained adolescents in Mississippi indicated that 11 percent of males and 5 percent of females reported having sex with a partner who injects drugs. This same study found that 60 percent of the males and 36 percent of the females reported having sex with a partner whom they knew concurrently had other sex partners. Eighteen percent of the males and nine percent of the females reported ever exchanging sex for money. Overall, HIV risk profiles of detained adolescents in this study were significantly greater than adolescents sampled from homeless shelters (St. Lawrence, Crosby, and O'Bannon 1999).

Pack and colleagues found that the median number of cumulative sex partners reported by a sample of detained adolescent males was eleven (Pack et al. 2000). Despite these high-risk behaviors, low rates of condom use have consistently been reported for samples of detained youth (Magura, Kang, and Shapiro 1994; Morris, Baker, et al. 1998; Rickman et al. 1994; St. Lawrence, Crosby, and O'Bannon 1999). These high-risk behavioral profiles are compounded by detained adolescents' high rates of STDs because these infections facilitate acquisition and transmission of HIV (CDC 1998; Wasserheit 1992). Evidence suggests that health education programs designed to promote STD-protective behavior among female adolescents are feasible and beneficial in detention facilities. These programs should emphasize the benefits of condoms for pregnancy prevention as well as STD prevention, address adolescents' negative perceptions about condom use, and promote condom use with steady as well as non-steady boyfriends (Gilmore et al. 1994).

Pregnancy

As is true for STDs, pregnancy is a relatively common event among female juvenile offenders. A study of 261 juvenile detention facilities found that one to five pregnant adolescents were held in about two-thirds of these facilities during any given day. Collectively, these facilities held about 2,000 pregnant adolescents and 1,200 adolescent mothers over the course of one year. Forty-five percent of the facilities reported they do not release female juvenile offenders based on established pregnancy. Of these facilities, 60 percent reported obstetric complications, 31 percent did not provide prenatal care, and 70 percent did not provide education relevant to parenting (Breuner and Farrow 1995).

Pregnancy certainly is a unique health care issue for female juvenile offenders, although parenting and the provision of those related skills should be universal to both male and female offenders. All females should receive pregnancy testing at intake. Girls should be counseled on pregnancy options to include adoption and abortion. Referral resources should be identified with services available for the pregnant girl. Access to abortion services during incarceration may vary with legal status of the girl and local consent requirements. In general, minors can consent to pregnancy-related services and sexually transmitted infection diagnosis and treatment. Parental notification may be required and not necessarily parental consent for abortion services. Each facility should be aware of all requirements in advance of the need for services. Appropriate prenatal care must be provided if the pregnancy is continued. These pregnancies may be high risk due primarily to age, lack of prenatal care, substance abuse, and inadequate nutrition. A good birth outcome is desired. Arrangements for child care must be made for the baby after delivery with support services for the mother.

Pregnancy prevention efforts should focus on education and treatment. Educational information should include all birth control methods as well as messages to encourage abstinence. Discussion and encouragement of condom use is essential in this population. Treatment options for pregnancy prevention should be available to incarcerated girls based on length of stay, release date, and compliance. If in a short-term placement, contraceptive treatment should be continued or initiated in adequate time prior to placement. The modality of the pregnancy prevention treatment (oral, injection, transdermal) should be based on clinical and compliance factors.

Substance Abuse

Data from a variety of sources suggest that substance abuse is highly prevalent among incarcerated adolescents. A recent study found that incarcerated adolescents' reports of recent substance abuse (including alcohol, marijuana, crack/cocaine, hallucinogens, stimulants, and barbiturates) exceeded rates reported by a geographically similar sample of homeless and runaway adolescents and a sample of high-risk community adolescents (St. Lawrence, Crosby, and O'Bannon 1999). Other evidence has suggested that alcohol use is considerably higher among juvenile offenders as compared to nonoffenders (Council on Scientific Affairs 1990). Nonetheless, surveillance systems that comprehensively document the prevalence of substance abuse among incarcerated adolescent females have not been developed.

However, in 2000, the federal Arrestee Drug Abuse Monitoring (ADAM) program released its first public report that detailed findings from drug tests conducted among incarcerated adolescent females. Data for five drug assays (marijuana, cocaine, methamphetamines, opiates, and PCP) administered to female offenders were reported from six cities throughout the United States (Denver, Colorado; Phoenix and Tuscon, Arizona; Portland, Oregon; San Antonio, Texas; and San Diego, California). Marijuana was the commonly detected substance, with 20 percent testing positive across the six sites. Cocaine use was the second most prevalent substance detected, with rates as high as 17 percent (Tucson). Methamphetamines were the third most commonly detected substance. Compared to male offenders, females were much more likely to test positive for methamphetamines. Opiate use was rare and PCP was not detected among females at any of the six sites (ADAM 2000).

The ADAM report also found that substance abuse was more common among female juvenile offenders who were not enrolled in school compared to those currently enrolled. Seventy percent of those not enrolled tested positive for at least one of the five substances assayed, compared to only 36 percent of those enrolled in school (ADAM 2000). This finding suggests that peer associations may be an important determinant of substance abuse among adolescent female offenders. Indeed, at least one study has identified a positive association between substance abuse among adolescent female offenders and their reports of substance abuse among their peers (Sigda and Martin 1996).

Evidence suggests that substance abuse, juvenile offenses, and sexual activity are interrelated among adolescent females (Elliot and Morse 1989). Although, the relationship of substance abuse with sexual activity and legal offenses is complex, investigations suggest that adolescents' substance abuse may be independently related to both their sexual activity and their legal offenses (Elliot and Morse 1989; Oh, Reynolds, et al. 1991). Thus, substance abuse among adolescent female offenders constitutes an important behavior that creates its own morbidity and may predispose adolescents to a variety of other risk behaviors. For example, a study of juvenile offenders in thirty-nine correctional facilities found that females were significantly more likely than males to ever inject drugs; 20 percent of the females reported injection drug use as compared to only 10 percent of the males (Morris, Harrison, et al. 1995). Given that injection drug use is an important risk factor for the acquisition of hepatitis B, hepatitis C, and HIV infection (Ambroziak and Levy 1999; Lemon and Alter 1999), this finding suggests that adolescent female offenders experience excessive risk of the long-term morbidity and premature death associated with these viral infections based on their propensity for injection drug use. In their study of adolescents in these thirty-nine facilities, Morris et al. also found that females were significantly more likely than males to use cocaine (42 percent vs. 30 percent) or crack (9.6 percent vs. 3.3 percent). The use of cocaine and crack among adolescent female offenders has been associated with

biologically confirmed STDs (Oh et al. 1991). One probable reason for this association is the exchange of sex for crack/cocaine or the exchange of sex for money,
which, in turn, is used to buy crack/cocaine (Lown et al. 1995). Morris et al. also
found high rates of alcohol use, including binge drinking, among females. Previous studies have identified strong associations between alcohol use among juvenile offenders and risky sexual behavior (Shafer et al. 1993). Further, a recent study
found that marijuana use may be more common than alcohol use among juvenile
offenders and that marijuana use may be strongly related to unprotected sex
among incarcerated adolescent females (Kingree, Braithwaite, and Woodring
2000).

Mental Health

Closely related to substance abuse issues are the mental concerns of female juvenile offenders. Mental health issues have become a prominent concern among
federal officials and agencies charged with protecting the health and welfare of
juvenile offenders. The Society for Adolescent Medicine also advocates the provision of mental health services for acute and chronic psychiatric and emotional
disorders (SAM 2000). Yet there is a dearth of research investigating the prevalence of mental illness among adolescent offenders (Cocozza and Skowyra 2000).
In a review of studies conducted across the country by the National Mental Health
Association (NMHA), the prevalence of mental disorders among juvenile offenders was consistently high (77 percent in one state). These juveniles are not just
"sad" about being locked up but met the psychiatric diagnostic criteria of mental
health disorders such as major depression. Bipolar disorder, anxiety disorders,
substance abuse disorders, attention deficit hyperactivity disorder, and eating
disorders are among other mental health disorders represented by girls in the
system. Many of them carry more than one mental health diagnosis. Levels of severity range from conduct disorders that can be managed with behavior modification to major depression requiring psychotropic medications and one on one
observation to prevent a suicide (NMHA 2005).

While rates of mental illness in the general population of adolescents may
range from 9 to 13 percent, rates among incarcerated adolescents appear to be
substantially higher (Otto et al. 1992). A recent report conservatively estimated
that 20 percent of all juvenile offenders experience some form of mental illness
(Cocozza and Skowyra 2000). Another recent study found that 80 percent of a
sample of female juvenile offenders had symptoms of an emotional disorder or
underlying substance abuse problem (Kataoka et al. 2001). Further, evidence suggests that mental illness and substance abuse co-occur in about 50 percent of
juvenile offenders (Greenbaum, Foster-Johnson, and Pertila 1996).

Female juvenile offenders are considerably more likely to have a history of
mental health issues; many of these problems may become manifest or progressively intensify during periods of incarceration. In a study of female juvenile offenders by Kataoka et al. in 2001, 80 percent had symptoms of an emotional

disorder or substance abuse problem and 63 percent had a history of recidivism. Of those with emotional symptoms or a substance use problem, 51 percent had used specialty mental health services and 58 percent had been in a special education program during their lifetime. Among the group of recidivists, 82 percent had a history of a substance abuse problem and 47 percent had used specialty mental health services in their lifetime. A recent study found that female juvenile offenders were 1.6 times more likely than female juvenile nonoffenders to be hospitalized as a result of physical trauma, with the form of trauma often being intentional injury attributable to guns or drug overdoses (Conseur, Rivara, and Emanuel 1997). This comparatively high rate of self-inflicted trauma suggests that underlying mental illness may be common among offenders.

A particularly insidious cause of mental illness among female juvenile offenders may be physical and sexual abuse. A history of victimization, for example, indicates a need to screen for emotional concerns, such as flashbacks to the abuse, suicidal thoughts, and other possible symptoms of post-traumatic stress disorder (Acoca 1998). A recent study found that about 75 percent of a sample of female juvenile offenders reported a history of physical abuse and nearly as many (68 percent) reported a history of sexual abuse (Mason, Zimmerman, and Evans 1998). Physical abuse, unfortunately, may also be a consequence of adolescents' incarceration (Woolf and Funk 1985).

Sexual abuse is approximately three times more prevalent among adolescent females compared to adolescent males (OJJDP 1998). A considerable body of literature has firmly established the relationship of adolescents' reports of physical and sexual abuse with multiple forms of subsequent mental illness (Beitchman et al. 1992; Briere and Runtz 1993; Green 1993; Kendall-Tackett, Williams, and Finkelhor 1993). Further, childhood sexual abuse has been associated with subsequent risky sexual behaviors (Boyer and Fine 1992; Nagy, DiClemente, and Adcock 1995), teen pregnancy (Stock et al. 1997), and juvenile offenses (Boyer and Fine 1992; Nagy, DiClemente, and Adcock 1995; Widom and Kuhns 1996). Further, sexual abuse of female juvenile offenders may frequently occur during periods of incarceration (Acoca 1998).

Other emotional disorders (for example, conduct disorders, learning disabilities, depression) are also found disproportionately among juvenile offenders (Council on Scientific Affairs 1990). Past and present symptoms indicating major depression have been observed for about 20 percent of juvenile offenders in correctional facilities; a rate far higher than would be expected from the general population of adolescents (Chiles, Miller, and Cox 1980; Council on Scientific Affairs 1990; Hyde, Mitchell, and Turpin 1986). Another study found that 18 percent of incarcerated adolescents met DSM-III diagnostic criteria for major depression (Kashani et al. 1980). Some girls may have a dual diagnosis of both substance abuse and a co-occurring psychiatric disorder (Acoca 1998), such as an eating disorder or a tendency to self-mutilate. All issues will need to be addressed in treatment.

"Can You Help Me?"

The vast majority of female juvenile offenders have been underserved by their families, schools, and communities. Indeed, periods of incarceration may often comprise the only opportunity these adolescents have for the receipt of medical and dental care and preventive services (for example, screening for diseases and health education). Acoca argues that the juvenile justice system has missed valuable opportunities to meet the needs of young female offenders who have a complex set of mental and physical health problems (1998). Gender-specific prevention and treatment programs, tailored to the unique needs of female juvenile offenders, constitute an essential starting point for addressing these missed opportunities. Indeed, the Juvenile Justice and Delinquency Prevention Act specifies that programs should be established that meet the full range of health needs (for example, mental health, substance abuse, physical and sexual assault) experienced by female offenders (OJJDP 1998). Effective programs provide girls with comprehensive health services, promoting physical and mental wellness.

The detention period offers the opportunity to present disease prevention and health promotion messages to youth engaging in high-risk behaviors. Information on sexual behaviors should not be limited to "abstinence only" messages among this population. The opportunity to provide intervention in this population will hopefully reduce the spread of HIV and other STIs since we know a large proportion of persons that become infected do so during adolescence. Other health education programs should address smoking and alcohol and drug use, with resources for treatment programs available. Behavioral management programs are essential since most juvenile offenders have difficulties with anger management and nonviolent conflict resolution.

Programs that focus on wellness promote good nutrition, exercise, reproductive health, disease prevention, and stress management. Health care also teaches girls to value and respect their bodies. Girls need to understand what is happening to their bodies during puberty as a positive, normal aspect of becoming a woman. Knowledge of basic anatomy and physiology should not be assumed in this adolescent population.

Because early sexual experimentation puts girls at increased risk of delinquency, sexuality education is a component of effective programs. Gender-specific educational programs teach girls that their bodies belong to them; that they have choices about how and when to explore their sexuality; and that they have the power to set limits in relationships. Because so many girls who become delinquent have a history of sexual abuse, sexuality education can also help them separate past abuse from healthy sexual relating (OJJDP 1998).

Specific Treatment Concerns

Delinquent girls may need specific treatment to address serious issues that can have long-term consequences. Gender-specific programs use a combination of individual and group therapy to help girls address and overcome personal issues that have interfered with positive development during adolescence. Issues may be interwoven and complex. Specific issues that may require additional treatment include but are not limited to:

- *Substance abuse* may be both cause and consequence of delinquency. Treatment needs to address underlying issues related to substance abuse, such as a girl's history of sexual abuse or substance abuse and codependency within her family. Effective programs include highly structured phases linked to clearly defined tasks, privileges, and consequences (Acoca 1995). In gender-specific programs, these phases are based on an understanding of female adolescent development. An individual treatment plan should be developed for each girl and her family. Treatment should be integrated with medical care, especially for girls dually diagnosed (experiencing substance abuse and co-occurring psychiatric problems). Case management can help girls receive the ongoing care they need both during and after treatment.

- *Prenatal and postpartum care*: Comprehensive programming addresses the needs of both the teenage mother (or mother-to-be) and her baby. For the mother, prevention focuses on wellness during pregnancy and postpartum, parenting skills to reduce the likelihood of child abuse, and reduction of risky behaviors that could lead to another unplanned pregnancy before she reaches adulthood. Whenever possible, the father should be included in programming.

- *Well-baby and day care*: Programs serving teen parents need to include comprehensive health care for babies and toddlers. Day care allows teen mothers time to focus on their personal issues, such as education and therapy. Involving mothers in day-care programs also offers them an opportunity to practice parenting skills in a safe, structured environment while maintaining a strong bond between mother and child.

- *Group therapy*: Effective programs use therapy groups because this delivery method offers specific benefits to girls, not because groups are more time efficient or cost-effective than individual therapy. In particular, group therapy settings provide a safe, secure place for girls to address painful experiences related to family dysfunction, sexual abuse, substance abuse, or other situations in which they may have felt isolated, ashamed, or at fault. In group work, girls discover they are not alone in dealing with these issues. They can safely break their silence and express themselves openly.

- *Aftercare*: Effective programs provide a seamless continuum of care that does not end when girls return to the community. Keys to aftercare are "graduated support" (a gradual withdrawal of services rather than an abrupt end) and long-term monitoring by an aftercare worker. A structured program for helping girls return successfully to the community includes discussions, presentations, and counseling to prepare them for reentry. Aftercare workers who help develop the girls' overall service plan and stay informed of their progress throughout their stay in the program spend time with the girls before they leave the program in order to build trust and rapport (Cowles, Castellano, and Gransky 1995; Milan 1996). Facility staff should also participate in developing a treatment plan continuum that include health care—including psychiatric and dental care—sexual and substance abuse treatment services, and educational and family services for the juvenile offender upon her return to the community. These community linkages may enhance the female offender's opportunity for success and reduce recidivism. (OJJDP 1998)

For youth with a high likelihood of repeat offenses, the Intensive Aftercare Program model developed with the Office of Juvenile Justice and Delinquency Prevention supports five principles to cut the risks of recidivism:

- preparing the youth for progressively increased responsibility and freedom in the community
- facilitating the involvement of and interaction between the youth and the community
- working with both the offender and community support systems, including families, peers, schools, and employers, on the qualities needed for constructive interaction and a youth's successful community adjustment
- developing new resources and support
- monitoring and testing the youth and the community on their ability to deal with each other productively (Altschuler and Armstrong 1995)

Resiliency skills should be developed for girls through programming that allows discovery of their strengths and abilities. Hidden talents and abilities may lie in art, music, mathematics, creative writing, sports, or vocational programs. The ability to identify just one strength in a girl who has been made to feel weak and powerless all her life gives instant gratification and encouragement.

Group work should be encouraged to develop positive peer relationships, effective communication skills, and problem solving. As they learn to relate to each other's experiences, they may feel less isolated and ashamed of their own experiences of sexual, physical, and substance abuse.

Providing positive role models and opportunities for appropriate role playing will break old stereotypes and help develop leadership skills, self-confidence, and assertiveness. By promoting positive family and peer relationships, community involvement, and spirituality, girls will be better prepared for successful reentry into their communities.

More research is needed to determine the onset and course of female juvenile delinquency and to draw conclusions about the effectiveness of gender-specific program models. Community-based programs serving this population may lack the evaluation resources to determine program effectiveness. College or university researchers may be able to provide these services in exchange for access to research populations. Creating links between service providers and researchers can provide an important mechanism for advancing gender-specific research and, eventually, helping to reduce the number of female delinquents. There is a critical need for advocates for providing health services to this special population of adolescents. Greater involvement by the medical and legal community may assist in this effort. The impact that we make upon the health and wellness of these youth during their period of incarceration will have a direct effect on the health and wellness of the emerging adult as well as the community to which they return.

REFERENCES

21st Century Department of Justice Appropriations Authorization Act. 1992. Pub. L. No. 107-273 (reauthorization of the Juvenile Justice Delinquency Prevention Act).

Acoca, L. 1998. Outside/inside: The violation of American girls at home, on the streets, and in the juvenile justice system. *Crime and Delinquency* 44: 561–89.

Altschuler, D. M., and T. L. Armstrong. 1995. Challenge activities program areas—Challenge Activity 1. Washington, DC: U.S. Department of Justice, Office of Juvenile Justice and Delinquency Prevention.

Ambroziak, J., and J. A. Levy. 1999. Epidemiology, natural history, and pathogenesis of HIV infection. In *Sexually transmitted diseases,* 3rd ed., ed. K. K. Holmes, P. F. Sparling, P. Mardh. New York: McGraw-Hill. 251–58.

American Bar Association. [2001]. Justice by gender: The lack of appropriate prevention, diversion, and treatment alternatives for girls in the justice system. A full report. http://www.abanet.org/crimjust/juvjus/justicebygenderweb.pdf (accessed July 30, 2004).

Anderson, B., and J. A. Farrow. 1998. Incarcerated adolescents in Washington state: Health services and utilization. *Journal of Adolescent Health* 22: 363–67.

Arkin, E. B. 1989. Making health communications. National Cancer Institute. National Institutes of Health. U.S. Department of Health and Human Services.

Arrestee Drug Abuse Monitoring (ADAM) Program. 2000. 1999 annual report on drug use among adult and juvenile arrestees. http://www.adam-nij.net (accessed July 2, 2001).

Beitchman, J. H., K. J. Zucker, J. E. Hood, G. A. daCosta, D. Akman, and E. Cassavia. 1992. A review of the long-term effects of child sexual abuse. *Child Abuse and Neglect* 16: 101–18.

Bergsmann, I. R. 1989. The forgotten few: Juvenile female offenders. *Federal Probation* 53, no. 1: 73–78.

Bergsmann, I. 1994. Establishing a foundation: Just the facts. 1994 Juvenile Female Offenders Conference: A time for change. Lanham, MD: American Correctional Association. 3–14.

Boyer, D., and D. Fine. 1992. Sexual abuse as a factor in adolescent pregnancy and child maltreatment. *Family Planning Perspectives* 24: 11–19.

Breuner, C. C., and J. A. Farrow. 1995. Pregnant teens in prison: Prevalence, management, and consequences. *Western Journal of Medicine* 162: 328–30.

Briere, J., and M. Runtz. 1993. Childhood sexual abuse: Long term sequelae and implications for psychological assessment. *Journal of Interpersonal Violence* 8: 312–30.

Campbell, J. R. 1995. Conference focuses on issues facing female juvenile offenders. *Corrections Today* 57, no. 1: 72.

Canterbury, R. J., E. L. McGarvey, A. E. Sheldon-Keller, D. Waite, P. Reams, and C. Koopman. 1995. Prevalence of HIV-related risk behaviors and STDs among incarcerated adolescents. *Journal of Adolescent Health* 17: 173–77.

Centers for Disease Control and Prevention (CDC). 1999. High prevalence of chlamydial and gonococcal infection in women entering jails and juvenile detention centers: Chicago, Birmingham, and San Francisco, 1998. *Morbidity and Mortality Weekly Report (MMWR)* 48: 793–95.

CDC. 1998. HIV prevention through early detection and treatment of other sexually transmitted diseases: United States. Recommendations of the advisory committee for HIV and STD prevention. *MMWR* 47: 1–24.

CDC. 1996. HIV/AIDS education and prevention programs for adults in prisons and jails and juveniles in confinement facilities: United States, 1994. *MMWR* 45: 268–71.

Chesney-Lind, M. 1988. Girls and status offenses: Is juvenile justice still sexist? *Criminal Justice Abstracts* 20, no. 1: 144–65.

Chiles, J. A., M. L. Miller, and G. B. Cox. 1980. Depression in an adolescent delinquent population. *Archives of General Psychiatry* 37: 1179–84.

Cocozza, J. J., and K. Skowyra. 2000. Youth with mental health disorders: Issues and emerging responses. *Juvenile Justice* 7, no. 1: 3–13.

Community Research Associates. 1997. Juvenile female offenders: A status of the states report. Northglenn, CO: Community Research Associates.

Conseur, A., F. P. Rivara, and I. Emanuel. 1997. Juvenile delinquency and adolescent trauma: How strong is the connection? *Pediatrics* 99: e5.

Council on Scientific Affairs. 1990. Health status of detained and incarcerated youth. *Journal of the American Medical Association* 263: 987–91.

Cowles, E. L., T. C. Castellano, and L. A. Gransky. 1995. "Boot camp" drug treatment and aftercare interventions: An evaluation review. Washington, DC: U.S. Department of Justice, National Institute of Justice.

Davidson, S. 1982. *Justice for Young Women.* Tucson, AZ: New Directions for Young Women.

Davis, K., C. Schoen, L. Greenberg, C. Desroches, and M. Abrams. 1997. The Commonwealth Fund survey of the health of adolescent girls. New York: Commonwealth Fund.

DiClemente, R. J., M. M. Lanier, P. F. Horan, and M. Lodico. 1991. Comparison of AIDS knowledge, attitudes, and behaviors among incarcerated adolescents and a public school sample in San Francisco. *American Journal of Public Health* 81: 628–29.

Dryfoos, J. G. 1990. *Adolescents at risk.* New York: Oxford University Press.

Elliott, D. S., and B. J. Morse. 1989. Delinquency and drug use as risk factors in teenage sexual activity. *Youth and Society* 21: 32–60.

Eng, T. R., and W. T. Butler, eds. 1997. *The hidden epidemic: Confronting sexually transmitted diseases.* Washington, DC: National Academy Press.

Federal Bureau of Investigation. 2003. Summary of Uniform Crime Reporting Program, 1980–1999. http://www.fbi.gov/ucr/cius-99/ww99tblol.xls (accessed June 22, 2005).

Feinstein, R. A., A. Lampkin, C. D. Lorish, L. V. Klerman, R. Maisiak, and M. K. Oh. 1998. Medical status of adolescents at time of admission to a juvenile detention center. *Journal of Adolescent Health* 22: 190–96.

Gilmore, M. R., D. M. Morrison, C. Lowery, and S. A. Baker. 1994. Beliefs about condoms and their association with intentions to use condoms among youth in detention. *Journal of Adolescent Health* 15: 228–37.

Girls, Incorporated. 1996. Prevention and Parity: Girls in juvenile justice. Indianapolis: Girls Incorporated National Resource Center.

Green, A. H. 1993. Child sexual abuse: Immediate and long-term effects and intervention. *Journal of the American Academy of Child Adolescent Psychiatry* 32: 890–902.

Greenbaum, P. E., L. Foster-Johnson, and A. Pertrila. 1996. Co-occurring addictive and mental disorders among adolescents: Prevalence research and future directions. *American Journal of Orthopsychiatry* 66: 52–60.

Greenwood, P. W., K. E. Model, C. P. Rydell, and J. Chiesa. 1996. Diverting children from a life of crime: Measuring costs and benefits. Santa Monica, CA: Rand Corporation.

Hein, K., M. I. Cohen, I. F. Litt, S. K. Schonberg, M. R. Meyer, A. Marks, and A. Sheehy. 1980. Juvenile detention: Another boundary issue for physicians. *Pediatrics* 66: 239–45.

Huerta, K., S. Berkelhamer, J. Klein, S. Ammerman, J. Chang, and C. G. Prober. 1996. Epidemi-ology of herpes simplex virus type 2 infection in a high-risk adolescent population. *Journal of Adolescent Health* 18: 384–86.

Hugo, K. E., and R. B. Rutherford Jr. 1992. Issues in identifying educational disabilities among female juvenile offenders. *Journal of Correctional Education* 43: 124–27.

Hyde, T., J. R. Mitchell, and E. Turpin. 1986. Psychiatric disorders in a delinquent population. Washington, DC: National Commission on Correctional Health Care.

Irwin, Charles E., Jr., Claire D. Brindis, Susan G. Millstein, Elizabeth M. Ozer, David Knopf, M. Jane Park, and Tina Paul. 1996. Fact Sheet on Out-of-Home Youth-Foster Care, Incarcer-ated, Homeless/Runaway Adolescents. National Adolescent Information Center.

Kashani, J. H., G. W. Manning, D. H. McKnew, L. Cyton, J. F. Simonds, P. C. Woodcrson. 1980. Depression among incarcerated delinquents. *Psychiatry Research* 3: 185–91.

Kataoka, S. H., B. T. Zima, D. A. Dupre, K. A. Moreno, X. Yang, and J. T. McCracken. 2001. Mental health problems and service use among female juvenile offenders: Their rela-tionship to criminal history. *Journal of the American Academy of Child Adolescent Psychiatry* 40: 549–55.

Kendall-Tackett, K. A., L. M. Williams, and D. Finkelhor. 1993. Impact of sexual abuse on chil-dren: A review and synthesis of recent empirical studies. *Psychiatry Bulletin* 113: 164–80.

Kingree, J. B., R. Braithwaite, and T. Woodring. 2000. Unprotected sex as a function of alcohol and marijuana use among adolescent detainees. *Journal of Adolescent Health* 27: 179–85.

Lemon, S. M., and M. J. Alter. 1999. Viral hepatitis. In *Sexually transmitted diseases*, 3rd ed., ed. K. K. Holmes, P. F. Sparling, P. Mardh. New York: McGraw-Hill. 361–84.

Loper, A. B. 2000. Female juvenile delinquency: Risk factors and promising interventions (Juvenile Justice Fact Sheet). Charlottesville, VA: Institute of Law, Psychiatry, and Public Policy, University of Virginia.

Lown, E. A., K. Winkler, R. E. Fullilove, and M. T. Fullilove. 1995. Tossin' and tweakin': Women's consciousness in the crack culture. In *Women and AIDS: Psychological perspec-tives*, ed. C. Squire. Thousand Oaks, CA: Sage. 90–106.

Magura, S., S. Kang, and J. L. Shapiro. 1994. Outcomes of intensive AIDS education for male adolescent drug users in jail. *Journal of Adolescent Health* 15: 457–63.

Maguire, K., and A. L. Pastore, eds. 1997. Sourcebook of criminal justice statistics 1996. Wash-ington, DC: U.S. Department of Justice, Bureau of Justice Statistics.

Mason, W. A., L. Zimmerman, and W. Evans. 1998. Sexual and physical abuse among incarcer-ated youth: Implications for sexual behavior, contraceptive use, and teenage pregnancy. *Child Abuse and Neglect* 22: 987–95.

Milan, M. A. 1996. Working in institutions. In *Clinical approaches to working with young offend-ers*, ed. C. R. Hollin and K. Howells. Chichester, England: John Wiley and Sons.

Miller, D., C. Trapani, K. Fejes-Mendoza, C. Eggleston, and D. Dwiggins. 1995. Adolescent fe-male offenders: Unique considerations. *Adolescence* 30, no. 118: 429–35.

Moore, J. 2003. Management and administration of correctional health care. In *Health Issues of Juvenile Offenders*, ed J. Moore. Kingston, NJ: Civic Research Institute.

Morris, R. E., E. A. Harrison, G. W. Knox, E. Tromanhauser, D. K. Marquis, and L. L. Watts. 1995. Health risk behavioral survey from 39 juvenile correctional facilities in the United States. *Journal of Adolescent Health* 17: 334–44.

Morris, R. E., C. J. Baker, M. Valentine, and A. J. Pennisi. 1998. Variations in HIV risk behaviors of incarcerated juveniles during a four-year period: 1989–1992. *Journal of Adolescent Health* 23: 39–48.

National Commission on Correctional Health Care (NCCHC). 2004. Standards for Health Ser-vices in Juvenile Detention and Confinement Facilities.

National Mental Health Association (NMHA). 2005. Prevalence of mental disorders among children in the juvenile justice system. http://www.nmha.org/children/justjuv/prevalence.cfm (accessed June 22, 2005).

Nagy, S., R. J. DiClemente, and A. G. Adcock. 1995. Adverse factors associated with forced sex among southern adolescent girls. *Pediatrics* 96: 944–46.

Office of Juvenile Justice and Delinquency Prevention (OJJDP). 1998. Guiding principles for promising female programming: An inventory of best practices. http://www.ojjdp.ncjrs.org/pubs/principles/contents.html (accessed November 28, 2003).

OJJDP. 2001. *OJJDP Research 2000.* Washington, DC: Office of Juvenile Justice and Delinquency Prevention.

Oh, M. K., K. R. Smith, M. O'Cain, D. Kilmer, J. Johnson, and E. W. Hook. 1998. Urine-based screening of adolescents in detention to guide treatment for gonococcal and chlamydial infections: Translating research into intervention. *Archives of Pediatric and Adolescent Medicine* 152: 52–56.

Oh, M. K., G. A. Cloud, L. S. Wallace, J. Reynolds, M. Sturdevant, and R. Feinstein. 1994. Sexual behavior and sexually transmitted diseases among male adolescents in detention. *Sexually Transmitted Diseases* 21: 127–32.

Oh, M. K., J. Reynolds, D. Kilmer, B. Cotton, M. Rouse, and R. Feinstein. 1991. Substance use and sexually transmitted diseases among juvenile delinquents. Poster presentation at the annual meeting for the Society of Adolescent Medicine, Washington, DC, March 17–22, 1991. Reprinted in the *Journal of Adolescent Health* (1992): 13, 54.

Otto, R., J. Greenstein, M. Johnson, and R. Friedman. 1992. Prevalence of mental disorders among youth in the juvenile justice system. In *Responding to the mental health needs of youth in the juvenile justice system,* ed. J. Cocozza. Seattle: National Coalition for the Mentally Ill in the Criminal Justice System.

Pack, R. P., R. J. DiClemente, E. W. Hook, and M. K. Oh. 2000. High prevalence of asymptomatic STDs in incarcerated minority male youth: A case for screening. *Sexually Transmitted Diseases* 27: 175–77.

Poe-Yamagata, E., and J. A. Butts. 1996. Female offenders in the juvenile justice system. Statistics summary. Washington, DC: U.S. Department of Justice, Office of Juvenile Justice and Delinquency Prevention.

Prescott, L. 1997. *Adolescent girls with co-occurring disorders in the juvenile justice system.* New York: Policy Research, Inc.

Rickman, R. L., M. Lodico, R. J. DiClemente, R. Morris, C. Baker, and S. Huscroft. 1994. Sexual communication is associated with condom use by sexually active incarcerated adolescents. *Journal of Adolescent Health* 15: 383–88.

St. Lawrence, J. S., R. A. Crosby, and R. O. O'Bannon. 1999. Adolescent risk for HIV infection: Comparison of four high risk samples. *Journal of HIV/AIDS Prevention and Education of Adolescent Children* 3: 63–85.

Shafer, M. A., J. F. Hilton, M. Ekstrand, J. Keogh, L. Gee, L. DiGiorgio-Haag, J. Shalwitz, and J. Schachter. 1993. Relationship between drug use and sexual behaviors and the occurrence of sexually transmitted diseases among high risk male youth. *Sexually Transmitted Diseases* 20: 307–13.

Sigda, K. B., and S. L. Martin. 1996. Substance use among incarcerated adolescents: Associations with peer, parent, and community use of substances. *Substance Use and Misuse* 31: 1433–45.

Society for Adolescent Medicine (SAM). 2000. Health care for incarcerated youth: Position paper of the Society for Adolescent Medicine. *Journal of Adolescent Health* 27: 73–75.

Stock, J. L., M. A. Bell, D. K. Boyer, and F. A. Connell. 1997. Adolescent pregnancy and sexual risk taking among sexually abused girls. *Family Planning Perspectives* 29: 200–203, 207.

Wasserheit, J. N. 1992. Epidemiological synergy: Interrelationships between human immunodeficiency virus infection and other sexually transmitted diseases. *Sexually Transmitted Diseases* 9: 61–77.

Widom, C. S., and J. B. Kuhns. 1996. Childhood victimization and subsequent risk for promiscuity, prostitution, and teenage pregnancy: A prospective study. *American Journal of Public Health* 86: 1607–12.

Woolf, A., and S. G. Funk. 1985. Epidemiology of trauma in a population of incarcerated youth. *Pediatrics* 75: 463–68.

Yoshikawa, H. 1994. Prevention as cumulative protection: Effects of early family support and education on chronic delinquency and its risks. *Psychological Bulletin* 115, no. 1: 28–54.

PART TWO

Mental Health and Addictive Behaviors

6

Mood Disorders in
Incarcerated Women

SAUNDRA MAASS-ROBINSON
PAMELA EVERETT THOMPSON

It is well established in research literature that women are at greater risk for depression than are men, especially during the reproductive years (Kornstein and Wojcik 2000). Lifetime prevalence rates approximating a two-to-one ratio of depressed women to depressed men is a robust figure that has remained constant even in the most recent international study conducted by the World Health Organization (WHO) in fourteen countries (Maier et al. 1999). Studies have also shown women to be more likely than men to experience the onset of depression following a stressful event involving self or others (Nazroo, Edwards, and Brown 1997). Given the propensity of women to experience clinical depression over the course of their lifetimes, the incarceration of females represents a particularly exacerbating event for mood disorders, defined as conditions "that have a disturbance in mood as the predominant feature" (American Psychiatric Association 2000, 345).

Incarceration poses extreme and uncontrollable challenges in the areas empirically determined to be the most likely precipitants for depression in females. In addition, incarceration creates unique challenges for mental health professionals who are working in an environment that often reinforces the very factors associated with the development of mood disorders. These disturbances in mood may include features of depression, mania, hypomania, and/or mixed episodes.

There are a number of clinical conditions that present primarily as a depressed mood. The hallmark of these disorders is major depressive disorder or MDD. Other conditions include dysthymic disorder, depressive disorder NOS (which includes premenstrual dysphoric disorder), adjustment disorder with depressive features, bipolar I or bipolar II disorder characterized by one or more depressive episodes, cyclothymic disorder, schizoaffective disorder, and/or depression secondary to substance use or a medical condition.

Unfortunately, the proportion of women who are in jails and prisons has grown at an alarmingly greater rate than men since 1990 (Greenfield and Snell 1999; Weiner and Ano 1992). A paucity of empirical data exists on this population regarding mood disorders. This chapter attempts to present what little there is, though it by no means represents an exhaustive search through all available literature. The purpose of this chapter, based on extrapolations from the literature and the clinical work experiences of the authors, is to draw thoughtful conclusions about proper assessment and appropriate treatment in a hostile environment that is unlike what the average clinician may encounter. The following discussion will include (1) prevalence data on depression in incarcerated females; (2) importance of accurate diagnosis; (3) contributing, confounding, and exacerbating factors; (4) salient clinical features of a depressive disorder; (5) the unique challenges of suicidal and parasuicidal sequelae; (6) differential characteristics of one depressive disorder from another; (7) treatment options for the incarcerated population; and (8) summary and conclusions.

Prevalence Data on Depression in Incarcerated Females

Fogel examined the mental health of female offenders at the time of incarceration and six months later (1993). She found high levels of depression (24.7 percent) upon entrance and high levels six months later (21.46 percent). Although depression scores decreased from the time of admission, they remained elevated over time compared with the general population. Fogel posited that sources of the high depression scores included separation from family, worries about children, and loss of control of their own lives. Hurley and Dunn (1991) screened ninety-two incarcerated women for psychological distress and stressful life events. They found high levels of depressive symptoms and that there was an association between stressful life events and depression. Singer, Bussey, Song, and Lunghofer (1995) explored psychosocial issues in a large population of jailed females. Findings indicated that almost two-thirds (59.2 percent) met the criteria for clinical depression. Jordan, Schlenger, Fairbank, and Caddell (1996) found depression rates of 13 percent in a comprehensive study of convicted felons entering prison. Lastly, Teplin, Abram, and McClelland (1996) identified a large majority of women awaiting trial with significant mental illness. More than three-quarters of the population were classified as having a psychiatric diagnosis, with 20.4 percent of that suffering from a mood disorder (namely major depressive disorder and dysthymia).

These data indicate that 13 percent to 59.2 percent of women arriving at prison or awaiting trial were experiencing depressive symptoms or mood disorders. The wide range of women diagnosed as depressed raises some concern about the criteria used for diagnosis. One may speculate that the very idea of coming to prison is enough to provoke a depressive episode or disorder. However, appropriate feelings of intense sadness, regarding the loss of one's freedom and relational disruptions introduced by incarceration, do not necessarily constitute a clinical presentation.

Importance of Accurate Diagnosis

Screening by a professional trained to listen and observe for mood disorders is essential when determining diagnosis and need for treatment. This includes a comprehensive clinical history as well as a review of other factors, which may be the basis for the patient's presenting complaint.

The importance of careful diagnostic questioning cannot be overstated when assessing for (1) the number and duration of symptoms in accordance with criteria outlined in the *DSM-IV* (1994), (2) mental health treatment history including suicidal or parasuicidal behavior, (3) level of functioning before coming to prison, and (4) ability to identify precipitating events that may or may not be related to prison. Recurring themes such as "I miss my kids so much," "I've never been to prison before," "I just can't believe I'm here and I can't stop crying" in lieu of specific description of symptoms generally demonstrate an appropriate reaction to incarceration rather than an actual mood disorder. As Maass-Robinson stated, "[we] are not talking about simply having a bad day or a bad week. Nor [are we] referring to those occasional moments of sadness or despair when you wonder where the next breath will come from in order to make it through the day. No, as difficult as these times are, they may only be *symptoms* of depression but not necessarily the *full expression* of the disease" (2001, 46). While a clinician cannot assume that observable tearfulness and agitation within a presenting inmate constitutes a mood disorder, a clinician also cannot assume that most or all of an inmate's presenting distress is *only* the result of incarceration and related adjustment. The evaluation of women who are incarcerated and who present complaints of "feeling depressed" should be no less comprehensive or clinically focused than the evaluation of *any* individual who presents with similar complaints. When a clinician is in doubt, follow-up with the inmate over time as well as documentation of mental status are crucial.

It is often the case at Metro State Prison in Atlanta, Georgia, where the authors of this chapter were employed at one time, that inmates will conceal their psychiatric symptoms and their need for treatment because they mistakenly believe that being on the mental health caseload will negatively affect their living arrangements as well as potential for parole and/or transfer to another facility. Hence, treatment is delayed and unnecessary suffering is experienced by the inmate. Therefore, thoughtful and patient questioning about an inmate's refusal of services in light of reported or observed symptoms may uncover the reasons for her resistance to psychiatric intervention and put her at ease in asking for help.

Contributing, Confounding, and Exacerbating Factors

Abuse History

A history of sexual abuse is more common in women than in men and is considered to be a major risk factor for depression and other psychiatric disorders

(Bifulco, Brown, and Adler 1991; Weiss, Longhurst, and Mazure 1999). Research also suggests that childhood and adult victimization of girls and women frequently is a precursor to female criminality (Louise 1998). Results derived from a national sample showed that 48 percent of jailed women reported having been physically or sexually abused before admission, and 27 percent had been raped (Harlow 1996). McClellan and colleagues conducted a survey of 500 women in Texas prisons and found that 57.4 percent had been abused as children (McClellan, Farabee, and Crouch 1997). This does not begin to include the abuse these women may have experienced as adults. At Metro State Prison in Atlanta, the percentage varies between 60 percent and 80 percent of the 905 women detained in this facility who have experienced physical or sexual abuse as children or adults.

The fact that girls and women tend toward an inward, ruminative coping style in response to feelings of sadness (Nolen-Hoeksema 1994; Nolen-Hoeksema, Larson, and Grayson 1999), indicates that they may be more inclined when they are abused to internalize their feelings. Hoagwood (1990) found that women who blamed themselves as children for having been abused had poorer overall adjustment as adults and were more depressed. This supports the findings of McClellan, Farabee, and Crouch (1997), whose study of Texas inmates revealed a significant relationship between childhood sexual abuse and adult depression, particularly in female inmates. Her survey revealed that even though men and women associated childhood abuse with depression, women's depression was more strongly associated with childhood abuse than was men's depression. Similar findings were reported by Sigmon, Greene, Rohan and Nichols (1996) in a study of nineteen nonincarcerated female survivors of childhood sexual abuse.

Prison life comes with a loss of space and privacy. At Metro State Prison, women generally reside in six-person cells the size of small dormitory rooms with an exposed commode and sink in the corner. These inmates experience unpredictable strip searches for contraband—either on the person of the inmate or among her possessions. This invasion of space, coupled with the ceaseless presence of intimidating officers and the potential for sexual or physical assault by officers or inmates, offers a poor environment for abuse recovery. Security concerns that dictate acts of dominance, such as ransacking lockers and storage spaces or stripping beds and going through personal items, can be retraumatizing for women with an abuse history. Heney and Kristiansen (1997) posit that incarcerated survivors of childhood abuse are likely to be reexposed to the traumatizing processes associated with their early abuse, including powerlessness, stigmatization, and betrayal. The powerlessness that most of these women already feel as a result of their previous abuse and exploitation is further exacerbated by the necessity to comply with prison procedures. Reexposure to these dynamics is met with a variety of coping responses including substance abuse, violence, self-injury, and suicide, thus further complicating many of the psychological problems with which they arrived in prison. Unfortunately for correctional staff, security concerns usually override treatment concerns, so security-related intrusiveness with women already vulnerable to mood disorders is difficult to alleviate.

Stressful Life Events

As previously noted, studies have shown women to be more likely than men to experience the onset of depression following a stressful life event. These events are likely to involve children, housing, and reproductive problems (Nazroo, Edwards, and Brown 1997), a history of sexual abuse (Bifulco, Brown, and Adler 1991) as well as social status and roles (Brown and Moran 1997; Shrier 2002) and unhappy marriages (Wu and DeMaris 1996). Additionally, women are more likely to report a stressful life event in the six months preceding a major depressive episode (Bebbington et al. 1998).

Women in prison frequently lose their husbands, boyfriends, children, and housing when incarcerated. Children, for instance, are often put in the custody of social service agencies, friends, distant relatives, ex-husbands, biological fathers, or in-laws. Houck and Loper (2002), in a study of 362 incarcerated mothers, found stress related to limited contact with children as well as concerns about parental competence to be related to higher levels of depression. Disconnection from family may be especially devastating for the female inmate, in that women have a unique need for extensive social support. They are more vulnerable than men, for instance, to the effects of divorce, in which case they demonstrate higher rates of depression (Horwitz, White, and Howell-White 1996). Since divorce affects women in general more profoundly than men, one may extrapolate that the emotional effect of divorce is much more intense while incarcerated. The feelings associated with such a loss are further exacerbated by the very limited and often nonexisting external support systems available to incarcerated women in general. The nonexistence of external supports or the lack of contact with them creates a need in incarcerated females to form intense emotional and sexual bonds with other females that becomes an important support system (Maeve 1999; Morgan 1997). These connections help stabilize mood when the relationships are satisfying, but they tend to unleash extreme mood instability when the relationships sour or when someone is transferred or paroled.

Alcohol Abuse and Other Substances

Women who abuse alcohol and drugs are more likely to attribute their drinking to a traumatic event or a stressor than men who abuse alcohol and drugs (Lex 1991). They also are more likely than nonabusers to have been sexually or physically victimized. Additionally, alcoholic females are twice as likely as other women to have experienced beatings or sexual assaults as children (Brienza and Stein 2002; Galaif et al. 2001; Stein, Burden, and Nyamathi 2002). The increased risk of substance abuse in women associated with traumatic events such as sexual assault may be affected by emotional experiences such as discouragement, feelings of inadequacy, and demoralization, often associated with depression (Cooper et al. 1997).

The Epidemiologic Catchment Area study found that 37 percent of women with alcohol use disorders had co-morbid mental illness, and major depression was the most common psychiatric co-morbidity among these women (Regier et al. 1990). The onset of psychiatric disorders precedes the onset of substance use disorders more often in women than in men (Dunne, Galatopoulos, and Schipperheijn 1993; Kessler et al. 1996). Moreover, when women in alcohol treatment have been asked about their reasons for seeking help, the most often cited reason is deepening depression (Turnbull and Gomberg 1991).

Unfortunately, women are less likely to seek treatment for addiction than men because they fear the loss of their children or harsh judgment if their addiction is known (Lowinson et al. 1997). Mere abstinence from substances, without psychological intervention or psycho-educational instruction in coping skills, does little to help these women with underlying depression stay clean after release. About two-thirds of arrestees with a history of chronic drug use return to a pattern of drug use and crime within three months after release from incarceration (Wexler 1994).

Compared to men entering treatment for substance addiction, women are more likely to be depressed, to have encountered more opposition to treatment from family and friends and to perceive higher personal psychosocial costs such as losing their children and being stigmatized after admitting the substance abuse problem (Allen 1995). If this is the experience of addicted women entering *treatment,* one may extrapolate from this that the same is true of women entering *prison,* perhaps with even more intense experiences of depression as the psychosocial stakes are higher.

When considering the relationship between abused women and incarceration discussed earlier as well as the relationship between abused women and addiction, a picture emerges for the average female inmate. Typically, there is a downward spiral that began with sexual or physical abuse without mental health intervention, followed by development of depressive disorders, followed by self-medication through substance abuse or dependence, followed by criminal activity to support the addiction, followed by incarceration.

Whether depression is a cause or consequence of drinking or other substance use, screening for it is critical during intake. The alert clinician should be wary of the fact that depression may mask signs of alcohol or drug abuse as they share many common symptoms such as depressed mood, markedly diminished interest or pleasure, weight loss, insomnia/hypersomnia, or psychomotor agitation (Stein and Cyr 1997). Differentiating symptoms of depressive disorders from the physiological expression of alcohol or other substance use is difficult and usually takes time and observation to clarify. Intense feelings of sadness may result from the intersection of alcohol/substance abuse or dependence and the bio-psycho-social impact of heavy use on that individual's quality of life (Canterbury 2002).

Nuances of Assessment and Treatment in a Correctional Setting

As one may imagine, assessing an inmate for placement and maintenance on the mental health caseload due to the diagnosis of a mood disorder is conducted differently in a correctional facility than in private practice. To begin, the limited resources and bulging caseloads often found in correctional settings, at least throughout the state of Georgia, necessitate attention to the most disturbed cases first and foremost. This means symptom presentation has to be more pronounced than one may observe in a private practice setting in order to merit clinical intervention. Clinicians must also pay greater attention to secondary gain issues (that is, factors that may motivate a sudden presentation or increase in depressive symptoms such as the "need" for a phone call, or the "need" for medication that may be "cheeked" and later "sold" to others for wanted goods, or the "need" to be moved from one location to another where a certain girlfriend happens to live).

Fortunately, in the prison setting, there is ample opportunity to obtain collateral data from correctional officers, psychiatrists, counselors, activity therapists, social workers, and clerical staff. All of these sources may provide valuable clues about symptom presentation and an inmate's ability to function and comply with procedures outside of the presence of the attending clinician.

Additionally, inmates should be able to provide a snapshot of a day in their lives, complete with adequate descriptions of symptoms apart from an *exclusive* focus on what they are missing in the free world. Many "symptoms" may be related to conflicts with a roommate, worries about placement upon release, or lack of contact with family. Obviously, these can be addressed without psychological or pharmacological intervention.

Diagnosis pertaining to mood disorders and the most appropriate treatment is always a challenge for those with a chronic substance abuse/suicidal/psychiatric history including multiple diagnoses. A recent study of chronically depressed patients found a greater severity of illness in women across several measures, as well as greater functional impairment, a younger age of illness onset, and greater family history of mood disorder (Kornstein 1997). These findings suggest that chronicity of depression may affect women more seriously than men. In support of this, a study by Berndt et al. (2000) found that early onset of chronic MDD adversely affects the educational attainment and expected lifetime earnings of women but not men. Of course, limited education coupled with low socioeconomic status are strongly correlated with women in the correctional system (Greenfield and Snell 1999). Hence, it stands to reason that some, if not many, incarcerated females may have experienced chronic depression at an early age that stymied their socioeconomic advancement and contributed to criminal behavior.

Other factors that challenge diagnosis of mood disorders and treatment include low IQ, personality disorders, a history of significant and/or repeated head trauma, physical disorders, and medication noncompliance. Many incarcerated females have all of the above. Therefore, psychological testing, timely cooperation from medical staff for tests and procedures, as well as the test of time and the reports of many observers must all work together to overcome the difficulties of differential diagnoses. Getting all parties to operate on the same page is more of a challenge in some facilities than in others, but likely a challenge to some degree in them all.

Salient Clinical Features of a Depressive Disorder

Major depressive disorder (MDD) should be considered the standard for defining depression as a disease. It is distinguished by several essential clinical features. Many of these features are also present in the other depressive disorders, although those disorders also have their own distinct criteria. Therefore, understanding and using the diagnostic criteria of MDD will allow for a comprehensive evaluation while also considering the various other possibilities within the differential diagnosis.

First and foremost, the symptoms of a depressed mood or the loss of interest or pleasure in nearly all activities must have been present for a period of at least two weeks. In addition, other symptoms (see following) must be present to the extent that they have significantly interfered with or impaired normal functioning. The challenge for the clinician working with an inmate population lies with being able to distinguish real and treatable disease from symptoms that, if generated only by the inmate's current situation, are likely to resolve on their own as adjustment to incarceration occurs.

Most depressed patients will present complaining of feeling sad, down in the dumps, hopeless, or overwhelmed. Other complaints include feeling like crying "for no reason." With incarcerated women this complaint is of serious concern as the presence of tears may create a feeling of vulnerability that places them, in their minds, at risk of being seen as weak by other inmates.

Insomnia is the most common of complaints expressed by this population as a symptom of their depression. Quite naturally, it leads to requests for medication "to help me sleep." On its own, insomnia is not significant enough to merit either a diagnosis of depression or treatment of the insomnia. However, insomnia associated with severe depression is often characterized by not only difficulty falling asleep but with middle-of-the-night awakening and inability to fall back asleep. There may be terminal insomnia where the individual awakens before a full and restful night's sleep has occurred. In addition, although less frequently, individuals may complain of hypersomnia or excessive sleepiness. In either situation, sleep problems secondary to depression create a unique situation for inmates as their inability to perform their assigned duties, because of inadequate sleep, may put them at risk of disciplinary action. Therefore, complaints regarding sleep should be thoroughly evaluated in order to be aware of a potentially treatable component of a depressive disorder.

Other complaints suggesting a depressive disorder include loss of energy (anergia) often described as feeling fatigued or tired, appetite changes that can present as either significant weight loss or weight gain, social isolation and withdrawal, psychomotor changes (agitation or retardation), and problems with memory, concentration, paying attention, and/or making decisions. Suicidal thoughts, wishes, plans, or intent must also be assessed in the initial evaluation. If present, then the inmate may need protective care and/or isolation until the depression is stabilized.

A useful tool that may be of assistance in circumstances where a brief, focused examination is necessary is the mnemonic "SADAFACES" (Montano and Montano 2002):

S – Sleep problems
A – Appetite or weight changes
D – Depressed or sad mood
A – Anhedonia or lack of interest, pleasure in daily activities
F – Fatigue
A – Agitation/psychomotor retardation
C – Concentration problems
E – low self-Esteem
S – Suicidal thoughts

Any of these symptoms, on their own, can significantly affect an individual's quality of life. When they occur as a cluster, along with the presence of a depressed mood, then there is adequate clinical evidence to support a diagnosis of depression.

The Unique Challenges of Suicidal and Parasuicidal Sequelae

Female inmates seen by the authors of this chapter frequently have a long and severe history of self-harm, which may include up to ten or more lifetime suicide attempts or chronic self-mutilation. The most popular methods of suicide attempts for incarcerated females at Metro State Prison are wrist cutting and hanging or suffocation with a bra or sheets tied around the neck. Marcus and Alcabes (1993) found in a study of forty-eight suicides committed by inmates in the custody of the New York City Department of Corrections between 1980 and 1988 that 42 percent occurred within the first thirty days of incarceration and 50 percent occurred within three days of a court appearance.

The symptoms most predictive of severe suicide attempts are hopelessness and insomnia; severe, relentless anxiety often with intermittent panic attacks; and a depressed mood (Hall, Platt, and Hall 1999). Depression, in fact, along with alcohol abuse are the most frequently made diagnoses in persons who commit suicide (Rich and Runeson 1992). As reported earlier, women are at far greater risk for depression as compared to men. Therefore, women are at greater risk for suicide attempts. In support of this, Moscicki (1997) found women to be three times more likely than men to attempt suicide, though men account for 65 percent of completed suicides.

Inmates frequently report suicidal thoughts, oftentimes without any intention of follow-through. Hence, therapeutic exploration of suicidal thoughts should include questions that expose the intention behind the thoughts—to actually end life or rather to end the pain and discomfort currently experienced. When confronted, inmates will usually offer immediate clarification with a statement like, "I don't want to kill myself and would never do it, but I just want to stop hurting." Clinicians may use this opportunity to offer hope through discussing available treatment, thus sending a vital message that help is on the way. Clinicians may also offer a reframe of the prison experience as useful time away from the madness of their lives on the street, where they may begin to rebuild their lives. The authors often hear reports from soon-to-be-released inmates that their incarceration was actually one of the best things that could have happened to them because they realize it saved their lives.

Reports of suicidal thoughts must be investigated even when the inmate is known to "cry wolf" when her desires for attention or some type of adjustment are not met. It can *never* be assumed that an inmate is "just being manipulative" and therefore attention from mental health staff is not warranted. While the follow-up attention is reinforcing of the suicidal behavior, a report of suicidal ideation is a serious matter. It leaves mental health professionals with no choice but to attend to the threat as though this report could be *the* time that the inmate's intentions are sincere. One never knows what inmates will actually do, even if they have no intention of killing themselves. For instance, some inmates who are accustomed to expressing their distress and frustration through cutting themselves may accidentally nick an artery and bleed to death.

When in doubt of an inmate's intention following an expression of suicidal thoughts, mental health professionals should be directed to reassess the inmate the next day and/or continue exploring an inmate's potential for imminent threat to self, in which case seclusion with frequent monitoring is necessary. Continued psychiatric evaluation with documentation is required until normal functioning has returned.

When evaluating for the potential for self-harm, a clinician must distinguish between self-injurious thoughts and thoughts that are suicidal in intent by asking, "Have you ever tried to hurt yourself without actually trying or wanting to kill yourself?" An affirmative response to this question, which may include head banging, cutting, burning, or stabbing oneself, often reveals layers of poor coping or problem-solving skills. Hence, if one only asks an inmate about her suicidal history, one only receives part of the story. Questions directed at parasuicidal behavior help the clinician to explore the inmate's potential for violence against herself, whether lethal or not. Treatment, therefore, should provide the inmate with a healthier understanding of how to manage her emotions and receive what she needs without resorting to self-injurious behaviors and suicide.

Differential Characteristics of One Depressive Disorder from Another

The next step in the psychiatric evaluation is to determine whether this is a major depressive episode, the depressive phase of a bipolar illness, a dysthymic disorder, depression associated with drug use, or depression of a different clinical entity such as occurring in conjunction with another medical illness. The successful treatment of any mood disorder rests upon the clinician's ability to identify, understand, and differentiate between the various clinical features of each disorder.

The assessment for any mood disorder should be detailed and comprehensive. Any complaints suggesting an abnormality of mood need to be assessed as to both severity and duration. In the incarcerated population, obtaining a full and honest history is often difficult. The inmates' histories of abuse, neglect, and poverty as well as feelings of hopelessness, shame, and guilt associated with their current incarceration may greatly compromise the validity of their information.

In addition, recent and recurring illegal drug use can easily confuse the clinical picture. The clinician is confronted with the question of which came first, the depression or the drug use. For these women, all too often the most readily available "treatment" for their lifelong pain and suffering has been illegal drugs often obtained through prostitution or other criminal activity. However, when depression is a part of the presenting complaint, most patients will be able to recall that their depressive symptoms and absence of contentment in their lives started long before their drug use, as discussed earlier.

The incarcerated woman may be experiencing a drug-free existence for the first time as well as the experience of a "normal" mood stabilized by medication. Although successful treatment of their depression may not be adequate to prevent relapse in all cases, it does begin to offer insight on their illness and treatment options not previously understood by them. Therefore, it is important that an accurate clinical profile is created that can then properly dictate treatment. In some cases, simple screening instruments such as the Zung Self Rating Scale for Depression or the Beck Depression Inventory may be either self-administered or verbally self-reported by the inmate, thereby giving some further indications of which symptoms are present and to what degree. Once the depressive symptoms have been identified, and where possible quantified, then a differential diagnostic assessment should be considered.

Depression and Bipolar Disorders

Although this chapter does not allow for a detailed discussion of the bipolar disorders, it is important to appreciate that a growing body of knowledge (Hirschfeld 2003) has identified significant numbers (69 percent) of treatment-resistant depressed patients who are actually suffering from a bipolar depression. Therefore, in addition to the self-assessments already listed, it is recommended that the Mood Disorder Questionnaire (Hirschfeld et al. 2000; Hirschfeld 2001) be given as an important screening instrument for bipolar disorder. In these patients, should they have a bipolar disorder, their depression would more likely be resistant to treatment by standard antidepressants alone.

Equally important in diagnosis is the fact that, in the incarcerated population, many features exhibited by these women, including mood liability, irritability, impulsivity, and low frustration tolerance, may actually be secondary to a bipolar type disorder with depressed mood. In that case, appropriate treatment with a mood stabilizer along with antidepressant medication would significantly improve their level of functioning, their ability to cope with their incarceration, and possibly reduce their risk of relapse upon release.

Depression Secondary to a Medical Illness

Another depressive disorder to consider as part of the differential diagnosis is depression secondary to a medical illness. As in the general population, both HIV and hepatitis C are increasing in prevalence in certain populations. Specifically, there is clear evidence that individuals with HIV and hepatitis B and C are at increased risk for a serious mental illness (Osher et al. 2003). While it is beyond the scope of this chapter to discuss these diseases in detail, it is important to emphasize here the increasing clinical evidence (Evans et al. 2002) that these medical illnesses have an associated risk of developing a major depression. Other medical conditions including malignancy, cardiovascular diseases, diabetes mellitus, and obesity have also been well established as creating an increased incidence of depression in at-risk populations (Anda et al. 1993; Barefoot et al. 1996; Carpenter et al. 2000; Frasure-Smith, Lespernance, and Talajic 1993; Koike, Unutzer, and Wells 2002; Maass-Robinson 2003). In the incarcerated population, obesity and diabetes are also highly prevalent and should be treated with as great a concern as any of the other conditions listed.

The incarcerated female, as noted, is more likely than the general public to exhibit excessive risk for depression. When coupled with a co-morbid medical condition, then this risk is, naturally, greatly enhanced. Therefore, a comprehensive medical evaluation that also includes an assessment for depression in the chronically medically ill inmate represents responsible medical care.

Dysthymia

Dysthymia differs from MDD primarily in its severity, chronicity, and persistence. The mood disturbance in this condition is present, not every day for two weeks as with MDD, but for most days over a two-year period. In addition, whereas MDD is defined by discrete periods of depression, dysthymia is more chronic and without these discrete episodes. These individuals have also never experienced any type of manic, mixed, or hypomanic episode. Otherwise, many of the same symptoms of MDD occur in dysthymia, often making it difficult to differentiate between the two.

In this population, the problem can be further complicated by a variety of factors that affect the inmate's perception of her depression, its duration, and severity. Patients with dysthymia will often report feelings of low energy or easy fatigue, poor sleep patterns, and a depressed mood as normal, stating, "I have always been like this" or "I have always felt like this . . . I thought that was normal." As a result, there may be little to no evidence of successful treatment of the depression as well as a greater likelihood of substance use to temporarily elevate an otherwise chronically depressed mood.

It should be noted that, in some studied populations, up to 75 percent of individuals diagnosed with dysthymia develop MDD within five years (*DSM-IV-TR*). Therefore, when making this diagnosis, it is appropriate to manage this condition much like MDD, both in the acute as well as chronic phases.

Depression Secondary to Substance Use (Substance-Induced Mood Disorder)

"Although manic patients seldom use sedatives to dampen their euphoria, depressed patients often use stimulants, such as cocaine and amphetamine, to relieve their depression" (Kaplan and Sadock 1998). Depression is common among women who have substance use, abuse, or dependence in their history. The choice of substances is usually determined by their social context (African American women are more likely to use cocaine while Caucasian women are users of amphetamines and methamphetamines). Often their incarceration is directly or indirectly related to their substance use (for example, arrests for drug possession, crimes committed to support addiction, such as theft or prostitution, and sale of drugs). Therefore, identifying and successfully treating a clinical depression in this population has value in several areas, including potentially reducing recidivism by controlling patients' use of drugs to self-medicate.

A substance-induced mood disorder is characterized by a disturbance in mood, in this case, depression, that is shown to be *the direct physiological effect of an ingested substance* (that is, drugs of abuse, medications, and steroids). As substance-induced depression arises only in association with the use of drugs or medications, then a history that reveals symptoms that preceded the substance use suggests a depressive disorder independent of the substance use. An evaluation for a substance-induced depression should seek to identify specific temporal factors that will then aid in distinguishing this depression from that of a primary mood disorder.

Upon initial incarceration, an inmate may be under the influence of her drug of choice. Therefore, an examiner should anticipate that the inmate might be experiencing withdrawal from drug use. The complaints of depression, insomnia, and agitation should be monitored but not medicated for a period of several weeks. After that time, a reassessment of the symptoms is necessary in order to ensure that the depression and associated symptoms have resolved. Their continued presence would support further evaluation and treatment.

Inmates being remanded to state prisons, once adjudicated, will often request that the medications prescribed for them in county jails now be discontinued. The reasons given may be that either the response to the medication has been inadequate, that the side effects are intolerable, or that they no longer need any medications. These recurring situations raise important questions as to how and when to treat inmates with a current history of substance use while held in county jails.

Treating depression in the presence of a history of substance abuse is often complicated by the complaint that the medication doesn't give the same "high" as the patient's street drugs. The goal of treatment, therefore, is to create an understanding of what normal mood is and, once established, to learn to accept the fluctuations that occur in any life experience without resorting to street drugs.

Treatment Options for the Incarcerated Population

Severe clinical depression, or MDD, is a serious medical illness that, if left untreated, will profoundly alter the quality of life of the individual and may lead to suicide attempts and death. The despair of this condition is difficult to appreciate either if one has not experienced it or if one ignores the reality of this disease and believes the patient's symptoms are all under volitional control.

In a prison or jail setting, treatment options are considerably limited, both in terms of medication choices as well as multidisciplinary therapy opportunities. Although this can create a sense of performing twenty-first-century medicine with a nineteenth-century formulary, it can also be seen as an opportunity to creatively integrate and augment medication choices in order to achieve stabilization and improve baseline functioning.

As to the type of treatment, medication or psychotherapy, the answer is not either/or but both. Clinical data (Nierenberg, Petersen, and Alpert 2003) have clearly shown that neither psychotherapy nor medication alone will successfully control depression over the long term. This same data has shown that therapy *and* ongoing medication management together can significantly reduce the morbidity and mortality of this disease. Therefore, the most successful approach is that which provides for both treatments.

The decision to initiate medication management is not to be made simply because of an expressed need by the inmate. As has been discussed previously, the final diagnosis may not support immediate or continuing medication management. The American Psychiatric Association, in its *Practice Guidelines for the Treatment of Psychiatric Disorders* (2002), suggests that medication may be the preferred treatment if the following features are present: (1) history of prior positive response, (2) severe symptomatology, (3) anticipation of need for maintenance therapy, (4) patient preference, and (5) lack of available alternative treatment modalities. Although in the jail or prison setting other factors may also be a consideration, these guidelines can serve to direct decision making in the acute situation.

For long-term maintenance, it is best to continue an inmate on her medication for no less than nine to twelve months once full remission has occurred. Here again, the prison setting may present such a level of recurring daily stress that normalizing of brain function is not possible in this time frame, and medication management may be needed indefinitely. Long-term maintenance can be problematic as inmates will often make decisions regarding their medications based upon pressure from other inmates, frustration with pill-call lines, or a need to express personal control by "doing it on my own" as opposed to full symptom relief. As with any patient management situation, these issues of noncompliance may be resolved only with a positive therapeutic alliance between the inmate and her provider.

Medication and Side Effects

The primary goal of treating depression with medication is to normalize mood while limiting or controlling for side effects. In spite of significant advances in the treatment of depression since the introduction of Prozac in the mid-1980s, medications are not without potentially disturbing or disruptive side effects. For an inmate population, the development of unexpected or disabling side effects is especially problematic. The absence of sympathetic corrections staff and the limited access to follow-up medical appointments may create a resistance to treatment that is difficult to overcome. Therefore, when medication is initiated, the possibility of side effects as well as the potential delay in achieving the desired benefits should be carefully explained to the inmate.

The choices in medication, as noted, are often limited to what is in the facility's formulary. Some formularies may only carry several of the serotonin reuptake inhibitors (fluoxetine, paroxetine, sertraline, or citalopram) as these are the older, original, and perhaps less expensive antidepressants. Others may also include a dopaminergic enhancer such as buproprion or a noradrenergic enhancer such as venlafaxine. Although the older tricyclic and tetracyclic medications continue to have a place in psychiatric medicine, they should be limited in their use in the correctional setting. Their high potential for lethal dosing as well as disturbing side effects supports their use only in very specific and well-controlled situations.

Nonpharmacologic Treatment

The consensus among mental health practitioners is that the use of medication combined with psychotherapy is the most efficient approach in treating mood disorders. However, few studies have investigated gender differences in response to psychotherapy for mood disorders (Kornstein and Wojcik 2002). Interestingly, one study found that in women under forty years old, there was no advantage of combined treatment over psychotherapy alone, whereas women over age fifty responded to combined treatment as well as men (Thase et al. 2000). It was noted that the use of tricyclic antidepressants as the medication component in these studies may be a confounding factor in these results because younger women tend to have a poorer response to tricyclics. One may also speculate that the need that women have, as opposed to men, for extensive social supports may predispose them for better response to psychotherapy alone when they feel appropriately heard and attended to by a warm and empathic therapist. Additionally, it may be that depression, left untreated until later age, in combination with a perimeno-pausal status, may necessitate the need for more intense treatment, which includes medication.

At Metro State Prison, as with most penal institutions, individual therapy is a luxury with a lengthy waiting list. Therefore, it is offered to those believed to gain the most benefit (that is, inmates who are motivated, verbal, insightful). Since individual therapy is available to only a few in a correctional setting, attempts should be made to steer inmates with marginal treatment needs toward group therapy. These groups help to make therapy available to everyone on the caseload and encourage inmates to develop a support system that sustains them when certain mental staff are unavailable. In groups, inmates begin to understand, perhaps for the first time, that they are not alone in their struggles with mood instability.

Group therapy for the mood disorders track at Metro State Prison include groups with foci such as "Self-Esteem," "Coping Skills," "Healing Life's Hurts," "Forgiving Yourselves," "Choosing to Live," and "Picture Your Life" (an innovative group that watches films with a therapeutic purpose in order to help those challenged by verbal expression to articulate certain feelings). Well-planned groups have proven to be well received by most inmates, and they serve as the primary nonpharmacological treatment modality. Recent studies evaluating the efficacy of group psychotherapy with incarcerated women (Bradley and Follingstad 2003) and incarcerated offenders in general (Morgan and Flora 2002) indicate positive treatment effects for mood disturbances. Data from Morgan and Flora indicate that the use of homework exercises significantly improves outcomes.

Summary and Conclusions

Women in general are at much greater risk than men for depression by a ratio of two to one. Incarceration represents a particularly exacerbating event for depression in females. It is a source of extreme stress as well as a challenge to the inmate's social support, which, for women, is especially important. However, distress and appropriate sadness about one's incarceration does not constitute a clinical presentation.

A number of clinical conditions include a depressed mood, and they have to be differentiated from a normal response by the use of a specific set of criteria as outlined in the *DSM-IV*. The hallmark of these disorders is major depressive disorder (MDD). Other conditions include dysthymic disorder, depressive disorder NOS, adjustment disorder with depressive features, bipolar I or bipolar II disorder, cyclothymia, schizoaffective disorder, and depression secondary to substance use or a medical condition.

In many cases, the use of screening instruments may help determine the true character of an inmate's mood disorder. These instruments include the Zung Self-

Rating Scale for Depression and the Beck Depression Inventory. Either of these may be self-administered or verbally self-reported by the inmate. The results may aid in quantifying which symptoms are present and to what degree. In addition to accurate diagnosis, screening for suicidality soon after an inmate's arrival is essential for effective treatment. Therefore, an inmate's report of suicidal thoughts must always be investigated further and differentiated from (1) a history or desire for acts of self-harm *without* intention of suicide, or (2) an expression of a desperate desire for the pain of life to end rather than for life itself to end. Appropriate and immediate psychiatric/psychological intervention must follow a careful assessment of suicidal risk.

Proper diagnosis of mood disorders in women is uniquely challenged by incarceration for many reasons. To begin with, inmates often begin their incarceration experience with a mistrust of all persons in positions of authority, including mental health professionals. This mistrust is so intense that inmates often attempt to wear the mask of wellness in order to avoid being singled out for treatment, regardless of how severe their depression may be. Therefore, in order to encourage inmates to take advantage of available mental health treatment in correctional facilities, it may be helpful to enlist the support of other inmates who have benefited from mental health services. One solution may be to designate inmates with a positive treatment experience and subsequent model behavior to become "inmate ambassadors." They may participate in the orientation process by advising inmates to be honest about their symptoms, to dispel myths regarding treatment, and to help inmates see that working with mental health professionals is in their best interest.

Other unique challenges in treating incarcerated females for mood disorders include the fact that most female inmates enter prison with a history of physical and sexual abuse that leaves them vulnerable to retraumatization in a prison environment that is hostile by design and nature. Inmates therefore need education about the boundaries that neither correctional staff nor peers should violate. This information should include grievance procedures in the event that violations occur. Understanding grievance procedures also gives the characteristically depressed/powerless and abused inmate a sense of empowerment, which in itself is therapeutic. Ultimately, proper management of inmates' fears and vulnerability serves to enhance all mental health treatment. It is the responsibility of the mental health staff to prepare and support inmates, beginning with intake, to learn appropriate coping skills. Through both group as well as individual therapy, inmates may learn to cope with intrusive inspections that are a regular occurrence in the prison setting. However, although group and individual therapy are critical to learning new skills, often they are not enough.

Treatment in a correctional setting, as in the free world, has a greater potential for success if medication, when indicated, is combined with psychotherapy. Because of the extensive substance abuse history of incarcerated women, acceptance of recommended medication will require unusual patience, careful selection of medications from a specified formulary, and attentive follow-up by treatment providers. Acceptance of treatment recommendations may also be complicated by

- co-morbid medical illness
- chronic self-injury or a history of head trauma
- past history of alcohol abuse or dependence
- failure of prior treatment efforts
- a general lack of trust in the system or anyone for that matter due to past experiences with physical or sexual assaults

However, the benefits of successfully treating female inmates for a mood disorder will be evident throughout the facility. Normal mood allows for normal functioning. This, of course, allows for the entire correctional system to operate more effectively in managing large numbers of inmates and returning stable inmates to society with a better chance of becoming gainfully employed, more responsible parents, and contributors to society at large.

REFERENCES

Allen, K. 1995. Barriers to treatment for addicted for African American women. *Journal of the National Medical Association* 87: 751–56.

American Psychiatric Association. 2002. *Diagnostic and statistical manual of mental disorders,* 4th ed. text revision. Washington, DC: American Psychiatric Association.

American Psychiatric Association. 2002. *Practice guidelines for the treatment of psychiatric disorders.* Compendium 2002. Washington, DC: American Psychiatric Association.

American Psychiatric Association. 1994. *Diagnostic and statistical manual of mental disorders,* 4th ed. Washington, DC: American Psychiatric Association.

Anda, R., D. Williamson, D. Jones, C. Macera, E. Baker, A. Glassman, and J. Marks. 1993. Depressed affect, hopelessness, and the risk of ischemic heart disease in a cohort of U.S. adults. *Epidemiology* 4: 285–94.

Barefoot, J. C., M. J. Helms, D. B. Mark, J. A. Blumenthal, R. M. Califf, T. L. Haney, C. M. O'Connor, I. C. Siegler, and R. B. Williams. 1996. Depression and long term mortality risk in patients with coronary artery disease. *American Journal of Cardiology* 78: 613–17.

Bebbington, P. E., G. Dunn, R. Jenkins, G. Lewis, T. Brugha, M. Farrell, and H. Meltzer. 1998. The influence of age and sex on the prevalence of depression conditions: Report from the national survey of psychiatric morbidity. *Psychological Medicine* 28: 9–19.

Berndt, E. R., L. M. Koran, S. N. Finkelstein, A. J. Gelenberg, S. G. Kornstein, I. M. Miller, M. E. Thase, G. A. Trapp, and M. B. Keller. 2000. Lost human capital from early-onset chronic depression. *American Journal of Psychiatry* 15: 940–47.

Bifulco, A., G. W. Brown, and Z. Adler. 1991. Early sexual abuse and clinical depression in adult life. *British Journal of Psychiatry* 159: 115–22.

Bradley, R. G., and D. R. Folllingstad. 2003. Group therapy for incarcerated women who experienced interpersonal violence: A pilot study. *Journal of Traumatic Stress* 16: 337–40.

Brienza, R. S., and M. D. Stein. 2002. Alcohol use disorders in primary care: Do gender-specific differences exist? *Journal of General Internal Medicine* 17: 387–97.

Brown, G., and P. M. Moran. 1997. Single mothers, poverty, and depression. *Psychological Medicine* 27: 21–33.

Canterbury, R. J. 2002. Alcohol and other substance abuse. In *Women's Mental Health,* ed. S. G. Kornstein and A. H. Clayton. New York: Guilford Press. 222–43.

Carpenter, K. M., D. S. Hasin, D. B. Allison, and M. S. Faith. 2000. Relationship between obesity and DSM-IV major depressive disorder, suicide ideation and suicide attempts: Results from a general population study. *American Journal of Public Health* 90, no. 2: 251–57.

Cooper, M. L., M. R. Frone, M. Russell, and R. S. Pierce. 1997. Individual and social perspectives. In *Gender and alcohol,* ed. R. W. Wilsnack and S. C. Wilsnack. Piscataway, NJ: Rutgers Center of Alcohol Studies. 199–224.

Dunne, F. J., C. Galatopoulos, and J. M. Schipperheijn. 1993. Gender differences in psychiatric morbidity among alcohol misusers. *Comprehensive Psychiatry* 34: 95–101.

Evans D. L., T. R. Ten Have, S. D. Douglass, D. R. Gettes, M. Morrison, M. S. Chiappini, P. Brinker-Spence, C. Job, D. E. Mercer, Y. L. Wang, D. Crusess, B. Dube, E. A. Dalen, T. Brown, R. Bauer, and J. M. Petitto. 2002. Association of depression with viral load, CD8 lymphocytes, and natural killer cells in women with HIV infection. *American Journal of Psychiatry* 159, no. 10: 1752–59.

Fogel, C. I. 1993. Hard time: The stressful nature of incarceration for women. *Issues in Mental Health Nursing* 14: 367–77.

Frasure-Smith, N., F. Lespernance, and M. Talajic. 1993. Depression following myocardial infarction. *JAMA* 270.15: 1819–25.

Galaif, E. R., J. A. Stein, M. D. Newcomb, and D. P. Bernstein. 2001. Gender differences in the prediction of problem alcohol use in adulthood: Exploring the influence of family factors and childhood maltreatment. *Journal of Studies on Alcohol* 62: 486–93.

Greenfield, L. A., and T. L. Snell. 1999. Women offenders. Bureau of Justice Statistics Special Report NCJ 175688.

Hall, R.C.W., D. E. Platt, and R.C.W. Hall. 1999. Suicide risk assessment: A review of risk factors for suicide in 100 patients who made severe suicide attempts. *Psychosomatics* 40: 18–27.

Harlow, C. W. 1998. Profile of Jail Inmates 1996. Bureau of Justice Statistics Special Report NCJ 164620.

Heney, J., and C. Kristiansen. 1997. An analysis of the impact of prison on women survivors of childhood sexual abuse. *Women and Therapy* 20: 29–44.

Hirschfeld, M. A. 2001. Bipolar spectrum disorder. Improving its recognition and diagnosis. *Journal of Clinical Psychiatry* 62, (Suppl. 14): 5–9.

Hirschfeld, M. A. 2003. Screening for bipolar disorder in the community. *Journal of Clinical Psychiatry* 64: 53–58.

Hirschfeld, Robert M. A., Janet B. W. Williams, R. L. Spitzer, J. R. Calabrese, L. Flynn, P. E. Keck Jr., L. Lewis, S. L. McElroy, R. M. Post, D. J. Rapport, J. M. Russell, G. S. Sachs, and J. Zajecka. 2000. Development and validation of a screening instrument for bipolar spectrum disorder: The Mood Disorder Questionnaire. *American Journal of Psychiatry* 157, no. 11: 1873–75.

Hoagwood, K. 1990. Blame and adjustment among women sexually abused as children. *Women and Therapy* 9: 89–110.

Horwitz, A.V., H. R. White, and S. Howell-White. 1996. The use of multiple outcomes in stress research: A case study of gender differences in responses to marital dissolution. *Journal of Health and Social Behavior* 37: 278–91.

Houck, K., and A. B. Loper. 2002. The relationship of parenting stress to adjustment among mothers in prison. *American Journal of Orthopsychiatry* 72: 548–58.

Hurely, W., and M. P. Dunne. 1991. Psychological distress and psychiatric morbidity in women prisoners. *Australian and New Z Psychiatry* 25: 461–70.

Jordan, B. K., W. E. Schlenger, J.A. Fairbank, and J. M. Caddell. 1996. Prevalence of psychiatric disorders among incarcerated women: Convicted felons entering prison. *Archives of General Psychiatry* 53: 513–19.

Kaplan, H. I., and B. J. Sadock. 1998. *Synopsis of Psychiatry,* 8th ed. Baltimore, MD: Lippincott Williams and Wilkins.

Kessler, R., C. Nelson, K. McGonagle, M. Edlund, R. Frank, and P. Leaf. 1996. The epidemiology of co-occurring addictive and mental disorders: Implications for prevention and service utilization. *American Journal of Orthopsychiatry* 66, no. 1: 17–31.

Koike, A. K., J. Unutzer, and K. B. Wells. 2002. Improving the care for depression in patients with co-morbid medical illness. *American Journal of Psychiatry* 159, no. 10: 1738–45.

Kornstein, S. G. 1997. Gender differences in depression: Implications for treatment. *Journal of Clinical Psychiatry* 58 (Suppl. 15): 12–18.

Kornstein, S. G., and B. A. Wojcik. 2000. Gender effects in the treatment of depression. *Psychiatric Clinics of North America Annual of Drug Therapy* 7: 23–57.

Lex, B. W. 1991. Some gender differences in alcohol and polysubstance users. *Health Psychology* 10: 121–32.

Louise, B. 1998. The victimization and revictimization of female offenders. *Corrections Today* 60: 106–11.

Lowinson, J., R. Ruiz, R. Millman, and J. Langrod, eds. 1997. *Women: Clinical aspects in substance abuse: A comprehensive textbook.* Baltimore, MD: Williams and Wilkins.

Maass-Robinson, S. 2001. An open letter to my sisters: Why don't we get help for depression? *American Journal of Health Studies Special Issue: The Health of Women of Color* 17: 46–49.

Maass-Robinson, S. 2003. Integrated health care must consider mental health to reduce rates of cardiovascular disease. *Ethnicity and Disease* 13, no. 3: 309.

Maeve, K. 1999. The social construction of love and sexuality in a woman's prison. *Advances in Nursing Science* 21: 46–65.

Maier, W., M. Gansicke, R. Gater, M. Rezaki, B. Tiemens, and R. F. Urzua. 1999. Gender differences in the prevalence of depression: A survey in primary care. *Journal of Affective Disorder* 53: 241–52.

Marcus, P., and P. Alcabes. 1993. Characteristics of suicides by inmates in an urban jail. *Hospital and Community Psychiatry* 44: 256–61.

McClellan, D., D. Farabee, and B. M. Crouch. 1997. Early victimization, drug use, and criminality: A comparison of male and female prisoners. *Criminal Justice and Behavior* 24: 455–76.

Montano, C. B., and M. B. Montano. 2002. A new paradigm for treating depression in the primary care setting; Medscape CME activity, September 18, 2002.

Morgan, D. 1997. Restricted love. *Women and Therapy* 20: 75–84.

Morgan, R. D., and D. B. Flora. 2002. Group psychotherapy with incarcerated offenders: A research synthesis. *Group Dynamics* 6: 203–18.

Moscicki, E. K. 1997. Identification of suicide risk factors using epidemiologic studies. *Psychiatric Clinics of North America* 20: 499–517.

Nazroo, J. Y., A. C. Edwards, and G. W. Brown. 1997. Gender differences in the onset of depression following a shared life event: A study of couples. *Psychological Medicine* 27: 9–19.

Nierenberg, A. A., T. J. Petersen, and J. E. Alpert. 2003. Prevention of relapse and recurrence in depression: The role of long-term pharmacotherapy and psychotherapy. *Journal of Clinical Psychiatry* 64, no. 15: 13–17.

Nolen-Hoeksema, S. 1994. An interactive model for the emergence of gender differences in depression in adolescence. *Journal of Research on Adolescence* 4: 519–34.

Nolen-Hoeksema, S., J. Larson, J., and C. Grayson. 1999. Explaining the gender difference in depressive symptoms. *Journal of Personality and Social Psychology* 77, no. 5: 1061–72.

Osher, F. C., R. W. Goldberg, L. A. Goodman, and S. D. Rosenberg. 2003. Hepatitis C and individuals with serious mental illness. *Psychiatric Annuals* 33, no. 6: 394–400.

Regier, D., M. Farmer, D. Rae, B. Locke, S. Keith, L. Judd, and F. Goodwin. 1990. Co-morbidity of mental disorders with alcohol and other drug abuse: Results from the epidemiologic catchment area (ECA) study. *Journal of the American Medical Association* 264: 2511–18.

Shrier, D. K. 2002. Career and workplace issues. In *Women's Mental Health,* ed. S. G. Kornstein and A. H. Clayton. New York: Guilford Press. 527–41.

Sigmon, S. T., M. P. Greene, K. J. Rohan, and J. E. Nichols. 1996. Coping and adjustment in male and female survivors of childhood sexual abuse. *Journal of Child Sexual Abuse* 5: 57–76.

Singer, M. I., J. Bussey, L. Song, and L. Lunghofer. 1995. The psychosocial issues of women serving time in jail. *Social Work* 40: 103–13.

Stein, J. A., L. Burden, and A. Nyamathi. 2002. Relative contributions of parent substance use and childhood maltreatment to chronic homelessness, depression, and substance abuse problems among homeless women: Mediating roles of self-esteem and abuse in adulthood. *Child Abuse and Neglect* 26: 1011–27.

Stein, M. D., and M. G. Cyr. 1997. Women and substance abuse. *Medical Clinics of North America* 81: 979–98.

Teplin, L. A. 1996. Prevalence of psychiatric disorders among incarcerated: Pretrial jail detainees. *Archives of General Psychiatry* 53: 505–12.

Teplin, L., K. Abram, and M. McClelland. 1996. Prevalence of psychiatric disorders among incarcerated women: I. Pretrial jail detainees. *Archives of General Psychiatry* 53, no. 6: 505–12.

Thase, M. E., E. Frank, S. G. Kornstein, and K. A. Yonkers. 2000. In *Gender and its effects of psychopathology,* ed. E. Frank. Washington, DC: American Psychiatric Publishing, Inc. 103–29.

Turnbull, J. E., and E.S.L. Gomberg. 1991. The structure of drinking-related consequences in alcoholic women. *Alcoholism: Clinical and Experimental Research* 11: 74–79.

Weiner, J., and B. Anno. 1992. The crisis in correctional health care: The impact of the drug control strategy on correctional health services. *Annals of Internal Medicine* 117: 71–77.

Weiss, E. L., J. G. Longhurst, and C. M. Mazure. 1999. Childhood sexual abuse as a risk factor for depression in women: Psychosocial and neurobiological correlates. *American Journal of Psychiatry* 156: 816–28.

Wexler, H. K. 1994. Progress in prison substance abuse treatment: A five-year report. *Journal of Drug Issues* 24: 349–60.

Wu, X., and A. DeMaris. 1996. Gender and marital status differences in depression: The effects of chronic strains. *Sex Roles* 34: 299–319.

7

Anxiety Disorders and
Major Thought Disorders

CASSANDRA F. NEWKIRK

Anxiety is often experienced as a normal emotion of everyday life because as Kaplan and Sadock (2002) state, anxiety is an alerting signal warning of impending danger that serves as an adaptive function to allow one to get out of harm's way. Pathological anxiety exists when the response to a situation is inappropriate in intensity and duration. Kaplan and Sadock describe anxiety as an awareness of physiological sensations such as palpitations, sweating, and awareness of being nervous. The anxiety causes cognitive changes such that a person has difficulty thinking and learning new information because of a sense of confusion.

The American Psychiatric Association *Diagnostic and Statistical Manual of Mental Disorders* (2000) lists the following anxiety disorders: panic disorder, with and without agoraphobia, agoraphobia, specific phobia, social phobia, obsessive-compulsive disorder, post-traumatic stress disorder, acute stress disorder, generalized anxiety disorder, substance-induced anxiety disorder, anxiety disorder secondary to a medical condition and anxiety disorder not otherwise specified. Anxiety disorders may be difficult to distinguish from other major mental disorders, as anxiety can be associated with several diagnostic categories such as schizophrenia and depression. Anxiety may also be induced by medical conditions such as certain inflammatory diseases, or it may be an adverse reaction to medications.

Several surveys have estimated the prevalence of anxiety disorders in the population, and women are affected by them more than men. The National Institute of Mental Health's Epidemiologic Catchment Area study showed that anxiety disorders had the highest overall prevalence rate among the mental disorders with a lifetime prevalence of 14.6 percent (Mendlowicz and Stein 2000). The National Comorbidity Study showed that women have a lifetime prevalence rate of 30.5 percent compared to 19.2 percent for men (Kaplan and Sadock 2002). Estimating the number of inmates suffering from anxiety disorder or any specific mental disorder has often been difficult due to strict guidelines relating to the gathering of research data. Teplin (1994) found that 6.1 percent of male and 12.3 percent of women entering the Cook County Department of Corrections had a serious mental illness. Pinta (2001) reviewed several articles and reports and surveyed several state prison systems regarding the number of mentally ill inmates they had identified. He concluded that 10 percent of men and 18 percent of women had had symptoms of a serious mental disorder within the year prior to the study. He considered these figures to be only a minimum as they did not include those inmates that may have been suffering from mental retardation and other disorders that were not labeled as serious but were the focus of attention. These studies imply that a fair percentage of incarcerated women will suffer from some sort of anxiety disorder during their incarceration whether in the jail or prison setting. Post-traumatic stress disorder is one of the anxiety disorders that are more prevalent among incarcerated women than in the general population because of the high incidence of abuse in the lives of women prior to incarceration. Post-traumatic stress disorder will be discussed later in the chapter.

Several theories exist as to the development of pathological anxiety. Kaplan and Sadock (2002) reflect on Freud's theory that anxiety is the result of psychic conflict between aggressive wishes and corresponding threats from external reality. Behavioral theory states that anxiety is a conditioned response to specific stimuli. An example of such a conditioned or learned response is that of women who were abused as children. Initially the anxiety associated with the abuse was a normal response to a dangerous and threatening stimuli, namely the abuse. Repeated abuse leads to what Herman (1997) calls the "formidable tasks of adaptation." Even in situations that may be safe, the child or adult has no belief that any place or person is safe and therefore continues to respond to nonthreatening situations with intense anxiety.

Women in correctional settings are admitted with a myriad of problems and issues. Greenfeld and Snell (1999) report that approximately 70 percent of incarcerated women have minor children and most were the primary caretakers prior to arrest. Fifty percent have never been married. Approximately 66 percent are women of color—black, Hispanic, or other races. Only 40 percent report working prior to incarceration, and 30 percent were on public assistance. Forty-four percent of the women stated that they had experienced physical or sexual abuse prior to incarceration with 69 percent reporting that the abuse occurred prior to the age of eighteen. Forty percent of the women admitted to using drugs at the time of arrest. The average woman entering a correctional setting in the United States is a woman of color that has two children, is unemployed, and may receive public assistance. Many have been abused, which has led to substance abuse to help deal with the pain of the abuse. Many became pregnant at an early age and contracted sexually transmitted diseases, including the virus that causes AIDS. In Greenfeld and Snell's 1999 sample of incarcerated women, 3.5 percent were HIV positive.

These demographics increase the likelihood of an incarcerated woman developing one or more mental disorders prior to her entry into the criminal justice system. The most common disorders seen in this population are mood disorders, which are covered in another chapter, and anxiety disorders. Generalized anxiety disorder, substance-induced anxiety disorder, and post-traumatic stress disorder are the most common anxiety disorders diagnosed in this population and will be discussed in more detail below. The treatment of these disorders in women's correctional facilities will be addressed as well.

Substance-Induced Anxiety Disorder

The diagnosis of substance-induced anxiety disorder requires, according to *DSM-IV-TR* (2000), the presence of prominent anxiety, panic attacks, obsessions, or compulsions. The symptoms should have developed during the use of a substance or within a month of its cessation. As many women entering the jail setting are using addictive substances shortly prior to their arrests, anxiety secondary to this use is common. Clinicians often misdiagnose this disorder as some sort of chronic anxiety disorder because of failure to illicit an adequate substance abuse history upon intake into the correctional facility. Often the addictive substance, such as cocaine, is used in an attempt to self-medicate anxiety or depression secondary to other causes. Clinicians have to ask questions about drug use and abuse as well as symptoms when the patient is drug free to make accurate diagnoses. All too often in the busy environment of a jail or prison intake area, there is not enough time or direction given to gather this information. Given the numbers of women with histories of abuse, it is also crucial that these histories are taken into consideration. Histories of abuse would lead clinicians to consider anxiety disorders or depression as probable primary problems and the substance abuse as secondary. Medical staff at intake should ask screening questions regarding current and past use of addictive substances and alcohol as well as questions relating to past interpersonal trauma. If any of these areas of inquiry are positive, referrals should be made to substance abuse and mental health services for further evaluation.

It is important to remind clinicians that if there is no known history of a mental disorder, a specific diagnosis should not be made whenever displayed symptoms may be secondary to addictive substances. In an ideal setting, the addicted person is withdrawn from the particular drug or alcohol, observed drug free for several weeks, and reassessed as to the continuing presence of symptoms, which may indicate a mental disorder rather than a substance-induced problem. In the reality of the correctional setting, most women will be seen for medical intake and physical examination within the first two weeks. If symptoms of anxiety exist, the woman will be referred for mental health screening and assessment. In a jail setting, she may not be seen again because of the short length of stay for most offenders. In the prison setting, it is much easier to differentiate the symptoms because the majority of the women entering prison have spent some time in jail prior to entering prison. Substance-induced symptoms are usually dissipated by the time someone is admitted to the prison. In this setting, more accurate diagnoses can be made. If the symptoms abate after a reasonable drug-free period, then substance abuse education should be offered and referrals made to substance abuse treatment programs. The reality is, however, that in most jails and prisons these programs do not exist. Groups such as Alcoholic Anonymous (AA) and Narcotic Anonymous (NA) do have volunteers that offer sessions inside many jails and prisons.

Generalized Anxiety Disorder

DSM-IV-TR (2000) diagnostic criteria for generalized anxiety disorder include excessive anxiety and worry occurring more days than not for at least six months about several events or activities. The person finds it difficult to control this worry and the symptoms cause clinically significant distress or impairment in social, occupational, or other areas of functioning. This is probably the disorder that most often coexists with another mental disorder, and anywhere between 50 to 90 percent of patients with generalized anxiety disorder have another mental disorder (Kaplan and Sadock 2002). Women more often suffer from this disorder than men. Because of the high co-morbidity of generalized anxiety disorder with other disorders, it might be better conceptualized as a prodrome rather than a discrete disorder. Data from two national surveys looking at the prevalence of generalized anxiety disorder and major depression showed that the majority of respondents who had generalized anxiety disorder also had major depression. Moreover, respondents who had both disorders had greater impairment than those with only one or neither of the disorders (Kessler et al. 1999). It is noted that both of these studies, the National Comorbidity Survey and the Midlife Development consisted of noninstitutionalized respondents. We can infer that persons that reside in institutions such as psychiatric hospitals or correctional settings are even more likely to suffer from co-morbid psychiatric disorders with greater impairment.

The diagnostic dilemma in correctional settings is that a certain amount of anxiety may be normal because incarcerated individuals have little control of anything in their environment. For incarcerated women who have histories of abuse, one expects to encounter depression and anxiety in the majority of women entering this environment. Recalling that one of the hallmarks of making diagnoses of mental disorders is the presence of major impairments in daily functioning, it becomes even harder for clinicians in correctional settings to discern how much impairment really exists. Given that incarcerated individuals cannot make many independent decisions regarding their daily activities, the assessment of functioning is often inadequate. The key to making accurate diagnoses, especially in the case of incarcerated women, is for clinicians to become familiar with the many issues that the women bring in with them upon their incarceration. Acknowledging that most of the women have children whom they are separated from and have concerns about their well-being puts the symptoms of worry and anxiety into perspective. Concerns about medical disorders that were not addressed prior to incarceration because of lack of access to health care in the public system is also an area of worry and anxiety for many women. Recalling that many women used addictive substances prior to arrest, they were unable to focus their attention fully on their lives or their children because of their focus on survival. All too often clinicians in correctional settings hear the complaints of "I'm worried about my children" or "I feel depressed." When asked why such feelings are present, many women are unable to talk about these issues succinctly and it becomes much easier for a clinician to prescribe medication to alleviate some of the surface anxiety and worry. What the women need at this point is someone to listen and understand. Medications without an opportunity to address the issues only serve to mask the problems. Medical staff should make referrals to mental health staff for further assessment and possible treatment, which will be discussed later in the chapter.

Post-Traumatic Stress Disorder

According to the *DSM-IV-TR* (2000), the essential criteria for a diagnosis of post-traumatic stress disorder is the development of symptoms following exposure to an extreme traumatic stressor involving direct personal experience of an event that involves actual or threatened death or serious injury. The response must involve intense fear, helplessness, or horror. The symptoms resulting from the trauma include persistent reexperiencing of the traumatic event, persistent avoidance of stimuli associated with the trauma and numbing of feelings, and persistent heightened arousal. The symptoms must be persistent for more than one month with significant distress or impairment in the activities of daily living. Post-traumatic stress disorder has a lifetime prevalence of 1 to 3 percent in the United States in the general population with higher rates found in some groups such as veterans who faced combat situations (Kaplan and Sadock 2002).

Kessler, Sonnega, and Bromet (1995) report that the lifetime prevalence rate for post-traumatic stress disorder in women is twice that for men, possibly secondary to high rates of interpersonal violence toward women. These acts of violence include childhood sexual abuse, rape, and battering, which challenges the clinical perception that military combat is the most common etiology. Butterfield, Becker, and Marx (2002) note that traumas such as rape or physical injury are associated with an 8.5-fold increase in developing post-traumatic stress disorder compared with other types of trauma. Butterfield et al. note that other risk factors include a history of severe and repeated trauma, lack of social support, minority status, poor education, history of psychiatric illness, and negative parenting in addition to childhood abuse. These risk factors reflect the issues that many incarcerated women face as they enter the criminal justice system in the United States.

There is a close relationship between the presenting symptoms of borderline personality disorder and the proposed diagnostic construct of complex post-traumatic stress disorder (Butterfield, Becker, and Marx 2002; McLean and Gallop 2003; Zlotnick, Franklin, and Zimmerman 2002). *DSM-IV-TR* (2000) describes the essential features of borderline personality disorder as a pervasive pattern of instability of interpersonal relationships, self-image, and affects and marked impulsivity that begins by early adulthood. Like PTSD, borderline personality disorder is diagnosed more often in women than men (Kaplan and Sadock 2002); over 90 percent of people with borderline personality disorder have a history of childhood abuse with a resultant overlap of the diagnosis of severe or complex post-traumatic stress disorder (Butterfield et al. 2000). McLean and Gallop (2003) found in their study of a group of women who were survivors of childhood sexual abuse that virtually all of them met the diagnostic criteria for both borderline personality disorder and post-traumatic stress disorder. They further suggest that instead of the current practice of using two distinct diagnoses, the construct of complex post-traumatic stress disorder may be more applicable. The definition of what constitutes post-traumatic stress disorder is not without problems, however: Van der Kolk (2002) states that the PTSD Field Trial was unable to demonstrate that the criteria delineated in the diagnosis of post-traumatic stress disorder captured the most essential elements seen after traumatic events. In several studies looking at psychiatric symptoms and diagnoses of abused children, none of the labels given them captured the profound developmental disturbances seen in this group. These children seem to have pervasive problems with attachment, attention, and managing physiological arousal. Van der Kolk (2002) summarizes the symptoms of complex post-traumatic disorder as occurring in children and adults who were abused and neglected who present with an impairment of affect regulation described as the inability to be emotionally upset without harming themselves, becoming aggressive or dissociating. Another symptom is having chronic destructive behavior such as self-mutilation. They exhibit distorted relationships with others and experience episodes of amnesia, dissociation, and somatization. This symptom construct for complex post-traumatic stress disorder is a mirror image of the current diagnostic criteria for borderline personality disorder as outlined in *DSM-IV-TR* (2002). The concept of considering the symptoms of borderline personality disorder and complex post-traumatic stress disorder seems reasonable. Clinicians are much more comfortable treating PTSD than they are a personality disorder. Herman (1997) states that repeated trauma in childhood forms and deforms the personality, which is borne out in van der Kolk (2002) and the review of data from the field trials for PTSD.

One of the symptoms of post-traumatic stress disorder is the experience of flashbacks of the abuse during which the feelings and other sensations associated with it are relived. As more attention has been paid to the existence of post-traumatic stress disorder in incarcerated women, it has become apparent that oftentimes there are cues in the correctional environment that trigger traumatic flashbacks. These can include the male officers assigned to various areas of most women's correctional facilities. Often a male officer's appearance or mannerisms may be similar to a perpetrator of abuse from a woman's past and serve as a trigger for flashbacks of this abuse. There may be a female officer that resembles an abusive mother. The cramped living quarters of most facilities or a single cell that a woman is placed in because she has broken a rule may serve as a trigger. Locked in a single cell twenty-three hours a day as punishment can be reminiscent of being locked in a closet as a form of punishment as a child. As women talk more about their abuse histories, it has come to light that many incarcerated women are sexually and psychologically abused by corrections staff, most often men. Human Rights Watch Women's Rights Project (1996) reports that this abuse has taken the form of vaginal, anal, and oral rape. Male officers use threatened and actual physical force as well as their authority to provide or deny goods and privileges to compel the women to have sex with them. Male officers may use mandatory pat-frisks or room searches to grope women and to view them inappropriately while in a state of undress in the housing or bathroom areas. The situations described above inadvertently serve to retraumatize many women who already have problems dealing with their issues.

Treatment and Interventions

Below are common scenarios in women's correctional facilities:

A twenty-one-year-old woman scratches her wrists at least two times a week with various objects. She is observed doing this repeatedly, and when she begins to bleed she will not stop unless someone intervenes. She appears expressionless while engaging in this behavior. When asked why she does this and what is she feeling, she answers that she does not know why and cannot explain her feelings. On intake screening, she admitted to daily use of cocaine for two years prior to her arrest. During the first two weeks of her incarceration, she complained of feeling extremely anxious and fearful and was unable to sleep. She asked for medications for sleep. She was prescribed antidepressants as the psychiatrist thought that her anxiety and fear were secondary to her recent incarceration. The medications have not helped decrease the self-injurious behavior, but her anxiety is less intense.

A thirty-one-year-old woman has become verbally and physically assaultive towards a male officer in her housing area for no apparent reason. These incidents happen suddenly with no warning. It usually takes four to six officers to subdue her, and she is subsequently given an infraction and spends time in administrative segregation for assault. She tells corrections and mental health staff that she has no memory of fighting with anyone. She is taking antipsychotic medication because the psychiatrist believes these episodes are psychotic in origin. The medication has not alleviated the behavior.

A mental health counselor is seeing a twenty-five-year-old woman once a week for individual sessions. At times she engages the therapist and talks about many issues in her life, and on other occasions she tells the counselor she is the most despicable person she has ever met. Eventually the counselor asks to be removed from the case because she does not like the patient. The inmate was initially referred for counseling because she often tells clinicians and officers that she wants to kill herself, yet when she is placed on suicide observation she adamantly denies such feelings. She self-injures herself by scratching various parts of her body until she bleeds. She has experienced periods of crying in her dormitory to the point where she could not go out on her work detail. She refuses to take medication for any reason. Medical has seen her on many occasions for nonspecific complaints, and she screams at them for not finding anything wrong with her.

The scenarios described above occur in the lives of incarcerated women no matter their ethnic or racial backgrounds and in various combinations of symptoms. Often the interventions on the part of medical or mental health staff are ineffective because clinicians do not understand the impact of the histories of these women prior to incarceration on their present symptomatology.

No matter the symptoms, women must have access to adequate and appropriate health and mental health care in correctional institutions. Jails and prisons are constitutionally mandated to provide adequate care and the first step towards this is assuring that adequate medical and mental health care is available to the women offenders if needed. The care provided should be gender specific, which means that medical and mental health care staff recognize that there are psychological as well as physical differences that have to be taken into consideration when rendering health care to this population. Bloom and Covington (1998) reviewed several groups' suggestions for gender-specific programming and care related to health services for women in correctional settings. A fundamental suggestion included promotion of support systems and relationships that help women to develop healthy connections. Health care staff can show that they listen to the complaints that the women present to them, and they can explain procedures, medications, and the care given in a respectful manner as a means of building trust. This behavior is counterintuitive to correctional rules that imply that staff are to keep their distance from the inmates. However, women thrive and grow in trusting relationships with others, especially other women. Trust is built upon respect, which is lacking in the lives of many of these women. All clinical as well as correctional staff must be trained about the differences that are specific to gender. Administrators must not make the assumption that staff of either gender are sensitive to the issues that women deal with daily and how these affect them when incarcerated. Education is the first step to understanding and thus increasing the likelihood of the provision of more adequate services.

All inmates should receive a medical screening and physical examination upon entry into a jail or prison. Medical professionals should ask all patients about violence in their lives. If any of these areas of inquiry elicit a positive response and the inmate admits to having any sort of psychological problems (which should also be included in the medical screening), they should be referred for assessment by a mental health professional. At that time, a more in-depth inquiry can be made about issues of concern. Bloom and Covington (1998) suggest that a gender-specific program would address the unique treatment issues of women such as trauma, coping skills, and self-worth. These are the issues that mental health staff have been trained to deal with by the nature of their disciplines. However, it should not be assumed that just because mental health staff address psychological issues that they are familiar or comfortable dealing with the gender-specific issues that women offenders are dealing with.

Many jails and prisons do not have regular mental health professionals at the facility. Facilities that have mental health staff on a regular basis providing general mental health care usually do not offer services such as group or individual counseling or therapy that deals with the myriad of issues that have affected women offenders. Where services are not adequate, administrators should look for alternative means of providing more than just emergency mental health care. Many jail systems coordinate the provision of mental health services in their facilities with the local community mental health agency. This often provides more continuity of care as many of the women were receiving services in this system prior to their incarceration. Many women's advocacy agencies will volunteer to train medical and mental health staff about the issues of violence in the lives of the women and how to make assessments, as well as providing referral sources for further care upon release. Most correctional facilities have volunteer departments, and tapping into this resource and targeting community agencies that deal with women can be a valuable resource.

It is crucial that mental health staff make accurate diagnoses in order to provide the most appropriate treatment. An important aspect of the diagnostic process is an adequate history. Butterfield, Becker, and Marx (2002) remind clinicians to ask about childhood abuse and trauma as an adult. The duration of exposure to trauma can be important in assessing the levels of distress secondary to the trauma. Staff must be sensitive to the fact that survivors of trauma usually have a difficult time talking about their experiences, and, as Butterfield et al. reiterate, clinicians need to become comfortable acknowledging this difficulty. Because of the intensity of such interviews, it is often necessary to allow the history of abuse to surface over time rather than trying to gather as much information as quickly as possible. Any collateral information can be reviewed as well because parts of the history may have been shared with other clinicians in different settings. Formal assessment tools may be used to elicit symptoms of many of the major mental disorders such as depression, bipolar disorder, and post-traumatic stress disorders, but there are seldom resources or time to do this in most correctional settings.

The women presented in the cases at the beginning of this section all have symptoms of post-traumatic stress disorder. The first woman also had symptoms of substance-induced anxiety disorder. She displayed the numbness of feelings and self-injurious behavior often seen in survivors of abuse with post-traumatic stress disorder. The second woman was experiencing episodes of dissociation. One of the male officers on her unit reminded her of the man who abused her, and the officer's presence became a trigger for a dissociative reaction of which this woman had no memory. This is fairly common among survivors of abuse, but the lack of recall is often seen as an excuse for the behavior rather than the truth. This behavior was misperceived as a psychotic episode by the psychiatrist and thus antipsychotic medication had no effect. The third woman's presentation is of someone with borderline personality traits or complex post-traumatic stress disorder. She was abused as a child and displays ambivalence towards people in her environment. She self-injures but does not understand why. She has somatic complaints for which the medical staff have no explanations. Accurate diagnoses will be made in these cases only if mental health clinicians review documentation from the various clinicians these women have had contact with as in-depth a history of abuse is elicited and there is an understanding of the connectedness of the symptoms with co-morbid psychiatric diagnoses. Once accurate diagnoses are made, assessment for treatment needs can be accomplished.

Given that so many of these women have multiple vulnerabilities and diagnoses, it is important to design treatment interventions that will best address the needs of women. Bloom and Covington (1998) present a model of treating addiction in women in the criminal justice setting that is also applicable to women with other mental disorders. This model of treatment is based on the interrelatedness of the issues of addiction, women's development, and trauma, and it comes from the relational model of women's development from the Stone Center at Wellesley College. It purports that women are motivated to establish relationships throughout their lives and that the group process of treatment based on this theory are more therapeutic than individual therapy sessions alone. A gender-specific treatment program must integrate services to address addiction and psychological disorders that traditionally have been provided from separate sources. Such a program needs to be safe and free from physical, emotional, and sexual harassment with appropriate boundaries. There must be a connection between group facilitators and the women. The facilitator cannot be in a role of authoritarian figure but be one who respects the women and their stories and is able to empathize with the group but not be consumed by the information. The facilitator also needs to be a model of how a woman can use power with and for others. There must be firm limits and respect of all group members. Bloom and Covington believe that these elements can be found in the correctional environment, even if only in a part of the environment.

Individual sessions do have their place in a correctional setting. It is often easier to gather historical data on a one-to-one basis than in a group. The individual session can also serve as a motivational and educational opportunity to encourage a woman to join a group. For those individuals that may need medication, individual sessions with a psychiatrist should be afforded. Medications that are most effective in treating generalized anxiety symptoms are the benzodiazepines. However, they are seldom used because generalized anxiety is seldom seen alone as a symptom and benzodiazepines can be addictive. The selective serotonin reuptake inhibitors (SSRIs) are the most effective in treating symptoms of post-traumatic stress disorder: several studies of specific SSRIs show a reduction in the symptom presentation of post-traumatic stress disorder, especially in women (Butterfield, Becker, and Marx 2002). Psychiatrists must be trained to recognize the co-morbid symptom presentation of anxiety and depressive disorders in order to decrease the prescription of multiple medications for interrelated symptoms. Multiple medication regimens serve only to reinforce the notion that a pill will solve the problem, which is reminiscent of the behavior prior to incarceration that drugs will solve the problem.

Anxiety disorders are the most prevalent mental disorder seen in women in the general population as well as in correctional settings. It is very important that these disorders be recognized and treated, and the women are educated about the disorders. The majority of incarcerated women will return to their communities. It is possible to reduce the likelihood they will not return to prison if they are given tools of self-empowerment that will help them to gain a place in society that many never had prior to incarceration.

REFERENCES

American Psychiatric Association. 2000. *Diagnostic and statistical manual of mental disorders*, 4th ed., text revision. Washington, DC: American Psychiatric Association Press.

Bloom, B., and S. Covington. 1998. Gender-specific programming for female offenders: What is it and why is it important? Paper presented at the Fiftieth Annual Meeting of the American Society of Criminology. Washington, DC.

Butterfield, M., M. Becker, and C. Marx. 2002. Posttraumatic stress disorder in women: Current concepts and treatments. *Current Psychiatry Reports* 4: 474–86.

Greenfeld, L., and T. Snell. 1999. *Bureau of Justice Statistics Special Report: Women Offenders.* U. S. Department of Justice, Office of Justice Programs.

Herman, J. 1997. *Trauma and recovery.* New York: Basic Books.

Human Rights Watch Women's Rights Project. 1996. *All too familiar: Sexual abuse of women in U.S. state prisons.* New York: Human Rights Watch.

Kaplan, H., and B. Sadock. 2002. *Synopsis of psychiatry,* 9th ed. Philadelphia: Lippincott Williams and Wilkins.

Kessler, R., R. DuPont, P. Berglund, and H. Wittchen. 1999. Impairment in pure and comorbid anxiety disorder and major depression at twelve months in two national surveys. *American Journal of Psychiatry* 156: 12.

Kessler, R., A. Sonnega, and E. Bromet. 1995. Posttraumatic stress disorder in the National Comorbidity Survey. *Archives of General Psychiatry* 52: 1048–60.

McLean, L., and R. Gallop. 2003. Implications of childhood sexual abuse for adult borderline personality disorder and complex posttraumatic stress disorder. *American Journal of Psychiatry* 160, no. 2: 469–70.

Mendlowicz, M., and M. Stein. 2000. Quality of life in individuals with anxiety disorders. *American Journal of Psychiatry* 157: 669–82.

Pinta, E. 2001. The prevalence of serious mental disorders among U.S. prisoners. In *Forensic mental health*, ed. G. Landsberg and A. Smiley. Kingston, NJ: Civic Research Institute.

Teplin, L. 1994. Psychiatric and substance abuse disorders among male urban jail detainees. *American Journal of Public Health* 84: 290–93.

Van der Kolk, B. 2002. Assessment and treatment of complex PTSD. In *Treating Trauma Survivors with PTSD*, ed. R. Yehuda. Washington, DC: American Psychiatric Association Press.

Zlotnick, C., C. Franklin, and M. Zimmerman. 2002. Is comorbidity of posttraumatic stress disorder and borderline personality disorder related to greater pathology and impairment? *American Journal of Psychiatry* 159, no. 11: 1940–43.

8

Substance Use Disorders

JACKIE BUTLER AND KISHA BRAITHWAITE

Female offenders are an increasingly large proportion of the incarcerated population, and their needs are different from those of men in correctional facilities. The goal of this chapter is to discuss the relationship of drug abuse to the increasing rates of female incarceration, to identify the challenges in meeting the unique needs of imprisoned substance-dependent women, and to provide descriptions of a promising intervention approach for this population.

The number of incarcerated women tripled between 1985 and 1997 (Richie 1999). On any given day in 1994, over 800,000 women were under some type of correctional supervision in the United States (Beck and Gilliard 1995). This total includes women on probation, in jail, in prison, and on parole. For women, the chances of going to prison were six times greater in 2001 (p = .018) than in 1974 (p = .003), and for men, the chances of going to prison were over three times greater in 2001 (p = .113) than in 1974 (p = .036) (Bonczar 2003). Among the percentage of all persons ever confined in prison, the proportion of women increased from 7.8 percent in 1974 to 10.3 percent in 2001 (Bonczar 2003). For a number of years, women have been entering prison at a faster rate than men (Beck and Gillard 1995). The number of incarcerated adult females rose from 142,000 in 1974 to 581,000 in 2001. Also, the number of white (non-Hispanic) incarcerated women rose from 86,000 in 1974 to 225,000 in 2001 while the number of black women in prison rose from 51,000 to 231,000 (Bonczar 2003).

Incarcerated women are disproportionately women of color (particularly black and Hispanic/Latina) from low-income communities who have been subjected to a disproportionately high rate of violence (Richie 1999). Adult black females are nearly two and a half times more likely than adult Hispanic females and five and a half times more likely than adult white females to have ever served time in a state or federal prison. Among adult U.S. residents in 2001, an estimated 1.7

percent of black females versus 0.7 percent of Hispanic females and 0.3 percent of white females had ever been incarcerated in a prison. The chance of a black woman going to prison in 2001 was 5.6 percent (nearly as high as for white males) versus 1.1 percent in 1974 (Bonczar 2003).

Women in the Criminal Justice System

Female offenders—sometimes called "the forgotten few"—have received relatively little research attention over the years. However, incarcerated women have been included in the samples of a few large epidemiological studies. The Research Triangle Institute's Women Inmates' Health Survey (WIHS) was the first large-scale epidemiological study of women prison inmates in the United States. Previous studies of women inmates paid little attention to sociodemographic characteristics and the relationship between these characteristics and the rates of substance use disorders. Findings from the WIHS study reveal variations of substance abuse by age and education. The African American proportion of the prison population was approximately three times the proportion in the mainstream North Carolina community (60 percent versus 20 percent). About half of the sample was thirty years or older; those with a high school diploma or GED held a small majority over those without (Jordan et al. 1996).

The WIHS study found that the rates of alcohol, substance abuse, and most psychiatric disorders were higher for non-Hispanic whites than for African Americans. However, these racial disparities may suggest that only the most disturbed and deviant white women are incarcerated while women of color face imprisonment for less serious offenses.

Overwhelmingly, women of all races are incarcerated primarily for nonviolent offenses (that is, for violating laws that prohibit the sale and possession of specific drugs) (Richie 1999). Some investigators argue that this pattern of illegal behavior is gender-related—that drug sales and other nonviolent crimes are "survival crimes" committed by women to earn money, feed a drug-dependent habit, or escape abusive intimate relationships and substandard social conditions (Richie 1999). In the WIHS study, drug offenses were the most frequent offenses resulting in imprisonment. These drug offenses, which include drug use and the manufacturing and sale of drugs, were also the most common reasons for previous incarceration of the women in the study. Only a small percentage (11 percent) were imprisoned due to violent crimes (Jordan et al. 1996).

Behavioral Health Status and Violence against Incarcerated Women

Research suggests that substance abuse and dependence are much more prevalent among women inmates than among women in the general population (Jordan et al. 1996). Furthermore, studies indicate that drug use is more prevalent among female inmates than among males (U.S. Department of Justice 1991).

Investigators suggest that the disproportionately high rates of substance abuse, as well as post-traumatic stress disorder (PTSD) symptoms among women inmates compared to women in the general population, may reflect incarcerated women's higher exposure to psychological trauma and traumatic events. Researchers involved in the WIHS study hypothesized that the elevated rate of substance abuse disorders of the North Carolina inmate population (as compared to the community sample) may have contributed to the criminal behavior that led to the incarceration of these women. Many inmates in the study had a substance abuse disorder as well as a personality disorder, and although co-morbidity data was not studied, the combination does impact the level of deviant behavior (Jordan et al. 1996).

The number of incarcerated women experiencing psychological trauma and the correlation between such trauma and psychiatric disorders including substance abuse substantiate the need for programs in women's prisons that address trauma and its consequences. Trauma and the resulting disorders such as PTSD and substance abuse are linked to behaviors connected to incarceration such as illegal drug use. Also, the high rates of substance abuse among incarcerated women and the proportion of arrest due to drug related charges reinforces the necessity of substance abuse programs in correctional facilities.

According to the National Clearinghouse for the Defense of Battered Women, one of the few national organizations that collect data on the relationship between violence against women and women's involvement in illegal activity, at least 50 percent of all women in jails and prisons have been physically or sexually abused before their imprisonment—a much higher rate than reported for the overall population (20 to 30 percent by the age of eighteen; Briere and Elliot 2003; Richie 1999). There is evidence that the burden of substance abuse disorders is heavier in women with a history of physical and/or sexual abuse. For example, a Bureau of Justice Statistics study reported significant rates of drug and alcohol use among abused women in state prisons. Nearly 70 percent of the abused women serving time in correctional facilities said that they used illegal drugs during the month before their current offense compared with 54 percent of the women who had not been abused (U.S. Department of Justice 1994).

Of the seventeen- to eighteen-year-old girls in the justice system, 74 percent to 95 percent have been victims of abuse (Richie 1999). Girls who have been sexually abused suffer from a painful and profound lack of self-esteem. These girls participate in disempowering and self-defeating behaviors, which propel them into a cycle of prostitution, addiction, drug dealing, and violence. Typically having never received the valuable life-skills training that a healthy family environment provides, these girls accept violence and sexual exploitation as a normal way of life. Many of them have never known responsible, respectful, caring adults and peers. They have not had the opportunity to learn how to form long-lasting relationships based on mutual support and affection. Without trust and healthy self-esteem, neither the girls nor the women they become learn to use available support systems. This is where the role of drug courts becomes evident and this is where judicial officers can provide the impetus and monitoring necessary for interventions to take place (Richie 1999).

Sentencing and the Role of Drug Courts

The U.S. Sentencing Guidelines (USSG), "while commanding that gender never be a relevant factor in sentencing . . . base their core sentences on predominately male behavior patterns" (Wald 2001, 1). Due to some of the differences in male and female offenders (for example, child custody, a greater prevalence of some psychiatric disorders, and a history of physical and/or sexual abuse), when the same sentence is levied on a female and a male offender, it can impose far greater deprivation on the female (Sherman 2001).

The discussion about women in the criminal justice system tends to focus on prisons and, secondarily, on jails. However, there are more offenders under community supervision than are incarcerated, and most prisoners will, at some point, return to the street. To construct a law-abiding life, a woman offender is likely to require the assistance of a large number of public systems, including public assistance, homelessness services, family court, child care, public education, drug treatment, health and mental health. If we are to help women succeed in the community, the criminal justice system must work more effectively with the other public systems that shape the lives of women. Competing demands must be reconciled. "In [federal] sentencing, the deletion of gender assumes a world in which men and women have equal custody of children and where the noncustodial parents are willing and able to take responsibility for the care of their children" (Sherman 2001, 2).

U.S. Justice Department statistics show that the ratio of female offenders who are single parents is much greater than that of male offenders (Wald 2001, 2). Other studies show that the minor children of male offenders almost always continue in the mother's care, whereas children of female offenders usually are taken in by relatives, friends, or put in foster care (Sherman 2001). The Bureau of Justice Statistics (1997) indicated that of the female offenders who lived with their children at the time of incarceration, 94 percent said that their children's current caretakers were the children's grandparents, other relatives, friends, or foster parents, while 31 percent said that the current caretaker was the children's father (the total is greater than 100 percent because some prisoners had several children living with multiple caretakers). In comparison, 92 percent of male offenders said that their children's current caretaker was their mother. The pattern of family separation starts at sentencing when a substitute caretaker is required for an extended period. Eleven percent of children of incarcerated mothers experience at least two changes in caretaker during the period of incarceration, exacerbating the trauma of separation (Sherman 2001, 2).

The Federal Adoption and Safe Families Act accelerates termination of parental rights and, under 42 U.S.C. 671 (a)(20)(A), bars individuals with certain convictions from being foster or adoptive parents . . . [The law] has a
potentially devastating effect on families in which the mother is involved in
the criminal justice system. Pursuant to 42 U.S.C. 675 (5)(E), the law requires
states to seek termination of parental rights when a child has been in foster
care 15 of the previous 22 months . . . [Thus], a single mom serving more
than 15 months would have serious [difficulty] reuniting with her children.
(Sherman 2001, 2)

The Role of Correctional Personnel in Linking Women to Services

The differences between female and male offenders apply to both the front and
back ends of sentencing (that is, presentence report, institutional recommendation, and postsentence supervision) and to pretrial services supervision. Since
female defendants facing prison terms may be primary caretakers of young children, the pretrial services officer's role should include helping the defendant gain
stability and arrange child custody and dispersion of child support payments. The
pretrial services officer could assist in referring the defendant to mental health/
substance abuse counseling as the time of imprisonment nears, so she can deal
effectively/emotionally with the impending separation. When the female defendant faces probation or is reentering society to begin a term of supervised release,
she may also need the help of her pretrial services and probation officers in
obtaining child support. Also important if probation violations are to be avoided,
probation officers must be prepared to help women offenders reconnect
with their children (where permitted) and to help avert crises related to housing,
substance abuse and mental health treatment, transportation, and unemployment.

Treating women offenders "equally but differently" means that the court, pretrial, and probation services understand the unique barriers and needs confronted by many women in this population. Although courts cannot sentence on
the basis of gender, they can select an alternative sentence where the guidelines
permit and tailor special conditions of supervision to meet the needs of individual
female offenders. It is not surprising that research now indicates that addiction
treatment programs that address women's unique needs—such as their relationship with their partners, families, and children as well as any history of physical
and sexual abuse—are more effective for women than traditional programs
(Carten 1996; Center for Substance Abuse Treatment 1994a and b; Covington
2000a and b; Finklestein 1993). The Helping Women Recover Program, for example, incorporates three theories into its programming: (1) theory of addiction,
(2) theory of women's psychological development, and (3) theory of trauma. The
program is designed to be used in community-based and criminal-justice-based
programs for women (Covington 2000a).

Treatment of Substance Abusing Offenders

Drug courts began with an experiment in Dade County, Florida (National Institute of Justice 1993). There are now over 750 programs throughout the United States. More are being developed every day, and there is significant evidence to suggest that drug courts work. Recidivism among substance-abusing offenders has been reduced, and retention rates in treatment have improved by mandating defendants to judicially supervised treatment instead of incarceration. Drug courts have moved from experimentation to institutionalization as the number of women arrested for drug violations continues to climb. Consequently, the needs of female drug court participants must be addressed. According to the National Institute of Justice, during the 1980s, the number of women arrested on drug charges more than tripled the number of seventeen- to eighteen-year-old girls in the justice system—a growth rate approximately double that of men. Similarly, according to the Bureau of Justice Statistics, from 1990 to 1996, the number of women convicted for drug trafficking increased by 34 percent and by 41 percent for drug possession (D'Angelo 2002).

Female drug court participants typically have little education, less money, and are likely to be homeless, unemployed, and suffer from mental illness and/or abuse. They are also likely to have health problems and family responsibilities (which can distract their focus from recovery). Research has shown that women felony offenders are more likely to be addicted to a serious substance than male felony offenders. Thus, the majority of women that arrive in drug courts are in crisis and have multiple problems and barriers to successful recovery (D'Angelo 2002).

Women graduating from drug courts do so with several disadvantages. They may not have a house or a job but they usually do have children that need care and attention. This situation can create tremendous pressure, which may ultimately lead to relapse. Another disadvantage for women is that treatment programs were, at least in part, built by and designed for men. This reality is evident in various programming and treatment elements. Therapeutic approaches to recovery that work for men often may not be suitable for women. Linda Fox, who runs the guidance clinic at the Kalamazoo Drug Court in Michigan, maintains that "treatment programs are geared for men and tend to emphasize breaking down the person, while women need programs that will empower them if they're going to get sober" (D'Angelo 2002, 386). According to Mary Bombich, coordinator of the Kalamazoo Women's Drug Court, the women's court, established in Kalamazoo in 1992 and supported in part by the Office of Justice Programs, was developed because "there were a lot of services for men in the criminal justice system but not for women." She indicates that in this gender-specific setting, "women [are] more inclined to offer personal revelations in the courtroom, and the judge can act on this information to help women succeed" (D'Angelo 2002, 386). Another disadvantage is the lack of support for participants with children, almost always women, who might be struggling to care for a family or coping with the stress of a family court case while trying to get healthy and sober.

Services Offered to Women in Drug Courts

Case Study 1: The Santa Clara County Drug Treatment Court

The Santa Clara County Drug Treatment Court in California has found success for women defendants. There are four major factors contributing to its success. First, the court includes local correctional facilities in the recruitment of women who are eligible to participate. Thus, almost all women in local correctional facilities are given the chance to receive drug treatment services. The second factor contributing to the success of this court is the segregation of male and female defendants. According to the project manager, "by handling women on a separate court calendar, court planners have found that female participants are less distracted, more able to develop a productive relationship with the judge, and better able to develop a support network with other female defendants" (D'Angelo 2002, 386).

Third, the Santa Clara County Drug Treatment Court attempts to ameliorate difficulties many women have with issues such as child care and/or custody battles. Partnering with a dependency court, which handles family cases, ensures that "mandates for women with cases pending in both courts are consistent, and that the dependency court stays up to date on each participant's progress in recovery" (D'Angelo 2002, 387). Finally, the Santa Clara court partners with the local health department to ensure that the health needs of women defendants are met. These four factors illustrate the importance of a well-rounded approach to drug treatment. The success of the Santa Clara County Drug Treatment Court transcends the raw percentages of women who are sober at any given point in time; true success lies in women's sobriety, their relationships with children and families, their ability to support themselves after treatment, and their physical health.

Case Study 2: The Brooklyn Treatment Court

Another drug court finding success for women defendants is the Brooklyn Treatment Court (BTC). Sponsored by the Federal Center for Substance Abuse Treatment, BTC ensures that women with psychiatric problems are accurately identified and that women are enrolled in treatment programs shortly after the court mandate. Despite the successes of the drug court itself, the clientele are often extreme cases. For example, one woman, weighing "only eighty six pounds; had lost custody of her three children, including a baby born addicted to crack; and had been battered for years by a boyfriend . . . Women come to court on their last dying knees. If you blow on them, they look like they'll fall down" (D'Angelo 2002, 388). Women completing the mandated drug treatment option are dismissed of all charges and no longer have to serve time in jail. This option is enticing for all but 9 percent of eligible women defendants (D'Angelo 2002).

Periodically, participants must return to the treatment court for drug testing, appearances before the judge, and meetings with their court case managers who offer counseling, make referrals to treatment programs and social services, and monitor overall program compliance. The court uses sanctions (that is, spending a day in the jury box to observe what happens to other offenders or writing essays on how drugs have affected their lives) and rewards (that is, applause in the courtroom, fewer court appearances, advancement through the court's various phases of treatment, and formal certificates of achievement) to encourage success. The judge may also order extra court visits or require participation in more intensive treatment programs. The most powerful sanction is a short-term jail sentence, which can run between one and twenty-eight days. Though sanctions can be strong incentives to treatment, the BTC tries to engage participants as much as possible in the Brooklyn courthouse where clients have access to on-site psychological evaluations, medical treatment, legal assistance, and job-related services.

Women tend to be much further along in their addiction than men when they finally get arrested on a drug-related felony charge (CSAT 1994a and b). One reason for this may be that the task of selling drugs is usually reserved for men—particularly young men who, if they are addicted, have not had a chance to progress far on the path of self-destruction. Women, however, initially shoplift and resort to prostitution to pay for their drug addiction, and only as addiction and desperation spiral out of control, do they get involved in the drug trade itself. When women are finally arrested on a drug charge, they most often already have a lengthy criminal history and years of suffering caused by their drug use, experiences as prostitutes and living the life of a petty criminal. "When women get to court they are absolute wrecks," said Valerie Raine, an attorney with the BTC from 1996 to 2000 (D'Angelo 2002, 389). "Women who come here tend to have more serious addictions than the men, [they] have lost more in their lives and have fewer resources," said Judge Ferdinand of the BTC. "The women are in worse shape . . . They have no self-respect, -esteem, or -confidence. They don't believe they can be clean or deserve to be. They feel hopeless. It's not uncommon to hear women say [about going into treatment], 'I can't do this'" (D'Angelo 2002, 389).

Men are more likely to have some basis of support—a job, school, girlfriend, or mother—to help them keep their lives together. Women have usually "lost it all—employment, family ties, children, and homes. 'Women [who reach drug court] usually don't have people in their lives who step in and say, "I'll keep your life afloat while you go get treatment." And they don't have a lot of men who come forward to help them make bail'" (Covington in D'Angelo 2002, 389). The BTC's evaluation of male and female offenders revealed gender differences in the following areas:

- Poverty: 84 percent of females at BTC versus 65 percent of males have an annual income less than $3,000.
- Education/Unemployment: 95 percent of women are unemployed or not in school versus 75 percent of men.

- Marital status: only 5 percent of women and 11 percent of men say they are married and living with their spouses.
- Homelessness: 35 percent of women versus 22 percent of men say they are or have been homeless.
- Addiction: 53 percent of women and 24 percent of men list crack as their drug of choice. Marijuana, considered a less serious drug, is listed as the primary drug for 4 percent of the women and 19 percent of the men.
- Mental Illness: 30 percent of the women versus 19 percent of the men report having attempted suicide, having been institutionalized, or having received counseling.
- Abuse: 40 percent of women versus 8 percent of men report having been physically, sexually, or emotionally abused. (D'Angelo 2002, 390)

A woman's mental health status can have a profound effect on her interaction with the court and her chances for long-term sobriety. The court's research has shown that female participants are more likely than male participants to have mental health problems (D'Angelo, 2002, 391). Upon intake in particular, there is a need to ensure that pressing mental health issues are identified. Even if a woman is correctly identified as having a mental disorder, the problem then becomes a lack of resources. In New York City, for example, there are few treatment programs for women who need psychological or mental health services. "The average court participant waits only nine days for a place in a treatment program, yet a thorny batch of regulation has relegated women with severe mental illness to months in jail while case managers search for an appropriate slot" (D'Angelo 2002, 392). When these women wait too long in jail, they lose their motivation to go into treatment and may opt to spend the rest of their sentence in jail (D'Angelo 2002). It is ironic that a woman's arrest is an opportunity to turn her life around. But the opportunity is fleeting and will disappear quickly if she is not placed in an appropriate drug treatment facility or program. Delayed diagnosis due to lack of treatment openings are issues that have caused women at BTC to wait twice as long as men to get into substance abuse programs.

To speed things up, the BTC revised its intake form to include questions that flag syndromes relating to the sexual and emotional abuse that often affect women. With a grant from CSAT, the court hired a psychologist to expand the questions from eight to twenty-five. If any of the responses to this more sophisticated psychometric instrument indicate mental illness, the case manager refers the participant to an on-site psychiatric nurse practitioner for a more in-depth psychological evaluation. Having the nurse practitioner on site has helped the BTC be able to place women appropriately and sometimes more quickly. Clients no longer have to wait up to a month for an off-site evaluation. Instead, they can be seen the first day they show up in court, and the window of opportunity to affect a deeper change in the female addict's life is not lost. The psychiatric nurse practitioner can evaluate clients immediately in the holding areas of the court or even from jail via videoconferencing. In addition, the court has been trying to encourage the development of new resources.

> Some experts, including staff at the treatment court, feel that addicts with milder psychological problems can benefit from individual psychotherapy. However, Medicaid and other insurers prefer a results-oriented, behavioral approach, which focuses on getting women clean, not helping them understand why they got high in the first place. "The old party line is: 'we deal with the addiction, then look at other issues.' That doesn't work," said Stephanie Covington, the expert on treatment programs for women. "The issues are interrelated . . . A woman with a history of abuse learns to survive by using alcohol and drugs. When she stops using she's flooded by feelings and memories of the prior abuse. You can't say to her, 'Let's put that on hold.'" (D'Angelo 2002, 394)

The physical health of female addicts is another focus of the court. Women substance abusers, especially those with histories of prostitution, face enormous health risks. Ten percent of women at the court report being HIV-positive versus only 3 percent of men. According to Kathy Morton, a family nurse practitioner from NYU, "some women have never had medical care, others have only had it the last time they came in contact with the [criminal justice] system." Even women with chronic conditions may have received only sporadic care in response to emergencies: "It's a problem when you have a woman who is diabetic and has seen a different doctor every time she needed care. Nobody has followed her and kept track of her medication. She could have a heart attack by the time she's 50 and nobody has taught her how to live with a chronic disease" (D'Angelo 2002, 393).

An addict is poorly equipped to get help for herself. Transportation is an issue as is the "chaos of their lives" (D'Angelo 2002, 394). In response to the problems female addicts have in accessing supportive medical services, the BTC decided that the treatment court should offer as many services as possible in the courthouse, thus minimizing the chance that participants would miss an appointment because of transportation problems, scheduling problems, or a simple lack of motivation. In 1997, BTC established an on-site health clinic through a partnership with NYU and the Brooklyn Hospital Center. The clinic provides physicals, pap smears, and tests for sexually transmitted infections. The NYC Department of Health also has staff on site, providing tests for communicable diseases like tuberculosis and hepatitis. The nurse practitioner on duty diagnoses illnesses and makes referrals to specialists. "When a case manager tells a client that she should have a physical to test for sexually transmitted diseases, she doesn't have to take a subway and two buses to get to a clinic where she'll wait for hours" (D'Angelo 2002, 395).

Broken families are a common, tragic consequence of drug addiction. Although 85 percent of the treatment court's female participants have children, many of those children have been placed in foster or kinship care. Prior to opening, court staff anticipated that the desire to reunite with their families would help motivate participants to recover. They found that the idea of possible reunification only played a role in the later stages of the recovery process. "I was surprised that the desire to reconnect with children isn't what's motivating women to go into treatment initially. But once women are in treatment and feel better about themselves they are driven to reconnect with their children," said a BTC judge (D'Angelo 2002, 396).

The process of reconnecting with children can be complicated and painful, and mothers face several emotional challenges. Children often get into trouble for acting out anxiety and anger caused by the absence of their mothers. Caregivers can feel overwhelmed and resent taking on the parenting role. The female offender may end up feeling guilty and helpless and may find it difficult to respond to the behavior of their children while she is taking on perhaps the biggest challenge of her life—getting clean. Many women are surprised if/when their children do not want to reconnect. Some reject their moms because they are hurt over having been abandoned and angry that they have had to become self-reliant or take care of younger siblings. The children might not trust that their mother will stay clean because of previous relapse experiences.

To help women reconnect with their children, the BTC has forged ties with the Brooklyn Family Court and the city's child welfare agency—the Administration for Children's Services. When a new client enters BTC, a case manager contacts the family court to determine if there is a case pending. If so, the case manager helps her work through the system. For example, if family court has ordered visitation, the case manager will make sure the treatment program knows about the visitation schedule and supports the participant's efforts to honor it. The case manager can also keep family court in the loop about the client's progress in treatment since achieving sobriety is usually one of the prerequisites for regaining custody. BTC has found that clients with pending family court cases hinging on their treatment outcome tend to be more engaged in their own recovery. BTC tries to refer participants with children to treatment programs that offer parenting support groups or workshops so they can get extra support concerning family issues as they work on their sobriety. BTC often refers women to Brooklyn Legal Services, a not-for-profit organization that represents parents with children in foster care. Brooklyn Legal Services hopes to offer workshops for women from BTC on parents' legal rights to plan for their children in foster care.

Planning a reunion can be particularly difficult for women who are trying to find/keep adequate paying jobs. Financial stability seems beyond the reach even of those who succeed in treatment, and welfare reform has only raised the stakes. BTC staff members have noticed a sense of urgency about getting/keeping a job even among clean, sober women. These women not only needed help finding jobs but also needed to be coached in the culture of work. Most of them have little education and no job experience. So BTC hired a vocational counseling specialist to work with both men and women. The specialist meets with individual participants to help them identify their career interests, compile resumes, and prepare for interviews. To address female needs for even more basic job-readiness skills, the vocational counselor created a sixteen-week workshop aimed at building self-esteem and developing positive attitudes toward work. It teaches concepts like being on time, dressing appropriately, following through on assignments, and dealing with anger on the job. It also provides women with concrete strategies for finding jobs that interest them. The counselor helps the women deal with the interview question "Have you ever been convicted of a crime?" and also offers strategies for finding affordable and quality child care.

BTC's goal is to use the incarceration as a teaching tool and to motivate offenders to seek help. The above methods are used for women with felonies, who make up only a small fraction of the female addicts arrested every day. The BTC also wanted to reach the women charged with misdemeanors such as loitering, prostitution, and shoplifting that were committed for the purpose of buying drugs. The BTC created the Treatment Readiness Program as a gateway to treatment for female addicts charged with misdemeanors. Judges handling arraignments in Brooklyn's Criminal Court identify substance-abusing women and order them to attend the Treatment Readiness Program. Judges have little legal leverage in these cases, so the program is designed as a short-term intervention with women sentenced to take part for only two days. Its purpose is to try to engage women, get them to acknowledge their addictions, and expose them to the idea of treatment. As part of the two-day program, women receive acupuncture to reduce cravings for drugs and alcohol. They are also required to attend workshops on drug and alcohol awareness and participate in group discussions where they examine how drug use has affected their lives.

From July 1997 to September 2002, 4,943 women were mandated to the Treatment Readiness Program and 2,777 completed it. This has astounded many observers at the treatment court who thought that without more coercive power, enrollment would be smaller. Raine, past director of BTC, says the power of the Treatment Readiness Program lies in its humanity. "Someone is paying attention to these women who isn't abusive, but is non-threatening and supportive" (D'Angelo 2002, 399). In addition, nearly one-third of the women who complete the Treatment Readiness Program request referrals for further treatment. It is unknown how many have gone on to achieve long-term sobriety because the court lacks the resources necessary to track participants after they have served their sentences (D'Angelo 2002).

A case manager for the Treatment Readiness Program indicates that the women who ask for referrals to the program are the ones who have hit bottom. They are tired of "hustling." "But the elevator stops at different floors. For one person it could be living on the street for two years and having lost everything. For someone else, it may be not being able to pay the rent" (D'Angelo 2002, 399). In addition to reaching low-level offenders, the court wanted to reach the women at the other extreme—those headed for prison. BTC created a "last-chance" program for women who had been repeatedly sanctioned by the court because they couldn't stay sober long enough to make it into treatment. "A lot of women were failing urine tests and getting sentenced before they had ever set foot in a program . . . They were stepping out the door of the court and getting high. We wanted to give these women a way to experience treatment" (D'Angelo 2002, 389). The BTC contacted city jail officials and asked if the court could send its poorest performing women to the therapeutic community housed at the city prison on Rikers Island. The program is normally offered to women at Rikers on a voluntary basis, and it can take many days to arrange placement. But staff set up an expedited placement process for treatment of court participants who are ordered to participate. From October 1998 through November 2002, the treatment court sent forty-nine women to the Substance Abuse Intervention Division at Rikers. Expediting placement has evidenced very positive results in getting women into drug treatment and motivating them to turn their lives around. "Research at the BTC and elsewhere has shown that delaying admission hurts the addict's chances for a drug-free future. For instance, a 1984 study that examined dropouts among 172 alcoholics attending an outpatient program found that a delay of more than fourteen days from assessment to first appointment was a key variable between those who did not show for treatment and those who kept at least one appointment" (D'Angelo 2002, 391).

The Brooklyn Treatment Center continues to look for ways to increase the likelihood of success for women. For example, the court may hire a housing specialist to help homeless participants find a permanent, affordable place to live. The court is also conducting research regarding the factors that help or hinder success in treatment on a continuous basis so that it can fine-tune its approach. As the BTC expands its services it raises questions about how far a court should go. There is a thin line between taking a hands-off distanced approach to court-ordered substance abuse treatment and getting into areas of life that some might say are out of the courts' jurisdiction. For Raines, a former defense attorney who represented hundreds of people whose lives were ruined by addiction, the line is always shifting. "If you would have asked me ten years ago if a court should provide mental health services, I would have said that's definitely going too far but now I think it's essential if you really want to have an impact on drug-related crime. You need to stop the revolving door—which means not merely punishing drug offenders, but helping them become productive, law-abiding members of the community" (D'Angelo 2002, 400).

Adverse Effects of Drug Courts for Women

As illustrated above, drug courts provide many resources for women with substance abuse disorders. The assistance of these courts and correctional personnel gives women a chance after recovery. However, there are a few downfalls to women's participation in drug court. These adverse effects contribute to an increased risk of failure of drug treatment programs for women and increase the likelihood that a woman may be unable to live independently after the treatment/incarceration period. First, research has shown that women prisoners enrolling in drug treatment programs are more likely than male prisoners to use drugs daily and to use hard drugs (for example, heroin and/or cocaine) when they start the program (Drug and Alcohol Services Information System Report 2001; Gender differences 2000). This heavier burden of advanced drug use among women prisoners, coupled with drug courts' lack of tolerance for relapse, places women at increased risk for failure.

Second, drug courts rarely mandate counseling or therapy for women. Women prisoners enrolling in drug treatment programs are more likely than men to report using drugs to cope with pain. Thus, there is a great need for mental health resources for women attending drug courts. In order to effectively help women replace an unhealthy coping mechanism (for example, drug use) with a healthier one, drug courts must understand the importance of incorporating general mental health resources with specific substance abuse related ones. Third, drug courts were initially designed with men in mind and, therefore, tend to treat men and women equally. However, research suggests that this trend is unfair and that gender should be taken into consideration during drug court sentencing. For example, a study by Lukas, Sholar, Fortin, Wines, and Mendelson (1996) showed that there are distinct differences in the effect of certain drugs on men and women. Specifically, women have a slightly higher tolerance for cocaine upon first use, which may cause them to use larger amounts and to use more frequently than men to achieve the same high. If drug courts do not consider the effects of gender on drug use and drug treatment, women may not gain as much from their treatment experiences as men.

Fourth, women's attendance in court-mandated drug treatment programs may be less effective than if the women had chosen to seek treatment themselves (Brumbaugh 1994). Jail sentences are often suspended if women choose to attend a drug treatment program. This offer is enticing and may persuade women who do not want help for their drug use to attend a treatment program in which they have no intention of fully participating. This lack of participation not only affects the treatment outcome for the woman but can also jeopardize outcomes for other women involved in the same program. Finally, sentencing women solely to drug treatment ignores the need for educational/vocational skills training. Women prisoners are less likely than male prisoners to have a high school degree or a GED (Gender differences 2000). This suggests that, even after successful completion of a court-mandated drug treatment program, women may have a more difficult time finding and maintaining a job that will sustain them and their families. Therefore, drug courts should consider mandating vocational training for women.

Conclusion

It is essential that treatment and justice professionals clearly understand the role of sociodemographic variables (that is, socioeconomic status, ethnicity, family life, mental health, education, and work experience) in substance abuse behaviors in women involved with the criminal justice system. These factors interact in complicated ways and the interrelationships among these factors vary for each woman. Awareness of the impact of these variables can facilitate more appropriate sentencing for women with substance abuse problems and, therefore, can help female addicts succeed during the treatment period and maintain sobriety afterward.

Female offenders need treatment that is gender-specific, culturally specific, and empowering. The Brooklyn Treatment Center's approach demonstrates that a comprehensive, multifaceted approach to understanding the obstacles facing this population of women is needed to stop the "revolving door" of substance abusing women offenders. Arrest provides a brief window of opportunity for such an understanding to take place. If a female addict is offered treatment during this period, she is far more likely to participate and succeed in treatment. This suggests that the courthouse has the potential to be more than just a courtroom.

REFERENCES

Beck, A. J., and D. K. Gilliard. 1995. Prisoners in 1995. Washington, DC: Bureau of Justice Statistics; BJS Bulletin NCJ-151654.

Bonczar, T. 2003. Prevalence of Imprisonment in the U.S. Population, 1974–2001. Washington, DC: Bureau of Justice Statistics; BJS Bulletin NCJ–197976.

Briere, J., and D. M. Elliott. 2003. Prevalence and psychological sequeale of self-reported childhood physical and sexual abuse in a general population sample of men and women. *Child Abuse and Neglect* 27: 1205–22.

Brumbaugh, A. G. 1994. Why Drug Courts Work. http://silcom.com/alexb/drugcrts.htm (accessed November 19, 2004).

Carten, Alma J. 1996. "Mothers in Recovery: Rebuilding Families in the Aftermath of Addiction." *Social Work* 42, no. 2: 214–23.

Center for Substance Abuse Treatment (CSAT). 1994a. "Practical Approaches in the Treatment of Women Who Abuse Alcohol and Other Drugs. *DHHS Publication No (SMA)* 94-3006. *Rockville, MD: CSAT, Substance Abuse and Mental Health Services Administration*

Center for Substance Abuse Treatment (CSAT). 1994b. "Screening and Assessment for Alcohol and Other Drug Abuse among Adults in the Criminal Justice System." *Treatment Improvement Protocol (TIP) Series, No. 7.*

Covington, S. 2000a. Creating gender-specific treatment for substance abusing women and girls in community correctional settings. In *Assessment to assistance: Programs for women in community corrections,* ed. M. McMahon. Lanham, MD: American Correctional Association. 171–233.

Covington, S. 2000b. Helping women recover: A comprehensive integrated treatment model. *Alcoholism Treatment Quarterly* 18: 99–111.

D'Angelo, L. 2002. Women and addiction: Challenges for drug court practitioners. *Justice System Journal* 23: 385–400.

Dowden, C., and K. Blanchette. 2002. An evaluation of the effectiveness of substance abuse programming for female offenders. *International Journal of Offender Therapy and Compara-tive Criminology* 46: 220–30.

Drug and Alcohol Services Information System Report. 2001. How men and women enter sub-stance abuse treatment. Substance Abuse and Mental Health Services Administration. Washington, DC: U.S. Department of Health and Human Services.

Finkelstein, N. 1993. "Treatment Programming for Alcohol and Drug-Dependent Pregnant Women." *The International Journal of the Addictions* 28, no. 13: 1275–1309.

Gender differences among prisoners entering drug treatment: Executive summary. 2000. Federal Bureau of Prisons Research Project. http://www.bop.gov/orepg.html (accessed July 14, 2004).

Jordan, K., W. E. Schlenger, J. A. Fairbank, and J. M. Caddell. 1996. Prevalence of psychiatric disorders among incarcerated women. *Archives of General Psychiatry* 53: 513–19.

Lukas, S. E., M. B. Sholar, M. Fortin, J. Wines, and J. H. Mendelson. 1996. Sex differences in plasma cocaine levels and subjective effects after acute cocaine administration in hu-man volunteers. *Psychopharmacology* 125: 346–54.

National Institute of Justice. 1993. Miami's drug court: A different approach. Washington, DC: U.S. Department of Justice, Office of Justice Programs NIJ: NCJ 142412.

Richie, B. E. 1999. Exploring the link between violence against women and women's involve-ment in illegal activity, *Research on Women and Girls in the Justice System: Plenary Papers of the 1999 Conference on Criminal Justice Research and Evaluation—Enhancing Policy and Prac-tice Through Research, U.S Dept. of Justice, Office of Justice Programs, National Institute of Jus-tice, NIJ Research Forum*, 3, 12–14.

Sherman, M. 2001. Women offenders and their children. Federal Judicial Center: *Special Needs Offenders Bulletin* 7: 1–3.

U.S. Department of Justice, Bureau of Justice Statistics. 1991. *Survey of Inmates in State Correc-tional Facilities.*

U.S. Department of Justice, Bureau of Justice Statistics: *Women in Prison. BJS, Special Report,* March 1994.

U.S. Department of Justice, Bureau of Justice Statistics: *Women Offenders: BJS, Special Report, December 1999, Mumola C.J. Incarcerated Parents and Their Children.*

Wald, P. M. 2001. *Special Needs Offenders Bulletin, No. 7 (September, 2001). U.S. Sentencing Guide-lines.*

9

Sexual Risk Behavior and Alcohol and Other Drug Use among Female Adolescent Detainees

Implications for Intervention

RHONDA C. CONERLY
ALYSSA G. ROBILLARD
RONALD L. BRAITHWAITE

Although male detention rates are significantly higher than female detention rates, the number of females involved in the juvenile court system has increased. Of the 2.5 million juvenile arrests made in 1999, 27 percent were of female offenders (Snyder 2001). According to data from 1997, less than 1 percent of the female adolescents were involved in the adult criminal system (Scahill 2000). During the period from 1989 to 1998, there was a 56 percent increase in the number of cases involving female delinquents entering detention compared to a 20 percent increase in male detention (Harms 2002). This increase was directly related to the number of females who committed person offenses.

This marked increase in the number of female detainees creates a population of young women in need of specific and appropriate intervention. Adolescent females placed in detention facilities typically engage in a number of risky behaviors including alcohol and other drug use and risky sexual behavior at very early ages. Alcohol and other drug use can impair judgment and lead to decisions that place one's health at risk, such as engaging in unprotected sexual behavior. Thus it is imperative to address these behaviors among adolescent female detainees. Female detainees exhibit many of the same risk factors of their male counterparts, including physical or emotional abuse, low economic status, and poor parenting (Bergsmann 1988, 1989; Crawford 1988; Sarri 1988), but they tend to receive fewer educational and vocational services, including fewer preventive services (U.S. General Accounting Office 1995). Early identification and treatment, long-term program commitment, individualized attention, skill enhancement, life options, vocational orientation, and greater community involvement are some possible means for increasing protective factors among girls (Burt, Resnick, and Matheson 1992).

In addition to these interventions designed to improve life skills and reduce delinquent behavior, interventions that address the specific risk behavior associated with HIV are sorely needed for adolescent detainees—especially female adolescent detainees. For young women with histories of physical, emotional, and sexual abuse who engage in sexual risk behavior, gender-specific interventions can have a significant behavioral impact. Examining substance use in the context of HIV risk behavior is also critical.

HIV and Adolescent Females

While early cases of HIV were diagnosed mostly in men, HIV/AIDS has increasingly affected women. In the United States, the proportion of all AIDS cases reported among adult and adolescent women has more than tripled from 7 percent in 1985 to 25 percent in 1999 (CDC 2002). In 2002, 26 percent of the estimated number of people living with HIV/AIDS among adults and adolescents based on the thirty areas with confidential, name-based HIV infection reporting were women (CDC 2003). Heterosexual sex is the leading avenue of transmission for AIDS among women. By the end of 2002, 72 percent of the 71,996 adult and adolescent cases among women with HIV/AIDS in the United States were exposed through heterosexual contact, and 26 percent were exposed through injection drug use. Sixty-eight percent of adult and adolescent women living with HIV/AIDS at the close of 2002 were black (CDC 2003).

Despite recent efforts to encourage testing, many adolescents and young adults are unaware of their HIV status. In 2002, 2,944 diagnoses of HIV/AIDS were reported among adolescents and young adults thirteen to twenty-four years of age in the thirty areas with confidential, name-based HIV infection reporting. From 1999 and 2002, there was an overall increase in the number of diagnoses of HIV/AIDS among black and Hispanic teens thirteen to nineteen years of age. The number of HIV/AIDS diagnoses was highest each year among black female teens (CDC 2004). Two groups are experiencing disproportionate rates of HIV/AIDS and are relevant to the group discussed in this chapter: women and minorities, especially blacks. Because African American youth are suffering a high incidence of HIV/AIDS (Bowler et al. 1992; Conway et al. 1993; Young et al. 1992) and disproportionate rates of HIV, especially among young women, appropriate measures are necessary to address their needs.

Among low-income adolescent females, increased HIV risk has been associated with older age, a weaker intention to reduce risk, high rates of substance abuse, lower risk-reduction skills, beliefs that their partner opposed risk-reduction behaviors, and higher risk-reduction outcome expectation (Sikkema et al. 2004). DiClemente et al. (2002) found that adolescents with previous diagnosis for an STD were less likely to engage in condom use, particularly during their most recent sexual encounter. Participation in social organizations, however, was found to be a protective factor for HIV risk behavior among low-income African American adolescents (Crosby et al. 2002).

Young women, especially those with histories of abuse and neglect who hail from poverty-stricken and crime-ridden neighborhoods and whose systems of social support are minimal at best, are especially at risk. Although HIV prevalence among detained youth is not high, many risk behaviors associated with it have been documented.

Sexual Risk Behavior in Adolescent Detainees

Adolescent detainees represent a subset of youth at high risk for substance use and risky sexual behaviors (Council on Scientific Affairs 1990), partly due to increased risk activity across a broad spectrum of behaviors, including substance use and sexual behaviors. Studies have shown that these youth are more sexually experienced and engage in fewer sexual protective practices than youth who are not incarcerated (DiClemente, Lanier, et al. 1991; Forrest et al. 2000), thereby placing them at increased risk for the negative health outcomes associated with unprotected sexual activity (sexually transmitted infections, including HIV, and unintended pregnancies). Several factors associated with these negative health outcomes have been identified in detained youth, including early onset of sexual activity, multiple partners, and lack of condom use (Bell et al. 1985; Canterbury et al. 1995; DiClemente 1991; Elfenbein, Weber, and Grob 1991; Forst 1994; Gillmore et al. 1994; Harwell et al. 1999; Kann et al. 2000; Kelly et al. 2000; Lanier, Pack, and DiClemente 1999; Magura, Shapiro, and Kang 1994; Morris, Baker, et al. 1998; Morris, Harrison, et al. 1995; Oh et al. 1994; Pack et al. 2000; Rickman et al. 1994; Shafer et al. 1993; Weber, Elfenbein, et al. 1989; Weber, Gearing, et al. 1992).

Several studies have documented sexually transmitted disease (STD) rates among detained adolescents, mostly males. Oh et al. (1994) reported rates of 6.9 percent for *Chlamydia trachomatis* and 4.5 percent for *Neisseria gonorrhoeae* among male adolescent detainees. Shafer and colleagues (1993) found that 15 percent of male detainees were infected with at least one STD at the time of their detention. Pack et al. (2000) found that 18 percent of detained male adolescents had either chlamydia, gonorrhea, or both. Failure to use condoms was significantly associated with positive STD results. Studies examining STD rates among female adolescent detainees are generally higher. Kelly and colleagues (2000) examined the prevalence of chlamydia in a juvenile detention facility and found it to be 22 percent among female detainees. A study by Bell and colleagues (1985) found gonorrhea in 18 percent of detained females; positive test results for chlamydia were found in 20 percent of the sample.

In addition to providing epidemiological data on STDs, many of these studies also report behavioral data highlighting the risk factors associated with these negative health outcomes. One study found a median number of eight lifetime partners for male adolescent detainees. Inconsistent condom use was also reported (Oh et al. 1994). This was also observed among female adolescent detainees. In a study by Bell and colleagues (1985), 68 percent of the female adolescent detainee population they interviewed reported no use of contraception. Shafer et al. (1993) found that male adolescent detainees engaged in risky sexual and drug use behaviors, identifying three factors that significantly place them at risk for STDs: multiple sexual partners, inconsistent condom use, and quantity of alcohol consumed per week.

In contrast to approximately half of high school youth who are sexually active (Kann et al. 2000), findings show that upwards of 80 percent of juvenile offender samples report initiation of sexual activity (Forst 1994; Harwell et al. 1999; Kelly et al. 2000; Lanier, DiClemente, and Horan 1991; Morris, Baker, et al. 1998; Morris, Harrison, et al. 1995; Weber, Elfenbein, et al. 1989; Weber, Gearing, et al. 1992). Harwell et al. (1999) found that 81 percent of males reported vaginal sex in the previous six months with 14 percent reporting insertive anal sex. In comparing youth with multiple corrections admissions versus first-time admissions, this study found that youth with multiple admissions were more likely to report eight or more lifetime partners, more likely to have exchanged drugs or money for sex and less likely to have used condoms with their last sex partner. Weber and colleagues (1989) examined sexual activity in delinquent adolescents and found that 83 percent reported previous sexual experience. More recent studies have found that over 90 percent of these youth report being sexually active (Harwell et al. 1999; Kelly et al. 2000): as high as 96 percent in a study examining risk behaviors among adolescent detainees over a four-year period (Morris, Baker, et al. 1998). Many of these youth initiated sexual activity before age thirteen.

A large majority of detained youth have initiated sexual activity at an early age. Several studies have found that the average age of initiation falls between twelve and thirteen (Forst 1994; Gillmore et al. 1994; Harwell et al. 1999). While the average age of initiation for female adolescent detainees was thirteen in a study by Weber and colleagues (1989), males commonly reported beginning sexual experience before age ten. Other studies have documented adolescent detainee populations as high risk due to their involvement with multiple sex partners. Canterbury and his colleagues (1995) found that 76 percent of youth in their sample reported having three or more sexual partners, while others found that almost half (46.5 percent) their sample had more than five lifetime partners.

Condom use has been measured in a variety of ways in studies with adolescent detainee populations. Researchers have measured condom use at last intercourse, condom use in the previous three to four months, as well as the frequency of condom use ranging from always to never. Studies indicate that detained youth are not consistent in their use of condoms. One study documenting condom use of females in a juvenile detention center found that 68 percent reported no use of any form of contraception (Bell et al. 1985). Studies have also found differences in condom use between steady and casual partners where condom use was less frequent with steady (or primary) partners (Gillmore et al. 1994; Oh et al. 1994; Shafer et al. 1993). Among jailed male adolescents, inconsistent condom use was most common with only 15 percent reporting consistent use (Magura, Shapiro, and Kang 1994). A more recent study found that 38 percent of youthful offenders surveyed did not use a condom at last intercourse (Kelly et al. 2000).

Alcohol and Other Drug Use in Adolescent Detainees

One factor that contributes to juvenile arrest and detention is substance use. Substance use and delinquent/criminal behavior are associated with one another. Substance use is associated with delinquent activity, level of violence, and recidivism among youth (Dembo et al. 1991; Ellickson, Saner, and McGuigan 1996; Harwell et al. 1999; Komro et al. 1999; Stice, Myers, and Brown 1998).

Efforts have been made to document the substance use patterns of adolescents in general and for at-risk adolescents. Data from the 1999 National Household Survey of Drug Abuse (NHSDA) administered by the Substance Abuse and Mental Health Services Administration (SAMHSA) for youth substance use documented that alcohol was the most commonly used substance among adolescents aged twelve to seventeen (Wright and Davis 2001). Approximately 16.5 percent of adolescents were classified as current drinkers (alcohol use in the past thirty days). In addition, 10.1 percent of the adolescents surveyed reported binge drinking (five or more drinks on the same occasion at least five different days in the past thirty days). The national average for alcohol initiation was 15.7 years for those aged 25 or younger. In the 2000 NHSDA, female adolescents reported a current alcohol use rate of 16.5 percent (SAMHSA 2001). Among adolescents, African Americans and Asians were the least likely to report current alcohol use. The rates were 8.8 percent and 7.1 percent, respectively, for African American and Asian adolescents and over 16 percent for adolescents in other racial/ethnic groups.

Recent data from the 2000 NHSDA shows that 9.7 percent of adolescents aged twelve to seventeen years reported illicit drug use in the past thirty days (SAMHSA 2001). Illicit drug use for girls was 9.5 percent. Inhalant use was reported by approximately 2.1 million adolescents (8.9 percent) aged twelve to seventeen in 2000. Marijuana use among girls was 6.6 percent. The 1999 NHSDA data demonstrated current marijuana use by 7.2 percent of adolescents aged twelve to seventeen and the national average for marijuana initiation was 16.2 years for those aged 25 and younger (Wright and Davis 2001).

The Youth Risk Behavior Survey of Alternative High Schools offers a glimpse into the substance use behavior of adolescents at risk. This survey offers data on youth who have been expelled from high school or those at risk for dropping out (Grunbaum, Lowry, and Kann 2001). Data from this survey revealed that 65 percent of the youth reported alcohol use in the past thirty days and cocaine use was reported by 15 percent in the last thirty days. Forty-six percent of youth reported the use of illegal drugs other than cocaine within the last thirty days. This data, however, does not capture the substance use patterns of adolescents currently detained.

Efforts to document substance use among adolescent detainees in the United States are made quarterly through the Arrestee Drug Abuse Monitoring Program (ADAM), administered in nine sites by the National Institute of Justice. The generalizability of these data, however, is limited due to the small number of sites. According to the 1999 ADAM annual report, over 20 percent of females tested positive for marijuana. Cocaine was the second most widely used substance with use ranging from 0 to 17 percent, depending on the site (National Institute of Justice 2000).

Health risk behaviors, including alcohol and other drug use, were examined among adolescents from thirty-nine correctional facilities in the United States using a modified version of the Youth Risk Behavior Surveillance System, or YRBSS (Morris, Harrison, et al. 1995). Results indicated that for most participants, alcohol consumption began by the age of fifteen, with the earliest onset being age nine. Thirty-two percent of the respondents reported using alcohol at least once a day for more than 100 days. Binge drinking (consuming five or more drinks at one time) was also common among this population, with approximately half reporting binge drinking within the last thirty days before incarceration. Marijuana use was also high; it was the illicit drug of choice. Forty percent reported using marijuana more than forty times. Females reported more cocaine (42 percent) and crack cocaine (9.6 percent) use than males (30 percent and 3.3 percent, respectively). They also reported an earlier initiation and more frequent use of cocaine. Gender differences were also found on use of other illicit drugs (PCP, ecstasy, speed, heroin, and so on) and injection drug use. These studies indicate high rates of substance use among at-risk and detained adolescents.

Alcohol and Other Drug Use and HIV Risk Behavior in Adolescent Detainees

When AOD use is combined with sexual activity, there is a greater chance for poor health outcomes such as STDs, including HIV, simply because an individual's judgment can be compromised. High levels of AOD use may predispose adolescent detainees to engage in risky sexual behavior by compromising the ability to recognize risk situations. For young women, AOD use may further compromise the ability to successfully communicate and negotiate protected sexual encounters or refuse sex altogether.

Evidence that AOD use is tied to HIV risk in this population comes from a study that examined predictors of risky sexual behavior among adolescent offenders (Barthlow et al. 1995). Of the twenty predictors examined, separate variables tapping marijuana and alcohol consumption were the strongest predictors of failure to use condoms. Other studies suggest that the more substances that sexually active young women have ever tried, the less likely they are to have used a condom the last time they had sex (Santelli et al. 2001). Among sexually active young women ages fourteen to twenty-two who had never used a substance, 67 percent used a condom. Among sexually active young women who reported ever having used five substances, 23 percent used a condom the last time they had sex (Santelli et al. 2001).

Sexual Risk and Drug Use in Female Adolescent Detainees: Project SHARP

Undoubtedly, juvenile detainees exhibit increased levels of high-risk behavior, including sexual behavior and substance use. Female adolescent detainees, an increasing proportion of the juvenile detainee population, engage in these behaviors at alarmingly high rates. It becomes important to characterize the sexual risk behavior and substance abuse behavior of female adolescent detainees to identify trends in risk activity and to determine best approaches to address these risks.

Project SHARP (Stop HIV and Alcohol Related Problems) was a prevention intervention developed to address HIV and alcohol and other drug use in adolescent detainees. The project was a randomized controlled investigation on the effects of an intervention designed to reduce future drug and alcohol use, risky sexual behavior, and delinquency. The intervention was delivered to adolescents while they were housed in Youth Development Campuses operated by the Georgia Department of Juvenile Justice. This chapter presents findings from Project SHARP that highlight both sexual risk and AOD use in female adolescent detainees.

Approximately 59 percent (N = 1,341) of the youth recruited to participate in Project SHARP were females. Participants had been sentenced to secured youth development campuses (YDCs) that served youth from the entire state. This study focused only on those youth in the juvenile system because they represent the vast majority of adolescent detainees. The youth were typically mandated to the YDCs for 90 days although sentences ranged between 30 and 180 days.

Female participants ranged in age from eleven to eighteen (M = 14.9, SD = 1.2). Approximately 2 percent were Hispanic (n = 26), less than 1 percent reported being Asian or Pacific Islanders (0.4 percent, n = 6) or Native American or Alaskan Native (0.4 percent, n = 6), and approximately 3 percent (n = 43) classified themselves as "other." Fifty-seven percent (n = 766) of the youth in this sample identified themselves as black, and 37 percent (n = 493) identified themselves as white. There was a significant difference in age among the racial/ethnic groups: $F (2, 1339) = 3.62$, $p < .05$, with white youth being significantly older than African American youth ($p < .01$). On average, these youth attained a median educational level of eighth grade (range: fourth to twelfth grade). Previous detention on a separate offense was reported by 53.5 percent of the sample.

Youth entering the YDC were informed of an opportunity to participate in a program addressing the prevention of HIV and alcohol-related problems. Youth who agreed to participate signed an assent form authorizing researchers to contact their parent or guardian to request permission for participation. Parents or guardians of these youth were then sent a letter that described the study and requested permission for their child to participate. (The Emory University Human Investigation Committee as well as the Department of Juvenile Justice Institutional Review Board approved the consent procedures.) During the enrollment period for this study, 4,031 youth were approached, and 2,766 gave personal assent and received parental consent to participate. Refusals after initial assents, releases, confinements, out-of-facility passes, kitchen duty, and simple misses resulted in a participation rate of 57 percent (n = 2,280).

Participants completed a baseline questionnaire before being randomized to either the experimental or comparison group. Trained interviewers residing in the communities located near the two Youth Development Campuses conducted face-to-face interviews to collect baseline information. All interviewers completed a criminal background check and participated in an eight-hour training session prior to conducting the interviews where the project director discussed interviewing techniques and reviewed and clarified each question in the interview protocol. Interviewers were gender-matched for female participants.

Among other variables, the baseline survey measured sexual risk behavior as well as alcohol and other drug use. Sexual activity was measured using a series of questions to assess whether youth had ever willingly engaged in each sex type—vaginal, anal, and oral (performed by them and received by them). Youth who reported participation in any of the individual sex type categories were then asked to provide the following information for each type: age at which they first willingly had sex, the number of lifetime partners, the number of times they had sex in the month before entering a detention center or youth development center, and the number of times they had not used a condom or latex barrier in the month prior to entering a detention center or youth development center. A rate of condom use in the month before entering a facility was calculated using the latter two variables.

Alcohol and other drug use were measured using an adaptation of the Centers for Disease Control's (CDC) Youth Risk Behavior Surveillance questionnaire. Adolescents were asked to recall how often they used a particular substance during the last month before entering the juvenile detention facility. There were six response categories measured on a Likert-type scale (0 to 5) ranging from no use to twenty to thirty-one days of use. For analysis purposes, the response categories were collapsed to reflect no use or use, which were coded as 0 and 1, respectively. Alcohol use was defined as consumption of beer, wine, wine coolers, grain alcohol, or hard liquor. Participants were asked about their lifetime consumption ("Ever had one drink of alcohol?"), as well as consumption during the last month before entering the facility. Age of alcohol initiation was measured by asking the age when they first had a drink of alcohol. Marijuana and other drug use were also measured using an adaptation of the Youth Risk Behavior Surveillance questionnaire and self-developed questions that were modeled after the Youth Risk Behavior Surveillance questionnaire. Participants were asked to indicate how often they used other drugs (cocaine, LSD, ecstasy, and so on) during the last month before entering the detention facility. Additional questions, identical to the items regarding alcohol use, were asked to assess age of initiation and lifetime use for marijuana only.

Sexual Risk Behavior in Female Adolescent Detainees

Approximately 88 percent (n = 1,159) of the young women in this sample had willingly engaged in vaginal sex. A much smaller percentage (4 percent; n = 57) indicated a history of willing anal sex. Participants did report consensual oral sex activity, and differences were observed between performing oral sex and receiving oral sex, 22 percent (n = 290) vs. 47 percent (n = 615), respectively. Differences on age of sexual initiation, number of lifetime partners, and condom use are presented for each type of sexual activity.

Age of Sexual Initiation

The mean age of sexual initiation for vaginal sex for females in this sample was 13.4 (SD = 1.4). The analysis of variances (ANOVAs) were conducted to examine differences on age of sexual initiation. Males (M = 12.8, SD = 1.8) were significantly younger than females at the age of initiation for vaginal sex observed (F [1, 2016] = 62.6, p < .001). Among girls, a significant difference among age categories on age of sexual initiation for vaginal sex was also observed (F [4, 1152] = 82.19, p < .01; see table 9.1). Post hoc analysis indicated significant differences between each age. Younger detainees in the sample had a lower mean age of sexual debut for vaginal sex than older detainees, indicating an earlier age of initiation for vaginal sex in younger girls. Significant differences among age categories were also observed for age of initiation of anal sex (F [4, 50]= 15.03, p < .01), and oral sex: performing on others (F [4, 282] = 31.07, p < .01) and receiving from others (F [4, 608] = 76.08, p < .01). Overall, for each type of sexual activity, younger detainees began having sex at earlier ages than older detainees. A significant difference was also observed among race/ethnicity categories (F [3, 1153] = 3.20, p < .05), particularly between white and black youth. White girls were younger than black girls at the age of initiation for vaginal sex (13.3 vs. 13.5 years old, respectively). This trend among female participants was also observed for oral sex.

Lifetime Number of Partners

A significant difference between males and females was observed on lifetime number of partners (H [1] = 138.18, p < .001) using a Kruskall-Wallis H test. Males had a significantly higher number of lifetime vaginal partners than females. As expected, for the overall sample (H [4] = 110.77, p < .001) and for female participants only (H [4] = 55.34, p < .01), the number of lifetime vaginal partners was significantly higher for older youth in the sample.

Among female participants, a significant difference among racial/ethnic

TABLE 9.1

Mean age of sexual initiation by age categories

	Age of Sexual Initiation M (SD)
Age Categories	
Vaginal (overall)	13.16 (1.5)
11–13	12.05 (1.0)
14	12.61 (1.4)
15	13.06 (1.4)
16	13.57 (1.9)
17–18	13.60 (1.6)
Anal (overall)	14.37 (1.4)
11–13	12.00 (1.0)
14	13.50 (0.7)
15	14.33 (0.8)
16	14.63 (1.7)
17–18	15.41 (1.4)
Oral (performing) (overall)	14.10 (1.6)
11–13	12.28 (0.8)
14	12.99 (1.4)
15	13.78 (1.1)
16	14.61 (1.4)
17–18	14.63 (2.2)
Oral (receiving) (overall)	13.93 (1.4)
11–13	12.16 (0.9)
14	13.09 (1.2)
15	13.74 (1.1)
16	14.31 (1.4)
17–18	14.48 (1.8)

groups was observed for vaginal sex (H [3] = 33.31, p < .01); black girls had the lowest number of lifetime partners compared to girls in all other groups. Racial/ ethnic groups also differed significantly for performing oral sex on others (H [3] = 13.38, p < .01). White youth had the highest number of lifetime partners, followed by youth categorized as "other," then Hispanic and black youth.

Condom/Latex Barrier Use

Females (68.1 percent) were more likely than males (31.9 percent) to not use condoms in the month preceding entrance into the Youth Development Campus (c^2 [2] = 16.10, p < .001). Table 9.2 presents categorized condom/latex barrier use in the month preceding entry into the facility for both males and females. Overall, more than half (52 percent, n = 761) of those who had engaged in vaginal sex in the month preceding entrance into the Youth Development Campus were consistent condom users (used condoms 100 percent of the time).

Among black girls, 55 percent were consistent condom users for vaginal sex compared to 20 percent who never used condoms; among white youth, 41 percent were consistent condom users for vaginal sex while 35 percent never used condoms (c^2 [6] = 27.74, p < .01). An alarming 56 percent of the females in this sample reported anal sex without the use of a condom, either never using them or inconsistently using them. In the month preceding entrance into the facility, 64 percent of white youth and 46 percent of black youth had not used condoms during anal sex activity (c^2 [4] = 25.76, p < .01).

TABLE 9.2

Condom/latex barrier use* by gender

	Condom Use (%)		
	Never	Inconsistent	Consistent
Vaginal (n = 1476)[†]	22.7	25.7	51.6
Male	17.5	57.0	55.5
Female	26.4	24.9	48.8
Anal (n = 52)	40.4	7.7	51.9
Male	29.6	11.1	59.3
Female	52.0	4.0	44.0
Oral (performing) (n = 289)[†]	69.9	4.5	25.6
Male	62.0	7.0	31.0
Female	76.3	2.5	21.3
Oral (receiving) (n = 695)[†]	70.4	3.3	26.3
Male	65.3	4.5	30.3
Female	74.7	2.4	22.9

*Includes only those who reported sexual activity in the month preceding detention

[†]Significant at p < .05

As expected, with both males and females, a greater percentage of youth reported "no use" for performing and receiving oral sex than consistent and inconsistent use combined.

Substance Use in Female Adolescent Detainees

ALCOHOL USE. Lifetime alcohol use was reported by 69.6 percent (n = 928) of the females in this sample. The mean age of alcohol use initiation was 12.9 years (SD = 2.1). Fifty-nine percent of the participants reported consuming alcoholic beverages between one and nineteen times, and almost 15 percent reported consuming alcoholic beverages 100 or more times during their lifetime. Recent alcohol consumption (the month prior to the current detention) was reported by 60.6 percent of the participants. Of those, 33.1 percent reported alcohol consumption on six or more days. Furthermore, 32.3 percent had five or more drinks during that time. Forty percent of the participants who reported alcohol consumption in the month prior to detention had five or more alcoholic drinks in the same day, with 64.8 percent engaging in this behavior between one and five days and the remaining 35.2 percent engaging in this behavior (binge drinking) between six and thirty-one days. Females were around thirteen years of age (M = 12.6, SD = 1.6) when they had their first drink of alcohol.

Alcohol use was further examined by gender and race/ethnicity. In general, males were significantly different in their alcohol use behavior than females, with more males engaging in detrimental behavior than females. More males reported lifetime alcohol use (c^2 = 126.8, p < .0001), more times drinking during their lifetime (c^2 = 50.3, p < .0001), the number of days they consumed alcohol in the last month (c^2 = 26.2, p < .0001), the number of drinks consumed the month before detention (c^2 = 20.4, p < .001), and consuming five or more drinks in the same day during their lifetime (c^2 = 40.3, p < .0001).

Chi-square analyses revealed significant racial/ethnic differences on the number of lifetime drinks, the number of drinks consumed in the month prior to detention, and consuming five or more drinks on the same day during their lifetime. White adolescents reported more lifetime drinks than all other racial/ethnic groups (c^2 = 72.5, p < .0001). Adolescents classified as "other" consumed more drinks in the month prior to detention (c^2 = 28.5, p < .05) and more often had consumed five or more drinks on the same day during their lifetime (c^2 = 14.5, p < .01). White adolescents (M = 12.5, SD = 2.1) were significantly younger than African American adolescents (M = 13.3, SD = 2.1) for alcohol initiation (F [3, 922] = 10.5, p < .0001).

MARIJUANA USE. The majority (72.2 percent) of the participants in this sample reported having tried marijuana in their lifetime. Approximately 30 percent had used marijuana 100 or more times in their lifetime and in the month prior to detention, 50 percent had used marijuana. Females were approximately thirteen years old (M = 12.9, SD = 1.7) the first time they used marijuana.

TABLE 9.3

Initiation of marijuana use by ethnicity

Race/Ethnicity	Age (mean years)
White	12.6 (SD = 1.7)
Black	13.4 (SD = 1.6)
Hispanic	12.3 (SD = 2.2)
Other	12.6 (SD = 1.9)

Analyses by gender revealed that males were more likely to report lifetime marijuana use ($c^2 = 112.8$, p < .0001), having used marijuana on more occasions during their lifetime ($c^2 = 128.9$, p < .0001), and marijuana use during the thirty days prior to incarceration ($c^2 = 89.1$, p < .0001). Marijuana use was further examined by ethnicity. White adolescents were more likely to have ever tried marijuana ($c^2 = 61.2$, p < .003) and to have used marijuana more times ($c^2 = 53.4$, p < .0001); while adolescents classified as "other" were more likely to have used marijuana in the month prior to detention ($c^2 = 24.3$, p < .0001). Analysis by race/ethnicity demonstrated a significant difference in age of initiation (F [3, 962] = 20.4, p < .0001). African American youth were significantly older when they began using marijuana than youth in all other racial/ethnic categories (see table 9.3).

OTHER DRUG USE. Use of other substances by this population was minimal. The only substance that was used by at least 10 percent of the sample was powdered cocaine (10.2 percent). The other substances on the list had been used by less than 10 percent of the sample (see table 9.4). The use of powdered cocaine was reported by more white adolescents ($c^2 = 85.7$, p < .0001) than by other ethnic groups. There were no gender differences in the use of powdered cocaine.

Convergent Risk Behaviors: Sexual Risk Behavior Coupled with AOD Use

Youth were also asked to report sexual risk behavior that occurred in combination with alcohol or marijuana use in the month preceding detainment. Sixteen percent of female participants reported alcohol use during sexual episodes where condoms were not used. Of those young women who were sexually active, 18 percent reported one or more partners with whom they used alcohol and used no condom. Twenty-one percent reported that their partners had used alcohol before sexual episodes that did not involve the use of a condom. Slightly more sexual risk behavior was reported with marijuana use. Twenty-four percent reported marijuana use during sex without the use of a condom. Twenty-five percent had one or more partners with whom they used marijuana during unprotected sexual episodes, and 28 percent had partners who used marijuana during unprotected sex.

TABLE 9.4

Self-reported frequency of other drug use by adolescent detainees

Substance	Use	No Use
Powder Cocaine	10.2%	89.8%
Crack	1.9%	98.1%
Inhalants	3.5%	96.5%
Heroin or Opium	1.6%	98.4%
LSD, Acid, or Hallucinogens	7.1%	92.9%
Speed or Uppers	7.7%	92.3%
Downers or Tranquilizers	4.0%	96.0%
PCP or Angel Dust	2.7%	97.3%
Ecstasy or other designer drugs	8.6%	91.4%

Conclusion

Adolescent substance use represents a serious concern, particularly as it relates to the health behaviors of adolescents with a history of detention. These youth are at increased risk for a myriad of health issues. Substance use combined with sexual risk behavior is an example of where two risk behaviors can merge to result in poor health consequences for this group. Rates of substance use are high among female adolescent detainees, and alcohol and marijuana were the substances of choice.

Sexual risk behavior is also prevalent among female adolescent detainees. Approximately 88 percent of the young women in this sample were sexually active, and while many used condoms consistently, others did not. Younger participants initiated sexual activity at younger ages for all types of sex indicating that youth have been steadily debuting at earlier ages. Also of note is the fact that sexual risk behavior is occurring in conjunction with AOD use.

The number of female participants in this study allows for more suitable gender comparisons and a more in-depth analysis of female adolescent detainees, although the small number of adolescents represented in the Hispanic and "other" racial/ethnic categories is a limitation. This is mainly due to geographic location; this study was conducted in a southeastern state with a small population of Hispanics, Asians, or Native Americans. In addition, participants self-reported their risk behavior to interviewers who administered the study instrument face-to-face. Recall bias and interviewer effects due to the sensitive nature of this topic should be acknowledged as possible limitations. Further, while participants were asked to report on consensual sexual behavior, it is possible that some mistakenly reported on sexually abusive activity instead.

Targeting HIV/AOD Prevention Interventions to Female Adolescent Detainees

Targeting relatively homogeneous groups allows for tailoring activities to address specific needs and risk behaviors that are common among group members (Braithwaite, Hammett, and Mayberry 1996). Female adolescent detainees represent a group with notable risk behavior. They are also a group of young women who for many have had life experiences that have challenged and debilitated their self-esteem. This often comes as a result of a wide range of abuses perpetrated against them. Targeted interventions that can enhance life skills while increasing self-esteem are a basis for interventions directed toward this population. These interventions can be built upon acknowledging the dynamics of male-female relationships as prescribed by society that can interfere with a young woman's ability to make the best possible choices.

Recommendations for HIV/AOD Interventions Using Theory-Driven Activities

A review of the literature indicates there are no published studies of HIV/AOD-focused interventions for adolescent female detainees. There are, however, many prevention interventions for adolescents that focus on risk around HIV or substance abuse (Kim et al. 1997; Office of Prevention, Program Development, and Evaluation 1996; Sherman et al. 1997; Stanton et al. 1996). One has been developed for alternative high school students (Sherman et al. 1997)—a population more like that of detained youth. Several of those aimed at substance abuse prevention also address other negative behavioral outcomes that may occur as a result of drug use (Kim et al. 1997; Sherman et al. 1997; Stanton et al. 1996). In general, interventions and prevention education that only emphasize information dissemination, fear, appeals to morality, or self-esteem and interpersonal growth are largely ineffective. But approaches that include training in resistance skills (for example, skills for effectively resisting social pressure) and broader-based life skills have been found to be effective (Kim et al. 1997). Activities designed to enhance negotiation skills should also be incorporated.

SOCIAL COGNITIVE THEORY. Social cognitive theory and its principles for behavioral change are especially germane for encouraging specific behaviors such as condom use. By concentrating on a specific health behavior, interventions that incorporate social cognitive principles are often successful in promoting that behavior across different situations. A major tenet of SCT is that behavior is dynamic and depends on characteristics of the individual as well as his/her environment (Glanz and Rimer 1995). Several concepts of this theory are relevant for encouraging and supporting changes in HIV risk behavior. Increasing behavioral capability for condom use and effective sexual communication is a basic goal in most HIV risk-reduction interventions. It is necessary to address expectations for social and sexual enhancement as they relate to substance abuse in interventions designed to change HIV risk behavior. Increasing self-efficacy for HIV preventive behavior is also a critical component. By increasing confidence in the youths' ability to perform behaviors such as condom use, they will have a greater likelihood for success. Through observational learning, positive peer role models can also be useful in assisting youth in the maintenance of protective behaviors.

An intervention can use social cognitive theory to alter sexual risk behavior by promoting positive attitudes, feelings of self-efficacy, and outcome expectancies in relation to condoms. Positive attitudes toward condoms can be shaped primarily through education about HIV and sexuality. Self-efficacy can be enhanced by teaching self-regulation skills (for example, coping with sexual triggers, monitoring self-talk), communication skills (for example, assertive expression, taking the view of others), and the mechanics of using condoms. Favorable outcome expectancies are instilled through the increased self-efficacy that comes from education and social-skills training, as well as by emphasizing the psychological gratification that people experience from practicing self-control and responsible intimacy.

PROBLEM BEHAVIOR THEORY. Problem behavior theory provides a cogent framework for addressing the tendency toward social deviance. This theory recognizes that behaviors such as delinquency, risky sex, and substance abuse tend to cluster among high-risk individuals, and it attributes these behaviors to an underlying disposition toward social deviance (Donovan and Jessor 1985; Resnicow, Ross-Gady, and Vaughn 1995). Problem behavior theory holds that the disposition for social deviance is associated with specific psychosocial risk factors, including poor self-esteem, low motivation for achievement in traditional domains (for example, school, organized sports), unsupportive family relationships, and a deprived neighborhood (Donovan and Jessor 1985; Jessor 1992). Given the multifaceted nature of this disposition, the theory calls for comprehensive interventions that address the risk factors for social deviance by enhancing self-concept and achievement motivation as well as family and community involvement.

Problem behavior theory can inform the design of the intervention to prevent risky sex and AOD use by addressing the generalized tendency to engage in these socially deviant activities. This is based on the premise that this underlying tendency must first be addressed to provide vulnerable youth with sufficient motivation to reduce their specific risks for HIV and AOD problems. Problem behavior theory views this tendency as a biopsychosocial phenomenon (Jessor 1992); however, an intervention can focus only on the psychological and social factors that are causes and consequences of social deviancy. Because these factors are difficult to change, the intervention can address them through multiple, as opposed to one-shot, sessions. In this way, the content of early sessions is reinforced by the content of later sessions.

The psychological concomitants of social deviancy (for example, stress, low self-esteem, hopelessness) are addressed by promoting general life skills such as stress management, effective decision making, and a future goal orientation. Stress management is enhanced by teaching cognitive (for example, imagery techniques, positive self-talk) and behavioral (for example, deep breathing, meditation) techniques as well as by highlighting the benefits of physical exercise. Decision-making skills are strengthened by encouraging the youth to consider alternatives before making decisions and then providing opportunities for them to role play effective decision making in hypothetical scenarios where pressures exist to engage in sex and/or AOD use. Future goal orientation is encouraged by directing the youth to make short-term goals for the upcoming week, as well as by asking them to monitor and subsequently report on their progress toward these goals. Self-concept is bolstered through all of these activities as well as through specific exercises designed to bolster ethnic identity. Moreover, the problem behavior theory intervention would seek to address social concomitants of deviancy (for example, parent conflicts, poor role models) by encouraging family and community involvement.

THEORY OF GENDER AND POWER. As members of modern society, female adolescents have observed and participated in the social dynamics of gendered relationships between males and females. The theory of gender and power addresses the social processes that compromise the health of women in disadvantaged circumstances (Wingood and DiClemente 2000). This theory has three main structures: the division of labor, the division of power, and the structure of cathexis. The division of labor includes the organization of child care, the distinction between paid and unpaid work, and wage inequalities between the sexes. To effect self-directed change, individuals must not only be provided with the skills for changing behavior but must also possess the resources and means to affect such change. For many adolescent females, economic stability is a very real concern that may be compromised by family responsibilities and expectations.

The division of power is manifested in the dynamics of authority within sexual relationships and supplies the machinery for authority, control, and coercion of men over women (Connell 1987). Protecting oneself against high-risk sexual practices requires a sense of power to exercise control over sexual situations. There are, unfortunately, numerous factors contributing to the power imbalances between men and women (Connell 1987). These include (1) the traditional gender power roles that reinforce male dominance and female submissiveness, (2) the threat of abuse to females, and (3) the dynamics of authority that are created since many adolescent females have sexual relationships with older men (Wingood and DiClemente 2000).

The structure of cathexis is society's gender-specified norms about what constitutes appropriate sexual conduct and what defines desire and desirability (Connell 1987). These norms are often reiterated for girls from disadvantaged backgrounds over and over through personal observations and through the media. Images (in reality or created in the media) that reinforce female submissiveness may aid in reducing a female adolescent's power to negotiate sexual protection and place her at increase risk for unprotected sexual intercourse (Wingood and DiClemente 2000).

The theory of gender and power seeks to characterize sexual relationships between women and men based on three social structures: the sexual division of labor, the sexual division of power, and the structure of cathexis (Wingood and DiClemente 2000). A gender-specific curriculum should maintain a theme of empowerment that would run through the entire intervention. Female adolescents have observed and participated in the social dynamics of gendered relationships between males and females. Therefore, the theory of gender and power would address the social processes that compromise the health of women in disadvantaged circumstances (Connell 1987). Specifically, the intervention would incorporate the constructs of division of power, division of labor, and structure of cathexis. Sessions would include role-playing and skill-building activities to enhance communication, negotiation skills, and condom-use self-efficacy skills. In addition, effective sexual communication would be highlighted as a way to voice sexual protection needs. Young women would participate in assertiveness training, role modeling responses to various sexual situations. Condoms should be made available upon release as a way to allow participants to exercise control over sexual situations.

Community-Based Education and Follow-up

Besides being multifaceted and comprehensive with a special emphasis on reducing substance abuse, HIV risk-reduction interventions delivered in juvenile detention facilities should include activities that will assist the youth after they return to the community. Aftercare or booster services are especially important for adolescent detainees as they are often sentenced to correctional facilities for short periods of time. HIV interventions have not typically incorporated aftercare or booster services (Stanton et al. 1996), which is surprising when considering two circumstances: (1) the effects of such interventions have usually deteriorated with time (Kalichman, Carey, and Johnson 1996; Kim et al. 1997), and (2) booster services have been shown to contribute to the maintenance of positive effects for other types of interventions such as substance abuse prevention programs (Dusenberry and Botvin 1992). While a "captive audience" in the facilities, youth are not faced with the opportunity to engage in risk behavior. Thus, community-based education that builds on education in the facility aids youth in using the prevention strategies they learn as they encounter risk situations "on the outside."

ACKNOWLEDGMENTS

The authors would also like to acknowledge the National Institute on Alcohol Abuse and Alcoholism (Grant RO1 AA11767) and the administration and staff of the Georgia Department of Juvenile Justice and Youth Development Campuses as well as those individuals who were instrumental in data collection and program implementation.

REFERENCES

Barthlow, D., P. Horan, R. DiClemente, and M. Lanier. 1995. Correlates of condom use among incarcerated adolescents in a rural state. *Criminal Justice and Behavior* 22: 295–306.

Bell, T. A., J. A. Farrow, W. E. Stamm, C. W. Critchlow, and K. K. Holmes. 1985. Sexually transmitted diseases in females in a juvenile detention center. *Sexually Transmitted Diseases* 12: 140–44.

Bergsmann, I. R. 1988. *State Juvenile Education Survey.* Washington, DC: Council of Chief State School Officers.

Bergsmann, I. R. 1989. The forgotten few: Female juvenile offenders. *Federal Probation* (March): 73–78.

Bowler, S., A. R. Sheon, L. J. D'Angelo, and S. Vermund. 1992. HIV and AIDS among adolescent in the United States: Increasing risk in the 1990s. *Journal of Adolescence* 15: 345–71.

Braithwaite, R., T. Hammett, and R. Mayberry. 1996. *Prisons and AIDS: A public health challenge.* San Francisco: Jossey-Bass.

Burt, M. R., G. Resnick, and N. Matheson. 1992. Comprehensive Service Integration Programs for At-Risk Youth. Washington, DC: U.S. Department of Health and Human Services.

Canterbury, R. J., E. L. McGarvey, A. E. Sheldon-Keller, D. Waite, P. Reams, and C. Koopman. 1995. Prevalence of HIV-related risk behaviors and STDs among incarcerated adolescents. *Journal of Adolescent Health* 17: 173–77.

Centers for Disease Control and Prevention. 2002. HIV/AIDS among US women: Minority and young women continuing risk. Atlanta, GA: Centers for Disease Control and Prevention.

Centers for Disease Control and Prevention. 2003. Cases of HIV infection and AIDS in the United States, 2002. *HIV/AIDS Surveillance Report* 2002; 14: 17–18.

Centers for Disease Control and Prevention. 2004. Cases of HIV infection and AIDS in the United States, by race/ethnicity, 1998–2002. *HIV/AIDS Surveillance Supplemental Report* 10, no. 1: 8–9.

Connell, R. W. 1987. *Gender and power: Society, the person, and sexual politics.* Stanford, CA: Stanford University Press.

Conway, G. A., M. R. Epstein, C. R. Hayman, C. A. Miller, D. A. Wendell, M. Gwinn, J. M. Karon, and L. R. Peterson. 1993. Trends in HIV prevalence among disadvantaged youth. *Journal of the American Medical Association* 269: 2887–89.

Council on Scientific Affairs. 1990. Health status of detained and incarcerated youths. *Journal of the American Medical Association* 263: 987–91.

Crawford, J. 1988. Tabulation of a Nationwide Survey of Female Inmates. Phoenix, AZ: Research Advisory Services.

Crosby, R. A., R. J. DiClemente, G. M. Wingood, K. Harrington, S. Davies, and R. Malow. 2002. Participation by African American adolescent females in social organizations: Association with HIV-protective behaviors. *Ethnicity and Disease* 12: 185–92.

Dembo, R., L. Williams, A. Getreu, L. Genung, J. Schmeidler, E. Berry, E. D. Wish, and L. La Voie. 1991. A longitudinal study of the relationships among marijuana/hashish use, cocaine use, and delinquency in a cohort of high-risk youth. *Journal of Drug Issues* 21, no. 2: 271–312.

DiClemente, R. J. 1991. Predictors of HIV-preventive sexual behavior in a high-risk adolescent population: The influence of perceived peer norms and sexual communication on incarcerated adolescents' consistent use of condoms. *Journal of Adolescent Health* 12: 385–90.

DiClemente, R. J., M. M. Lanier, P. F. Horan, F. Patricia, and M. Lodico. 1991. Comparison of

AIDS knowledge, attitudes, and behaviors among incarcerated adolescents and a public school sample in San Francisco. *American Journal of Public Health* 81: 628–30.

DiClemente, R., G. M. Wingood, C. Sionean, R. Crosby, K. Harrington, S. Davies, E. W. Hook, and M. K. Oh. 2002. Association of adolescents' history of sexually transmitted disease (STD) and their current high-risk behavior and STD status: A case for intensifying clinic-based prevention efforts. *Sexually Transmitted Disease* 29: 503–9.

Donovan, J., and R. Jessor. 1985. Structure of problem behavior in adolescence and young adulthood. *Journal of Consulting and Clinical Psychology* 53: 890–904.

Dusenbury, L., and G. Botvin. 1992. Applying the competency enhancement model to substance abuse prevention. In *The present and future of prevention,* ed. M. Kessler, S. Goldston, and J. Joffe. Newbury Park, CA: Sage.

Elfenbein, D. S., F. T. Weber, and G. Grob. 1991. Condom usage by a population of delinquent southern male adolescents. *Journal of Adolescent Health* 12: 35–37.

Ellickson, P., H. Saner, and K. A. McGuigan. 1996. Profiles of violent youth: Substance use and other concurrent problems. *American Journal of Public Health* 87, no. 6: 985–91.

Forrest, C. B., E. Tambor, A. W. Riley, M. E. Ensminger, and B. Starfield. 2000. The health profile of incarcerated male youths. *Pediatrics* 105: 286–91.

Forst, M. L. 1994. Sexual risk profiles of delinquent and homeless youths. *Journal of Community Health* 19: 101–14.

Gillmore, M. R., D. M. Morrison, C. Lowery, and S. A. Baker. 1994. Beliefs about condoms and their association with intentions to use condoms among youths in detention. *Journal of Adolescent Health* 15: 228–37.

Glanz, K., and B. K. Rimer. 1995. *Theory at a glance: A guide for health promotion practice* (95-3896): National Institutes of Health.

Grunbaum, J. A., R. Lowry, and L. Kann. 2001. Prevalence of health-related behaviors among alternative high school students as compared with students attending regular high schools. *Journal of Adolescent Health* 29, no. 5: 337–42.

Harms, P. 2002. *Detention in Delinquency Cases, 1989–1998.* Fact Sheet. Washington, DC: U.S. Department of Justice, Office of Justice Programs, Office of Juvenile Justice and Delinquency.

Harwell, T. S., R. Trino, B. Rudy, S. Yorkman, and E. L. Gollub. 1999. Sexual activity, substance use, and HIV/STD knowledge among detained male adolescents with multiple versus first admissions. *Sexually Transmitted Diseases* 26, no. 5: 265–71.

Jessor, R. 1992. Risk behavior in adolescence: A psychosocial framework for understanding risk and action. In *Adolescents at risk: Medical and social perspectives,* ed. D. Rogers and E. Ginzburg. Boulder, CO: Westview Press. 19–34.

Kalichman, S., M. Carey, and B. Johnson. 1996. Prevention of sexually transmitted HIV infection: A meta-analytic review of the behavioral outcome literature. *Annals of Behavioral Medicine* 18: 6–15.

Kann, L., S. A. Kinchen, B. I. Williams, J. G. Ross, R. Lowry, J. A. Grunbaum, and L. J. Kolbe. 2000. Youth Risk Behavior Surveillance—United States, 1999. *Morbidity and Mortality Weekly Reports* 49: 1–94.

Kelly, P. J., R. M. Bair, J. Baillargeon, and V. German. 2000. Risk behaviors and the prevalence of chlamydia in a juvenile detention facility. *Clinical Pediatrics* 39: 521–27.

Kim, N., B. Stanton, K. Dickersin, and J. Galbraith. 1997. Effectiveness of forty adolescent AIDS risk-reduction interventions: A quantitative review. *Journal of Adolescent Health* 20: 204–15.

Kingree, J. B., R. L. Braithwaite, and T. Woodring. 2000. Unprotected sex as a function of alcohol and marijuana use among adolescent detainees. *Journal of Adolescent Health* 27: 179–85.

Komro, K. A., C. L. Williams, J. L. Forster, C. L. Perry, K. Farbakhsh, and M. H. Stigler. 1999. The relationship between adolescent alcohol use and delinquent and violent behaviors. *Journal of Child and Adolescent Substance Abuse* 9, no. 2: 13–28.

Lanier, M. M., R. J. DiClemente, and P. F. Horan. 1991. HIV knowledge and behaviors of incarcerated youth: A comparison of high and low risk locales. *Journal of Criminal Justice* 19: 257–62.

Lanier, M. M., R. P. Pack, and R. J. DiClemente. 1999. Changes in incarcerated adolescents' human immunodeficiency virus knowledge and selected behaviors from 1988 to 1996. *Journal of Adolescent Health* 25: 182–86.

Magura, S., J. L. Shapiro, and S. Y. Kang. 1994. Condom use among criminally involved adolescents. *AIDS Care* 6: 595–603.

Morris, R. E., C. J. Baker, M. Valentine, and A. J. Pennisi. 1998. Variations in HIV risk behaviors in incarcerated juveniles during a four-year period: 1989–1992. *Journal of Adolescent Health* 23: 39–48.

Morris, R. E., E. A. Harrison, G. W. Knox, E. Tromanhauser, D. K. Marquis, and L. L. Watts. 1995. Health risk behavioral survey from thirty-nine juvenile correctional facilities in the United States. *Journal of Adolescent Health* 17, no. 6: 334–44.

National Institute of Justice. 2000. 1999 *Annual report among adult and juvenile arrestees.* [NCJ 181426]. Washington, DC: National Institute of Justice.

Office of Prevention, Program Development, and Evaluation. 1996. Program reviews: 90-day placement facilities. Georgia Department of Children and Youth Services.

Oh, M. K., G. A. Cloud, L. S. Wallace, J. Reynolds, M. Sturdevant, and P. A. Feinstein. 1994. Sexual behavior and sexually transmitted diseases among male adolescents in detention. *Sexually Transmitted Diseases* 21: 127–32.

Pack, R. P., R. J. DiClemente, E. W. Hook, and M. K. Oh. 2000. High prevalence of asymptomatic STDs in incarcerated minority male youth: A case for screening. *Sexually Transmitted Diseases* 26: 175–77.

Resnicow, K., D. Ross-Gady, and R. Vaughn. 1995. Structure of problem and positive behaviors in African American youth. *Journal of Consulting and Clinical Psychology* 63: 594–603.

Rickman, R. L., M. Lodico, R. J. DiClemente, R. Morris, C. Baker, and S. Huscroft. 1994. Sexual communication is associated with condom use by sexually active incarcerated adolescents. *Journal of Adolescent Health* 15: 383–88.

Santelli, J. S., L. Robin, N. D. Brener, and R. Lowry. 2001. Timing of alcohol and other drug use and sexual risk behaviors among unmarried adolescents and young adults. *Family Planning Perspectives* 33: 200.

Sarri, R. C. 1988. Keynote remarks. Conference on Increasing Education Equity for Juvenile Female Offenders. Washington, DC: Council of Chief State School Officers.

Scahill, M. C. 2000. *Female delinquency cases, 1997.* http://ncjrs.org/tstfiles1/ojjdpl/ fs200016.txt (accessed February 2, 2002).

Shafer, M. A., J. F. Hilton, M. Ekstrand, J. Keogh, L. Gee, L. Digiorgio-Haag, J. Shalwitz, and J. Schachter. 1993. Relationship between drug use and sexual behaviors and the occurrence of sexually transmitted diseases among high-risk male youth. *Sexually Transmitted Diseases* 20: 307–13.

Sherman, L. W., D. Gottfredson, D. MacKenzie, J. Eck, P. Reuter, and S. Bushway. 1997. Preventing crime: What works, what doesn't, what's promising. Washington, DC: U.S. Department of Justice, Office of Justice Programs, National Institute of Justice.

Sickmund, M. (2002). *Juvenile residential facility census, 2000:* Selected findings. [NCJ No. 196595]. Washington, DC: Office of Juvenile Justice and Delinquency Prevention.

Sikkema, K. J., M. J. Brondino, E. S. Anderson, C. Gore-Felston, J. A. Kelly, R. A. Winett, T. G. Heckman, and R. A. Roffman. 2004. HIV risk behavior among ethnically diverse adolescents living in low-income housing developments. *Journal of Adolescent Health* 35: 141–50.

Snyder, H. 2001. *Law Enforcement and Juvenile Crime.* Juvenile Offenders and Victims National Report Series Bulletin. Washington, DC: U.S. Department of Justice, Office of Justice Programs, Office of Juvenile Justice and Delinquency Prevention.

Stanton, B., N. Kim, J. Galbraith, and M. Parrott. 1996. Design issues addressed in published evaluations of adolescent HIV risk-reduction interventions: A review. *Journal of Adolescent Health* 18: 387–96.

Stice, E., M. G. Myers, and S. A. Brown. 1998. Relations of delinquency to adolescent substance use and problem use: A prospective study. *Psychology of Addictive Behaviors* 12, no. 2: 136–46.

Substance Abuse and Mental Health Services Administration. 2001. *Summary of findings from the 2000 national household survey on drug abuse.* [NHSDA Series H-13, DHHS Publication No. (SMA) 01-3549]. Rockville, MD: Substance Abuse and Mental Health Services Administration, Office of Applied Studies.

U.S. General Accounting Office. 1995. Juvenile Justice: Minimal Gender Bias Occurred in Processing Noncriminal Juveniles (GAO/GGD-95-56). Washington, DC: U.S. General Accounting Office.

Weber, F. T., D. S. Elfenbein, N. L. Richards, A. B. Davis, and J. Thomas. 1989. Early sexual activity of delinquent adolescents. *Journal of Adolescent Health Care* 10: 398–403.

Weber, F. T., J. Gearing, A. Davis, and M. Conlon. 1992. Prepubertal initiation of sexual experiences and older first partner predict promiscuous sexual behavior of delinquent adolescent males—unrecognized child abuse? *Journal of Adolescent Health* 13: 600–605.

Wingood, G. M. and R. J. DiClemente. 2000. Application of the theory of gender and power to examine HIV-related exposures, risk factors, and effective interventions for women. *Health Education and Behavior* 27, no. 5: 566–69.

Wright, D., and T. R. Davis. 2001. *Youth substance use: State estimates from the 1999 National Household Survey on Drug Abuse* [Analytic Series: A-14, DHHS Publication No. SMA 01-3546]. Rockville, MD: Substance Abuse and Mental Health Services Administration, Office of Applied Studies.

Young, R. A., S. Feldman, B. T. Brackin, and E. Thompson. 1992. Seroprevalence of human immunodeficiency virus among adolescent attendees of Mississippi sexually transmitted disease clinics: A rural epidemic. *Southern Medical Journal* 85: 460–63.

PART THREE

Sexual and Reproductive Health

10

Carrying in the Criminal Justice System

Prenatal Care of Incarcerated Women

RENATA FORTENBERRY
CARMEN WARREN
JOHN CLARK

Literature on the health outcomes of incarcerated women tends to include issues of prenatal care within the framework of overall health and also tends to recognize those characteristics of health care that are unique to women (gynecological, reproductive [birth control and abortion], and prenatal care; Brennan and Austin 1997; Wismont 2000). However, perhaps because women are only a small proportion of the inmate population, traditional correctional systems have failed to allocate substantial resources toward adequate health care for women, particularly pregnant women (Brennan and Austin 1997; Morash, Bynum, and Koons 1998; Understanding Prison Health Care 2002). In effect, there is some inconsistency in research and practice.

In taking the approach that incarcerated women—like all women and in fact all human beings—should have equal access to quality health care, we recognize that there is another point of view. Many individuals feel that, because these women were convicted of a criminal offense, they should not be given the same opportunities as women in the general population and they should not have access to quality health care. The current state of affairs in the U.S. health care system makes it seem almost unreasonable to mandate better care for these women than that which is often denied to other Americans (those who have not committed a crime) because of their race, class, or socioeconomic status. However, we believe that incarcerated women deserve quality care, despite what may not be available to women in the general population. As the saying goes, "two wrongs don't make a right."

Presently in the United States, women have the right to use various methods of birth control and, in effect, to choose whether they want to become pregnant.

And in cases where pregnancy is unintended, women may choose either to maintain or terminate it. Incarcerated women who are pregnant should be able to maintain their right to make reproductive decisions. When a pregnancy is maintained in a correctional setting, unique challenges arise. This chapter will tackle issues related to prenatal care; health care issues related to pregnancy termination in this setting will be discussed in chapter 11 on reproductive health. The purpose of this chapter is to review what is known about birth outcomes for pregnant inmates, to provide an overview of the prenatal services that are currently available in U.S. prison systems, to review the cost of health care in correctional facilities, to identify potential barriers to prenatal services, and to make recommendations as to what prenatal services should be offered in correctional facilities.

Birth Outcomes of Incarcerated Women

The health care needs of women in prison are unique, especially surrounding the labor and delivery process; however, very limited information is available regarding the birth outcomes of pregnant inmates (Egley et al. 1992). Currently, there is considerable debate regarding the effects of incarceration on pregnant women and their unborn children. While it is reasonable to contend that the incarceration of women leads to a host of negative birth outcomes, there is evidence that this is not always the case. There are aspects of the prison environment that may serve to produce positive birth outcomes as well.

Positive Outcomes

Some studies have shown that the birth outcomes for women in prison are better than outcomes for women outside the criminal justice system (Martin et al. 1997). In such studies, positive outcomes are often attributed to the prison environment itself, which may serve to buffer pregnant women from the adverse consequences associated with negative, unhealthy lifestyles. For example, incarceration may provide high-risk women with an environment where alcohol and illicit drug use is prohibited or at least restricted, physical stress is reduced due to limited demanding physical labor, and, in some cases, access to quality prenatal care is provided (Martin et al. 1997). Inconsistent shelter and food and exposure to intimate partner violence are examples of stressors in the home environment that contribute to negative birth outcomes (Cordero et al. 1991; Martin et al. 1997). Incarceration may promote healthy birth outcomes in women whose exposure to these stressors in the correctional facility is far less than their exposure at home.

One measure of positive birth outcomes is a normal infant birth weight. In studies that examined the effect of incarceration during pregnancy on infant birth weight, paired analyses of the differences between incarcerated women's birth outcomes and the birth outcomes of the same women when they were not incarcerated revealed that incarceration was positively associated with infant birth weight (Cordero et al. 1991; Martin et al. 1997). Also, women incarcerated for a longer period of time appeared to have a greater increase in the birth weight of their infant. These studies conclude that prison provides a structured environment and proves beneficial to pregnant women in that it promotes the adoption of healthy lifestyles, provides accessible and adequate prenatal care, improves nutrition, and facilitates the cessation of alcohol and drug use (Barkauskas, Low, and Pimlott 2002; Cordero et al. 1991). All of these factors ultimately lead to more favorable birth outcomes.

Negative Outcomes

In light of some studies that report the positive effect of incarceration on the health of pregnant women, other studies show that women who are pregnant during incarceration have increased health risks due to the stress produced from the prison environment, and that this increase in health risks ultimately leads to negative birth outcomes (Fogel 1992; Fogel and Harris 1986; Martin et al. 1997). These reports have shown that incarcerated pregnant women have a high incidence of certain conditions that result from poor nutrition, anemia, bleeding during early pregnancy, and multiple hospital admissions during pregnancy (Egley et al. 1992; Fogel 1992; Fogel and Harris 1986; Martin et al. 1997). In order to have an optimal pregnancy and birthing experience, there are certain factors that must be in place for pregnant women. These factors include the presence of social supports, low exposure to stress, and knowledge of the process of childbirth. When these factors are present, reports show that women have "less complicated, more psychologically satisfying labor" experiences and are able to foster more positive relationships with their babies (Fogel and Harris 1986). Unfortunately, these beneficial factors are often unavailable to incarcerated pregnant women, thus placing them—and their babies—at increased risk for experiencing negative birth outcomes.

It is widely accepted that the use of alcohol, drugs, and tobacco by pregnant women has adverse effects on their health as well as the health of the baby. Incarcerated women's risk of poor health outcomes is increased by the lifestyle many women lead prior to incarceration. This lifestyle often filled with unfavorable histories including previous obstetric and gynecological complications, exposure to numerous sexually transmitted diseases, inadequate health care, poor nutrition, low socioeconomic status, violence (including physical and sexual abuse), mental health problems, and poor overall health (Barkauskas, Low, and Pimlott 2002; Fogel and Harris 1986). The presence of these factors increases the chance that pregnant inmates will experience negative birth outcomes (Barkauskas, Low, and Pimlott 2002; Fogel 1992; Fogel and Harris 1986). Further documented negative birth outcomes for incarcerated women include high rates of fetal and infant mortality, intrauterine growth retardation, preterm labor and delivery, and numerous conditions that necessitate intensive care of the newborn (Siefert and Pimlott 2001).

Additionally, anticipation of the labor and delivery process and separation from their newborns immediately after delivery are major stressors that may influence the onset of negative birth outcomes experienced by incarcerated pregnant women. Incarcerated women who are in labor often must be transported to community hospitals to deliver their babies due to the lack of in-house medical facilities for childbirth in a majority of correctional facilities (Acoca 1998). Women are placed in restraints (that is, handcuffs and shackles) in transit to the hospital, and once at the hospital, women continue to experience the reality of a harsh, inhumane environment. As one woman stated in a report on women in prison:

> Giving birth while incarcerated was one of the most horrifying experiences of my life. . . . The shackles were not removed until 30 minutes prior to my delivery. . . . Not only was this painful, it was traumatizing, and very stressful for myself and also for my child. . . . Even animals would not be shackled during labor. . . . The birth of a child is supposed to be a joyous experience, and I was robbed of the joy of my daughter's birth. (Birth and Development of Children of Incarcerated Women in the United States 2004)

The use of restraints for incarcerated women in labor often poses unnecessary health risks for both the mother and her baby. The routine use of restraints during transport and labor is considered a "cruel, inhuman and degrading practice that seldom has any justification in terms of security concerns" (Shackling of Women in Labor 2004). Nevertheless, only fifteen state departments of corrections have policies explicitly barring the use of physical restraints on incarcerated laboring women. The stressful labor and delivery process is further exacerbated by the lack of encouragement and support provided during the birthing process.

Many pregnant inmates report that they are fearful and depressed due to the inevitable separation from their infants (Acoca 1998; American Correctional Association 2000a; Belknap 2000; Birth and Development 2004; National Women's Law Center 1995; Wismont 2000). According to Wismont, the mother-infant separation at the end of the hospitalization period is perhaps the most significant stressor that negatively affects the experiences and birth outcomes of incarcerated women and their children. This separation occurs within the realm of very limited or nonexistent education and preparation for the pregnant inmate (Birth and Development 2004). In light of reports that show the majority of incarcerated pregnant women are detained for at least six months following the birth of their child, the prison environment seems an adequate site for education and prevention programs (Wismont 2000).

As a consequence of the separation and lack of bonding, serious developmental problems may arise for the child as well as increased psychological distress for the mother (American Correctional Association 2004; Huft 1992; Huft, Fawkes, and Lawson 1992). Problems that arise for the child often result from the geographical and emotional distance from their mothers (Birth and Development 2004). Additionally, children of incarcerated mothers may be at greater risk for developing attachment difficulties later in life. In all stages of development, the children may experience a slow development of independence, which could lead to their inability to develop and maintain self-confidence, and a decreased ability to work and interact in group settings and to follow positive norms of social conduct. Past studies have shown a link between early child-parent separation and adults experiencing emotional and behavioral problems later in life (Birth and Development 2004). Finally, the separation of mother and infant places the child, as well as the mother, at increased risk for perinatal and postnatal morbidity and mortality (Understanding Prison Health Care 2002).

Many incarcerated mothers express the need to bond with their children; however, the prison environment threatens this bond and causes considerable stress and anxiety for mothers (Brennan and Austin 1997; Huft, Fawkes, and Lawson 1992). The levels of psychological distress, anxiety, and stress during and after a pregnancy in a correctional facility potentially influence numerous birth outcomes (Bell et al. 2001; Fogel 1992; Huft 1992). The adaptive responses of pregnancy are often affected by the increased stress experienced in the prison environment. The direct consequences of this increased stress include higher incidences of complications experienced in pregnancy, labor, and delivery (Huft 1992; Huft, Fawkes, and Lawson 1992). The restrictive nature of the prison environment is often transferred to the hospital during the woman's labor and delivery. Certain mothers are at risk for longer labor, needing medication due to increased discomfort during labor, and increased needs for medical intervention as a result of the physical and emotional limitations placed on them in labor and delivery (Huft 1992; Huft, Fawkes, and Lawson 1992). Finally, because existing policies dictate that incarcerated women do not have the right to care for their infants after birth, pregnant inmates experience altered maternal roles. Therefore, incarcerated mothers must learn to cope with the psychological effects of losing a child and losing identity as a mother (Huft, Fawkes, and Lawson 1992). The resulting outcomes for women who expect to give up their newborns in comparison to women who keep their babies include feelings of detachment and loss of bonding, loss of freedom, loss of privacy, and loss of self-esteem.

Available Prenatal Services in U.S. Correctional Facilities

Several associations have recognized the need for guidelines in the treatment of incarcerated mothers and pregnant women (for example, United Nations Minimum Rules for the Treatment of Prisoners, the American Correctional Association [ACA], the American Public Health Association [APHA], the American Medical Association [AMA], and the American Bar Association; Linder 1991). Currently, the Federal Bureau of Prisons (FBOP) follows guidelines set by the American College of Obstetrics and Gynecology (ACOG) when annual gynecological exams are requested by inmates (Anderson in press). However, ACOG also has standards for obstetric care that are not being implemented in correctional facilities in the United States. These standards specify services, health promotion and mainte-nance programs, guidelines for postpartum evaluation, and the facilities, equip-ment, and consultative services that should be available to all female patients.

It is necessary to contextualize the current status of prenatal care in correc-tional facilities by reviewing some of the historical issues and landmark legal cases on inmate health care. Documentation of women being mistreated in the criminal justice system dates back to before the 1870s when women were crowded into small cells in a corner of men's correctional facilities (Feinman 1986; Linder 1991). Because facilities of the time were staffed entirely by men and incarcerated women were viewed by society as depraved and deserving of every mistreatment, women giving birth under these conditions rarely—if at all—received medical treatment. A century later, literature documented similar conditions and treat-ment of women in prison. For example, McHugh (1980) tells of women being forced to perform hard labor while pregnant, being forced to terminate their preg-nancies, and being beaten and denied treatment for chronic conditions during and after pregnancy.

Legal opinion on the health care and treatment of women in prison has been dissonant. In 1976, the Supreme Court ruling in *Estelle v. Gamble* mandated that all prisons provide care for inmates' serious medical needs (Anderson in press; Linder 1991; McHugh 1980; Young 1977). One year later, the *Todaro v. Ward* decision declared that incarcerated women had "no real access to medical care or physi-cians in the New York Penal system" (Anderson in press). This was the first major legal case to challenge women's access to health care in correctional institutions, and it led to the formation of standards for prison health care by the AMA, APHA, and the ACA (Resnick and Shaw 1981). Also in 1977, as a result of the maltreatment of women at the Bedford Hills correctional facility, the Supreme Court added an amendment that made "cruel and unusual punishment" illegal. In 1980, the *Brown v. Beck* decision stated that medical care for prisoners "need only to be reasonable, not perfect, or even good" (Anderson in press). According to Linder (1991), McHugh noted in 1980 that even though several associations had set guidelines for the fair treatment of incarcerated women, improvement in the actual condi-tions and treatment of these women was minimal.

Indeed, women in the U.S. prison system do not receive regular gynecological, breast, or pelvic exams and/or sonograms, and they receive little education about prenatal care and nutrition (Understanding Prison Health Care 2002). Even if pregnant inmates are given adequate information regarding nutritional needs during pregnancy, they often cannot systematically alter their diets to increase their caloric or vitamin intake. Some correctional facilities allow women to con-tinue the drug treatment programs that they may have begun before they were incarcerated (that is, methadone maintenance), but these treatments are not tai-lored specifically to the needs of pregnant drug-abusing women (Acoca 1998; Fogel, RNC [WHCNP], FAAN and Belyea 2001).

Basic Prenatal Services

Many of the correctional facilities housing women today are equipped for basic prenatal and postpartum treatment, but these services are not required, nor are they provided to women who do not explicitly request them (ACA 2000a; Anderson in press; Mertens 2001). Nevertheless, as female inmates enter correctional institutions throughout the United States, it is universally essential to determine the current state of the patient's reproductive system; in other words, is the patient pregnant, if so, what is the gestational age, and is the patient receiving prenatal care? Given the nature of the criminal justice system, many female clients are not certain about their last menses. It is more likely than not that their reproductive systems are affected by the use and abuse of chemical substances, which can significantly impact the outcome of either an intended or unintended pregnancy. Therefore, the assessment of pregnancy status should be accomplished at the initial intake screening and a referral should be made to the appropriate provider for evaluation. Many times, this can be done by simply asking the inmate "Are you pregnant?" In other situations, a more detailed history and pregnancy test may be required. Once it is established that the patient is pregnant, the first prenatal visit should be scheduled as soon as possible. The following description and outline of prenatal services assumes that the facility has gone through the process of determining the feasibility of on-site versus off-site prenatal care or a combination of basic services on-site and special high-risk services off-site. In either event, the components below should be available through a trained women's health care specialist or a board-eligible or board-certified obstetrician.

The specific objectives of prenatal care are to prevent and manage conditions that result in poor prenatal outcomes. It is well documented that the earlier the prenatal care is started, the better, which is based on the principal that a complete risk assessment (Problem Oriented Prenatal Risk Assessment System [POPRAS]) can identify up to 70 percent of the risk factors that can result in poor prenatal outcome. This can be done using a standardized form and correlated with each prenatal visit, the findings on each physical examination, and the results of baseline and other laboratory tests.

There are nine essential components of prenatal care:

- complete risk assessment (using a standardized form)
- vitamin and iron supplementation
- dietary supplementation (that is, evening snack, extra milk, etc.)
- cervical cytology
- complete blood count
- urinalysis and screen for bacilluria
- blood type, Rh factor, and antibody screen
- RPR (syphilis serology), gonorrhea, and chlamydia screen
- HIV/AIDS testing

Other tests and services may be needed as indicated (for example, serum glucose, ultrasonography, tuberculin skin test, hepatitis panel), and ideally an inmate would take part in prenatal classes (for example, anatomy and physiology of pregnancy, family planning and parenting). Prenatal visits should occur monthly during the first twenty-eight weeks, every two weeks from twenty-eight to thirty-six weeks, then weekly during the remaining four weeks. They may occur more frequently as indicated by physician or maternal concern.

In addition to these components, it is imperative to indoctrinate the nursing staff to the concept that when dealing with a pregnant inmate/patient, there are two patients, the mother and the fetus. Following the principal of documenting each patient encounter, we must assess and document the status of the fetus each time we evaluate the mother. After the third and fourth month of pregnancy, we can auscultate fetal heart tones with a fetal stethoscope, as well as ascertain from the mother whether she can feel fetal movements. Another way to meet the goal of documenting the patient's health status is to establish a policy that routinely, each patient will have her vital signs (for example, blood pressure, temperature, pulse, respiratory rate, oxygen saturation, and fetal heart rate) documented in the medical record once each shift. Other necessary aspects of nurse staff training are the assessment of the onset of labor, emergency delivery, and resuscitation of the newborn infant.

When a pregnant inmate remains in custody after the thirty-second week of pregnancy, she should receive a copy of her "hospital papers" (POPRAS forms) to keep on person in the event that she unexpectedly goes into labor or gets released from custody unbeknownst to the medical staff, and instructed to present these papers when she is taken to the hospital for delivery. Most correctional facilities do not have birthing rooms, so laboring women are transported to hospitals for delivery and are often limited in their range of motion during the labor and delivery process due to physical restraints (Anderson in press; Birth and Development 2004). Few correctional facilities provide mental health care related to reproductive health, so postpartum depression—which is often heightened by incarcerated women's circumstances (the prison environment and the fact that they are denied biological urges, such as breast-feeding, after delivery)—can go undiagnosed and untreated. Following the birth, ACOG recommends that women be examined within four to eight weeks. This examination should include weight and blood pressure screenings and a thorough assessment of the breasts, abdomen, and external and internal reproductive organs. As each correctional facility develops a mechanism to provide prenatal services to the incarcerated female, postpartum follow-up and care should be negotiated as part of the service package. The responsible physician and health care administrator should maintain and monitor outcome data on all of the patients who received care and delivered while incarcerated and whenever possible on those inmate patients who received prenatal care but were released before delivery.

Existing Guidelines for Federal Facilities

All federal prisons are accredited by the Joint Commission on Accreditation in Health Care Organizations (JACHO), the National Commission on Correctional Health Care (NCCHC), or the ACA, but national standards are not upheld for state and local correctional facilities (Baldwin and Jones 2000). Therefore, prenatal care for women outside of federal prison systems tends to be substandard and inconsistent.

The Federal Bureau of Prisons has set the following guidelines for the health care of incarcerated female inmates:

1. All women inmates must receive a thorough examination within one month of admission into the facility.
2. This physical examination should include gynecological and obstetrical history, serology for syphilis, complete blood count, urinalysis, infectious disease tests, TB screening, and an audiogram.
3. Inmates may receive pregnancy tests and Pap smears upon request. (Morash, Bynum, and Koons 1998)

But again, non-federal facilities are not held accountable by these guidelines and therefore, care tends to be poor. Anderson (in press) summarizes the problems of access to health care for incarcerated women, which can be applied to those problems of pregnant incarcerated women as well: access to treatment is limited; when treatment is provided, it is substandard; and prison medical professionals are often underskilled and show little concern for the inmate and her individual needs. In a study of the real-life experiences of women in prison, Wismont (2000) interviewed twelve female inmates from a maximum security state prison in the Midwest. The participants were from twenty-two to thirty-six years old and the majority were African American. Participants believed that the inadequate prenatal care received in the correctional facility coupled with stressors related to imprisonment negatively impact the health of their unborn babies. They also indicated that receiving health care services within the facility was difficult and inconsistent. Not only were women denied the chance to choose their health care provider and play a role in the decision-making process, but they were also denied prompt transportation to the hospital during labor. Many women in correctional facilities are not given adequate postpartum treatment. For example, they are often denied the necessary medications to dry up breast milk, which, according to Acoca (1998) can lead to "painful breast engorgement, breast infections, and an increased sense of loss and depression upon returning to prison."

Health Promotion and Maintenance Programs

Health promotion and maintenance programs for pregnant women should include information on five specific areas of health. First, physicians should encourage patients to change negative health behaviors and should provide appropriate literature (with literacy, cultural, religious, and economic issues taken into consideration) on how to change behaviors during pregnancy as well as how to maintain healthy behaviors once the child is born. Second, women should be made fully aware of the nutritional needs of their bodies. For example, pregnant women require an average of 15 percent more kilocalories than nonpregnant women (ACOG 1989). Nutritional components of health promotion programs should identify those women who cannot meet vitamin/mineral requirements with their regular diet and prenatal vitamins should be made available to them. Since weight gain is an issue in prenatal care and it is often an indicator of healthy pregnancies, weight should be monitored periodically. ACOG also recommends that women be encouraged to exercise and that they be given the opportunity to participate in a comprehensive childbirth education program. Third, women should be made aware of the impact of their sexual health and sexual activity on the health of their unborn child. Finally, women should have access to comprehensive education regarding the impact of alcohol, tobacco, and other drugs on their health as well as the health of their unborn children.

Participants in the Wismont (2000) study report feeling controlled and unable to make decisions for themselves during pregnancy. The inability to make choices about which nutritious food and snacks to eat is inconsistent with the guidelines outlined by ACA. Further, women expressed concern about the harm of their negative health behaviors on the health of their children. This indicates that women are aware of how their actions influence their children's health; however, such inclinations are not systematically reinforced in the correctional facility.

Facilities, Equipment, and Consultative Services
ACOG standards provide various guidelines regarding the equipment that should be available in

- the examining room area (i.e., scale, measuring tape, and an ultrasonic fetal pulse detector)
- each examining room (i.e., hand-washing facilities, exam table with disposable cover and stool, and gynecologic examination equipment and supplies)
- the utility room (i.e., locked medicine cabinets, refrigerator, and facilities for sterilization).

Each facility should also have the necessary equipment for emergency resuscitation, distinct plans and procedures for the disposal of contaminated supplies, and safe and reliable methods for transporting patients to other hospitals and facilities. In cases in which women do not have full access to imaging equipment, parenting consultation, gynecologic oncology consultation, or medical or surgical consultation services, referrals must be made. Correctional facilities often do not have adequate space and/or equipment to care for laboring women; therefore, they should provide laboring inmates with safe, adequate, and prompt transportation to local hospitals. According to participants in Wismont's study, however, this transportation is inadequate and often untimely. One woman wrote, "I not only think about my unborn child, I worry about how it will make it into this world. Will we make it to the hospital on time?"

The Cost of Inmate Health Care

According to the ACA (2000b), forty-one U.S. correctional facilities spend over $82 billion on inmate health care (ACA 2000b). Women's health care costs per capita exceed those of men, but unique services for women are often being omitted from the budgets of prison systems. For example, every year, the District of Columbia and the State of Oklahoma house an average of 2,395 and 21,788 inmates, respectively. Although over $25 million is spent on inmate health care in Oklahoma (no data were available on the District of Columbia), correctional facilities in the District of Columbia and Oklahoma do not include ob/gyn services in their budget. Considering the fact that approximately 10 percent of these inmates are female, it can be assumed that more than 2,000 women are denied appropriate obstetric/gynecological care in the State of Oklahoma annually (ACA 2000a). Despite great improvements in health care policy and technology, there remains a gap between policy and practice in U.S. correctional systems. This gap may be attributable to many variables, but an exploration of some of the barriers to care may help to explain inadequacies in the delivery of health care services in correctional systems.

Barriers to Prenatal Care in Correctional Settings and Recommendations

There are several barriers that prevent women from receiving appropriate prenatal care in correctional facilities. The ACOG and ACA policies and guidelines imply a comprehensive public health approach to women's health care, which would target the needs of the whole individual. Perhaps the different missions of public health and corrections may help to explain the discord between de jure and de facto treatment of pregnant women in correctional facilities. A public health approach to prenatal care for incarcerated women would require that resources be allocated to the prevention of negative birth and postpartum outcomes as well as to the treatment of said outcomes. Unfortunately, however, the main goal of corrections in the United States is not prevention, and this poses an obvious problem for women in need of preventative care. For example, women are often forced to miss prenatal care appointments due to facility policies such as periodic head counts, which, if missed, would result in punishment (Mertens 2001). Thus, communication between correctional staff and medical personnel must be improved. Oftentimes, health care appointments are scheduled during routine prison activities, and clinics are not informed when women are released from the facility. This lack of communication may prevent other women from being seen due to over scheduling.

Correctional systems are often limited in their financial resources. Without adequate monetary resources, they simply cannot afford to employ adequate medical personnel and to purchase expensive, up-to-date equipment for prenatal screenings and care. Also, when budget restrictions are imminent, extraneous health care programs are often the first to be cut. Lack of financial resources in correctional facilities poses an access barrier for incarcerated women seeking prenatal care and treatment.

Coinciding with the 1980 *Brown v. Beck* decision, there is a general apathy toward the health care needs of incarcerated women in the United States. There is such stigma and shame associated with being imprisoned that many individuals in the general public feel that inmates do not deserve good medical and/or prenatal care. As illustrated by Linder's use of a quote by a prison chaplain in the 1840s, this attitude toward incarcerated women has existed for decades: "But no one, without experience, can tell the obduracy of the female heart when hardened and lost in sin. As women fall from a higher point of perfection so she sinks to a profounder depth of misery than man" (1991, 33).

Unfortunately, this disdainful detachment penetrates the prison walls and can also be the bias of prison guards, medical personnel, and other staff. According to a participant in Wismont's study: "If you are having trouble with your pregnancy, they act like they don't care or it's not a big deal. I had an incident of vaginal bleeding 2 weeks ago [at 29 weeks gestation]. Health Care told me to go back and lay down. When they finally took me to the hospital, I was having contractions" (2000, 295). Another participant recounted, "They make it real evident they don't care for me or my baby" (Wismont 2000, 295).

When a woman feels that she is not cared for, she is unlikely to play an active role in the prenatal care process. Facilities should require annual sensitivity training for all staff and medical personnel and should create policies that explicitly forbid inappropriate treatment and/or mistreatment of inmates. Prison staff and medical personnel should be aware of the impact of stigma and negative stereotypes on incarcerated women's health and the health of their unborn children.

Recommendations

> As society chooses a social policy of incarceration to assess the problems of violence and drug use, there is solid public health reason to design and implement comprehensive prenatal programs in correctional facilities with connections to community-based health services.
>
> –Safyer and Richmond, "Pregnancy behind Bars"

There is a lack of resources and trained staff in correctional facilities in the United States (Baldwin and Jones 2000). Oftentimes, the inability of women to access adequate prenatal care in correctional facilities is a resource issue. By increasing monetary resources for prenatal and reproductive care, prison systems could not only build the necessary infrastructure but could also hire more trained medical professionals and could purchase the imaging and screening equipment necessary to ensure proper care.

It would be erroneous to assume that all incarcerated women have knowledge about how to keep their bodies healthy, or even to assume that all incarcerated women value their health. Therefore, reproductive health education should be an essential component in prenatal care for incarcerated women. Approximately 75 to 80 percent of incarcerated women are mothers, but most of these women have never had a child in a correctional setting and, therefore, do not know what to expect as far as the labor, delivery, and separation processes. Prenatal educational in every correctional system should include prebirth counseling to prepare women for the physical limitations of labor and delivery as an inmate as well as for the inevitable separation from their babies. Given that 70 percent of incarcerated women report having ever abused substances and 50 percent report using alcohol and/or drugs at the time of their arrest, women should also be educated about the potential negative health effects of alcohol, tobacco, and other drug use on the health of their unborn child (Birth and Development 2004; Beck, Karberg, and Harrison 2002).

Many women lose their social support networks upon incarceration. Correctional facilities should attempt to increase social capital in pregnant inmates by providing financial assistance to family members who visit prisons and by offering support groups during the period of incarceration. Increasing social support can decrease the stress and isolation that often lead to negative birth and postpartum outcomes. Currently, prenatal and obstetric care and screening guidelines are not governed by one entity; therefore, the quality of prenatal care received by incarcerated women varies widely (Baldwin and Jones 2000). Also, state and local correctional facilities are not under the jurisdiction of the federal government and are not held accountable by the accreditation bureaus mentioned earlier. Therefore, we recommend that federal correctional facilities standardize obstetric/gynecological care and substance abuse and reproductive health screening services according to the guidelines set by the ACOG and ACA. As for state and local facilities, the importance of inmate health care on local communities should be stressed to state leaders (that is, governors, health care advocates, and so forth). The health of the children of incarcerated women will impact the health of the society in which they live; therefore, prenatal care for incarcerated women should be high on the priority list of state health care agencies, advocates, and leaders.

According to Linder (1991), most incarcerated mothers are not aware of their parental rights in a correctional setting. Therefore, they do not know how to regain custody of their children upon release—or even where to find their children in cases in which children were placed in the foster care system. Pregnant women in correctional facilities should have access to legal counseling concerning the placement of their children with family members, friends, or foster care. Prenatal programs in correctional settings should be standard and comprehensive, targeting the physical, mental, and social well-being of the female inmate. Women should be active participants in their prenatal care and treatment as well as in the labor and delivery decision-making processes. Involving women in these processes could decrease stress and depression caused by their loss of parenting rights and their lack of control in the prison environment. Involvement could also lead to better birth outcomes and could increase the overall physical and mental health status of the woman.

Conclusion

Women are a growing proportion of the incarcerated population, but the specific and unique health care needs of incarcerated women are often overlooked. One unique need, comprehensive prenatal care, is rarely provided and is inadequate when provided. Many variables in the prison environment lead to increased stress for pregnant inmates and increase their risk for adverse birth outcomes. The lack of resources for women coupled with the stigma of being an inmate puts pregnant incarcerated women low on the health care priority list and, in turn, jeopardizes their health as well as the health of their unborn children. The ACOG summarizes the qualities of an ideal prenatal care program:

> Pregnancy is a dynamic process, and a comprehensive program of obstetric care should be structured to permit appropriate responses to the individual needs of each patient. The ideal program begins before conception, continues during pregnancy, and extends through the postpartum period. The earlier pregnancy can be diagnosed, the earlier efforts can be undertaken to modify behavior, assess risk factors, ameliorate problems, and establish a management plan appropriate to the individual. Prenatal care should involve family members in a support role to foster the concept of pregnancy and childbirth as a family experience. (1989, 13)

It is clear that the real-life experiences of pregnant incarcerated women are inconsistent with the recommendations made by organizations such as the ACOG and the ACA. So it seems that little has changed from the 1970s and 1980s. Although we realize that a complete system overhaul would be difficult, to say the least, we recommend that the current approach to prenatal care in correctional systems—or the lack thereof in some cases—be more inclusive of the prevention and promotion components of the public health approach to health care and of the guidelines set forth by these associations. Prenatal care can be improved in correctional systems in the United States. Given the different emphases of corrections and public health, some systematic changes would have to take place. In addition, implementing existing guidelines would require reallocating monetary resources and engaging multiple stakeholders (that is, political and public health representatives, activists, and so forth).

REFERENCES

Acoca, L. 1998. Defusing the time bomb: Understanding and meeting the growing health care needs of incarcerated women in America. *Crime and Delinquency* 44: 49–69.

American College of Obstetricians and Gynecologists. 1989. *Standards for obstetric-gynecologic services,* 7th ed. Washington, DC: American College of Obstetricians and Gynecologists.

American College of Obstetricians and Gynecologists. 2002. *Guidelines for perinatal care,* 5th ed. Washington, DC: American College of Obstetricians and Gynecologists.

American Correctional Association (ACA). 2000a. Inmate health care, part 1. *Corrections Compendium* 10: 1–34.

American Correctional Association. 2000b. Inmate health care, part 2. *Corrections Compendium* 11: 1–35.

American Correctional Association. 2004. ACA Resolutions and Policies. http://www.aca.org/pastpresentfuture/resolutions.asp (accessed May 6, 2004).

Anderson, T. L. In press. Issues in the availability of health care for women prisoners. In *Female prisoners in the United States: Programming needs, availability, and efficacy,* ed. S. Sharp. Englewood Cliffs, NJ: Prentice Hall.

Baldwin, K. M., and J. Jones. 2000. Health issues specific to incarcerated women: Information for state maternal and child health programs. Johns Hopkins School of Medicine. http://www.med.jhu.edu/wchpc (accessed May 3, 2003).

Barkauskas, V. H., L. K. Low, and S. Pimlott. 2002. Health outcomes of incarcerated pregnant women and their infants in a community-based program. *Journal of Midwifery and Women's Health* 47: 371–79.

Beck, A., J. Karberg, and P. Harrison. 2002. Prison and jail inmates at midyear 2001. Washington DC: Bureau of Justice Statistics. U.S. Department of Justice. http://www.ojp.usdoj.gov/bjs/pub/pdf/pjim01.pdf (accessed May 11, 2004).

Belknap, J. 2000. *The invisible woman: Gender, crime, and justice,* 2nd ed. Belmont, CA: Wadsworth.

Bell, J. F., F. J. Zimmerman, M. L. Cawthon, C. E. Huebner, D. H. Ward, and C. A. Schroeder. 2001. Jail incarceration and birth outcomes. The Conference Exchange. http://apha.confex.com/apha/129am/techprogram/paper_30464.htm (accessed May 10, 2004).

Birth and development of children of incarcerated women in the United States. 2004. Dickenson College. http://www.dickinson.edu/~egica/researchprisons.htm (accessed March 1, 2004).

Brennen, T., and J. Austin. 1997. Women in jail: Classification issues. National Institute of Corrections. U.S. Department of Justice. http://www.nicic.org/pubs/1997/013768.pdf (accessed May 3, 2004).

Cordero, L., S. Hines, K. A. Shibley, and M. B. Landon. 1991. Duration of incarceration and perinatal outcome. *Obstetrics and Gynecology* 78: 641–45.

Egley, C. C., D. E. Miller, J. L Granados, and C. Ingram-Fogel. 1992. Outcome of pregnancy during imprisonment. *Journal of Reproductive Medicine* 37: 131–34.

Feinman, C. 1986. *Women in the criminal justice system,* 2nd ed. New York: Praeger.

Fogel, C. I. 1992. Pregnant inmates: Risk factors and pregnancy outcomes. *Journal of Obstetric, Gynecologic, and Neonatal Nursing* 11: 33–39.

Fogel, C. I., and B. G. Harris. 1986. Expecting in prison: Preparing for birth under conditions of stress. *Journal of Obstetric, Gynecologic, and Neonatal Nursing* (Nov/Dec): 454–58.

Fogel, C. I., RNC (WHCNP), FAAN and M. Belyea. 2001. Psychological risk factors in pregnant inmates: A challenge for nursing. *American Journal of Maternal/Child Nursing* 26: 10–16.

Huft, A. G. 1992. Psychosocial adaption to pregnancy in prison. *Journal of Psychosocial Nursing* 30, no. 4: 19–21.

Huft, A. G., L. S. Fawkes, and W. T. Lawson Jr. 1992. Care of the pregnant offender. *Federal Prisons Journal* (Spring): 49–53.

Linder, K.R.M. 1991. An evaluation of correctional policies related of incarcerated mothers. Master's thesis, University of Cincinnati, Cincinnati, Ohio.

Martin, S. L., R. H. Rieger, L. L. Kupper, R. E. Meyer, and B. F. Qaqish. 1997. The effect of incarceration during pregnancy on birth outcomes. *Public Health Reports* 112: 340–46.

McHugh, G. 1980. Protection of the rights of pregnant women in prisons and detention facilities. *New England Journal of Prison Law* 6: 231–63.

Mertens, D. J. 2001. Pregnancy outcomes of inmates in a large county jail setting. *Public Health Nursing* 18: 45–53.

Morash, M., T. Bynum, and B. Koons. 1998. Women offenders: Programming needs and promising approaches. Washington, DC: U.S. Department of Justice, National Institute of Justice. http://www.ncjrs.org/pdffiles/171668.pdf (accessed May 5, 2004).

National Women's Law Center. 1995. Women in prison fact sheet. Washington DC: The Center.

Resnick, J., and N. Shaw. 1981. *Prison Law Monitor* 3, no. 3/4: 57, 68, 83, 89, 104, 115.

Safyer, S. M., and L. Richmond. 1995. Pregnancy behind bars. *Seminars in Perinatology* 19: 314–22.

Shackling of women in labor. 2004. Doula World Site. http://doula.ws/prison.html (accessed March 1, 2004).

Siefert, K., and S. Pimlott. 2001. Improving pregnancy outcomes during imprisonment: A model residential care program. *Social Work* 46: 125–37.

Understanding prison health care: Women's health. 2002. Project funded by Stanford School of Medicine Arts and Humanities Medical Scholars Program. http://www.movement building.org/prisonhealth/womens.htm (accessed March 1, 2004).

Wismont, J. M. 2000. The lived pregnancy experience of women in prison. *Journal of Midwifery and Women's Health* 45: 292–300.

Young, R. L. 1977. Supreme Court report. *American Bar Association Journal* 63: 91–104.

11

Reproductive Health among Incarcerated Women

JOHN CLARK

There is no doubt that the rapid rise in the numbers of individuals incarcerated in the United States over the past several years has been a challenge to all correctional professionals in every facet of the correctional industry. Given the magnitude of the increasing numbers coupled with the fact that health care issues for female prisoners have traditionally been an afterthought of male-oriented correctional officials, there is no wonder that female offenders have and are receiving health care services that fail to adequately address the totality of reproductive health. In fact, it is only in recent years that the issue of prenatal care has been perceived as a high priority and provided as an essential service for the pregnant inmate. And, as the provision of prenatal health services becomes more accessible, basic reproductive health services for incarcerated women aged fourteen through forty-four need to be reorganized and provided in such a fashion that they also can be delivered cost effectively and efficiently.

In order to accomplish this task, it is vital to draw upon the experiences and efforts of providers of prenatal and reproductive health services in the free community. In this regard, there are two highly recommended offerings to be used as basic references for those who are developing, reviewing, and revising reproductive health services. They are the guidelines published by the American College of Obstetrics and Gynecology for prenatal care and for women's health care services (ACOG 2002a and b).

Next, it is crucial to understand and accept the principle that jails and prisons are uniquely different and at the same time very similar. It is important to be knowledgeable about the operational characteristics and the clinical morbidity and mortality in both types of institutions. As delivery systems for any type of health care service are developed, there are many policies, procedures, protocols, and forms available for use specific to this environment so it is not necessary to reinvent the wheel. However, because each system/agency has some unique characteristics, there is a need to fine tune and tailor policies for the individual facility/agency.

Intake Screening

The importance of intake screening in both jail and prison settings cannot be over emphasized, as this is the one best opportunity to proactively evaluate potential problems and to implement steps to avert disaster. The entire intake process is fraught with the urgency to get people into the system, classified, ready for court, and assigned appropriate housing. Linked with the fear and anxiety of being incarcerated, getting detailed health information is not always at the top of the priority list for either staff or patients. Therefore, it is imperative that we take advantage of the opportunity to gather important information at the time of booking. The most widely used correctional health care standards stress the efficacy of using a well-developed screening tool with a minimal number of questions to identify anyone in need of health care services or at risk for suicide or exacerbation of mental illness (National Commission on Correctional Health Care 2003). Most of these screening tools inquire about medical problems, current medications, hospitalizations, communicable diseases, and thoughts of harming one's self. In the case of the female inmate, this list obviously leaves the area of reproductive health unexplored for potential problems.

When we consider the fact that up to 80 percent of the females arrested may be chronic substance abusers and under the influence of illegal drugs at the time of arrest, and given the fact that many of these abused substances affect the regularity of the menstrual cycle, it is not unusual for an arrestee to have no clue as to the last normal menstrual cycle and whether there is a possibility of an unknown pregnancy. As a part of the intake process, it is necessary to establish a good baseline reproductive history. This can be accomplished fairly simply, although not ideally, by asking a few well-structured questions. A case example follows:

- gravity (how many pregnancies) = 6
- parity (how many live births) = 4
- last normal monthly period (LNMP) = 7/1/2004
- last monthly period (LMP) = 7/1/2004
- birth control method, if any = none
- C/O (complaints of) = none
- medications = none

One of the important tasks in the practice of medicine is that of concisely describing or defining the patient and their problems in a systematic manner, which in turn helps organize our thoughts and actions especially in situations where it is very busy and multiple tasks must be completed such as screening, booking, classification, and housing. Using the aforementioned format for sum-

marizing the patient's overview provides a good baseline for evaluating reproductive health needs and establishing appropriate priorities for care giving. Given the
sample information above, we have a "thirty-four-year-old Caucasian female, who
has had six pregnancies with four live births. The patient's last menses and last
normal menses was on July 1, 2004 [we will assume that the date of this sample
assessment is August 26, 2004], and she is currently not using any contraceptive
method, nor is she taking any prescribed medication. She presents with no complaints at this time."

The health professional who reviews the intake information can then make
the appropriate determination of which steps to take next, including ruling out
whether the inmate may be pregnant by doing a urine and/or blood pregnancy
test. Irrespective of the test results, it is important at this point to assess what
prescription medications the client may be taking as well as taking a good drug
and alcohol use history. Drug use is so prevalent that the practitioner must be
comfortable asking the patient direct questions regarding addictive substance
use. It is most helpful if such questions are included on the intake medical screening and history form.

As we go through this process of gathering and processing information, there
are a few important things to remember:

- Many of the arrests involving female detainees are related to drug use and
  prostitution. Many abused substances are morphologically similar to the hormones that control the reproductive cycle. Therefore, it is important to rule
  out/confirm pregnancy.
- Drug use is very commonplace in our society.
- Most abusers are poly drug abusers.
- Fetal wastage in patients who withdraw from opiates "cold turkey" approaches
  50 percent.

In lieu of the principles and assertions established thus far, there must be
equal concern at intake screening to the linkage between drug use, prostitution,
and communicable diseases. For this reason, normally in the correctional environment we ask about tuberculosis, HIV, hepatitis, and sexually transmitted diseases in general. There is a need to make an in-depth assessment about genital
herpes, gonorrhea, chlamydia, syphilis, and human papillomavirus. Many of the
items here can be included as a part of the health assessment because of the need
to collect specimens and samples, which cannot always be done at intake screen-
ing/booking.

Once again, it does not matter if it is a jail or a prison:

- Receipt of intake screening is the best opportunity to begin the process of
  providing reproductive health services.
- Review the clinical morbidity and mortality of the female inmates in your
  agency (reviewing several years is best).

- Take a basic reproductive history (develop a format and ensure that the persons doing the screening are trained).
- Take a basic substance abuse history.
- Focus on communicable diseases that impact the reproductive tract.

Initial Health Assessment

In most jails and prisons, the receiving/intake process is very hectic and is not the best environment in which to conduct an in-depth assessment of the clients' health status. The conventional thinking is that this type of comprehensive assessment should be performed near the two-week point in one's incarceration. There are, however, some jurisdictions that perform the assessment sooner for a variety of reasons. The important factor is that this health assessment is intended to be above and beyond the cursory screening at the time of intake. If a facility is able to accomplish this level of assessment at intake, then the goal and objective of the complete health assessment will be met.

It is very clear from looking at anecdotal data regarding the deaths of female prisoners that there are specific concerns that should be reviewed as a part of the initial health assessment and annual examination. These concerns are also important in the jail setting, given lifestyle behaviors and limited access to health maintenance services prior to incarceration. In some jail and the prison environments, the ability to conduct a complete assessment after two weeks of incarceration is much more conducive to getting information than during the initial booking/screening process. In addition, the patient has more time and opportunity to focus on details important to medical problems and personal health care. Keep in mind that the issues and concerns discussed here are items that should be reassessed on an annual basis as incarceration continues.

Much of the initial health assessment/annual examination should focus on metabolic, surgical, and infectious problems and how they may impact the reproductive system. Again, a well-structured historical review can identify most of the potential factors that require in-depth evaluation and follow-up. Unfortunately, in many correctional settings, the provider designated to provide care for the female inmate is not a trained women's health care practitioner and in many instances is not interested in or oriented to assessing the reproductive system. Delivery of service is much more effective when whoever provides this care has a vested interest in reproductive health. Whoever is the care provider, a thorough history and review of systems should be completed and a panel of laboratory tests performed as indicated. It should also be kept in mind that women are just as susceptible to the same problems and risks as the male patients, especially with regard to cardiovascular disease, diabetes, and hyperlipidemia. In reviewing over 400 in-custody deaths at the Los Angeles County jail during the author's nineteen years as the chief medical officer there, it is well documented that over 70 percent of in-custody deaths occur in that 25 percent portion of the inmate population that are over forty years of age, and this clearly suggests that this over-forty population warrants a higher level of both intake screening and health assessment/ annual examination (Los Angeles County Sheriff's Department 2000).

The initial health assessment/annual examination specific for the female inmate should include at least the following:

SCREENING FOR ABNORMAL CERVICAL CYTOLOGY

The primary objective for cervical screening is to exclude the presence of invasive carcinoma. This should be followed by (1) pelvic examination, (2) repeat cytology as indicated, (3) colposcopic examination as indicated, and (4) endocervical curettage as indicated.

EVALUATION FOR BREAST DISORDERS

- Elicit a history related to breast disorders inclusive of (1) family history, (2) duration, onset, signs, and symptoms, (3) menstrual and reproductive history, (4) hormone use, (5) dietary habits, and (6) breast implants
- breast examination
- educate, counsel, and teach self breast examination
- referral as indicated
- mammography as indicated
- referral and follow-up as indicated.

SEXUALLY TRANSMITTED DISEASES

- elicit detailed history
- counsel effectively on strategies to prevent infections
- screen, diagnose, and treat
- adhere to local regulations regarding screening and reporting
- adhere to Centers for Disease Control and Prevention (CDC) guidelines for treatment
- counsel regarding partner notification. (CDC 2002; ACOG 2002b)

GYNECOLOGIC PROBLEMS

There are numerous medical and surgical conditions related to the reproductive health of female inmates that will present from time to time, and as a correctional health professional, it is recognized that even in the best of circumstances with the maximum amount of resources, every service cannot be provided at the facility in the correctional institution. There are, however, several things that each agency can do to ensure that there are policies and practices in place to address these problems in a timely fashion.

- First and foremost, the level of sensitivity and awareness to reproductive health care issues must be raised to a significantly higher level among all correctional professionals (executive, middle management, and line staff).

- Correctional health professionals and correctional staff with health-related responsibilities (such as intake/booking screening) must receive specific training related to recognizing and obtaining help for potentially serious gynecological problems such as pelvic inflammatory disease, genital trauma, lower genital tract infections (vaginitis), miscarriages, ectopic pregnancy, and abnormal vaginal bleeding.
- Specific policies, procedures, and protocols should be developed to address access to commonly required measures, such as (1) aspiration of breast cyst, (2) biopsies, (3) cervical colposcopy, (4) cryosurgery, (5) culdocentesis, and (6) abscess incision and drainage and so forth.

Problematic Reproductive Health Issues

There are several issues that present themselves that require a significant degree of forethought and planning. Frequently these issues involve interagency negotiations, legal opinions, and specific financial arrangements. It is absolutely essential that the correctional health care professional who is the responsible health authority for the correctional agency is knowledgeable in regard to the regulations that govern correctional institutions in that jurisdiction. In addition, one must be familiar with all professional standards that impact on the delivery of services in the specific correctional environment. Since corrections is a very litigious environment, it is not unusual that the health authority must seek legal counsel on occasion from the county/state attorney on these situations. Fortunately, in the author's case as the chief medical officer for the Los Angeles County Sheriff's Department, an excellent working relationship with the attorneys assigned to the sheriff's department has been developed over the years; and as questions and situations arose, we were able to craft thoughtful solutions, responses, and policies that were legally sound and defendable. The message here is clear: to the extent possible, forge a positive working relationship with your legal team/resources, and as you problem solve, ensure that your work gets reviewed and approved by counsel.

Pregnancy Termination

The first scenario that should be addressed is pregnancy termination. As a fundamental principle established by the American College of Obstetricians and Gynecologists, "if a pregnancy is to be terminated, it should be performed safely and as early as possible." A woman has the right to choose to have a pregnancy terminated, and access to this service should be unencumbered by obstacles such as

- bans on public funding for abortion
- bans on specific procedures
- lack of availability of practitioners
- mandatory waiting periods, and
- parental notification or consent. (ACOG 2002b)

Each agency should develop a written policy on this issue, taking into consideration the jurisdiction's penal code and the written opinion of counsel. Once this is accomplished, a procedure for carrying out the policy must be written, detailing what steps must be taken and how these services will be reimbursed. I would advise any agency providing these services to ensure that they are performed off-site, away from the institution by another agency. The use of an outside agency ensures that the procedures are done in a medically safe environment and decreases the perception of any coercion on the part of correctional medical staff. These policies will require some significant sit-down negotiations and annual review. Remember, this is a very controversial, highly political subject, and each agency's practice needs to be defendable from every angle.

Methadone Withdrawal/Maintenance for the Pregnant Inmate

On occasion, your system may be confronted with an inmate who is pregnant and is an opiate addict, and who may be enrolled in a methadone maintenance program or at risk for withdrawing "cold turkey" from opiates. While this is largely an issue related to prenatal care services, sometimes a patient may elect to terminate her pregnancy and will still need some degree of management of the addiction problem. To this end, the agency policy on methadone maintenance should be comprehensive, addressing each of these contingencies. There are several dilemmas the agency must resolve, including but not limited to

- applying to the Drug Enforcement Agency for a license to prescribe and dispense methadone (a complex and difficult process in and of itself)
- providing/arranging for an acute hospital setting to facilitate detoxification from opiates and initiation of methadone maintenance
- choosing which methodology/regime for opiate detoxification and methadone maintenance to achieve the best possible prenatal outcome. It is highly recommended that each agency review the current literature as well as survey the professional community to keep these protocols up to date and in line with the community standard of practice.
- ensuring a mechanism to provide maintenance medication through a certified program in the community in the absence of a license to prescribe methadone
- exploring the alternatives to incarceration for the pregnant offender when the agency is not equipped to manage these issues.

Again, one of the key parts of this process is review by counsel to ensure that the policy has a sound legal basis in addition to sound clinical principles. Management staff must affirm that safeguards are in place to prevent methadone in the facility from becoming problematic.

Transsexual/Transgender Issues

Sexual identification can and will be a problem when it comes to correctional facilities. Many of the difficulties with this dilemma are custodial and legal in terms of classification and housing, and in some cases the health provider will be asked to make the call as to whether they are dealing with a male or female inmate. Needless to say, having to make this call in the middle of the night is not always the best circumstance in which to make a quality, sound decision. For the most part, these issues must be resolved based on the facts of the case, the nature of the offense, and the state of surgical transition from one gender to the other.

Most often the health care provider is asked by the client to prescribe hormonal therapy to help facilitate the nonsurgical development of breasts. While one could simply say yes or no, there is a great chance that either answer will subject correctional agency to litigation. On the one hand, there is the correctional health care standard of "continuity of care" (that is, if a patient is receiving a legally prescribed treatment from a licensed physician in the community, then it is a violation of the inmate's civil rights to refuse to continue this medication while the patient is incarcerated). On the other hand, it is well known that there are serious potential side effects and complications that may result from this type of hormonal therapy. If we fail to verify that this treatment is a part of a sexual reassignment protocol, and that the patient has had informed consent, are we negligent in our duty as caregivers to provide adequate informed consent? Formulating sound policy is essential to ensure that we can defend the position that we establish for the agency on these issues.

Family Planning/Emergency Contraception

It is not uncommon to screen inmates into the system (jail) who indicate that they are taking birth control pills for contraception and desire to continue, particularly if they have been free of problems and complications. When the provider writes a script for birth control pills, the provider may be questioned as to why they are spending money for a medication that the patient will not need in jail. As we all know, the jail is a high volume/high turnover environment and many inmates are in the system for only a few days. Once again, the principle of continuity of care comes into effect. Moreover, questions of this nature show that there is a lack of understanding how these medications work. This is an opportunity to raise the level of awareness about reproductive health issues. As the female inmate population growth rate continues, and as the penal system continues to undergo a number of reforms, there will be many discussions regarding programming for inmates and parallel gender-related services for male and female inmates. For example, should conjugal visitation, which for many years has been afforded to male prisoners, be available for female offenders? If so, what is the role and responsibility of the health provider to provide access to contraceptive methods? Once again, these are issues that require thoughtful development and legal review. Beyond the contraceptive purpose, it is important to understand and articulate to others the fact that birth control pills (hormones) are often used to manage reproductive problems such as frequent irregular uterine bleeding. The bottom line is the recognition that a comprehensive selection of contraceptive methods should and must be available to female inmates. Equally important is ensuring that there are provisions for patient counseling and education as it pertains to family planning, the anatomy and physiology of pregnancy, parenting, and domestic violence.

A brief word is necessary about emergency contraception ("morning-after pill"). Since the incorporation of the morning-after pill in standard contraceptive practices, there have been significant changes in the timelines of the initial ingestion of the first dose from within 72 hours to within 120 hours (five days) of intercourse. Several types of emergency contraceptives are available in the United States. The copper-containing intrauterine device (IUD) is a nonhormonal method that can also be used for emergency contraception. There may be a rare instance in a jail or prison where an inmate has had unprotected sexual intercourse within 120 hours of incarceration and may require counseling regarding the risks of sexually transmitted diseases and pregnancy. This education and counseling should include providing the option of emergency contraception should the patient request or desire such. If possible, this should be prescribed within the first 120 hours, and the patient should be evaluated for pregnancy if menses has not occurred within twenty-one days after emergency contraception.

In summary, it is very clear that the female inmate has many health issues that are not addressed in an organized fashion, and while there has been some emphasis on the importance of determining whether an inmate is pregnant and then providing adequate prenatal care, much remains to be accomplished towards providing reproductive health services. Perhaps the most formidable task is raising the level of awareness about women's reproductive health care issues and convincing the decision makers/resource allocators that the investment of appropriate funding will positively impact the quality of the services we provide and represent a major step toward proactive risk management.

REFERENCES

American College of Obstetricians and Gynecologists (ACOG). 2002a. *Guidelines for Perinatal Care,* 5th ed. Washington, DC: ACOG.

American College of Obstetricians and Gynecologists (ACOG). 2002b. *Guidelines for Women's Health Care,* 2nd ed. Washington, DC: ACOG.

Centers for Disease Control and Prevention. 2002. CDC Sexually Transmitted Disease Guidelines. Atlanta: CDC.

Los Angeles County Sheriff's Department. 2000. *Executive Summary. Los Angeles: Los Angeles County Sheriff's Department, Medical Services.*

National Commission on Correctional Health Care. 2002. *National Commission on Correctional Health Care for Juvenile Facilities.* Chicago, IL: NCCHC.

National Commission on Correctional Health Care. 2003a. *National Commission on Correctional Health Care Standards for Jails.* Chicago, IL: NCCHC.

National Commission on Correctional Health Care. 2003b. *National Commission on Correctional Health Care Standards for Prisons.* Chicago, IL: NCCHC.

PART FOUR

Infectious Diseases

12

Tuberculosis

No Longer the "White Plague"

SHARON BAUCOM
KAREN BAUCOM
PAULA BROWN
HAROLD MOUZON

If the first woman God ever made was strong enough to turn the world upside down all alone, these women together ought to be able to turn it back and get it right-side up again. And now that they are asking to do it, the men better let them!

—Sojourner Truth, Ain't I a Woman?

Sojourner Truth, an African American former slave and outspoken advocate of women's and civil rights, gave her famous Ain't I a Woman? speech at the 1851 Women's Convention. Her words of empowerment have inspired black women and poor people the world over to this day. As an abolitionist and a feminist, Truth defied the notion that slaves were male and women white, expounding a fact that still bears repeating: among blacks, there are women; among women, there are blacks.

Never more cogent today are her words as they relate to the incarcerated population, as among inmates there are women, and among women, there are those of color who are shackled worldwide by an ancient killer once known as the white plague. This disease, tuberculosis, is preventable and 90 percent curable when treated with the appropriate antibiotics.

This chapter will review the global and national impact of tuberculosis on the health of women. The pathophysiological, epidemiological, transmission, and treatment challenges associated with tuberculosis for incarcerated women will also be discussed. The potential impact of gender disparity and cultural bias on women of color behind bars will also be a component of this discussion.

TB: The Comeback Bug

Tuberculosis has been described as "the comeback bug." Although many attribute the long-standing decline of TB to the discovery of antituberculin drug therapy, chroniclers of the history of the disease observed that TB rates declined dramatically during the nineteenth and first half of the twentieth century. This was well before the discovery of streptomycin.

The antibiotic era only slightly accelerated the reduction in tuberculosis. Many theorists suggest that significant improvements in the social environment— better housing, nutrition, and sanitation—were largely responsible for the long-term decline in TB. This theory also explains the long-recognized correlation between lower socioeconomic status and high rates of tuberculosis (Gostin 1995).

A thorough understanding of the role of overcrowding and underventilated congregate facilities in the spread of TB infection, along with the recognition of the nuances of the correctional site itself as a potential breeding environment for TB, allowed public health and correctional health care workers to recognize the need to work more closely together to identify and treat aggressively in a most holistic manner the women we serve in correctional settings (Gostin 1995).

Global and National Impact

Thirty-three percent of the world's population is infected with TB. There are 8 million new cases of TB yearly and 2 million deaths. In most of the world, more men than women are diagnosed with TB and die from it (Uplekar, Rangan, and Ogden 1999). Worldwide, tuberculosis is the single biggest killer of young women of childbearing age (Reichman and Tanne 2001; World Health Organization n.d.). Tuberculosis represents 9 percent of deaths of women between the ages of fifteen and forty-four globally compared with 3 percent for HIV. Of the world's 6 billion people, 2 billion are infected with latent TB, including 15 million in the United States. Of those in the United States, 4 to 7 percent are in correctional facilities.

In 1993, tuberculosis was declared a global health emergency by the World Health Organization (WHO). TB had progressed almost unabated in many parts of the world (Gostin 1995; WHO n.d.). The U.S. Public Health Service Tuberculosis Program was first created in 1944, when there were over 126,000 reported cases of TB in the United States. Industrialized countries had experienced some decline in the burden of the disease by 5.6 percent each year from 1953 to 1985 (Gostin 1995).

Correctional facilities in all countries have recognized the association of tuberculosis and other infectious diseases. Outbreaks of TB in prisons in Russia, Spain, China, and India as well as other countries have been seen throughout this century. Russia continues to reject the global standard for TB treatment (WHO n.d.). U.S. prisons saw a resurgence of TB in the mid-1980s, coincident with the growth of the HIV epidemic. TB and AIDs are copromoters of each other and are considered "deadly twins" (Reichman and Tanne 2001). In the New York State correctional system, the incidence rate of TB increased sevenfold between 1976 and 1986. Because of the increase, the rate of TB in New York City approached the incidence of tuberculosis in parts of sub-Saharan Africa (Centers for Disease Control and Prevention [CDC] 2003a).

TB, Poverty, and Gender

As the greatest single infectious cause of death for women, the magnitude of the global TB epidemic is enormous (WHO n.d.). One finds a profound synergy between TB, poverty, and gender in incarcerated women of color (Gostin 1995). The association of overcrowed living environments, homelessness, foreign birth/immigration, stress, alcoholism, malnourishment, substance abuse, cigarette smoking, indoor air pollution, and heightened exposure to coinfections such as HIV or HCV through shared high-risk behavior with the transmission of TB is overwhelming from a public health perspective.

Tuberculosis was once a universal affliction that was the leading cause of death in Europe. It was also called the "social leveler" because it affected all races and social and economic classes (Gostin 1995). Eleanor Roosevelt, a social activist and widow of President Franklin D. Roosevelt, died of drug-resistant TB in 1962. She spent a lot of time among the poorest groups of citizens in this country— foreign-born, ethnic, and minority populations—championing their rights (Reichman and Tanne 2001).

Today, as noted, tuberculosis disproportionately burdens ethnic and racial minorities. Inner cities' homelessness rates range from 18 to 79 percent. These citizens are in daily contact with other individuals who are also at higher risk for TB. The lack of a fixed residence, multiple health issues, and erratic behavior related to substance abuse as well as depression or schizophrenia undermine compliance opportunities on all levels for follow-up care from health care workers. In fact, the impact of poverty among non-white females worldwide, and among incarcerated women in particular, is more intractable. The burden of ill health makes women more susceptible to more infectious diseases attributable to poverty of which TB remains a primary one. Among the leading threats to women's health, TB may be the most affordably controllable disease (WHO n.d.).

Racial and Ethnic Disparity

U.S.-born non-Hispanic blacks comprise the largest number of TB cases among both foreign-born populations and U.S.-born. U.S.-born non-Hispanic blacks represent 46.7 percent of TB cases in U.S.-born persons and 25 percent of all cases of TB. Among U.S.-born racial and ethnic populations, rates of tuberculosis among non-Hispanic blacks were 7.5 times higher and 2.1 times higher respectively than those among whites and Hispanics, the two other U.S.-born groups that account for the majority of TB cases (CDC 1992).

Five states—California, Florida, Illinois, New York, and Texas—accounted for 52.5 percent of cases and 68 percent of the overall decrease in the number of cases. Case rates declined an average of 50 percent from 1992 to 2002 (CDC 2003a). In the nation's largest correctional systems—California, Florida, New York, and Texas—foreign-born prisoners make up a significant number of the total detainees (Bick 2002).

In 2002, for the first time, TB cases among foreign-born persons accounted for the majority of TB cases in the United States at 51 percent (those born in Mexico 24 percent of the cases, Philippines 11.3 percent, Vietnam 8.6 percent). Despite a 68 percent decline in rates from 1992, however, U.S.-born non-Hispanic blacks in 2002 continue to have the highest TB rate of any U.S.-born racial ethnic population (CDC 1992).

TB and Its Relationship to Correction's Ethnic Minorities

African American women are seven to eight times more likely to be incarcerated in their lifetime than white females (Chicago Legal Advocacy for Incarcerated Mothers 2000). Rates of TB among incarcerated females reflect the racial and ethnic disparity found in the general population. Nationally, the rate of active TB cases in incarcerated men and women is 100 times greater than that of the general population (Bick 2002). So although the social and environmental factors previously referenced have been identified with the resurgence of TB, the most common denominators among the victims of tuberculosis that incarcerated women share are race, gender, poverty, and drugs.

Prison Overcrowding and Race

The dramatic growth in women's prison population has contributed to making the particular needs of incarcerated women and TB prevention a priority. A disproportionate number of women of color (who are usually previous victims of homelessness, alcohol, cigarettes, drugs, HIV/AIDS, and violence) are housed in overcrowded conditions in prisons and jails and, along with children, represent the indigent among the affluent in this country. Since 1995, the female population for prisons has grown at an average rate of at least 10 percent in thirteen states (Harrison and Beck 2002).

Twenty-two states reported operating correctional facilities at 100 percent or more of their highest capacity. California and Montana, reported operating at 91 percent over their lowest previously reported capacity, had the highest percent of capacity occupied (Harrison and Beck 2002). Female incarceration rates reveal racial and ethnic disparities with non-Hispanic black females leading the groups. Black non-Hispanic females have an incarceration rate of 200 per 100,000. That is five times that of white non-Hispanic females (36 per 100,000) and three times that of Hispanic females (60 per 100,000). These differences were consistent across all age groups (Chicago Legal Advocacy for Incarcerated Mothers 2000). More than one-third of all female inmates in this country are held in three correctional systems. They are Texas (12,369), the Federal Bureau of Prisons (10,973), and California (9,921) (Harrison and Beck 2002).

Gender Insensitivity and Custody Challenges

Gender is what it means to be male or female and how that defines a person's opportunities, roles, responsibility, and relationships. The influence of gender on health and treatment in jails and prisons is similar as that experienced by women of color in our society at large. Social ills that affect women's lives spill over to the prisons that house them and shape the kind of problems they present to staff, the services they need, and their potential compliance with drug regimes.

Gender itself is not the cause of morbidity or mortality in TB. But it is a powerful indicator of disadvantage and a marker of the many factors that influence health and use of health services. Women's social histories and experiences prior to incarceration strongly affect their health needs, which in turn affect the manner in which the medical staff delivers its services (Ammar and Erez 2000).

The importance of gender in the epidemiology of TB, as well as its impact on access to treatment in an incarcerated setting, has been largely ignored previously. Gender was not just a missing factor in research; it was considered unnecessary (Uplekar, Rangan, and Ogden 1999). In May 1998, the Nordis School of Public Health convened an international research workshop on gender and TB. With the reemergence of TB onto the international and correctional communities already concerned with HIV and multiple-drug-resistant TB (MDR-TB), a national public health agenda has begun to focus on the role of gender for this disease (WHO n.d.). Medical staff who were advocating adherence when treating incarcerated women who have TB and/or HIV may find themselves negotiating with patients/inmates who have different agendas and who see the disease as an opportunity to barter, bargain/beg for other needs as a trade-off (Ammar and Erez 2000). These negotiations become harder under the conditions that can be demanded to treat a case of TB: a patient may have to be isolated for months, and it can be a challenge to convince inmates to participate in the medication regimen for that long.

The reason for the inmate's resistance to the approach to treatment may never be discovered. It could be anger related to a perceived loss of timely return to the social support system of the other women in her unit. It could also be the return of problems with power that haunted her on the outside, where so much energy was used maintaining a sphere of control. Submission in corrections is associated with loss of personal possessions and relationship positions that may protect against unwanted domination (Bloom and Owen 2002). Alpha females in prison control and conduct services that depict position of power within the matriarchy.

Precautions taken by corrections staff to prevent transmission result in repeated compromises of confidentiality in the treatment of TB as well as HIV. The stigma attached to any disease is much more devastating to women than to men, as it extends more often to her children and her family than males. Double standards regarding male and females within the African American and Hispanic ethnic groups prevail (Uplekar, Rangan, and Ogden 1999).

Even the times medications are administered contribute to an erosion of the dignity of the patient. Successful treatment means administering medications on a schedule, and a 4:30 a.m. dose time frequently means women inmates are not yet dressed before the doors open for an officer of either gender to deliver medication. The multiple assaults on the respect/dignity of incarcerated women is well known. These women come from backgrounds of sexual and physical abuse (Uplekar, Rangan, and Ogden 1999). Women inmates often have a basic lack of health education and comprehension regarding the impact of diseases on health. This adversely impacts the values attached to well-being and oftentimes impacts the understanding of the need to consent to treatment for TB or testing for HIV. The incarcerated female inmate may feel overwhelmed by the challenges posed by chronic diseases or other health conditions. TB treatment is not grasped as an opportunity for wellness but another burden while incarcerated. What is to be gained by treatment intervention from a public health perspective is oftentimes not embraced as valuable by the inmate, who is isolated and usually intimidated by just the pill load (Maruschak and Beck 2001).

Lack of respect is an issue seldom addressed, but it is often the guiding force behind resistance to treatment. If there is the perception that the inmate has not been treated fairly by the medical staff discussing treatment, the inmate who did not feel respected will withhold her cooperation, even if it means self-harm. This is because the lack of understanding regarding the health risk is lost in the cultural pathos that is part of the inmate's decision-making process. Staff who are unaware of the cultural issues may dismiss the resistance as attitude. That is why both gender and cultural sensitivity training is essential for those personnel who work with incarcerated women. The cultural interpretation of the reasons or motivations for staff to insist upon medication intervention may inhibit cooperation by the inmate. Even the difference of the economics of a provider who is of the same racial group may separate him or her from understanding the inmate. Regardless of the differences in the cultures, race, or ethnicity, all women inmates are expected to incorporate the gender-based norms, values, and behaviors of the dominate culture into their lives (Bloom and Owen 2002).

There is embarrassment for some females associated with the hacking up of sputum for smear and culture for a TB diagnosis. There is more stigma and shame in having to be isolated from others for females than males. On occasion, one may run into a "culture of silence," a tendency to suffer silently. A female inmate may perceive the constraints of communication with the medical staff as something that cannot repair the condition, so they do not report problems (Uplekar, Rangan, and Ogden 1999; Hudelson 1996).

For an inmate who has to be treated for TB, there is the loss of more than control. When isolating women under respiratory measures, we remove more than the opportunity of self-choice. Incarceration and respiratory isolation removes a vital source of support for women in crisis: other women. Gender differences regarding isolation are demonstrated in the attitude of males who would prefer to "tough it out" alone from their tribe. Women seek other female companionship when facing major stressors. Women inmates feel additional isolation socially that can become an opportunity for medical staff or a challenge (Uplekar, Rangan, and Ogden 1999).

Getting Infected: Drugs

Drug offenses accounted for the largest portion of the total growth of numbers of female inmates at 33 percent compared to 19 percent among male inmates. Injecting drug use and substance abuse, high-risk behavior, unprotected sex, and needle sharing account for the major routes of transmission of HIV virus to women. Injection drug users increase their risk for TB infection as well as HIV disease.

Drug abuse contributes to unemployment and homelessness. A number of women with mental health issues will use illicit substances to ward off depression or compensate for manic episodes through alcohol abuse. Crowded shelters or the streets become the haunts of these women. Depressed immune status along with malnourishment make someone more susceptible to infectious diseases. In addition, without help to enroll in public assistance or find employment, women may lapse into prostitution for food and a drug fix. They are much more likely to share needles with sexual partners or other women. Injecting drug use is one of the major routes of infection with the viruses that transmit HIV and hepatitis C.

Coinfection: HIV/AIDS

TB is the single biggest killer of people living with HIV/AIDS (Gostin 1995). TB and women of color have a strong association with HIV; African American women represent 64 percent of new infections with the virus that causes human immune deficiency. Injectable drug usage accounts for 25 percent cases of HIV among heterosexuals. There is a disparity in the rate and transmission of HIV that is gender and racial (CDC 1992).

There is evidence that the HIV epidemic is a major factor associated with the recent increase in TB cases. Immune suppression resulting from HIV infection allows a person with latent TB infection and newly infected persons to progress rapidly to clinical TB disease. The prevalence of HIV infection is higher among racial ethnic minorities than non-Hispanic whites. Clinical TB is more common in the HIV-infected minority population than among HIV-infected non-Hispanic whites.

In December 2000, there were 774,467 AIDS cases in the United States; of these 134,441 were women. There were 448,060 deaths related to HIV/AIDS; 66,448 were female (CDC n.d.).

In 1995–1996, the California Department of Corrections and the local health department investigated two outbreaks of drug-susceptible TB in a facility housing unit dedicated to HIV inmates. Each outbreak was linked via DNA fingerprinting of MTB isolates. Thirty cases of TB were diagnosed (Bick 2002). In 1999–2000 in a housing unit for HIV-infected prisoners, thirty-one prisoners and one medical student developed TB. TB among incarcerated women coinfected with HIV remains a major potential reservoir for outbreaks of drug-resistant TB.

Multiple-Drug-Resistant TB

The proportion of MDR-TB decreased from 3 percent of 17,684 cases in 1993 to 1 percent of 12,056 cases in 2000. However, the MDR cases in foreign-born persons increased from 31 percent in 1993 to 72 percent in 2000 (Bick 2002). The first documented transmission of MDR-TB occurrence in a correctional system was in New York prisons in 1991, when eight cases of MDR-TB were diagnosed. Seven of the cases were inmates who were all infected with HIV who had CD4 counts less than 60. All eight cases of MDR-TB died.

Resistance to TB medications can occur by random spontaneous mutation of the bacterial chromosome. However, in the correctional setting as well as public and private settings, the following scenarios are also associated with resistant strains of TB. Primary drug resistance occurs when a previously uninfected person becomes infected with organisms that are already resistant to one or more drugs, for this individual, the standard treatment will fail (CDC 2000). Secondary drug resistance results when there is sporadic dosing, suboptimal dosing, or ineffective anti-tuberculosis drug therapy. This can be related to

1. Inappropriate treatment regimes prescribed by private or public sector physicians
2. Poor compliance: the patient does not adhere to prescribed treatment regimes
3. Insufficient number of effective drugs in the regimen that allow the TB bacillus to survive, multiply, and become drug resistant
4. Multiple-Drug-Resistant TB associated with the immigration of persons from countries with high incidence of resistant TB already resistant to INH and/or rifampin
5. Patient with occult HIV infection with CD4 count < 100 placed on weekly or twice-weekly treatment instead of following the new CDC recommendations (CDC 2000; Chaisson 2003)

A Brief History of the Battle with TB

In 1882, Robert Koch discovered that consumption, an infectious disease, was caused by the rapid multiplication of the *Mycobacterium tuberculosis* bacillus and was transmitted from person to person through airborne particles. It was called consumption because those infected with it wasted away; it consumed the body. The devastation of this disease to communities globally led one official from the World Health Organization to describe it more recently as "Ebola with wings" because of how rapidly active TB cases could be transmitted among patients who were HIV infected and had low CD4 counts (Reichman and Tanne 2001).

Tuberculosis is an airborne disease, and human beings are the only known transmitters of it. It is transmitted when an individual with active disease in his lungs or laryngeal area sneezes, coughs, sings, speaks, or does anything that could propel droplets of sputum into the air. Because Koch showed that TB was spread person to person, early identification and isolation of infected people from others was one of the first lines of defense in protecting others from contracting the disease. Identification of people with tuberculosis became possible in 1890, when Koch developed the tuberculin skin test that could determine that someone was infected (Gostin 1995). The TB skin test is still used today. Up into the late 1970s, mass testing of adults and children for TB had been done. This was abandoned to allow for a more targeted approach by identification of high-risk groups of which incarcerated women are one. The nomenclature has been changed to reflect the change in approach. The phrase targeted tuberculin skin testing has replaced screening (CDC 2000; Maryland Department of Health and Mental Hygiene 2002a).

Antimicrobial Therapy

The development of biological agents to fight disease that was launched in 1929 by the isolation of penicillin was fortified in 1944 with the isolation of streptomycin by Selman Abraham Waksman. Its capacity to suppress one of the oldest and most vicious enemies of mankind led to an accelerated search for biological strategies to combat the TB epidemic (Gostin 1995).

Isoniazid (INH) prevention treatment was introduced in the 1950s to treat tuberculosis infection to prevent the development of the clinically active disease. Ethambutolin (EMB) soon followed, and the availability of rifampin and the rediscovery of pyrazinamide (PZA) in the 1960s and 1970s allowed for five front-line drugs to be taken in combinations. A new drug, Rifapentine (RPT), is similar to rifampin (RIF) but has a half-life of twenty hours. A weekly dosing schedule is possible because of this longer half-life. There are additional second-line drugs that are generally less effective and more toxic, but they serve important therapeutic functions when called upon.

To effectively control TB, it is very important to detect, isolate, and treat infectious cases as quickly as possible. There are several approaches appropriate in correctional settings that include

- the assignment of supervisory responsibility for TB control to nursing staff in partnership with doctors

- clear guidelines and protocols regarding the management of woman inmates who are suspected of infection and disease. These policies and procedures should be reviewed and revised with updates related to community and CDC standards.
- administrative measures that reduce the risk of exposure through symptom screening, TB isolation procedures, and prompt intervention and treatment of persons with TB disease
- engineering control methods to inhibit the spread and reduce the concentration of infectious droplet nuclei in the air via high-efficiency particulate air filtration (HEPA filtration), UV germicidal irradiation (UGV), and adequate ventilation systems
- personal respiratory protective equipment in areas where there is an increased risk of exposure to *M. tuberculosis,* such as isolation rooms
- medical staff and custody staff education on the signs and symptoms of tuberculosis. Education programs must reoccur periodically to combat staff turnover and complacency.
- guidelines for the prompt detection of persons who have symptoms suggestive of TB that include reception, screening, routine sick call. (Maryland Department of Health and Mental Hygiene 2002a)

Inmates who chronically cough and look sick to custody officers or medical staff are not always considered infectious for TB so a high index of suspicion is necessary to be successful in diagnosing cases.

Targeted Tuberculin Skin Testing (TST)

TB skin testing using the Mantoux tuberculin skin test (PPD) is the preferred method of testing for TB infection. It should be targeted towards high-risk populations who would benefit from treatment of latent TB infection (CDC 2000).

Correctional healthcare staff must be trained to administer and interpret the TST. Often times in transport of inmates between facilities or coming back into the system, there is no record of the test being administered. There are occurrences when an inmate says there was a reaction, describes the procedure for the test, and advises that she had a problem. There may be difficulty retrieving the record and/or there is no other documentation.

It is appropriate to repeat the test unless the inmate describes a blister or even sloughing at the site. A chest x-ray, along with a system review and risk factors for TB, should help determine if there is a need to do anything further if the TST cannot be repeated. The tuberculin skin test is a valuable tool but it is not perfect.

Do Not Rule Out Diagnosis Based on Negative Skin Test Results

Anergy is the absence of a reaction to the TB skin test. HIV infection, sarcoidosis, Hodgkins disease, steroids for asthma or other viral infections, as well as TB dis-

TABLE 12.1

False positive and negative reaction

Factors that May Cause False-Positive and False-Negative Reactions to the Tuberculin Skin Test

Type of Reaction	Possible Cause
False-positive	Nontuberculous mycobacteria
	BCG vaccination
False-negative	Anergy
	Recent TB infection
	Very young age (< 6 months old)
	Live-virus vaccination
	Overwhelming TB disease

Source: Centers for Disease Control and Prevention (2000)

ease itself can cause a negative reaction in 10 to 25 percent of patients. Inmates have other conditions that may hamper their responses to skin testing. The absence of a reaction does not rule out the diagnosis of TB infection or disease (CDC 2000). However, in some circumstances, testing for TB disease with chest radiographs or sputum smears may be more appropriate than testing for infection with the tuberculin skin test.

The example in corrections is high-turnover jails or when the objective is to identify persons quickly who have current pulmonary TB or when treatment for latent TB infection is not the primary goal. High-volume turnaround jails or prisons hold challenges regarding tracking down lab and x-rays, but every effort should be made to get old medical records and chest x-rays to aid in the evaluation of the patient. Electronic medical records or database retrieval of treatment histories would be helpful in any correctional institution. If the system does not have the IT support to facilitate records review, the relationship with city and state health departments offers opportunities for disease intervention specialists to help obtain records for some inmates.

The Bacilus Calmette-Guerin (BCG) Vaccine

In 1908 two French researchers developed a vaccine to prevent TB. The BCG vaccine is the most widely used vaccine in the world. The World Health Organization has recommended the BCG vaccine since 1950. It is a compulsory vaccine in 64 countries and officially recommended in 118 others. The vaccine does not prevent initial infection with TB. Rather, it boosts the cellular immune response to *M. tuberculosis* infection, which theoretically reduces the risk of developing active TB. BCG vaccination is not a contradiction for TST. The efficacy ranges from 0 to 80 percent with an average risk reduction of 50 percent. In the United States, BCG vaccination is not recommended because of the low incidence of infection with *M. tuberculosis*, the variability in the effectiveness, and the vaccine's interference with the ability to determine tuberculin reactivity. It should also not be used in inmates who are HIV positive.

However, foreign-born inmates who have had the vaccination who are given a TST and have induration considered positive for TB should be treated as having infection with *M. tuberculosis* after active TB disease has been ruled out. If the individual has other risk factors, apply the same guidelines for interpretation for individuals who have not been vaccinated. The evaluation and workup should proceed according to the guidelines provided by the Centers for Disease Control (Maryland Department of Health and Mental Hygiene 2002b).

Treatment for Latent TB Infection (LTBI)

Priority candidates who constitute high-risk groups, regardless of age, if TST positive, should be considered for treatment for latent TB infection (TLTBI) if there are no contraindications. These are the high-risk groups:

- close contacts with persons known or suspected to have TB
- foreign-born persons from areas where TB is common
- health care workers who serve high-risk congregate settings
- medically underserved, low-income populations
- high-risk racial or ethnic minority populations
- persons who inject illicit drugs
- children exposed to adults in high risk categories

HIV pre- and post-counseling and testing should be offered to all inmates known to have a positive tuberculin test result. A woman who is HIV positive or at high risk for HIV but whose status is unknown should be encouraged to complete a longer course of preventative therapy and should have chest x-ray and/or sputums to rule out active TB. Anergy testing is not recommended.

A clinical provider should examine every woman inmate who has a positive skin test reaction. There should be an emphasis placed upon the TB symptom review, chest x-ray, and HIV counseling and testing as well as a review of co-morbid disorders that could compromise treatment options or place the inmate at greater risk for adverse reactions.

Isoniazid given for six to twelve months has been the mainstay of treatment for LTBI in the United States for more than thirty years. However, the application of isoniazid for LTBI has been limited because of poor adherence due to the relatively long duration of treatment required and because of concerns about toxicity.

Therefore, there has been interest in the development of shorter, rifampin-based regimens as alternatives to isoniazid for the treatment of LTBI. During the past decade, a series of studies of "short-course" treatment of LTBI in persons with human immunodeficiency virus (HIV) infection has been undertaken.

Although a nine-month regimen of isoniazid is the preferred regimen for the treatment of LTBI, a six-month regimen also provides substantial protection and has been shown to be superior to placebo in both HIV-negative and HIV-positive persons. In some situations, treatment for six months rather than nine months may provide a more favorable outcome from a cost-effectiveness standpoint. Thus, based on local conditions, health departments or providers may conclude that a six-month rather than a nine-month course of isoniazid is preferred. Both the nine-month and six-month isoniazid regimens may be given intermittently (that is, twice weekly). When isoniazid is given intermittently, it should be administered only as directly observed therapy (DOT).

The two-month daily regimen of rifampin and pyrazinamide is recommended on the basis of a randomized trial of treatment of LTBI in HIV-infected persons that showed the two-month regimen to be similar in safety and efficacy to a twelve-month regimen of isoniazid. Twice-weekly treatment with rifampin and pyrazinamide for two or three months may be considered when alternative regimens cannot be given. This intermittent regimen should always be administered as DOT. Some experts recommend that the two-month regimen of daily rifampin and pyrazinamide also be given by DOT, which can consist of five observed and two self-administered doses each week. In situations in which rifampin cannot be used (for example, HIV-infected persons receiving protease inhibitors), rifabutin may be substituted (CDC 2000).

American Thoracic CDC Guidelines

Directly observed therapy (DOT) can facilitate the compliance of women inmates with TB. DOT involves providing the anti-tuberculin drugs personally to the patient and watching as he/she swallows the medication. It is the preferred core management strategy for all patients with tuberculosis (American Thoracic Society et al. 2003, 615; Panel on Clinical Practices for the Treatment of HIV Infection 2001; Ruby 2002). In correctional settings:

- Staff will watch the inmate with TB swallow each dose of TB medication, making sure that no pills remain in the pill cup and that the inmate has not palmed or otherwise concealed the medications.
- The inmate will not be permitted to use his or her own cups or glasses to take TB medications.
- After observing pills being swallowed, staff will ask the inmate to talk to ensure that pills do not remain in the inmate's mouth and inspect his oral cavity.

- If the inmate is not present at the pill line, staff will follow up immediately to locate the inmate and ensure that doses of TB medications are not missed.

Often DOT is compromised by security. Shortages of staff or security levels of inmates may mean that corrections officials do not want to open the cell door or force nursing to administer the medication through a slat in the door or under the door. (This is not true DOT.) The number of doses of medication administered under DOT is five days in most public health sites, and patients may be given weekend doses to take on their own. Correction facilities order DOT drug therapy for seven days. CDC is counting five-day DOT equivalent to seven-day treatment (Panel on Clinical Practices 2001).

Treatment for latent TB infection should be given to pregnant inmates who have high-risk medical conditions, especially HIV infection, as soon as TB infection is documented and TB disease has been ruled out. This should be in concert with a high-risk ob/gyn consultant and an infectious disease HIV/TB consultant guiding and supporting the treatment interventions, labs, and medications (Ruby 2002).

HIV-infected inmates have the highest risk for developing TB including MDR-TB. DOT therapy with a nine-month regimen of isoniazide (INH) or a two-month regimen of rifampin/pyrazinamide daily or twice weekly is recommended. Some precautions prior to treatment of latent TB infection must be taken:

- treat high-risk females regardless of age
- do a thorough history and physical exam with gender-sensitivity-related questions and concerns raised
- determine if the female is at higher risk for adverse reactions, if there is previous history of treatment for TB infection or disease
- check for contraindications to particular treatment regimens such as previous INH-associated hepatic injury; history of severe adverse reaction to INH such as a drug fever, rash, or arthritis; or acute or unstable liver disease of any cause
- screen for HIV and hepatitis C and B along with routine biochemical screening, UA, pregnancy test, blood work, and chest x-ray
- determine if other chronic diseases are present
- enroll patient in chronic care clinic

On a monthly basis, throughout the entire period of therapy monitoring, the following should occur for inmates who are receiving DOT:

- education regarding signs and symptoms of TB disease and medication adverse reactions or side effects
- determine adherence to the prescribed regimen
- watch for signs and symptoms of hepatitis such as a combination of nausea, loss of appetite, vomiting, persistently dark urine, yellow skin or whites of the eyes, malaise, elevated temperature, abdominal tenderness in the right upper quadrant

- watch for signs of neurotoxicity due to INH such as paresthesia of the hands or feet

Some evidence suggests that women, particularly black and Hispanic, are at increased risk for fatal hepatitis associated with INH. This risk may be increased during the postpartum period (CDC 2000). Some mild asymptomatic elevation of liver enzymes will occur in 10 to 20 percent of the people taking INH. These abnormalities tend to resolve even if the INH is continued. One should consider discontinuation of the drug, however, if the measurement exceeds three to five times the upper limit of normal or if the patient reports symptoms of adverse reactions.

Tuberculosis Disease

Signs and symptoms of TB disease may include hemoptysis, cough, night sweats, weight loss, fatigue, chest pain, and chills. Extra pulmonary TB can have site-specific symptoms and represent 15 to 25 percent of TB cases depending on the organs affected. Atypical chest x-ray and symptoms in HIV-infected inmates is not unusual. The following inmates are at higher risk of developing TB diseases:

- HIV positive
- recently infected with TB
- history of injecting illicit drugs
- history of inadequately treated TB

The Role of Sputum Analysis and Culture in the Diagnosis of TB Disease

Suspected cases of pulmonary TB should have at least three sputum specimens examined for AFB (acid-fast bacilli) smear and culture on three consecutive days. It is preferred in corrections and elsewhere to collect sputum in the early mornings. Provisions should be made for individuals who require assistance in situations where the sputum has to be induced. Staff should use appropriate protective respiratory protection. If there is not a sputum induction booth, then an AFB isolation room can be used. The specimens should go to the lab as soon as possible. If immediate transportation is not available, they can be refrigerated for a day.

A smear of the sputum that reveals acid-fast bacillus allows a consideration of active TB diagnosis. Other mycobacteria can be mistaken for *M. tuberculosis,* including *M. bovis* and *M. africanum* (Maryland Department of Health and Mental Hygiene 2002a; Sprinson, Lawton, and Flood 2003). DNA probes, NAP inhibition tests, or liquid chromatography tests like HPLC are used to assist in the identification of the AFB-positive organism.

State labs may do conventional tests that yield results in six to twelve weeks or may use methods that give results in ten to fourteen days (Maryland Department of Health and Mental Hygiene 2002). Several tests can be used, but a positive culture for *M. tuberculosis* confirms the diagnosis of TB. One should not wait for confirmation to initiate treatment as the clinical signs and symptoms should drive the decision to treat. However, it is vital that drug-sensitivity testing be done on all positive cultures. Cultures and sensitivities are mandatory components of sputum specimen analysis regardless of AFB smear results.

Follow-up sputum examinations are important to assess response to treatment as well as infection. In the first two months of therapy, one to three sputum exams should be collected on three different days at least monthly or a demonstration of culture conversion from positive to negative by three consecutive negative cultures should be documented before changes in approach to treatment should be considered (CDC 2000; Maryland Department of Health and Mental Hygiene 2002a).

Abacillary TB

Just as a negative smear does not rule out TB, negative sputum cultures do not preclude a diagnosis of TB disease. If there is a clinical suspicion of TB with clinical signs, system review, and x-ray changes consistent with the disease, then do not delay treatment irrespective of a negative smear and/or culture. If there is clinical improvement of the chest x-ray and the previous signs and symptoms that presented as part of the complex, continue treatment for this culture-negative tuberculosis for a total of four months (Maryland Department of Health and Mental Hygiene 2002a).

Again, the support of the state and local health department TB specialists cannot be emphasized enough. It is vital that the primary consultants use all of the modalities available to conference on females with these conditions. Telemedicine communication can help facilitate tertiary consultations without outside transport. There are mutual benefits that are particularly unique to corrections.

Drug Therapy for TB Disease

There are four recommended regimens for treating patients with tuberculosis caused by drug-susceptible organisms. Because of the relatively high proportion of adult patients with tuberculosis caused by organisms that are resistant to isoniazid, four drugs are necessary in the initial phase for the six-month regimen to be maximally effective. Thus, in most circumstances, the treatment regimen for all adults with previously untreated tuberculosis should consist of a two-month initial phase of isoniazid (INH), rifampin (RIF), pyrazinamide (PZA), and ethambutolin (EMB). If (when) drug susceptibility test results are known and the organisms are fully susceptible, EMB need not be included for "adult-type" (upper-lobe infiltration, cavity formation) tuberculosis. If PZA cannot be included in the initial phase of treatment, or if the isolate is resistant to PZA alone (an unusual circumstance), the initial phase should consist of INH, RIF, and EMB given daily for two months. (Examples of circumstances in which PZA may be withheld include severe liver disease, gout, and, perhaps, pregnancy.) EMB should be included in the initial phase of regimen 4 until drug susceptibility is determined.

The initial phase may be given daily throughout (regimens 1 and 4), daily for two weeks and then twice weekly for six weeks (regimen 2), or three times weekly throughout (regimen 3). For patients receiving daily therapy, EMB can be discontinued as soon as the results of drug susceptibility studies demonstrate that the isolate is susceptible to INH and RIF (American Thoracic Society et al. 2003). When the patient is receiving less-than-daily drug administration, expert opinion suggests that EMB can be discontinued safely in less than two months (that is, when susceptibility test results are known), but there is no evidence to support this approach.

Although clinical trials have shown that the efficacy of streptomycin (SM) is approximately equal to that of EMB in the initial phase of treatment, the increasing frequency of resistance to SM globally has made the drug less useful. Thus, SM is not interchangeable with EMB unless the organism is known to be susceptible to the drug or the patient is from a population in which SM resistance is unlikely.

The continuation phase of treatment is given for either four or seven months. The four-month continuation phase should be used in the large majority of patients. The seven-month continuation phase is recommended only for three groups: patients with cavitary pulmonary tuberculosis caused by drug-susceptible organisms and whose sputum culture obtained at the time of completion of two months of treatment is positive; patients whose initial phase of treatment did not include PZA; and patients being treated with once-weekly INH and rifapentine and whose sputum culture obtained at the time of completion of the initial phase is positive.

The continuation phase may be given daily (regimens 1a and 4a), two times weekly by DOT (regimens 1b, 2a, and 4b), or three times weekly by DOT (regimen 3a). For HIV-seronegative patients with noncavitary pulmonary tuberculosis (as determined by standard chest radiography) and negative sputum smears at completion of two months of treatment, the continuation phase may consist of rifapentine and INH given once weekly for four months by DOT (regimens 1c and 2b).

If the culture at completion of the initial phase of treatment is positive, the once-weekly INH and rifapentine continuation phase should be extended to seven months. All of the six-month regimens, except the INH-rifapentine once-weekly continuation phase for persons with HIV infection (Rating EI), are rated as AI or AII or BI or BII, in both HIV-infected and uninfected patients (CDC n.d.).

Special Clinical Conditions and Tuberculosis

Each case should be approached with the information regarding that specific inmate in collaboration with the specialists for these patients directly involved in care decisions. Medical staffs that consult for these specialists to come on site make the risks associated with custody transport staff missing the appointment or taking them on the wrong day less likely.

Renal Dialysis

Renal failure is a complicated condition that should be treatment-assisted with the consultant in renal disease and the dialysis center subcontracting with the correctional facility. On-site dialysis is the most desirable situation for correctional females. However, most dialysis centers will accommodate dosing medication post-dialysis. Custody officers are also trained in medication administration. Usually the nurse will administer the TB medications upon return to the site after each dialysis treatment, three times weekly.

The standard initiation and completion phases of TB treatment remain the same. The maximum for INH dosing is 900 mg at 15mg/kg, 600mg RIF at 10mg/kg, 25–30mg/kg for PZA and 15 mg/kg for EMB.

Pregnancy

In general, preventative therapy should not be given to pregnant women who are found to be tuberculin positive until after delivery. Although INH is considered safe to give to pregnant women in general, if a woman becomes pregnant while on treatment for latent TB infection the treatment is stopped except as noted below:

- close contacts to a person who has pulmonary/laryngeal TB and who is TST positive
- HIV positive and maybe TST negative or positive, but in close contact with an active TB case

A chest x-ray should be done on inmates who have symptoms suggestive of TB disease with the usual precautions taken for pregnancy. Post-first-trimester lower-risk TST-positive pregnant inmates should have a chest x-ray. Treatment should be in consultation with an infectious disease consultant or pulmonary specialist who is familiar with correctional medicine and TB where possible and always in conjunction with the local and state health departments. Pregnant women should not be placed on streptomycin because of potential harmful effects on the fetus. Pyrazinamide (PZA) should not be used routinely because of unknown effects on the fetus, except in the case of HIV-positive women. The small concentrations of TB drugs in breast milk do not have a toxic effect on nursing newborns, and breast-feeding should not be discouraged for inmates undergoing anti-TB therapy.

An infectious disease/TB expert is critical to resolve the potential complications associated with this pregnancy and TB. Because this combination of conditions is so complicated, one should make sure that the general considerations outlined for the approach to care in this chapter are not used as specific recommendations for treatment.

METHADONE. Pregnant inmates who have abused opiates may come into the system on methadone to protect the fetus from the stresses of withdrawal. Because of the interactions between rifampin and methadone, pregnant inmates on TB therapy with rifampin may require up to a 50 percent increase of their methadone while on treatment. One may have to titrate the dose upward by small increments every other day to prevent withdrawal symptoms. Jails without infirmaries may have to transport these inmates to places where twenty-four-hour nursing coverage is available during the first few weeks of treatment (Maryland Department of Health and Mental Hygiene 2002b).

HIV-POSITIVE INMATES. HIV-positive pregnant inmates who have TB risk transmitting HIV to infants when their HIV treatment is not appropriate during the pregnancy. It is imperative that an HIV specialist who understands TB and works well within the framework of the correctional physician and local health and state public health consults in her management (CDC 2000; Maryland Department of Health and Mental Hygiene 2002b).

The challenges associated with pill loads that may contribute to side effects create opportunities for nonadherence or missed doses. Direct Observed Therapy (DOT) is a critical component of management in this subpopulation as well as ongoing patient education.

HIV/TB Short-Course Therapy

HIV/AIDS Broward County Jail had a short-course project to determine the effectiveness of a targeted TST project to determine the effectiveness of a two-drug/two-month regimen on completion rates. From among 8,812 HIV infected persons receiving a TST, 242 (3 percent) were identified with LTBI from February 1999 to January 2003 and put on biweekly medication administration under DOT. Patients received either a rifabutin or a rifampin treatment regimen: 86 percent of the patients on rifabutin/pyrazinamide completed treatment, and 73 percent who received rifampin/pyrazinamide completed treatment for a combined completion rate of 82 percent. Ninety-three persons received INH for twelve months and 61 percent completed treatment.

Prior to the project's implementation, the previous five-year average of TB cases coinfected with HIV was 47.8 cases per year. The average has decreased over the three years since the project began to 33.6 cases per year. The project's conclusion was that targeted testing and treatment of a high-risk population is an effective TB prevention and control strategy. In addition, they concluded that along with the short-course therapy and DOT, the establishment of community partnerships was an essential component of an effective TB program (Murray et al. 2003).

Isolation Cell Admissions

TB suspects should be placed when possible in a respiratory isolation cell with negative airflow relative to other parts of the facility. The negative flow should be documented each shift to ensure proper airflow. Inmates as well as custody staff should receive education about the transmission of TB, the reasons for isolation, and the importance of staying in the room with the door shut. Engineering controls are based primarily on the use of adequate ventilation systems.

The lack of traditional incentives—vouchers for fast foods, phone cards, candy and so forth—for women in TB isolation can be overcome. The director of nurses and ID coordinator in collaboration with the medical director and the warden/custody staff can help promote compliance by making sure the following amenities are not denied while the patient is in isolation:

- no loss of "good time" (as infirmary settings sometimes preclude earning these points)
- dietary services that duplicate food choices found in the commissary; access to the commissary list
- access to children if parental rights have not been severed; flexibility when possible to accommodate family
- arrangements to spend time in the yard, mask and all (Maryland Department of Health and Mental Hygiene 2002)

Inmates who require transport who have TB infection should wear surgical masks that cover the mouth and nose during transport. They should also be given tissues and asked to cover their nose and mouth when coughing or sneezing to contain droplet nuclei before they are expelled into the air. The officers do not need to wear respiratory protection outside of TB isolation rooms (Maryland Department of Health and Mental Hygiene 2002).

High custody staff turnover supports incorporation of infectious disease and universal precautions as part of officer training in the curriculum as well as at roll call. Medical staff is often called in to educate jittery officers who worry that the inmate's mask will not protect them in transport even with the windows down in the car.

Case Management

Correctional facilities have a public health responsibility to be part of the surveillance system for state and local health departments who have the primary responsibility for prevention and control of TB. All cases of suspected TB disease or infection should be reported to the health department. Prevention and control efforts should include

- the identification and treatment of all inmates who have TB disease
- finding and evaluating inmates who have been in contact with TB patients to determine whether they have TB infection or disease and treating them appropriately
- testing high risk-groups for TB infection to identify candidates for treatment

of latent infection and to help ensure the completion of treatment (CDC 1996; Gibson 2003)

Jails and prison personnel may not always have an appreciation of the need to maintain documentation of who has been in what housing units with other female inmates prior to movement or relocation to other cells. In jails, inmates may move rapidly in groups from place to place including out to court, other housing units in separate buildings within the same complex, and worse, out into the community. To place inmate movement on hold while staff completes interviews and reviews for symptoms related to TB or to have to retest individuals and read TSTs creates tension between security and health care staff. It promotes anxiety among inmates as well. Inadequate number of isolation cells at some overcrowded female jails or prisons make transport of mask-wearing inmates an additional problem for containment of disease.

Chest x-ray ability may not be easily obtained. Changes of shift, lockdowns, and so forth create challenges for medical and public health officials who are working with custody to follow up on what inmates worked, ate, or played with the woman suspected of TB disease. Often the area for isolation is a single cell, and the mask-wearing female waiting to be transported is embarrassed and angry at the public humiliation associated with a disease. Older jails' or prisons' ventilation and lighting systems are less than adequate for environmental containment to prevent airborne transmission of TB. Many women will be missed or not considered suspicious for TB transmission directly related to gender bias and cultural factors.

Shortages of medical staff create additional burdens related to contact tracing and TST planting and reading. Public health department support can be solicited especially in county jails to help in the TST reading. Other methods to get identification and containment underway include staff incurring overtime and other shift coverage while the efforts are in process.

TB nurse case management is an essential part of the correctional as well as public health approach to the incarcerated TB patient. The relationship of the nurse to the inmate in securing compliance is vital. The nurse can help develop a treatment plan that will accomplish the following:

- promote adherence and completion of therapy
- track AFB smears, chest x-ray results, culture and sensitivities with the infectious disease coordinator
- coordinate with health department personnel including infectious disease, pulmonary, and other specialists depending upon the other conditions the inmate may have
- identify and manage isolation-related problems; use policy and procedures to ensure safety of all staff and avoid premature release of the inmate back to population

- educate and communicate with the custody and transport staff involved with treatment planning for appointments on and off site
- coordinate case conferences and telemedicine evaluations surrounding the treatment plan
- identify interpreters for foreign-born inmates or those who have language barriers; TB information should be given to the inmate in the language they speak. Translators or public health assistance in getting this information in the language is important. (CDC 1992; CDC 1996)

Inmates see the nurse much more often than they do the doctor. However, there may be a drawback in that some women inmates will minimize the serious nature of the condition if they are primarily seen by nurses. Some feel if they are not ill enough to see the doctor, then the condition must not be life threatening. Cultural and gender bias may thwart attempts to reach medication adherence without staff training regarding these possibilities.

Contact Investigation and Contract Tracing

The role of DNA fingerprinting is to identify or confirm outbreaks and to detect unsuspected transmissions between inmates' cases of TB. If the cases have the same strain of M.TB and know each other or have been contact, they might have transmitted the disease to each other (Maryland Department of Health and Mental Hygiene 2002). Tuberculosis-targeted testing in jails and prisons serves to identify women who may have infectious TB so they can be isolated immediately to prevent the spread of disease and to receive treatment. Jails may not target females who are incarcerated less than seventy-two hours for skin testing and may use chest x-ray to rule out active TB disease expeditiously or not (Maryland Department of Health and Mental Hygiene 2002).

Many smaller jails may not have an infectious disease surveillance program at all and depend upon local health department personnel to help. Women who are bailed out before local hospital labs or state health departments can get results are often lost to follow-up despite case management. As many women experience recurrent arrests, however, the opportunity may present itself again to identify if these women have TB infection or disease. Medical provider staff is most often part time in smaller jails, and, except for nursing staff and some mid-level providers, do not constitute continuity of care. Crisis intervention is reactive and not proactive.

As the female jail population increases it becomes more likely that there will not be enough isolation cells for women. More county jail systems have developed agreements with their state prison system to borrow isolation cells and services to accommodate TB suspects when there is not a respiratory isolation room on site or available at the local hospital. Likewise, many county budgets cannot cover the expense of the long-term treatment of TB and the jail inmate may be housed at the state facility until she is released from isolation or evaluated and found noninfectious by the infectious disease consultant for the prison. Dropping the charges on female offenders because of space problems further complicates follow-up in the community as does wrong addresses and the use of aliases.

Larger jails for female inmates have state-of-the-art equipment including radiology and isolation cells. Alameda County, California, has accelerated screening and radiographic ability to determine TB. Larger jails such as Cook County (Chicago) and Los Angeles County have overwhelming numbers of non-Hispanic black and foreign-born females who have cohort morbidities including substance abuse and HIV that make skin testing alone insufficient for identifying incubating TB disease. Rapid and early reception and screening processes that introduce radiology and telemedicine services help to facilitate early recognition of female inmates with potential higher risk for TB (CDC 1996).

Often, female inmates subsist in antiquated, poorly vented, suboptimally lit, and overcrowed dorms, where admitting officers administer reception-screening questionnaires with little medical training for signs and symptoms of TB. The questionnaire is not done confidentially: female prisoners are handcuffed to one another while the questions on the form are asked. The interviewer for this process is usually an officer. The questions are not culturally or gender sensitive with regard to TB (Bur et al. in press). These jails average twenty to thirty new prisoners a day and most are released within seventy-two hours. Eighty-five percent have substance-abuse-related arrests and high rates of HIV/AIDS. There are jail systems in which women are placed in holding cells that are confined spaces without ventilation and have ambient temperatures higher than 85 to 90 degrees in the summer. They breath the same air as fifteen other women in a 8' x 10' room and have greater susceptibility to the TB bacillus because of their drug and alcohol use as well as their ethnicity, race, and income level.

Provisions should be made for continuation of medication before a patient's release. Her case may need to be transferred to the health department or a receiving correctional facility to oversee completion of an appropriate course of preventive therapy. The release of an inmate who under the best DOT could "miss" some doses after prolonged confinement in a prison is a daunting prospect. Jail-released women may disappear to the street or some homeless shelter, flop house, or crack house. Outside of the correctional system, the interventions to assist patients in completing therapy include various vouchers for transportation and snacks, outreach workers who speak the same language, or arrangements for housing, food, coupons, books, clothes stipends, and so forth.

The Maryland department of corrections has had a very low rate of active TB cases and outbreaks directly related to an aggressive infectious disease/TB surveillance program. This was done in collaboration with the Department of Public Safety and Correctional Services (DPSCS) medical director (who was an infectious disease specialist) and direct involvement of the DPSCS Director of Infectious Diseases with the Department of Health and Mental Hygiene for the state of Maryland

(Bur et al. in press). The state health department staff facilitates case management and review of all suspicious cases of TB with weekly presentations to the state pulmonary consultant by the correctional ID staff with the DPSCS director of infectious diseases. In addition, the isolation cases are reviewed jointly as well.

The transition to the community of the inmate is accomplished as part of the discharge planning between the local agency, the state, the medical services contractor, and DPSCS. Correctional sites statewide are part of the network to provide a seamless transition back to the community and focus on treatment completion and monitoring. The state health department reviews and helps to draft the treatment protocols and guidelines for TB in the state of Maryland. Telemedicine opportunities to jointly manage TB coinfected patients with an HIV specialist from Johns Hopkins assigned to the corrections department are available as well via a grant from the state.

The state health department has a relationship with Johns Hopkins that also allows grants from the state health department to finance directly staff employed by Johns Hopkins to serve as TB coordinators, data management, and case management for DPSCS on site. The database to track and monitor TB infection and disease has been instrumental in retrieving information on inmates as they reenter the system or transfer back and forth to other counties or detention centers. There are studies conducted by the health department with correctional staff that yield valuable information regarding the surveillance of TB.

On-site case management and conferencing about complex cases whose treatment profile of nonadherence is managed jointly by the DPSCS director of infectious diseases, the private medical contractor staff, and the state and local public health agencies has been a wonderful model of collaboration. The state health department assists in TB training, and correctional staff is made aware of all TB updates and considerations for CME credit.

Most contact investigations tracing routes of transmission are done using the traditional concentric circle model. However, a presentation made at the June workshop showed an STD surveillance model used for TB that yielded more correct information for correctional investigations. So the application of that model may be pursued in the future (Maryland Department of Health and Mental Hygiene 2002; Bur et al. in press).

Compulsory Incarceration for Nonadherence

Since the beginning of the recognition that tuberculosis was an airborne disease and because of outbreaks of TB throughout the country, the reporting to the state of citizens who had known TB disease or were suspected to be infectious has been required. The recognition of this disease by the judicial system as a public health issue has allowed most states the authority to enforce treatment both for the infectious citizen with TB as well as those who are infectious to the public because of noncompliance.

Maryland's authority for requirement for tuberculosis treatment is outlined in the Maryland Code of Regulations (COMAR) 10.06.01 and in Health-General 18-324,325. The local health departments document and explain the patient's legal responsibility to comply with treatment and problems with a tuberculosis patient/provider agreement form. The patient signs this agreement before treatment initiation or continuation. DOT refusals or no shows threaten successful completion of TB treatment and continuation or a relapse into an infectious state would place the community at risk.

Progressive steps are taken that include an order for treatment that could result in the citizen being placed in mandatory quarantine. This could be in a health care facility or a hotel if the person is homeless. If the individual violates the order for quarantine, the person has committed a misdemeanor that can result in prosecution and incarceration until treatment completion. The local state and correctional personnel coordinate these situations through a network of calls to one another. One never is sure when this event will occur until the call is received from the police that the patient is at the booking desk (Maryland Department of Health and Mental Hygiene 2002).

When possible, the correction staff should work with the health care staff to take the individual with a mask directly to an isolation room and do the commitment at bedside/isolation cell. This avoids exposure of the patient to at-risk inmates sharing a holding cell with her. Woman inmates can be placed in state correctional isolation units if there is not an available negative air pressure cell in the jail. This is done through a local jail and state memorandum of agreement. If the state agency has a site where the individual cannot simply walk off the premises because of security, they might accommodate citizens who need treatment without the help of a correctional connection.

Conclusion

Tuberculosis is disproportionately represented in woman of color who are incarcerated in this country and others. Although TB is represented in ethnic minorities and foreign immigrants outside of the confined population, African American and non-white Hispanic women have become the faces of TB among the confined female populations in most state facilities. This is directly related to the increased rate of incarceration of women secondary to substance abuse. Tuberculosis co-morbidity with HIV/AIDS is increased in the jail and state correctional female populations.

Correctional women affected by tuberculosis are more likely to be poor, substance abusing, homeless, and victims of sexual and domestic violence. They are less likely to be educated or previously employed prior to their incarceration. Women have gender disparities directly related to the correctional environment that impact their potential compliance to various treatment options related to TB and other diseases. These women have unique cultural and social interactions with medical providers and custody staffs that provide increased barriers to treatment and care while incarcerated. These barriers include anger, stigma, reading and language skills, male-constructed correctional facilities, sexual dominance and power plays, trust factors, low self-esteem and manipulation using TB medication compliance as a bargaining chip for other freedoms. Many women of color do not have a reference for wellness. Additional chronic diseases, asthma, hypertension, diabetes, and high-risk lifestyle patterns among other factors make tuberculosis just one of many ongoing battles regarding health they have.

Directly observed therapy (DOT), a mainstay of WHO and CDC recommendations for TB treatment, is often compromised in jail as well as in state prisons. This could be related to inadequate staffing, physical barriers blocking the nurses' ability to confirm swallowing, security rushing medication rounds, and so on. Public health tools to increase TB medication adherence among ethnic minorities include giving patients phone cards, vouchers for clothes or food, or coupons for McDonalds. These options are not always available to women when incarcerated. The interaction or partnership of public health agencies with correctional centers is invaluable for continuity of care as well as assistance in contact tracing. It should be sought, fostered, and nourished.

Social isolation from other women inmates who may serve as support may be severed when an inmate is placed in respiratory isolation. This compulsory segregation may be difficult for women who are already isolated from children they single parent and adds to defiance if one cannot offer increased visitation with children or members of the patient's family as an incentive. The medical providers who are directed to promote compliance to TB medication regimens with incarcerated women are more likely to be challenged with providing incentives within the correctional setting to females. These interactions may affect adherence and compliance with drug regimes.

TB was called the social leveler in the early part of the epidemic in this country because it traversed all social classes and ethnic groups. It was called the white plague because the dominant culture was affected as much as any other group. As public health reforms and sanitation efforts grew, TB became a disease of ethnic minorities, women and children of poverty, and the foreign born. The conditions of correctional facilities for most women inmates mimic the environmental conditions that public health reforms were to eradicate.

For those seeking more in-depth treatment guidance for tuberculosis, I refer you to the official joint statement of the American Thoracic Society, Centers for Disease Control and Prevention, and the Infectious Diseases Society of America in the *American Journal of Respiratory Critical Care Medicine* (2003, 167: 603–62, appendix A). The information in this chapter is not a specific reference for treatment per se but a guideline to prepare the reader for some of the challenges one needs to be aware of "behind the walls" that serve as additional barriers to treatment of tuberculosis for all incarcerated women.

REFERENCES

American Thoracic Society, Centers for Disease Control and Prevention, and Infectious Diseases Society of America. 2003. Treatment of Tuberculosis. *American Journal of Respiratory and Critical Care Medicine* 167 (February): 603–62.

Ammar, N. H., and E. Erez. 2000. Health Delivery Systems in Women's Prisons: The Case of Ohio. *Federal Probation* 19 (June). http://print.westlaw.com/delivery.html (accessed March 3, 2003).

Asthma: Tuberculosis – The Comeback Bug (n.d.). http://www.thedoctorwillseeyounow.com/articles/other/tb_10/ (accessed June 25, 2003).

Bick, J., ed. 2002. Tuberculosis in Corrections: 2002 Update (electronic version). HIV Education/Prison Project (March): 1–3.

Bloom, B., and B. Owen. 2002. Gender Responsive Strategies: Research, Practice, and Guiding Principles for Women Offenders. Unpublished manuscript, National Institute of Corrections.

Bur, S., J. Golub, J. Armstrong, K. Myers, B. Johnson, D. Mazo, et al. In press. Evaluation of an Extensive Tuberculosis Contact Investigation in an Urban Community and Jail. *International Journal of Tuberculosis and Lung Disease.*

Centers for Disease Control and Prevention. 2003b. Trends in Tuberculosis Morbidity: United States, 1992–2002. *Morbidity and Mortality Weekly Report* 52, no. 11 (March 21): 217–22.

Centers for Disease Control and Prevention. 2003a. Treatment of Drug-Susceptible Tuberculosis Disease in Persons not Infected with HIV. http://www.cdc.gov/tb/ (accessed March 2, 2003).

Centers for Disease Control and Prevention. 2000. *Core Curriculum on Tuberculosis: What the Clinician Should Know,* 4th ed. Atlanta, GA: Author.

Centers for Disease Control and Prevention. 1996. Prevention and Control of Tuberculosis in Correctional Facilities Recommendations of the Advisory Council for the Elimination of Tuberculosis (electronic version). *Morbidity and Mortality Weekly Report* 45, no. RR-8 (June 7): 1–27.

Centers for Disease Control and Prevention. 1992. Prevention and Control of Tuberculosis in U.S. Communities with At-Risk Minority Populations Recommendations of the Advisory Council for the Elimination of Tuberculosis (electronic version). *Morbidity and Mortality Weekly Report* 41, no. RR-5 (April 17): 1–6.

Centers for Disease Control and Prevention. n.d. A Glance at the HIV Epidemic. http://www.cdc.gov/nchstp/od/news/At-a-Glance.htm (accessed June 25, 2003).

Chaisson, R. 2003. Principles of Chemotherapy and Treatment of TB Disease. In Maryland TB Today. Symposium presented at the annual Maryland TB Today conference, Marriottsville, MD, April 29–May 1, 2003.

Chicago Legal Advocacy for Incarcerated Mothers. 2000. *Women in Prison Fact Sheet.* http://www.beyondmedia.org/VV/ (accessed June 25, 2003).

Gibson, J. 2003. TB Nurse Case Management Model 2002 for Ensuring Completion of Therapy: Care Practice and Standard Terminology. *TB Notes* 1: 15–18. http://www.cdc.gov/nchstp/tb/notes/tbn_1.03.

Gostin, L. O. 1995. The Resurgent Tuberculosis Epidemic in the Era of AIDS: Reflections on Public Health, Law, and Society (electronic version). *Maryland Law Review* 54, no. 1.

Harrison, P., and A. J. Beck. 2002. Prisoners in 2001. Bureau of Justice Statistics Bulletin, NCJ 195189 (July), 1–16.

Hudelson, P. 1996. Gender Differentials in tuberculosis: the role of socioeconomic and cultural factors. *Tubercle and Lung Disease* 77, no. 5 (October): 391–400.

Maruschak, L. M., and A. J. Beck. 2001. Medical Problems of Inmates, 1997. Bureau of Justice Statistics Special Report, NCJ 181644 (January), 1–12.

Maryland Department of Health and Mental Hygiene. 2002a. Guidelines for Prevention and Treatment of Tuberculosis. Baltimore: Author.

Maryland Department of Health and Mental Hygiene. 2002b. Controlling TB in Correctional Institutions, 1995. http://www.cdc.gov/nchstp/tb/pubs/corrections.htm.

Maryland Department of Health and Mental Hygiene. 2002c. The Role of BCG Vaccine in the Prevention and Control of Tuberculosis in the United States. *Morbidity and Mortality Weekly Report* 45, no. RR-4 (April 26): 1–18.

Panel on Clinical Practices for the Treatment of HIV Infection. 2001. *Guidelines for the Use of Antiretroviral Agents in HIV-Infected Adults and Adolescents.* Washington, DC: U.S. Department of Health and Human Services/Henry J. Kaiser Family Foundation.

Reichman, L. B., and J. H. Tanne. 2001. TB's Dangerous Secrets. http://www.tbtimebomb.com/secrets.html (accessed June 25, 2003).

Ruby, W. H. 2002. Do's and Don'ts in Correctional HIV Care. Symposium at the meeting of the Intensive Review in Correctional Medicine, Baltimore, Maryland, July 12–14, 2002.

Sprinson, J., E. Lawton, and J. Flood. 2003. Discontinuing Isolation: The Value of Three AFB Sputum Smears in Evaluation of Hospitalized Pulmonary TB Suspects. Symposium presented at the 2003 National TB Controllers Workshop, Washington, DC, June 8–12, 2003.

Truth, Sojourner. 1851. Ain't I a Woman? http://www.webcom.com/~duane/truth.html (accessed November 7, 2001).

Uplekar, M., S. Rangan, and J. Ogden. 1999. Gender and Tuberculosis Control: Towards a Strategy for Research and Action. Draft strategy paper prepared for the Communicable Disease Prevention, Control, and Eradication, World Health Organization, Geneva, Switzerland, December.

World Health Organization. n.d. TB/HIV. http://www.who.int/gtb/policyrd/TBHIV.htm (accessed June 25, 2003).

13

Hepatitis C Virus Infection among Incarcerated Women

GRACE E. MACALINO

Given the overlap of hepatitis C–infected and incarcerated populations, it is difficult to discuss either one without mention of the other. The inmate population is distinct in that it consists of individuals with greater risk factors for contracting blood-borne infections such as the hepatitis C virus (HCV) compared to the general population. Such characteristics include drug use, and in particular injection drug use, as well as commercial sex work (Butler, Spencer, et al. 1999). Although female inmates comprise a much smaller segment of the incarcerated population compared to males, they may actually represent an incarcerated population with higher risk of contracting HCV. Courts have traditionally been relatively lenient on women for their early criminal offenses; when women reach the point of detention, they are often incarcerated for much more serious crimes and usually represent a higher-risk population as compared to men.

It is estimated that in 1997, 29 to 43 percent of inmates in the United States were infected with HCV (Hammett, Harmon, and Rhodes 2002). Thus, not only do jails and prisons house individuals with high-risk behaviors for HCV, they are also a reservoir of infection, primarily attributed to risk behaviors that occurred before incarceration (Anda et al. 1985).

This chapter will provide HCV prevalence and incidence estimates among correctional and community populations, an overview of HCV natural history, and methods for the screening, diagnosis, treatment, and prevention of HCV among correctional populations. In addition, it will highlight reasons why this is a pressing health concern for incarcerated individuals, particularly among women.

Epidemiology of HCV in Prisons

Hepatitis C is primarily transmitted parenterally—through percutaneous exposure to HCV-contaminated blood. The primary mode of HCV transmission in the

United States is now the sharing of needles and syringes among injection drug users (IDU). Although sexual transmission of HCV can occur, the efficiency of this route appears relatively low (Centers for Disease Control and Prevention [CDC] 1998).

Studies evaluating HCV prevalence among incarcerated populations reflect that HCV infection is endemic among prisoners worldwide. In published studies of incarcerated populations, HCV prevalence ranged from 4.8 percent in an Indian jail (Singh, Prasad, and Mohanty 1999) to 92 percent in two prisons in northern Spain (Pallas et al. 1999). The variance of HCV prevalence between different incarcerated settings internationally likely depends on a number of factors, including the stage of the HCV epidemic in the community, the local policy regarding the incarceration of drug injectors, and the sampling population used for the study.

Studies done to evaluate HCV prevalence in the incarcerated community consistently found HCV prevalence to be higher among prison inmates as compared to local comparison groups. Catalan-Soares, Almeida, and Carneiro-Proietti (2000) report HCV seroprevalence in Brazilian inmates of 6.34 percent in comparison to 0.57 percent of blood donors from the general population. Chang et al. (1999) found similar results, indicating that although HCV prevalence in non-IDU inmates was much lower than in IDU inmates (14.7 percent vs. 67.2 percent), it was still ten times higher than that of healthy blood donors in Taiwan. Allwright et al. (2000) report in their cross-sectional survey of HCV prevalence in Irish prisoners that 80 percent of IDUs were HCV positive compared to 52 to 76 percent prevalence in community surveys of IDUs.

For the studies that identified risk correlates of HCV seroprevalence, risk behaviors included self-reported past and present injection drug use, other substance use, and syringe sharing in prison. Studies that included information about self-reported injection drug use found injection drug use as a significant correlate of HCV infection. When comparing IDUs with noninjection drug users, HCV among IDUs ranged from 49 percent to 90 percent (Butler, Spencer, et al. 1999; Gore et al. 1999), while among non-IDUs from 3 percent to 14.7 percent (Chang et al. 1999). In fact, the study with the highest HCV seroprevalence (92 percent) comprised a study population with 100 percent self-reported IDUs (Pallas et al. 1999). Other correlates found to be significantly associated with HCV seroprevalence were age (Chang et al. 1999; Butler, Dolan, et al. 1997), incarceration history (Christensen et al. 2000; Weild et al. 2000; Malliori et al. 1998; Butler, Dolan, et al. 1997; Pallas et al. 1999), hepatitis B (HBV) infection (Butler, Dolan, et al. 1997), sexual behavior (Guimaraes et al. 2001; Chang et al. 1999), and history of tattooing (Holsen, Harthug, and Myrmel 1993; Pallas et al. 1999).

Most published studies that determined prevalence by gender showed HCV to be higher among female compared to male inmates (Weild et al. 2000; Allwright et al. 2000; Singh, Prasad, and Mohanty 1999; Ruiz et al. 1999; Crofts et al. 1995; Long et al. 2001; Huffman et al. 1999). This is similar to gender differences seen in HIV prevalence in prisons, often attributed to selection bias, where incarcerated women are often at even greater risk for blood-borne pathogens and sexually transmitted infections than their male counterparts.

A review of the literature shows that only two studies published to date have evaluated the incidence of HCV within the prison setting (intraprison transmission). Christiansen et al. (2000) reported an incidence rate in a Danish prison of 25.2 per 100 person-years (PY) (0.6–140, 95 percent CI). However, this seroconversion rate is related to only one inmate of eight persons at risk, with almost four years of follow-up. Vlahov et al. found in a U.S. prison (Maryland) an HCV seroconversion rate of 1.1 per 100 PY, though the authors hypothesize that a possible explanation for the low seroconversion rate could be related to a saturation of the susceptible population, with reports of HCV prevalence rates of 85 percent within the IDU community from which the prison draws (Vlahov et al. 1993). In a more recent study, Macalino et al. (in press) report HCV incidence of 0.4 per 100 PY in a U.S. prison (Rhode Island).

Additional studies have also investigated the issue of HCV seroconversion among incarcerated populations. Haber et al. (1999) documented four cases of HCV seroconversion after four to fifty-two months of continuous imprisonment. While two subjects had a history of IDU, the other two subjects had histories of possible exposure by physical assault and attack by barber shears. In contrast, Taylor et al. (2000) found that over a six-year follow-up period, new HCV infections occurred primarily within the community, rather than in prisons where access to syringes are limited. While HCV transmission does occur in prisons, the incidence reported is often much lower than among IDUs in the community.

Despite high levels of HCV, HIV, and HBV seen in the incarcerated population, imprisonment may actually reduce the overall risk of blood-borne pathogen transmission. Detention may ultimately interrupt patterns of drug use by decreasing the frequency of injection and limiting the size of sharing networks (Christensen et al. 2000; Malliori et al. 1998). Thus, although injection drug users who continue to inject in prison are at a higher risk for contracting blood-borne illnesses, the overall number of individuals who are injecting are substantially less due to the restrictive prison environment, and therefore the incidence of infection declines over the total prison population (Smyth 2000).

To provide a context for HCV prevalence among incarcerated populations, I outline the burden of disease among subpopulations in the community, limiting the discussion to the United States. Prevalence of HCV varies widely in the community, and table 13.1 shows the average prevalence of HCV among people with different risk factors for infection (CDC 1998).

Not surprisingly, the highest prevalence of HCV in the United States is seen among IDUs, as well as hemophiliacs and other recipients of HCV-infected blood transfusions. Rates of HCV infection among people of color are significantly higher than those among non-Hispanic whites (1.5 percent), with the rates of infection among Hispanics at 2.1 percent and African Americans at 3.2 percent (Williams 1999). HCV is more prevalent among men than women, and among

TABLE 13.1

Estimated average prevalence of hepatitis C virus (HCV) infection in the United States by various characteristics and estimated prevalence of persons with these characteristics in the population

Characteristic	%	HCV-infection prevalence (range, %)	Prevalence of persons with characteristic, %
General population	1.8	(1.5–2.3)	NA
Persons with hemophilia treated with products made before 1987	87	(74–90)	<0.01
Injecting drug users			
Current	79	(72–86)	0.5
History of prior use	No data		5
Persons with abnormal alanine aminotransferase levels	15	(10–18)	5
Chronic hemodialysis patients	10	(0–64)	0.1
Persons with multiple sex partners (lifetime)			
≥50	9	(6–16)	4
10–49	3	(3–4)	22
2–9	2	(1–2)	52
Persons reporting a history of sexually transmitted diseases	6	(1–10)	17
Persons receiving blood transfusions before 1990	6	(5–9)	6
Infants born to infected mothers	5	(0–25)	0.1
Men who have sex with men	4	(2–18)	5
Health-care workers	1	(1–2)	9
Pregnant women	1	–	1.5
Military personnel	0.3	(0.2–0.4)	0.5
Volunteer blood donors	0.16	–	5

Source: CDC (1998)

individuals between the ages of thirty and forty-nine than any other age cohort (CDC 1998). The majority of new HCV infections are among injection drug users, who account for 60 percent of new cases, and among adults between the ages of twenty and thirty-nine years (CDC 1998).

In addition to the epidemiologic evidence that demonstrates the problem of

HCV among the incarcerated population, other biological and social aspects of HCV infection also highlight the need to understand this disease in the context of incarcerated women. In the following sections, I will describe these aspects of the disease and discuss their unique relevance to incarcerated women.

Natural History of Infection

The precise natural history of hepatitis C remains largely undetermined due to limited prospective data, difficulties in determining onset of disease, and the influence of multiple cofactors on HCV progression. Based on existing data and current knowledge, figure 13.1 details the overall progression of hepatitis C infection with population estimates at each stage.

The first six to nine months after initial HCV infection are considered the acute phase. Although the vast majority of people infected with HCV remain asymptomatic throughout this period, approximately 20 to 30 percent of individuals experience symptoms of newly acquired HCV infection (acute HCV), including fatigue, nausea, abdominal pain, and, in some severe cases, jaundice. Only 15 to 30 percent of people will entirely clear the virus from their body within six to nine months of initial infection without any long-term impact from the infection—resulting in 70 to 85 percent of infected individuals progressing to chronic HCV. Presence and/or absence of symptoms during the acute phase is not predictive of progression to chronic HCV.

Chronic HCV infection is also frequently asymptomatic. This phase of HCV is characterized by highly variable rates of progression to liver fibrosis (scarring of the liver caused by ongoing liver inflammation). Of those chronically infected with HCV, 70 percent will likely progress to chronic liver disease over the subsequent twenty to thirty years. Fifteen to 20 percent of the individuals who develop chronic liver disease may develop cirrhosis, or irreversible scarring of liver tissue. In addition, a small number of chronically infected individuals will also develop additional extrahepatic medical conditions (that is, impacting organs other than the liver). Chronic HCV infection is currently the leading cause of hepatocellular carcinoma and liver transplantation in the United States (Lauer and Walker 2001). Three percent of HCV-infected individuals are likely to die as a result of chronic liver disease.

Research has found that several factors accelerate the progression of hepatitis C to cirrhosis. These factors include alcohol use, age over forty at time of initial infection, male gender, and coinfection with hepatitis B and/or HIV (Poynard, Bedossa, and Opolon 1997). While studies suggest that women have a decreased likelihood of progressing to severe liver damage (Wiese et al. 2000; Hayashi et al. 1998), a review of the literature shows that few studies have examined the different biological experience of women infected with HCV. HIV increases HCV replication and the rate of HCV transmission, as well as accelerates the course of disease and places individuals at higher risk of liver damage. Research has demon-

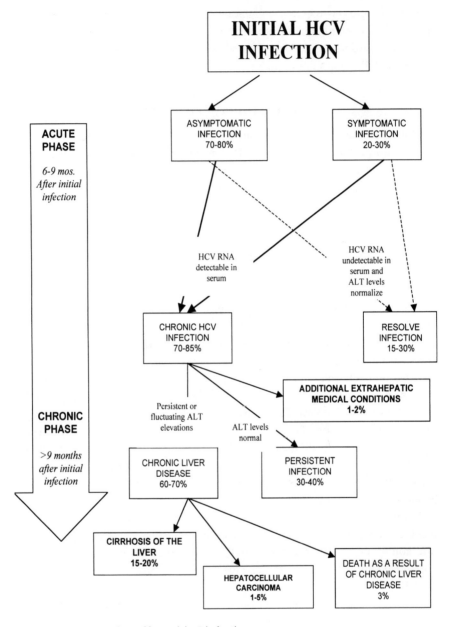

FIGURE 13.1. Progression of hepatitis C infection

strated that the progression to decompensated liver disease, hepatocellular carcinoma, and liver disease–related mortality are far more common among HIV/HCV
coinfected populations than among those infected with HCV alone (CDC 2001).

The effect of HCV on the course and progression of HIV is less clearly defined.
Nonetheless, there are important consequences related to HCV among HIV-

infected individuals. HCV and related liver disease have been shown to be significant causes of non-AIDS associated death among HIV-infected individuals. In coinfected patients who have benefited from treatment for their HIV infection (highly active antiretroviral therapy [HAART]), end-stage liver disease associated with HCV is a leading cause of death.

Due to the chronic nature of HCV and the long-term effects associated with it, the transient nature of incarceration does not lend itself to impacting the disease. This inconsistency is further exacerbated among incarcerated women. Women tend to have shorter lengths of stay than men in correctional facilities, limiting the opportunity to change the course of HCV infection.

Diagnosis

Diagnosis of HCV infection is primarily done by initially testing for HCV antibodies (anti-HCV) and then further evaluating anti-HCV positive persons for chronic HCV infection and liver disease. Screening for HCV antibodies is done by enzyme immunoblot assay (EIA), with positive tests confirmed by recombinant immunoblot assay (RIBA). Ninety percent of individuals infected with HCV develop HCV antibodies within six months after initial exposure. False negative anti-HCV results may occur among those in the early stages of infection and among immunocompromised patients (that is, advanced HIV infection). HCV infection can also be diagnosed by testing the amount of HCV virus in the blood using gene amplification techniques. A qualitative polymerase chain reaction (PCR) test confirms the presence of virus in the bloodstream, while a quantitative PCR test measures the amount of HCV RNA present in the blood.

Once infection with HCV is confirmed, the least invasive way of identifying liver damage during routine clinical evaluation is laboratory testing for elevated alanine aminotransferase (ALT) and aspartate aminotransferase (AST) as these enzyme levels rise as liver cells are being injured and/or destroyed. It is of note that women tend to have lower ALT levels than men, both in the absence and presence of HCV infection. In approximately 30 percent of patients with chronic HCV, normal or intermittently normal ALT/AST levels are found. Research suggests that these patients may be at lower risk of developing progressive liver disease compared to patients with recurrently elevated enzyme levels (Bacon 2002). Enzyme levels can only sometimes provide information regarding the extent of liver damage or disease progression among infected individuals. Liver biopsy is the definitive diagnostic procedure to assess the amount of damage to the liver and establish the stage of HCV infection. However, liver biopsies are invasive, expensive, and not without risk. It is often difficult to recommend that patients undergo a liver biopsy given current clinical options available to HCV patients (see "Treatment" section below).

Screening and diagnosis of hepatitis C in correctional facilities is strongly recommended by the Centers for Disease Control and Prevention (CDC 2003), graphically represented in figure 13.2. It is recommended that the algorithm be followed for all inmates entering an adult correctional facility.

The screening and diagnosis of HCV and evaluation of chronic infection and liver disease provides unique challenges for the incarcerated individual. Diagnosis involves multiple tests and likely occurs over an extended period of time. Medical appointments with specialists and liver biopsies may need to be scheduled far in advance. Some state correctional systems have facilities spread throughout the state with only one main medical facility. Transportation to either a centralized correctional medical facility or a medical facility on the outside is often required to fully diagnose the extent of infection and disease. This may lead to both logistical challenges (such as coordination with security staff) and a lengthy workup period.

Questions still remain regarding the extent of screening appropriate and adequate for HCV in correctional facilities. The primary reason why HCV testing is not routinely conducted, despite recommendations, is often related to what the particular correctional facility response would be if someone were found to be HCV seropositive. In addition, inmate attitudes may also prevent identification of HCV. Assessments of prison screening programs report an inmate refusal rate of nearly 50 percent (CDC 2003). Correctional physicians report that many inmates offered voluntary testing opt to not be tested because of their desire to limit involvement with the correctional system. Inmates may fear that acknowledgment of health problems could prolong incarceration, result in quarantine, or require additional tests and disclosure of prior drug use (Association of State and Territorial Health Officials 2003). Concerns about confidentiality and stigma also exist. Some inmates may already know their HCV status but do not wish to disclose this information in the prison setting. Moreover, ignorance surrounding HCV may result in inmates having an apathetic attitude toward testing.

Treatment

Hepatitis C viral treatment is recommended for individuals with detectable HCV RNA, sustained increased ALT levels, and a liver biopsy that shows one of the following outcomes: portal bridging, fibrosis, or moderate degrees of inflammation or necrosis (National Institutes of Health [NIH] 2002). While the primary goal of treatment for HCV is virus eradication, there are additional secondary goals of treatment, including decelerating disease progression, improving underlying histologic findings, and preventing hepatocellular carcinoma (Bernstein 2004).

There are currently three antiviral therapies approved for the treatment of chronic hepatitis C among adults: standard alpha interferon, pegylated alpha interferon, and standard or pegylated alpha interferon in combination with ribavarin. The rates of initial viral response of HCV infected persons to alpha interferon monotherapy have been high; however, problems with relapse and viral nonresponse have been associated with this course of treatment. These limita-

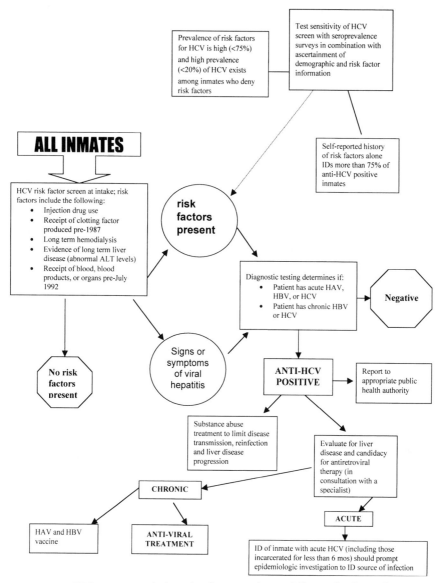

FIGURE 13.2. CDC recommendations for the screening and diagnosis of HCV in correctional facilities

tions are probably due to a drop in drug concentration between doses that allows the virus to replicate. This response led to the development of pegylated interferon. The pegylation process decreases the rate of drug release, resulting in prolonged concentrations of interferon in the bloodstream, without altering the effects of the drug, thus allowing for once-weekly dosing. Ribavirin, an antiviral, is used in combination with alpha interferon to increase the potency of HCV treatment. Ribavirin cannot be used alone to successfully treat HCV.

Recommended Treatment

The current regimen recommended by the NIH for HCV treatment is a combination therapy of once-a-week pegylated alpha interferon injections and oral ribavirin administered three times weekly (NIH 2002) for six to twelve months, depending on genotype and HIV status. Standard alpha interferon alone is recommended only when a patient cannot tolerate pegylated alpha interferon or ribavarin due to toxicities or side effects (Nerenberg 2002).

Side effects experienced by patients receiving interferon include headaches, nausea, loss of appetite, hair loss, muscle and joint pain, and, long term, potentially irreversible thyroid disease. Interferon can also suppress bone marrow production leading to neutropenia, which affects immune defense; this can result in possible increased susceptibility to other infections. Side effects associated with ribavarin include anemia and thrombocytopenia, which can lead to severe fatigue and weakness requiring medical evaluation. In addition, ribavarin is teratogenic and should not be prescribed to women who are pregnant or breastfeeding; women either being treated with ribavirin that are of sexually active reproductive age or with a sexual partner being treated with ribavarin should be prescribed birth control for the duration of treatment and at least six months after completion of therapy. Side effects are often a barrier to adherence to HCV treatment. In registration trials of pegylated interferon and ribavirin, significant side effects resulted in discontinuation of treatment in approximately 10 to 14 percent of patients (NIH 2002).

Mental health side effects are also related to HCV antiviral therapy. It is estimated that at least 30 to 50 percent of patients develop anxiety, depression, or insomnia that require medical or mental health intervention during the course of treatment. One of the most common side effects of interferon is depression, thus it is not recommended for those with current clinical depression and it is advised that physicians assess patients' mental health before beginning antiviral therapy and regularly monitor mental health throughout treatment. Although unstable psychiatric illness remains a contraindication to treatment, patients with clinically stable mental illnesses may be safely treated with regular psychiatric assessments (Bernstein et al. 2002).

Not all patients with chronic HCV infection are candidates for therapy. Alcohol abuse and pregnancy can complicate or even preclude HCV treatment. While the contraindication of HCV therapy for individuals with active substance abuse disorders was lifted in 2002, acknowledging that treatment should be considered for active substance users, substance abuse counseling remains an integral component of the HCV treatment protocol. Before treatment is initiated, genotype testing of the virus is often necessary to evaluate whether an infection is likely to respond to therapy. The duration of treatment required for a response also varies by genotype.

While treatment for HCV has improved greatly in the last decade, it remains effective for only 40 to 60 percent of patients. HCV is a rapidly mutating virus with eleven different genotypes and nearly ninety different subtypes, and only some genotypes respond to currently available treatments for HCV. While viral response rates differ depending on HCV genotype, response rates for genotype 1 (the most common in the United States) are between 40 to 50 percent, with HCV remaining undetectable for six or more months after the end of therapy (Barclay 2002).

Data indicate that the number of doses and duration of treatment influence the likelihood of sustained viral response to therapy. The "80/80/80" rule, as it is called, is based on data that demonstrate that patients who adhere to at least 80 percent of their ribavirin and 80 percent of their interferon for at least 80 percent of the recommended treatment interval have a much higher cure rate than those with lower rates of adherence to regimens (Manns et al. 2001; McHutchison et al. 2002a; McHutchison et al. 2002b).

In addition to the influence of HCV genotype and adherence on the success of HCV therapy, other factors that have been associated with an increased likelihood of response to HCV therapy include age less than forty-five years, female gender, mild (rather than advanced) chronic inflammation on liver biopsy, and lower baseline viral load (Fontana and Kane 2003).

HCV among Incarcerated Women

The correctional setting presents several challenges to the treatment of HCV-infected women. While incarceration does provide a brief "window of opportunity" during which to access health care, the two most common reasons that incarcerated individuals remain untreated for HCV are cost and length of treatment. The cost of HCV treatment is estimated to range from $15,000 to $30,000 per patient when taking into account the cost of drugs, management of adverse effects associated with treatment, and estimated health care resource use (Davis and Rodrigue 2001; Salomon et al. 2003). While this does not take into consideration the potential savings treatment could pose to the correctional system over time, few studies have been done to date, and current correctional system health care budgets may not be robust enough to absorb the expense of treating HCV-infected individuals. There is also a hesitance among correctional health care providers to treat inmates who do not have enough time left in their prison sentence to allow for completion of treatment. Many facilities require a period of fifteen to twenty-four months remaining in a sentence from the time of treatment initiation in order to start therapy. Women typically serve shorter sentences and have shorter lengths of stay in correctional facilities than men, both of which limit the likelihood for incarcerated women to be treated for HCV.

Female inmates are often housed in smaller facilities where it is more difficult to maintain confidentiality overall, and in particular regarding their health-seeking behaviors around HCV infection. The daily activities of an HCV-infected incarcerated woman, such as visiting health services, being transported to off-site facilities, and waiting in line for medications are more easily recognized by fellow inmates and correctional officers than would be the case if they were housed in larger, more anonymous facilities. The stigma associated with HCV infection and the desire of women to maintain the maximum level of privacy possible in an incarcerated setting may prevent them from accepting and/or adhering to treatment.

Even if eligible women initiate treatment for HCV while incarcerated, they may be released during the six- to twelve-month course of therapy. When trying to reintegrate into the community, HCV and/or continuation of treatment may not be their highest priority. HCV-infected women are faced with the same challenges that all women newly released from prison deal with; and unless HCV care is seen as a priority, the probability of continued HCV therapy is quite small. Women transitioning to the outside world are faced with a myriad of health and social concerns, including but not limited to housing, finances, education, and health care, while they are returning to their high-risk environment of substance use and potentially illegal activity such as commercial sex work. Additionally, over 75 percent of women in prisons are mothers and were primary custodians of their children prior to incarceration (Greenfeld and Snell 1999), and they may need to address reunification during the immediate post-release period. Finally, limited resources are available to HCV-infected women upon release for continuation of treatment, which often requires intensive discharge and transition planning.

Despite the limitations of providing HCV treatment in correctional settings, prisons do provide a unique setting in which to consider therapy for high-risk populations. There are distinct advantages to treating hard-to-reach individuals while they are in an environment where loss to follow-up is minimized. It is easier to locate women housed in smaller facilities, and treatment, adherence, and clinical needs can be closely monitored. Sobriety is enforced in correctional settings, making it a stable environment in which to treat HCV. Additionally, the close clinical follow-up available in correctional settings may provide a safe environment for treatment of patients with psychiatric illnesses and side effects. Through education provided and knowledge gained while in prison, incarcerated women may have the motivation and commitment to start and maintain HCV treatment to completion, thereby reducing the health risks to themselves and others.

Prevention

Correctional facilities offer an opportunity to implement the CDC's strategy to prevent and control hepatitis C virus infection and HCV-related disease. This strategy combines primary prevention activities (that is, screening and testing of blood products, risk-reduction counseling, and implementation of infection control practices), secondary prevention activities (that is, identification, counseling, and testing of persons at risk and medical management of infected persons), and surveillance and research. In addition to these system-level activities, professional and public education is a key element of the comprehensive strategy. Inmate health education and health promotion programs in prisons and jails allow for structured dissemination of information related to routes of disease transmission, risk factors for infection, methods of prevention, disease outcomes, and HCV treatment options (CDC 2003). Appropriately incorporating relevant aspects of this strategy into the policies and procedures of correctional facilities can help to prevent the transmission of HCV in the incarcerated setting.

Conclusion

Incarceration highlights and magnifies the challenges related to HCV prevention, diagnosis, and treatment, particularly for women. Clearly, hepatitis C is only one of many issues that may face this population; however, there are far-reaching benefits of addressing HCV in this context. HCV infection almost always occurs among IDUs, a high-risk population that is often hidden. Despite the lack of highly effective treatment, knowledge of one's HCV serostatus would be the first step in impacting change ranging from decreasing high-risk behaviors, increasing access to health care, and ultimately, decreasing HCV transmission.

In the 2000 Census of State and Federal Adult Correctional Facilities, almost 80 percent of state facilities reported having a policy to test inmates for hepatitis C. However, only 9 percent of the facilities broadly tested inmates; the remainder tested a targeted group of inmates based on clinical indication, inmate request, or risk factors (Stephan and Karberg 2003). The implications of HCV prevention and control activities in the correctional setting extend far beyond the prison walls. As the vast majority of inmates will return to the community, there is a public health opportunity to impact change on a broader level by addressing HCV among members of those communities at highest risk and often most difficult to find.

From a policy perspective, given the HCV prevalence among incarcerated populations, hepatitis C is a significant disease that urgently needs to be addressed. Existing guidelines need to be followed by correctional facilities and continually updated as the knowledge base expands. Prevention options, ranging from education and counseling regarding injection drug use and alcohol intake, to drug treatment and needle exchange, regardless of whether in or out of correctional facilities, can significantly decrease transmission and progression of hepatitis C. Treatment options for HCV are growing and the effects of existing antivirals are increasing. The effectiveness of current HCV prevention and treatment strategies has been proven and its scope needs to be widened to include the prison population. If a response is not made with urgency, a larger problem will have to be addressed eventually. Almost 80 percent of injection drug users have a history of an incarceration in their lifetime, and as people become chronically infected, society will have to deal with the adverse health outcomes associated with HCV infection, whether it is in the incarcerated or health care setting. It is early enough in the HCV epidemic where we can learn from our response to HIV over the past twenty years, tackling upfront the issues of lack of knowledge and stigma.

REFERENCES

Association of State and Territorial Health Officials. 2003. *Hepatitis C and incarcerated populations: The next wave for correctional health initiatives.* Washington, DC: Association of State and Territorial Health Officials.

Allwright, S., F. Bradley, J. Long, J. Barry, L. Thornton, and J. V. Parry. 2000. Prevalence of antibodies to hepatitis B, hepatitis C, and HIV and risk factors in Irish prisoners: Results of a national cross sectional survey. *British Medical Journal*: 78–82.

Anda, R. F., S. B. Perlman, D. J. D'Alessio, J. P. Davis, and V. N. Dodson. 1985. Hepatitis B in Wisconsin male prisoners: Considerations for serologic screening and vaccination. *American Journal of Public Health* 75: 1182–85.

Bacon, B. R. 2002. Treatment of patients with hepatitis C and normal serum aminotransferase levels. *Hepatology* 36: S179–S184.

Barclay, L. 2002. NIH Consensus Conference Notes HCV Treatment Advances. *Medscape Medical News.* http://www.medscape.com/viewarticle/436529.

Bernstein, D. 2004. Diagnosis and Management of Hepatitis C. Medscape. http://www.medscape.com/viewprogram/712_pnt.

Bernstein, D., L. Kleinman, C. M. Barker, D. A. Revicki, and J. Green. 2002. Relationship of health-related quality of life to treatment adherence and sustained response in chronic hepatitis C patients. *Hepatology* 35: 704–8.

Butler, T., J. Spencer, J. Cui, K. Vickery, J. Zou, and J. Kaldor. 1999. Seroprevalence of markers for hepatitis B, C, and G in male and female prisoners: NSW, 1996. *Australian New Zealand Journal of Public Health* 23: 377–84.

Butler, T. G., K. A. Dolan, M. J. Ferson, L. M. McGuinness, P. R. Brown, and P. W. Robertson. 1997. Hepatitis B and C in New South Wales prisons: Prevalence and risk factors. *Medical Journal of Australia* 166: 127–30.

Catalan-Soares, B. C., R. T. Almeida, and A. B. Carneiro-Proietti. 2000. Prevalence of HIV–1/2, HTLV-I/II, hepatitis B virus (HBV), hepatitis C virus (HCV), Treponema pallidum and Trypanosoma cruzi among prison inmates at Manhuacu, Minas Gerais State, Brazil. *Revista da Sociedade Brasileira de Medicina Tropical* 33: 27–30.

Centers for Disease Control and Prevention (CDC). 1998. Recommendations for prevention and control of hepatitis C virus (HCV) infection and HCV-related chronic disease. *MMWR* 47 (No. RR–19). http://www.cdc.gov/epo/mmwr/preview/mmwrhtml/00055154.htm.

CDC. 2001. *Frequently Asked Questions and Answers about Coinfection with HIV and Hepatitis C Virus.* http://www.cdc.gov/hiv/pubs/facts/HIV-HCV_Coinfection.htm.

CDC. 2003. Prevention and control of infections with hepatitis viruses in correctional settings. [Recommendation Report]. *MMWR* 52 (RR010, 1–33.

Chang, C. J., C. H. Lin, C. T. Lee, S. J. Chang, Y. C. Ko, and H. W. Liu. 1999. Hepatitis C virus infection among short-term intravenous drug users in southern Taiwan. *European Journal of Epidemiology* 15: 597–601.

Christensen, P. B., H. B. Krarup, H. G. Niesters, H. Norder, and J. Georgsen. 2000. Prevalence and incidence of bloodborne viral infections among Danish prisoners. *European Journal of Epidemiology* 16: 1043–49.

Crofts, N., T. Stewart, P. Hearne, X. Y. Ping, A. M. Breshkin, and S. A. Locarnini. 1995. Spread of bloodborne viruses among Australian prison entrants. *British Medical Journal* 310: 285–88.

Davis, G. L., and J. R. Rodrigue. 2001. Treatment of chronic hepatitis C in active drug users. *New England Journal of Medicine* 345: 215–17.

Decker, M. D., W. K. Vaughn, J. S. Brodie, R. H. Hutcheson Jr., and W. Schaffner. 1984. Seroepidemiology of hepatitis B in Tennessee prisoners. *Journal of Infectious Diseases* 150: 450–59.

Editorial. 1995, April 2. Imprisonment, injection drug use, and bloodborne viruses. *British Medical Journal* 310: 275–76.

Fontana, R.J., and B. Kane. 2003. Management of hepatitis C: Focus on minority populations. http://www.medscape.com/viewprogram2515.

Gore, S. M., A. G. Bird, S. O. Cameron, S. J. Hutchinson, S. M. Burns, and D. J. Goldberg. 1999. Prevalence of hepatitis C in prisons: WASH-C surveillance linked to self-reported risk behaviours. *Quarterly Journal of Medicine* 92: 25–32.

Greenfeld, L.A., and T. L. Snell. 1999. Women offenders. Bureau of Justice Statistics. [Special Report NCJ 175688]. http://www.ojp.usdoj.gov/bjs/pub/pdf/wo.pdf.

Guimaraes, T., C. F. Granato, D. Varella, M. L. Ferraz, A. Castelo, and E. G. Kallas. 2001. High prevalence of hepatitis C infection in a Brazilian prison: Identification of risk factors for infection. *Brazilian Journal of Infectious Diseases* 5: 111–18.

Haber, P. S., S. J. Parsons, S. E. Harper, P. A. White, W. D. Rawlinson, and A. R. Lloyd. 1999. Transmission of hepatitis C within Australian prisons. *Medical Journal of Australia* 171: 31–33.

Hammett, T. M., M. P. Harmon, and W. Rhodes. 2002. The burden of infectious disease among inmates of and releases from U.S. correctional facilities, 1997. *American Journal of Public Health* 92: 1789–94.

Hayashi, J., Y. Kishihara, K. Ueno, K. Yamaji, Y. Kawakami, N. Furusyo, Y. Sawayama, and S. Kashiwagi. 1998. Age-related response to Interferon Alfa treatment in women vs. men with chronic hepatitis C virus infection. *Archives of Internal Medicine* 158: 177–81.

Holsen, D. S., S. Harthug, and H. Myrmel. 1993. Prevalence of antibodies to hepatitis C virus and association with intravenous drug abuse and tattooing in a national prison in Norway. *European Journal of Clinical Microbiological Infectious Disease* 12: 673–76.

Huffman, S., J. Savage, S. Jacups, and S. LaBrooy. 1999. Hepatitis C virus in the NT prison population. *The Northern Territory Disease Control Bulletin* 6, no. 1: 8–10.

Hull, H. F., L. H. Lyons, J. M. Mann, S. C. Hadler, R. Steece, and M. R. Skeels. 1985. Incidence of hepatitis B in the penitentiary of New Mexico. *American Journal of Public Health* 75: 1213–14.

Lauer, G. M., and Walker, B. D. 2001. Hepatitis C virus infection. *New England Journal of Medicine* 345: 41–52.

Long, J., S. Allwright, J. Barry, S. R. Reynolds, L. Thornton, F. Bradley, and J. V. Parry. 2001. Prevalence of antibodies to hepatitis B, hepatitis C, and HIV and risk factors in entrants to Irish prisons: A national cross sectional survey. *British Medical Journal* 323: 1209–13.

Macalino, G. E., D. Vlahov, S. Sanford, S. Patel, K. Sabin, C. Salas, and J. D. Rich. 2004. Prevelance and incidence of Human Immunodeficiency Virus, Hepatitis B Virus and Hepatitis C Virus among males in Rhode Island Prisons. *American Journal of Public Health* 94, no. 7:1218–23.

Malliori, M., V. Sypsa, M. Psichogiou, G. Touloumi, A. Skoutelis, N. Tassopoulos, A. Hatzakis, and C. Stefanis. 1998. A survey of bloodborne viruses and associated risk behaviours in Greek prisons. *Addiction* 93: 243–51.

Manns, M. P., J. G. McHutchison, S. C. Gordon, V. K. Rustgi, M. Shiffman, R. Reindollar, Z. D. Goodman, K. Koury, M. Ling, and J. K. Albrecht. 2001. Peginterferon alfa–2b plus ribavirin compared with interferon alfa–2b plus ribavirin for initial treatment of chronic hepatitis C: A randomised trial. *Lancet* 358: 958–65.

McHutchison, J. G., M. Manns, K. Patel, T. Poynard, K. L. Lindsay, C. Trepo, J. Dienstag, W. M. Lee, C. Mak, J. J. Garaud, and J. K. Albrecht. 2002a. Adherence to combination therapy enhances sustained response in genotype–1-infected patients with chronic hepatitis C. *Gastroenterology* 123: 1061–69.

McHutchison, J. G., T. Poynard, R. Esteban-Mur, G. L. Davis, Z. D. Goodman, J. Harvey, M. H. Ling, J. J. Garaud, J. K. Albrecht, K. Patel, J. L. Dienstag, and T. Morgan. 2002b. Hepatic

HCV RNA before and after treatment with interferon alone or combined with ribavirin. *Hepatology* 35: 688–93.

Nerenberg R. 2002. HCV in corrections: Frontline or backwater? *HEPP News* 5, no. 4. http://www.thebody.com/hepp/apr02/hcv_corrections.html.

National Institutes of Health (NIH). 2002. National Institutes of Health consensus development conference statement. Management of Hepatitis C. http://consensus.nih.gov/cons/116/091202116cdc_statement.htm.

Pallas, J. R., C. Farinas-Alvarez, D. Prieto, and M. Delgado-Rodriguez. 1999. Coinfections by HIV, hepatitis B and hepatitis C in imprisoned injecting drug users. *Euopean Journal of Epidemiology* 15: 699–704.

Poynard, T., P. Bedossa, and P. Opolon. 1997. Natural history of liver fibrosis progression in patients with chronic hepatitis C. The OBSVIRC, METAVIR, CLINIVIR, and DOSVIRC groups. *Lancet* 349: 825–32.

Rotily, M., C. Delorme, A. Galinier, N. Escaffre, and J. P. Moatti. 2000. HIV risk behavior in prison and factors associated with reincarceration of injection drug users. *Presse Medical* 29: 1549–56.

Ruiz, J. D., F. Molitor, R. K. Sun, J. Mikanda, M. Facer, J. M. Colford Jr., G. W. Rutherford, and M. S. Ascher. 1999. Prevalence and correlates of hepatitis C virus infection among inmates entering the California correctional system. *Western Journal of Medicine* 170: 156–60.

Salomon, J. A., M. C. Weinstein, J. K. Hammitt, and S. J. Goldie. 2003. Cost-effectiveness of treatment for chronic hepatitis C infection in an evolving patient population. *Journal of the American Medical Association* 290: 228–37.

Singh, S., R. Prasad, and A. Mohanty. 1999. High prevalence of sexually transmitted and blood-borne infections amongst the inmates of a district jail in Northern India. *International Journal of STD and AIDS* 10: 475–78.

Smyth, B. P. 2000. Health effects of prisons. Many injectors stop injecting while imprisoned. *British Medical Journal* 321: 1406.

Stephan, J. J., and J. C. Karberg. 2003. Census of State and Federal Correctional Facilities, 2000. United States Department of Justice, Office of Justice Programs, Bureau of Justice Statistics. NCJ 198272 . http://www.ojp.usdoj.gov/bjs/pub/pdf/csfcf00.pdf.

Taylor, A., D. Goldberg, S. Hutchinson, S. Cameron, S. M. Gore, J. McMenamin, S. Green, A. Pithie, and R. Fox. 2000. Prevalence of hepatitis C virus infection among injecting drug users in Glasgow, 1990–1996: Are current harm reduction strategies working? *Journal of Infectious Disease* 40: 176–83.

Vlahov, D., K. E. Nelson, T. C. Quinn, and N. Kendig. 1993. Prevalence and incidence of hepatitis C virus infection among male prison inmates in Maryland. *European Journal of Epidemiology* 9: 566–69.

Weild, A. R., O. N. Gill, D. Bennett, S. J. Livingstone, J. V. Parry, and L. Curran. 2000. Prevalence of HIV, hepatitis B, and hepatitis C antibodies in prisoners in England and Wales: A national survey. *Communicable Disease and Public Health* 3: 121–26.

Wiese, M., F. Berr, M. Lafrenz, H. Porst, and U. Oesen. 2000. Low frequency of cirrhosis in a hepatitis C (genotype 1b) single-source outbreak in Germany: A 20-year multicenter study. *Hepatology* 32: 91–96.

Williams, I. 1999. Epidemiology of hepatitis C in the United States. *American Journal of Medicine* 107: 2S–9S.

14

HIV/AIDS Infection among Incarcerated Women

ANNE S. DE GROOT
RACHEL MADDOW

The "common wisdom" about HIV/AIDS in prisons is that prisons serve as "breeding grounds" or "incubators" for the HIV/AIDS epidemic ("Prisons are breeding ground" 2001; UNAIDS 1997; Weed 2001). It is often assumed that the main reason prisoners are four times more likely than the general population to have AIDS is because of unprotected sex, drug use, and other HIV risk behaviors behind bars (Maruschak 2002). If in-prison risk behavior was the main factor driving high HIV rates among prisoners, one might expect to find higher rates of HIV among male prisoners than among female prisoners because of the relatively high HIV transmission risk associated with unprotected sex between men. In fact, incarcerated women are almost twice as likely as incarcerated men to be HIV positive: at the end of the year 2000, 3.6 percent of women prisoners were known to be HIV positive, as compared with 2.0 percent of male prisoners (Maruschak 2002).

Experts maintain that the high rate of HIV/AIDS among male and female prisoners is due to the fact that there is a higher concentration of individuals at high risk for HIV infection within prisons and jails than in the community (Braithwaite, Hammett, and Mayberry 1996). While in-prison HIV risk behaviors occur, it is likely that most HIV-positive prisoners were infected in the community, not while they were incarcerated. Incarcerated women have higher rates of HIV infection than men because women have particularly high rates of HIV risk factors in the community both before and after incarceration, including drug use, sex work, childhood sexual abuse, and physical abuse (DeGroot 2000; Fogel and Belyea 1999).

In this chapter, we describe the prevalence of HIV/AIDS among women prisoners, discuss the risk factors that give rise to the high rates of HIV/AIDS in this population, and provide basic information about culturally appropriate management of HIV/AIDS in correctional facilities that house women. As advocates and practitioners in this field, we also recommend that readers seek out the many important documents in this field written by women prisoners themselves (Boudin 1993; Boudin et al. 1999; DeGroot and Cuccinelli 1997; Henry 1999, 2002; Members of the ACE Program 1998; Voices from Inside 1993).

Prevalence of HIV/AIDS among Incarcerated Women

The overall prevalence of known HIV infection among female state prisoners at year-end 2000 was 3.6 percent (Maruschak 2002). Because the overall prevalence of HIV among U.S. women is thought to be 0.18 to 0.27 percent, it can be estimated that women in state prisons are thirteen to twenty times more likely than women in the general population to be living with HIV (UNAIDS and WHO 2002). In specific correctional jurisdictions, primarily but not exclusively on the East Coast, HIV prevalence rates are much higher than the national average (see table 14.1). It should also be noted that figures provided by correctional facilities may underestimate the true prevalence of HIV infection. In facilities without mandatory testing, some inmates may prefer not to disclose their HIV status.

Occasionally, prevalence estimates are derived from blinded serosurveys. A survey might, for example, perform HIV testing on leftover serum from mandated syphilis tests (Maryland 2003). Blinded serosurveys that only consider new correctional admissions may understate the true prevalence of HIV/AIDS among women prisoners because the number of times a woman has been arrested can be an indirect measure of the likelihood of her exposure to HIV when her HIV risk behaviors (that is, drug use or sex work) are the same behaviors that put her at risk

TABLE 14.1
Highest HIV prevalence rates among women prisoners, year-end 2000

Location	%
Washington, DC	41.0%
New York (State)	18.2
Nevada	12.4
Connecticut	10.3
Maryland	9.8
Florida	9.0
Maine	8.1
New Jersey	6.8

Source: Maruschak (2002)

for arrest. The number of times a woman has been arrested may be linked both to the likelihood that she will be sentenced and the frequency of her HIV exposures (Stevens et al. 1995). Uninfected women (with fewer probable HIV exposures and fewer arrests) are more likely to be released due to their unencumbered criminal record, while women with more arrests and, therefore, more probable HIV exposures (who are more likely to be HIV infected) tend to accumulate sentences and time behind bars. Thus blinded studies of "new admissions" to a women's jail are likely to underestimate the number of women living with HIV/AIDS in a given correctional facility.

Underestimating the prevalence of HIV/AIDS among prisoners may contribute to the development of inaccurate correctional budgets for medication and personnel. More accurate estimates of the prevalence of HIV infection in correctional facilities might serve to dispel widely held beliefs that disproportionate money and effort are spent on HIV-positive inmates.

Understanding High Rates of HIV/AIDS among Women Prisoners

Understanding the reasons why incarcerated women have such high rates of HIV infection is the first step toward crafting culturally appropriate HIV/AIDS services for women in prison. The matrix of factors affecting the HIV prevalence rate is complex—it includes demographic considerations such as race, health, and behavioral issues including sex and drug use, as well as more complex social issues like poverty and sentencing laws. We describe some of the important factors affecting HIV/AIDS prevalence among incarcerated women to lay the groundwork for understanding how quality HIV/AIDS services for incarcerated women differ from those provided for incarcerated men.

Sentencing Changes

One factor underlying the high prevalence of HIV/AIDS among women prisoners is the shift in the nature of crimes for which women have been incarcerated over the course of the HIV/AIDS epidemic. Table 14.2 shows that since 1979, the proportion of female state prisoners incarcerated for drug offenses has risen, while the proportion incarcerated for violent and property offenses has declined. The overall rate of incarceration for women has also dramatically increased during the course of the HIV/AIDS epidemic. The rate of incarceration for U.S. women in 1979 was 10 per 100,000 population; in 2000, it was 59 per 100,000 (*Sourcebook* 2001). Having been convicted of a drug-related offense is not a risk factor for HIV/AIDS, but it is a marker for drug use and for involvement in street economies that may raise the risk of a woman's potential exposure to HIV/AIDS through sex and drug use.

Drug and Alcohol Use

Incarcerated women report high levels of involvement with drugs and alcohol. Women prisoners are five to eight times more likely to have abused alcohol than

TABLE 14.2

Proportion of female state prisoners, by offense category, 1979–1997 (%)

Offense	1979	1986	1991	1997
Violent	47.9	40.7	32.2	28.2
Property	36.1	41.2	28.7	26.6
Drug	12.3	12.0	32.8	34.4

Source: Greenfeld and Snell (1999)

women outside of prison, ten times more likely to have abused drugs, and twenty-seven times more likely to have used cocaine (Zlotnick 2002). More women prisoners than male prisoners report regular drug use and being under the influence of drugs when they committed the offense for which they were incarcerated; however, males tend to report more alcohol use than females (Bloom, Owen, and Covington 2003).

Sexual Health

Incarcerated women tend to have high rates of sexually transmitted infections (STIs), vaginal infections, and abnormal Pap smears. In one study, more than three-quarters of newly incarcerated women had abnormal Pap smears and a majority had vaginal infections or STIs (CDC 2003a). High rates of STIs are associated with high risk for HIV for three main reasons:

1. Unprotected sex that results in the transmission of an STI could also result in HIV transmission.
2. STIs can cause genital lesions that can increase a person's susceptibility to HIV infection. In addition, STIs increase the number of CD4 cells in a woman's cervical secretions—CD4 cells are target cells for HIV, and increased CD4s in vaginal secretions can increase a woman's susceptibility to HIV infection.
3. If a person is infected with both HIV and an STI, increased "shedding" of HIV can occur—which means that the person is more likely to infect another person if he or she engages in high risk behavior such as unprotected sex or sharing needles. (CDC 1998)

The high prevalence of STIs and other sexual health issues is a marker for HIV risk behaviors. Because of the crossover of risks for HIV and STIs, testing or diagnosis of an STI can offer an opportunity for health care providers to discuss the issue of HIV transmission with patients.

History of Abuse

An additional factor in the high rates of HIV infection among incarcerated women may be prior physical and/or sexual abuse. According to self-reported data, from 33 to 65 percent of incarcerated women report prior sexual abuse, and from 19 to 42 percent report a history of childhood sexual abuse (Brown, Miller, and Maguin 1999; Fogel and Belyea 1999; Stevens et al. 1995). These figures probably underestimate the prevalence of abuse histories among incarcerated women. In contrast, in studies of women who are not currently incarcerated, approximately one woman in seven (14.3 percent) reports a history of forced sex, one woman in five (20 percent) reports a history of childhood sexual abuse, and about one woman in four (25 percent) reports a history of physical abuse. These studies of women outside correctional facilities do not often request information on previous incarceration; thus, there may be some overlap between populations.

Prolonged physical and sexual abuse may have damaging effects on emotional development and social functioning and may lead to behaviors that increase the risk of HIV infection. A number of studies have linked prior childhood experiences of abuse and neglect with women's health care needs, mental health needs, and HIV risk behaviors (Clarke et al. 1999; Fogel and Belyea 1999; Johnson et al. 1999; Richie and Johnson 1996; Stevens et al. 1995).

Racial Demographics

Women of color, particularly African American women, are grossly overrepresented among women prisoners. Although the racially skewed demographics of the incarcerated female population do not mirror the racial balance of the general U.S. population, they do mirror the racial balance of women living with HIV/AIDS in the United States. CDC estimates that annual new HIV infections among U.S. women are 64 percent among African Americans, 18 percent among whites, and 18 percent among Hispanics (CDC 2002). Cumulative AIDS cases reported among women through 2002 in the United States are 59 percent among African Americans, 21 percent among whites, and 19 percent among Hispanics (CDC 2003b). Women involved in the criminal justice system are more likely to be women of color than the general population, and women of color are more likely to be living with HIV/AIDS than white women.

Other Issues, Further Study

Other determinants of incarceration and HIV infection in women include poverty, racism, the status of women in society, illiteracy, adolescent pregnancy, and lack of marketable job skills (Zierler and Krieger 1997). Each of these factors contributes to poorer health, decreased access to adequate and affordable healthcare, and/or increased exposure to community violence. The presence of these factors alone do not cause poor outcomes per se, but they each influence women's chances of participating in activities that lead to incarceration and put them at risk for HIV infection.

Culturally Appropriate HIV/AIDS Management
in Women's Correctional Facilities

For a variety of social and economic reasons, incarcerated women may have little access to HIV/AIDS services in the community. Therefore, time in prison or jail presents an important opportunity to learn about HIV infection, acquire prevention skills, get tested, and gain access to HIV/AIDS treatment and other health care. But for many individuals, it is difficult to consider sensitive and life-changing issues such as HIV/AIDS in a correctional setting. Incarcerated women who know they are HIV positive do not always seek care in the prison or jail health unit, preferring instead to postpone care until they are released and can return to the care of community-based clinicians who have engaged their trust. Trust and sensitivity are key ingredients to a successful HIV management program for incarcerated women (Mostahari et al. 1998). When the issue is approached in a sensitive manner, incarcerated women are often willing to be tested for HIV or to disclose their HIV status.

Identifying Risk

To identify women's risk factors for HIV/AIDS and other infectious diseases, medical evaluations in prisons or jails should include questions about a number of social factors that, in a male-focused environment, might not be seen as directly relevant to a patient's medical history. A woman's history of physical abuse, sexual abuse, sexual assault, domestic violence, commercial sex work, and drug use all may have a direct impact on her risk for HIV/AIDS as well as the appropriate course of HIV/AIDS counseling, education, testing, treatment, and case management. Because correctional environments are usually designed with male prisoners in mind, women's HIV/AIDS risk factors may not be recognized as "classic" HIV/AIDS risks for prisoners—just as gynecological or menstrual problems caused by HIV may not be recognized as "classic" HIV/AIDS symptoms.

Stigma

The incarcerated woman's fear of stigmatization by her peers and by correctional staff can have a negative impact on HIV/AIDS management in prisons and jails. The closed setting of correctional institutions makes confidentiality difficult to maintain (particularly if a clinic or care provider is identified as being associated with HIV), though total confidentiality should always be the goal. In some institutions, an HIV diagnosis may have overt negative consequences, such as segregated housing or limited access to prison programs. Alabama, Mississippi, and California, for example, are three states whose housing policies allow for segregation of HIV seropositive and seronegative inmates (Hammett, Harmon, and Maruschak

1999). Since Alabama and Mississippi require HIV screening for new inmates, they can effectively integrate these policies. In most facilities in California, inmates with AIDS live separately from the general population and asymptomatic HIV-infected inmates. These individuals may, however, attend work and vocational programs with the other inmates. From a public health perspective, discrimination on the basis of HIV infection is not necessary or appropriate, and it may discourage at-risk patients from getting tested. Peer HIV/AIDS education programs may reduce stigmatization among prisoners and increase the general awareness of HIV (and of the prevalence of infection among their peers) in the female prison or jail population (Members of the ACE Program 1998).

Testing

Factors that are likely to encourage incarcerated women to get tested include concern about the impact of HIV infection on their present or future children and about having contracted HIV in the context of having acquired other STIs. Many incarcerated women may have been tested for HIV in the course of prior pregnancies and may therefore be familiar with the concepts and procedures related to HIV tests. However, younger women (with fewer arrests, fewer pregnancies, and fewer opportunities to interact with HIV testers and counselors) may be less familiar with the concept of HIV testing and more fearful.

Because incarcerated women have a high prevalence of HIV, because they may have multiple sources of HIV risk in their lives, and because they may have limited access to HIV testing and counseling services outside of prison or jail, there should be multiple opportunities for women to say "yes" to HIV counseling and education while they are incarcerated. In particular, education and testing services should be offered on multiple occasions to women who

- are pregnant or who are seeking pregnancy testing
- have a current or prior STI diagnosis
- have abnormal pap smear test results
- have hepatitis B or C
- have a history of sex work
- have a history of physical and/or sexual abuse
- have a history of drug use and/or needle sharing behavior

In many facilities, this list of "risk factors" will include virtually every female prisoner in the institution. With HIV/AIDS prevalence rates thirteen to twenty times higher in prisons than the general population, voluntary HIV testing should be regularly offered and easily available to all women prisoners.

Language Barriers

Non-English-speaking women and women for whom English is not their first language can face significant barriers in obtaining medical care and social services. Written materials in languages other than English, "buddy" programs with bilingual peers, and bilingual medical and social service programs may be helpful. Bilingual providers who are culturally attuned and able to discuss HIV management with non-English speakers may be more likely to succeed at building patient-provider trust than their monolingual colleagues.

Literacy and Basic Skills

A basic skills and literacy assessment may help to determine if a woman's difficulty with reading and writing will reduce her ability to take advantage of medical and social services. Low literacy and picture-based written materials can be useful in this setting. HIV/AIDS programs in prisons can also offer an opportunity to develop literacy and basic skills (Boudin et al. 1999).

Pregnancy

In 1998, 1,400 women gave birth within prisons (U.S. General Accounting Office 1999). The number of these women who were infected with HIV is unknown. Vertical transmission of HIV infection has been all but eradicated in the United States as a result of the success of prenatal HIV testing programs in the community (Lindegren 1999). However, leading pediatric HIV researchers have repeatedly raised concerns about reaching high-risk women who seek care late in the course of pregnancy. In a 1997 survey of prisons and jails, HIV testing was mandatory for pregnant women in 39 percent of prisons and 2 percent of jails, routine in 8 percent of prisons and 15 percent of jails, and provided on request at 14 percent of prisons and 22 percent of jails; 10 percent of jails had no policy related to HIV testing during pregnancy (Hammett, Harmon, and Maruschak 1999). The correctional setting clearly provides a critical opportunity to reach a group of women who may not have accessed prenatal testing in the community.

Family Services

Most women prisoners are mothers, and family responsibilities are often the top priority for incarcerated parents and parents being released from prison. HIV/AIDS services for women prisoners and ex-prisoners should address family issues such as foster care, family reunification, parenting education, child care, guardianship planning, domestic violence prevention, and victim services. There is ample opportunity to provide counseling and other mental health services during the incarceration period and after release for the female inmate, her children, and the individuals who served as guardians for her children. Due to the complexity of the HIV/AIDS infection and the stigma attached to those infected, it may be difficult for mothers to

- accept their HIV status (for those who were tested upon entry into the facility)
- share necessary information with their children
- disclose their status (if necessary) to other people outside of the correctional facility

Access to adequate post-test and post-release counseling services will give inmates and their families a chance to learn effective coping strategies and could, ultimately, facilitate a smoother transition from the facility into the community.

Hepatitis

It has been estimated that up to 80 percent of HIV-positive male prisoners are also infected with hepatitis C (Rich, Chin-Hong, et al. 1997). Because women prisoners generally have higher rates of chronic hepatitis C than male prisoners, the HIV/HCV coinfection rate may also be higher among women (Maryland 2003; Massachusetts Public Health Association 2003). As hepatitis-related liver disease becomes a leading cause of death in some correctional facilities, the management of HIV/AIDS in prisons will become ever more entwined with the management of chronic viral hepatitis.

Discharge Planning

Discharge planning and transitional HIV/AIDS services can be a stabilizing force for HIV-positive women prisoners and ex-prisoners, ultimately easing the transition back to home communities after release. The issue of discharge planning has received increased attention in recent years, largely due to the evaluation of model programs and to the joint CDC/HRSA five-year demonstration project on "HIV Prevention, Intervention, and Continuity of Care within Correctional Settings and the Community" (Flanigan et al. 1996; Laufer et al. 2002; Rapposelli et al. 2002; Rich, Holmes, et al. 2001).

Conclusion

Incarcerated women are disproportionately affected by HIV. It is the crimes for which women are incarcerated—most often drug use and drug-related crimes— and the life circumstances that surround these crimes that put incarcerated women at risk for HIV infection. Correctional management of HIV-infected women must take into account the many reasons for their acute vulnerability to HIV: these include drug use, histories of physical and sexual abuse, and poverty. Therefore, correctional management of HIV can be viewed as a network of interconnected services that can address the various needs of an incarcerated woman. These services include clinical medical services as well as physical and sexual abuse recovery programs, drug treatment, and mental health services. They may also include vocational training and skills-building workshops that, by helping women to become socioeconomically more powerful, facilitate their ability to continue to effectively manage their health care needs and to prevent HIV transmission upon prison release. Finally, discharge planning programs initiated during incarceration can help connect women to community medical services; drug treatment and support services that provide child care; safe, affordable housing; and job training and employment opportunities that will all serve to increase a woman's ability to continue to care for her own health needs. Overall, incarceration provides a critical opportunity for the education, diagnosis, and medical care of HIV-infected women and high-risk HIV seronegative women as well as a public health opportunity to reduce the spread of HIV infection.

REFERENCES

Bloom, B., B. Owen, and S. Covington. 2003. *Gender Responsive Strategies: Research, Practice, and Guiding Principles for Women Offenders.* Washington, DC: National Institute of Corrections.

Boudin, K. 1993. Participatory literacy behind bars: AIDS opens the door. *Harvard Educational Review* 63: 207–32.

Boudin, K., I. Carrero, J. Clark, V. V. Flournoy, K. Loftin, S. Martindale, M. Martinez, E. Mastroieni, and S. Richardson. 1999. ACE: A peer education and counseling program meets the needs of incarcerated women with HIV/AIDS issues. *Journal of the Association of Nurses in Aids Care* 10: 90–98.

Braithwaite, R. L., T. M. Hammett, and R. M. Mayberry. 1996. *Prisons and AIDS: A Public Health Challenge.* San Francisco: Jossey-Bass.

Browne, A., B. Miller, and E. Maguin. 1999. Prevalence and severity of lifetime physical and sexual victimization among incarcerated women. *International Journal of Law Psychiatry* 22: 301–22.

Centers for Disease Control and Prevention (CDC). 1998. *Prevention and treatment of sexually transmitted diseases as an HIV prevention strategy: CDC Update.* Atlanta: CDC.

CDC. 2002. *A glance at the HIV epidemic: CDC HIV/AIDS update.* Atlanta: CDC.

CDC. 2003a. "Prevention and Control of Infections with Hepatitis Viruses in Correctional Settings." *MMWR* 52, no. RR–1 (January 24): 49.

CDC. 2003b. *HIV/AIDS surveillance report.* Vol. 14, Addendum: Table A3. Atlanta: CDC.

Clarke, J., M. D. Stein, M. Sobota, M. Marisi, and L. Hanna. 1999. Victims as victimizers: Physical aggression by persons with a history of childhood abuse. *Archives of Internal Medicine* 159: 1920–24.

DeGroot, A. S. 2000. HIV infection among incarcerated women: Epidemic behind bars. *AIDS Reader* 10: 287–95.

DeGroot, A. S., and D. Cuccinelli. 1997. Put her in a cage: Childhood sexual abuse, incarceration, and HIV infection. In *The gender politics of HIV in women: Perspectives on the pandemic in the United States,* ed. J. Manlowe and N. Goldstein. New York: New York University Press.

Flanigan, T. P., J. Y. Kim, S. Zierler, J. Rich, K. Vigilante, and D. Bury-Maynard. 1996. A prison release program for HIV-positive women: Linking them to health services and community follow-up. Letter to the Editor. *American Journal of Public Health* 86: 886–87.

Fogel, C. I., and M. Belyea. 1999. The lives of incarcerated women: violence, substance abuse, and risk for HIV. *Journal of the Association of Nurses in AIDS Care* 10: 66–74.

Greenfeld, L. A., and T. L. Snell. 1999. Women offenders: Special Report. Washington, DC: Bureau of Justice Statistics.

Hammett, T. M., P. Harmon, and L. M. Maruschak. 1999. 1996–1997 *Update: HIV/AIDS, STDs and TB in Correctional Facilities.* Washington, DC: National Institute of Justice.

Henry, B. 1999. Between a rock and a hard place. *Women Alive* (Spring), http://www.aegis.com/pubs/woalive/1999/WO990407.html.

Henry, B. 2002. Positive Empowerment. *Test Positive Aware Network* 13, no. 3: 23.

Johnson, J. C., P. Cohen, J. Brown, E. M. Smailes, and D. P. Bernstein. 1999. Childhood maltreatment increases risk for personality disorders during early adulthood. *Archives of General Psychiatry* 56: 607–8.

Laufer, F. N., K.R.J. Arriola, C. S. Dawson-Rose, K. Kumaravelu, and K. K. Rapposelli. 2002.

From jail to community: Innovative strategies to enhance continuity of HIV/AIDS care. *Prison Journal* 82: 84–100.

Lindegren, M. L. 1999. Trends in perinatal transmission of HIV/AIDS in the United States. *Journal of the American Medical Association* 282: 531–38.

Maruschak, L. M. 2002. HIV in Prisons, 2000. Bulletin. Washington, DC: Bureau of Justice Statistics.

Maryland Department of Health and Mental Hygiene and Maryland Division of Correction. 2003. *Examination of HIV, Syphilis, Hepatitis B, and Hepatitis C in Maryland correctional facilities*. Annapolis: Maryland Department of Health and Mental Hygiene.

Massachusetts Public Health Association. 2003. *Correctional health: The missing key to improving the public's health and safety*. Boston: MPHA.

Members of the ACE Program of the Bedford Hills Correctional Facility. 1998. *Breaking the walls of silence: AIDS and women in a New York State maximum-security prison*. Woodstock, NY: Overlook Press.

Mostahari, F., E. Riley, P. A. Selwyn, and F. L. Altice. 1998. Antiretroviral use among HIV-infected female prisoners. *Journal of Acquired Immune Deficiency Syndromes and Human Retrovirology* 18: 341–48.

Prisons are breeding ground for HIV, but officials ignore problem. 2001. *Body Positive Newsletter* 19, no. 9 (October).

Rapposelli, K. K., M. G. Kennedy, J. R. Miles, M. J. Tinsley, K. J. Rauch, L. Austin, S. Dooley, B. Aranda-Naranjo, and R. A. Moore. 2002. HIV/AIDS in correctional settings: A salient priority for CDC and HRSA. *AIDS Education and Prevention* 14 (suppl. B): 103–13.

Rich, J. D., P. V. Chin-Hong, K. A. Busi, K. H. Mayer, and T. P. Flanigan. 1997. Hepatitis C and HIV in male prisoners. *Journal of Acquired Immune Deficiency Syndromes and Human Retrovirology* 16: 408–9.

Rich, J. D., L. Holmes, C. Salas, G. Macalino, D. Davis, J. Ryczek, and T. Flanigan. 2001. Successful linkage of medical care and community services for HIV-positive offenders being released from prison. *Journal of Urban Health* 78: 279–89.

Richie, B. E., and C. Johnson. 1996. Abuse histories among newly incarcerated women in a New York City jail. *Journal of American Medical Women's Association* 51: 111–17.

Sourcebook of Criminal Justice Statistics. 2001. Washington, DC: Bureau of Justice Statistics.

Stevens, J., S. Zierler, V. Cram, D. Dean, K. H. Mayer, and A. S. De Groot. 1995. Risks for HIV infection in incarcerated women. *Journal of Women's Health* 4: 569–77.

United Nations Acquired Immune Deficiency Syndrome (UNAIDS). 1997. *Prisons and AIDS: UNAIDS point of view*. Geneva: UNAIDS.

UNAIDS and World Health Organization (WHO). 2002. Table of UNAIDS/WHO country-specific HIV/AIDS estimates, end–2001. *Report on the global HIV/AIDS epidemic* 2002. Geneva: UNAIDS.

U.S. General Accounting Office. 1999. *Report to Honorable Eleanor Holmes Norton: Women in prison. Issues and challenges confronting U.S. correctional systems*. Washington, DC: U.S. General Accounting Office. Publication GAO/GGD-00-22.

Voices from inside: Prisoners respond to the AIDS crisis. 1993. San Francisco: ACT UP/San Francisco.

Weed, W. S. 2001. *Incubating disease: prisons are rife with infectious illnesses—and threaten to spread them to the public*. Mother Jones.com Special Report: July 10, 2001. http://www.motherjones.com/prisons/disease.html (accessed June 24, 2003).

Zierler, S., and N. Krieger. 1997. Reframing women's risk: Social inequalities and HIV infection. *Annual Review Public Health* 18: 401–36.

Zlotnick, C. 2002. *Treatment of incarcerated women with substance abuse and post-traumatic stress disorder*. Rockville, MD: National Criminal Justice Reference Service.

15

Adherence to Antiretroviral Therapy in HIV-Infected Incarcerated Women

BECKY L. STEPHENSON

At least five percent of the HIV-infected women in the United States are incarcerated (Maruschak 2003). Many of these women are inmates in correctional facilities where antiretroviral therapy (HIV medication) is routinely provided (Hammett, Harmon, and Maruschak 1999). Most of these women represent underserved populations for whom access to care is poor. Incarceration may be the first time that these individuals have consistently received medical care. HIV care and treatment in correctional facilities can be challenging because of confidentiality issues, medical understaffing, and inflexible medication line hours (Spaulding et al. 2002). Interventions that are widely used in prisons may enhance adherence or become a barrier. Furthermore, most prisons were designed for men and are not gender specific (U.S. Government Accounting Office [U.S. GAO] 1999). This is important because women prisoners are disproportionately depressed, poorly educated, and sick when compared to their nonincarcerated counterparts (Conklin, Lincoln, and Tuthill 2000; Jordan et al. 2002). They also come from communities that historically have distrusted health care systems and providers (Altice, Mostashari, and Friedland 2001). Despite these challenges, there is data that shows incarcerated populations are able to adhere to HIV medication schedules and to achieve virological outcomes at least equivalent to their nonincarcerated counterparts (Kirkland et al. 2002; Wohl et al. 2003). This chapter reviews the definition, importance, measurements, determinants, and interventions associated with adherence to HIV medications in HIV-infected incarcerated women.

The use of recently developed combination antiretroviral therapy has been associated with decreased morbidity in both incarcerated and nonincarcerated populations (Maruschak 2003; Palella et al. 1998; Wright and Smith 1999). The National Commission on Correctional Health Care advocates the use of antiretroviral therapy in correctional settings in a manner that parallels its use in noncorrectional communities. When HIV medications are prescribed in certain combinations of three or more, they are highly active because they have the ability to kill most of the virus in the blood to very low levels. Thus, combination antiretroviral treatment is called "highly active antiretroviral therapy" or HAART. The degree of viral suppression is primarily determined by the ability of a patient to adhere to his or her HAART (Stone et al. 2002). Adherence to these complex regimens has been associated with increased survival and decreased hospitalizations (Paterson and Mohr 2000; Stone et al. 2002). Thus, it is of primary importance to understand adherence and the factors that are associated with adherence to HAART.

Adherence to antiretroviral therapy in nonincarcerated populations has been associated with many factors such as active substance abuse, antiretroviral pill burden, antiretroviral side effects, and the relationship between patient and health-care provider (Chesney 2000). Although there is limited data about these factors in incarcerated populations, evidence suggests that some of these variables may differ from nonincarcerated populations (Kirkland et al. 2002). Most commonly, the variables have been separated into system, treatment, and patient related. In order to design the needed interventions to achieve positive health outcomes in HIV-infected women prisoners, it is crucial to understand the many factors that affect HAART adherence in prisons.

Adherence: Definition and Measurements

Before the factors potentially affecting adherence in prisons can be understood, it is necessary to understand the definition of adherence, its relationship to viral resistance, and why "near-perfect" adherence is required. Adherence can be defined as "the ability to follow a prescribed treatment regimen that has been developed through a shared decision-making process between the client and the health care provider" (Frank 1999). It involves taking the right medication at the specific dose prescribed at the right time. In addition, it involves taking the medications with or without food as prescribed.

What distinguishes adherence in HIV disease from other chronic diseases is that poor adherence can lead to the development of resistance that can render the HIV medications ineffective. Resistance develops because of the very high replication and mutation rate of HIV (Peiperl and Volberding 2003). If the medications are missed, the drug levels become low. Low drug levels allow the virus to increase replication. The more the virus replicates or reproduces itself, the more mutations occur. Mutations in the viral genes may cause the virus to become unresponsive to some HIV medication. When this happens, the virus is said to be resistant to the medication. This can have lifelong consequences, since many of the medications are similar. Thus, resistance to one medication can confer resistance to other medications. This is called cross-resistance. This cross-resistance can limit future treatment options for these individuals, eventually leaving an individual with HIV without any effective treatment options (Peiperl and Volberding 2003). Furthermore, because resistant viruses can be transmitted from person to person, the potential to impact public health exists (Stone et al. 2002).

The degree of adherence required to forestall viral resistance is very high in comparison to other chronic disease states. Most studies show that HAART adherence needs to be greater than 90 to 95 percent to forestall viral resistance and therefore sustain viral suppression (Paterson and Mohr 2000). This is of concern since, in most chronic diseases, the majority of patients take only 50 percent of their prescribed doses (Stone 2001). Although some studies show that many HIV-infected individuals have HAART adherence rates of 70 to 80 percent, these adherence rates are suboptimal to maintain adequate viral suppression and prevent resistance. Thus, measuring adherence becomes very important.

Adherence Measurement in Prisons

How does one measure adherence? Measures of adherence can be divided into subjective, objective, and physiological measures. Subjective measures are self-reports of adherence by patients. Objective measures are pill counts of returned medications, medication refill data from the pharmacy, medication administration records as recorded by correctional staff, and electronic monitoring caps. Electronic monitoring caps are primarily used in research settings to record electronically the opening and closing of the medication container, which should correlate with medication taking. Physiological measures are the viral blood levels (viral loads) and antiretroviral drug levels.

The most commonly available measure in prison clinics is inmate self-reporting. Most studies have shown that HIV-infected individuals overestimate their adherence by self-report (Stone 2001). This has also been shown in prison cohorts. Wohl et al. found that the median self-reported HAART adherence of fifty-one men and women prisoners was 100 percent. When pill counts and eDems were used to measure adherence, adherence was significantly lower at 90 percent and 86 percent, respectively (Wohl et al. 2003). Patients often overestimate their adherence to their health care providers because of recall bias (difficulty remembering not-so-recent events) and social desirability (wanting to please their doctors). But when patients report poor adherence and/or admit to not taking medications, self-report data has been shown to be very reliable. Out-of-prison studies have shown that self-report data can also be helpful when adherence is confined to the last three days (Stone 2001). In general, self-report of nonadherence is helpful and recall of adherence within the past three days has been proven to be the most valid.

Objective measures have also been shown to be valid, but this measurement has not been fully evaluated in correctional settings. Most correctional health care providers do not have access to pill counts, but many have access to pharmacy refill data and medication administration records as many of the antiretrovirals are directly observed (Altice 1998). In a study of incarcerated women, pharmacy refill data has been associated with adherence in incarcerated and nonincarcerated settings (Mostashari et al. 1998). However, this may be less help-ful as some prisons switch to automatic refill policies. Medication administration records are used in many prisons to monitor adherence to many medications. Wohl and colleagues (2003) showed that medication administration records over-estimated adherence, as compared to validated objective measures such as pill counts and electronic monitoring caps in a prison cohort. This data suggests that medication administration records should not be the sole adherence measure.

Physiological measures such as viral loads and therapeutic drug monitoring can be used to measure adherence. Although many correctional facilities may not have ready access to HIV drug level monitoring, most have access to viral load data (Hammett, Harmon, and Maruschak 1999). Viral load data has been shown to cor-relate with adherence (Paterson and Mohr 2000). However, this can be mislead-ing. In patients new to HIV drugs, individuals who are less than 90 percent adherent for the first few months can have undetectable viral loads. If providers are relying solely on viral load data, they can be misled into attributing good ad-herence to poorly adherent patients. In summary, multiple measures should be used to access inmate adherence (Liu et al. 2001).

Determinants of Inmate Adherence

System-Related Issues

The primary goal of correctional institutions is to protect the public and punish the convicted offenders. This is done by detaining convicted offenders in a secure and controlled environment (Frank 1999). Security takes precedence over health care in most correctional systems, which can lead to a disruption of access, care, and treatment for HIV-infected women inmates. Because security is standardized, this has influenced medical care as well. Treatment is standardized by protocols with little individualization since this can indicate favoritism. In contrast, the practice of community medicine uses standardized treatment individualized for each patient.

Despite these differences, inmates are the only Americans guaranteed a right to health care by the U.S. constitution (Rold 1998). This unique access to care and treatment may be responsible for the success in HIV care in prisons. Correctional facilities also provide uniform access to care (Mostashari et al. 1998). Even more important is access to antiretrovirals. In the United States, many barriers exist in the procurement of antiretrovirals for individuals. For prisoners, access to antiretrovirals is guaranteed by the Eighth Amendment, unlike in nonincarcer-ated populations (Rold 1998). Thus, financial and access barriers are removed if not completely eliminated.

Correctional systems have a distinct history of providers. Traditionally, most providers have been correctional officers who attended to all health care needs.

With the advent of the modern prison health care system, officers have been replaced with nurses, physicians, and physician extenders. Understaffing has been
such a chronic problem that correctional facilities have been listed as
underserved areas by the federal government. Staff turnover is high—especially
among nurses—resulting in poor continuity of care. Treatment of HIV disease requires constant updates and education. Because of the nursing shortage, prisons
must again use correctional officers to perform many tasks reserved for nurses
outside of prisons. This can be a problem since inmates not surprisingly have an
adversarial relationship with their custody officers. In a study by Stephenson et al.
(2003), women inmates universally stated that they would rather have their medication given by a nurse than a custody officer. Also, many of the officers may not
understand the importance of adherence that is necessary for positive health outcomes in HIV-infected individuals.

Specialized correctional nurses may influence health care outcomes in HIV-
infected prisoners. Some prisons have specialized correctional nurses that are
specifically assigned to monitor HIV-infected inmates and medications and provide discharge planning services at prison release (Wohl et al. 2004). In the North
Carolina state prison system, a group of specialized nurses called "outreach
nurses" monitor the health of inmates between visits to their HIV health care providers. They assess inmates for medication side effects and adherence. In addition, they go to their prison facilities and help with facility-specific issues. Many
prisons have specialized HIV nurses that may contribute to the success of HAART
adherence in prisons.

Specialized nurses serve as educational resources on HIV for prison systems
in the absence of continuous educational updates. Many systems are not able to
send their nurses and health care providers to conferences because of lack of
funding. In addition, pharmaceutical companies (which provide support for educational activities in the community) are often not allowed to provide educational
seminars on site. (Although many pharmaceutical company presentations are biased, they are a common way that health care providers learn new information.)

Collaborations between correctional institutions and other health care agencies have evolved with providers affiliated with academic teaching hospitals, public health departments, and private practice. This has resulted in providers from
state-of-the-art institutions providing HIV care. These providers bring medical
expertise and experience often lacking in prisons. Experience of providers has
been associated with survival and in HIV infected individuals (Kitahata et al. 1996,
2003).

Patient-Related Factors
DEMOGRAPHIC FACTORS. The relationship between demographic factors (such as
age, race, gender, and education) and adherence have been measured in incarcerated HIV-infected women. In our study, we found no association between adherence and these demographic factors (Stephenson et al. 2003). Other prison

studies showed that male gender, higher education, and white race have been associated with better adherence (Altice, Mostashari, and Friedland 2001; Mostashari et al. 1998). The results are consistent with nonincarcerated results where demographic factors have not been consistently associated with medication adherence (Fogarty et al. 2002; Stephenson et al. 2003).

SOCIAL PSYCHOLOGICAL FACTORS. Medication adherence has been associated with social psychological factors such as substance abuse and depression. This is of particular importance to women because the prevalence of depression and substance abuse is higher in incarcerated women than in their nonincarcerated counterparts (Centers for Disease Control and Prevention [CDC] 2001). Both of these factors, when untreated, have been associated with poor adherence (Chesney 2000). In our group of women, depression and active substance abuse were cited as common reasons for missed medications (Stephenson et al. 2003). Although substance abuse correctional programs are not readily available, the increased access to mental health care and mental health medications offer an opportunity for correctional health care providers to facilitate adherence in this population.

Health beliefs and attitudes have been associated with adherence in women prisoners. Studies have shown that prisoners of both genders who trusted their medications showed higher adherence to antiretrovirals than those who did not (Altice et al. 2001; Stephenson et al. 2003). In contrast, in studies of women prisoners only, trust in antiretroviral therapy was not associated with adherence. However, interpersonal relationships between health care providers defined as the "belief that an HIV doctor always listens to her" and the "belief that an HIV doctor always understands her" were associated with adherence (Mostashari et al. 1998). Thus, positive beliefs and attitudes about health care providers may be more important for HIV-infected women than beliefs about antiretrovirals in facilitating adherence.

Social support has also been measured in women inmates. Studies have shown that men and women prisoners who were socially isolated or received no social support regarding HIV were less likely to be adherent to their antiretroviral regimen (Wohl et al. 2003). Studies that have examined women only have found that social support by peers was associated with adherence (Mostashari et al. 1998). This has been shown in studies outside of correctional institutions as well (Fogarty et al. 2002). Thus social support, especially peer support in prisons, is an important social correlate of adherence to antiretrovirals in women prisoners.

Treatment-Related Factors

The complexity of the regimen has been extensively studied. Many studies have examined the association of pill burden with adherence. In a systematic overview of clinical trials, Bartlett et al. (2001) showed that the number of pills (pill count) was negatively associated with viral load suppression (plasma HIV RNA < 50 copies/mL). Since adherence correlates with viral load suppression (Paterson and Mohr 2000), this study suggests that increasing pill burden is associated with poor adherence.

In some studies, complex dietary restrictions have been associated with poor adherence (Chesney 2000). For example, antiretrovirals such as lopinavir/ ritonavir and nelfinavir require a full stomach for adequate absorption. In contrast, didanosine requires an empty stomach for adequate absorption. These dietary restrictions are particularly concerning for incarcerated populations where meal times are predetermined at each correctional institution and thus less adaptable to the individual.

Medication side effects have been shown to be an important regimen-related factor associated with poor adherence. In a cohort of women prisoners, the third most common reason for missing medications was side effects (Stephenson et al. 2003, table 15.1). In another prison cohort, medication adherence in men and women was negatively correlated with the presence of side effects (Altice et al. 2001).

Interventions

Directly Observed Therapy

Directly observed therapy (DOT) has been proposed as an intervention to enhance HAART adherence levels because of its successful use in tuberculosis (TB) treatment programs. Although the cornerstone of TB DOT programs is to observe individuals swallowing medications, it has been most effective when a patient-centered approach is used. Patient-centered interventions are tailored to the patients' needs. They offer comprehensive case management that often includes substance abuse treatment, housing, transportation, and social services (CDC 2003). In a recent forum on directly observed therapy for HIV treatment, the overwhelming recommendation was that DOT programs should be voluntary and flexible (Forum for Collaborative HIV Research 2001). In contrast, many DOT programs in prisons are inflexible, involuntary, nonconfidential, and nonindividualized (Spaulding et al. 2002).

It is unclear if DOT is an effective intervention for enhancing antiretroviral adherence in prisons. One study compared prisoners on DOT HAART with nonprisoners on non-DOT HAART. Because 95 percent of the prisoners achieved viral load levels less than 400 copies/mL (compared to 75 percent of their nonincarcerated counterparts), it has been suggested that DOT was the intervention that resulted in these viral load levels (Fischl et al. 2001). But other observational studies in prisons have shown no difference in the adherence or viral loads of individuals on self-medications vs. directly observed medications (Altice et al. 2001; Dieckhaus 2002; Wohl et al. 2003). DOT is also labor intensive and costly for correctional facilities that are chronically understaffed and over budget. Fur-

TABLE 15.1

Reasons for missed medications in incarcerated women (N=14)

Have you ever missed any medications because:	% Agree
You were asleep when a dose was due	57
Busy or simply forgot	36
Medications made you sick	36
Away from facility	29
Do not want others to see	29
Drug reminds you that you have HIV	29
Ran out of medications	21
Using alcohol or drugs	21
Depressed or overwhelmed	21
Change in daily routine	14

Adapted from Preliminary Assessment of Health Beliefs and Attitudes about Antiretroviral Therapy Measures in a Sample of Prison Inmates, in submission 2004.

thermore, most women inmates in one study reported dislike of the intervention (Wohl et al. 2003). Thus, it is unclear if its expense is justified.

Peer Support

Peer support interventions may be the most promising given the correlation between social support and adherence. Peer support interventions are inexpensive for prisons. They also have been generally accepted by women inmates. Unfortunately, these interventions in HIV-infected women have not been rigorously studied and most of the data is anecdotal.

Conclusion

The greatest challenges to adherence to HAART in women inmates may not be in prison but after they are released where access to care is not uniform (Wohl et al. 2004). Correctional facilities vary greatly in terms of how much medication is dispensed to inmates upon release. If inmates are to remain adherent to therapy upon release, it is essential that comprehensive discharge planning be done so that they may be connected with medical services upon release (Braithwaite, Hammett, and Mayberry 1996; see chapter 19 for a discussion of discharge planning). Although the majority of state and federal systems offer discharge planning services for HIV-infected inmates being released, the evaluation of these services is weak and the extensiveness of these services varies greatly (for example, they range from making referrals to making appointments). Moreover, these services are rarely offered for inmates leaving city/county correctional systems.

In summary, adherence to HAART in women inmates can be challenging. Although issues such as confidentiality and inflexibility may be barriers to adherence, access to care and antiretrovirals may be more important in determining success for women inmates. Randomized studies are now needed to evaluate gender-specific interventions for HIV-infected incarcerated women. Although barriers exist in prisons, facilitators such as access to care/antiretrovirals and trust in health care professionals may offset these barriers.

REFERENCES

Altice, F. L. 1998. Overview of HIV care. In *Clinical Practice in Correctional Medicine,* ed. M. Puisis. St. Louis: Mosby.

Altice, F. L., F. Mostashari, and G. H. Friedland. 2001. Trust and the acceptance of and adherence to antiretroviral therapy. *Journal of Acquired Immune Deficiency Syndromes* 28, no. 1: 47–58.

Bartlett, John A., R. DeMasi, J. Quinn, C. Moxham, and F. Rousseau. 2001. Overview of the effectiveness of triple combination therapy in antiretroviral-naive HIV-1 infected adults. *AIDS* 15, no. 11: 1369–77.

Braithwaite, R. L., T. M. Hammett, and R. M. Mayberry. 1996. *Prisons and AIDS: A public health challenge.* San Francisco: Jossey-Bass.

Centers for Disease Control (CDC). 2001. *Women, injection drug use, and the criminal justice system.* August 2001.

CDC. 2003. Treatment of Tuberculosis. *MMWR.* Atlanta, GA: CDC.

Chesney, M. A. 2000. Factors affecting adherence to antiretroviral therapy. *Clinical and Infectious Diseases* 30 (suppl. 2): S171–76.

Conklin, T. J., T. Lincoln, and R. W. Tuthill. 2000. Self-reported health and prior health behaviors of newly admitted correctional inmates. *American Journal of Public Health* 90, no. 12: 1939–41.

Dieckhaus, K. D. 2002. *Adherence to self-administered antiretroviral therapy in incarcerated patients.* [Abstract 484] In: Abstracts of the Infectious Disease Society of America Fortieth Annual Meeting (Chicago). October 24–27, 2002.

Fischl, M., J. C., R. Monroig, E. Scerpella, L. Thompson, D. Rechtine, and D. Thomas. 2001. *Impact of directly observed therapy on long-term outcomes in HIV clinical trials.* [Abstract 528] In: Program and Abstracts of the Eighth Conference on Retroviruses and Opportunistic Infections (Chicago). Alexandria, VA: Foundation for Retroviruses and Human Health.

Fogarty, L., D. Roter, S. Larson, J. Burke, J. Gillespie, and R. Levy. 2002. Patient adherence to HIV medication regimens: A review of published and abstract reports. *Patient Education and Counseling* 46, no. 2: 93–108.

Forum for Collaborative HIV research. 2001. Examining the risk and benefits of Directly Observed Therapy for the treatment of HIV Disease. Washington, DC: April 14–17, 2001. http://www.hivforum.org.

Frank, L. 1999. Prisons and public health: Emerging issues in HIV treatment adherence. *Journal of the Association of Nurses in AIDS Care* 10, no. 6: 24–32.

Hammett, T. M., P. Harmon, and L. M. Maruschak. 1999. Issues and practices: 1996–1997

Update, HIV/AIDS, STDs, and TB in correctional facilities. Washington, DC: National Institute of Justice, the Centers for Disease Control and Prevention, and BJS. NCJ 176344.

Jordan, B. K., E. B. Federman, B. J. Burns, W. E. Schlenger, J. A. Fairbank, and J. M. Caddell. 2002. Lifetime use of mental health and substance abuse treatment services by incarcerated women felons. *Psychiatric Services* 53, no. 2: 317–25.

Kirkland, L. R., M. A. Fischl, K. T. Tashima, D. Paar, T. Gensler, N. M. Graham, H. Gao, J. R. Rosenzweig, D. R. McClernon, G. Pittman, S. M. Hessenthaler, and J. E. Hernandez. 2002. Response to lamivudine-zidovudine plus abacavir twice daily in antiretroviral-naive incarcerated patients with HIV infection taking directly observed treatment. *Clinical Infectious Diseases* 34, no. 4: 511–18.

Kitahata, M., T. D. Koepsell, R. A. Deyo, C. L. Maxwell, W. Dodge, and E. H. Wagner. 1996. Physicians' experience with the Acquired Immunodeficiency Syndrome as a factor in patients' survival. *New England Journal of Medicine* 334, no. 11: 701–6.

Kitahata, M., S.E.V. Rompaey, P. W. Dillingham, T. D. Koepsell, R. A. Deyo, W. Dodge, and E. H. Wagner. 2003. Primary care delivery is associated with greater physician experience and improved survival among persons with AIDS. *Journal of General Internal Medicine* 18: 95–103.

Liu, H., C. E. Golin, L. G. Miller, R. D. Hays, C. K. Beck, S. Sanandaji, J. Christian, T. Maldonado, D. Duran, A. H. Kaplan, and N. S. Wenger. 2001. A comparison study of multiple measures of adherence to HIV protease inhibitors.[Comment] [Erratum appears in *Annals of Internal Medicine* (2002, January 15) 136, no. 2: 175]. *Annals of Internal Medicine* 134, no. 10: 968–77.

Maruschak, L. 2003. *HIV in prisons, 2000.* Bureau of Justice Statistics Bulletin (NCJ 196023).

Mostashari, F., E. Riley, P. A. Selwyn, and F. L. Altice. 1998. Acceptance and adherence with antiretroviral therapy among HIV-infected women in a correctional facility. *Journal of Acquired Immune Deficiency Syndromes and Human Retrovirology* 18, no. 4: 341–48.

Palella, F. J., Jr., A. C. Moorman, M. O. Loveless, J. Fuhrer, G. A. Satten, D. J. Aschman, and S. D. Holmberg. 1998. Declining morbidity and mortality among patients with advanced human immunodeficiency virus infection: HIV Outpatient Study Investigators. *New England Journal of Medicine* 338, no. 13: 853–60.

Paterson D. L., and J. Mohr. 2000. Adherence to protease inhibitor therapy and outcomes in patients with HIV infection. *Annals of Internal Medicine* 133: 21–20.

Peiperl, L., and P. Volberding. 2003. AIDS Knowledge Base. http://hivinsite.ucsf.edu/ (accessed September 15, 2003).

Rold, W. J. 1998. Legal considerations in the delivery of health care services in prisons and jails. In *Clinical Practice in Correctional Medicine,* ed. M. Puisis. St. Louis: Mosby.

Spaulding, A., B. Stephenson, G. Macalino, W. Ruby, J. G. Clarke, and T. P. Flanigan. 2002. Human immunodeficiency virus in correctional facilities: A review. *Clinical Infectious Diseases* 35, no. 3: 305–12.

Stephenson, B., D. Wohl, R. D. Hays, C. E. Golin, H. Liu, C. N. Kiziah. 2003. Preliminary assessment of health beliefs and attitudes about antiretroviral therapy measures in a sample of prison inmates. In submission

Stone, D. R., C. Corcoran, A. Wurcel, B. McGovern, J. Quirk, A. Brewer, L. Sutton, R. T. D'Aquila. 2002. Antiretroviral drug resistance mutations in antiretroviral-naive prisoners. *Clinical Infectious Diseases* 35: 883–86.

Stone, V. E. 2001. Strategies for optimizing adherence to highly active antiretroviral therapy: Lessons from research and clinical practice. *Clinical Infectious Diseases* 33: 865–72.

U.S. Government Accounting Office (GAO). 1999. *Women in prison: Issues and challenges confronting U.S. correctional systems.* Washington, DC: U.S. GAO: GGD-00-22. http://www.gao.gov.

Wohl, D. A., B. L. Stephenson, C. E. Golin, C. N. Kiziah, D. Rosen, B. Ngo, H. Liu, and A. H.

Kaplan. 2003. Adherence to directly observed antiretroviral therapy among human immunodeficiency virus-infected prison inmates. *Clinical Infectious Diseases* 36, no. 12:
1572–76.

Wohl, D. A., B. L. Stephenson, R. Strauss, C. Golin, L. Shain, M. Adamian, et al. 2004. Access to
HIV care and Antiretroviral Therapy (ART) following release from prison. [Abstract] In:
Program and Abstracts of the Eleventh Conference on Retroviruses and Opportunistic
Infections (San Francisco). Alexandria, VA: Foundation for Retroviruses and Human
Health.

Wright, I. N., and P. F. Smith. 1999. Decrease in AIDS-related mortality in state correctional
system: New York, 1995–1998. *Journal of the American Medical Association* 281: 506–7.

PART FIVE

Chronic Conditions

16

Cardiovascular Disease

SYLVIA McQUEEN

Cardiovascular disease (CVD) is the number one cause of death in the United States and in women (AHA 2001). Despite this fact, early heart studies notoriously excluded women, partly due to concerns about exposing fertile women to the same radiation-based imaging, invasive surgeries, and medication side effects as men (Ting, McLartey, and Andersen 1999). The more lingering mantra is that estrogen confers immunity to cardiovascular disease. There is a lot to be said for the power of myths in a civilized society. The belief that heart disease is a man's problem and women are more likely to survive a heart attack is not an unfamiliar attitude in the current medical arena. It is true that cardiovascular events cause most deaths in men and women's heart disease presents ten to fifteen years later than men, but, in retrospect, cardiovascular disease has always been an equal opportunity threat. At least one-half million women die in the United States each year, and cardiovascular disease unequivocally ranks as the leading culprit, with a commanding chasm between it and the next nine causes of death (Haran 2003). Today, this crippling disease appears to affect more women than men (Centers for Disease Control and Prevention [CDC] 1998). The American Heart Association (AHA) reports that more women than men have died of heart disease every year since 1984. The second leading cause of mortality is breast cancer, which kills one in twenty-six women, compared to one in two from CVD (McKeown 2000). As if these staggering statistics were not enough, women also simultaneously suffer from one or more types of cardiovascular illnesses more frequently than men.

One would expect pathology in the incarcerated patient to be a direct sampling of the surrounding community, but such is not so for CVD in women. Women make up such a small percentage of the confined population that, in spite of an increasing rate of incarcerations, there is a dearth of information available regarding their cardiovascular status. Most studies only address substance abuse, mental health problems, and sexually transmitted infections in women behind bars. Confinement does not appear to influence the progression of cardiovascular disease and its associated co-morbidities: coronary artery disease (CAD), peripheral vascular disease (PVD), hypertension (HTN), adult-onset diabetes mellitus (AODM), hyperlipidemia, and cerebral vascular and kidney disease. These all maintain their innate pathophysiology, with or without external intervention.

Clinical Background

Much progress has been made in acknowledging the prevalence of heart disease in women, but more is needed in the areas of prevention and education about the atypical presentations and management. This may be a reflection of deficient knowledge on both patients' and practitioners' part regarding the importance of education, risk-factor modification and postintervention risk stratification, patient noncompliance, and an inadequate follow-up system of care. Hoffmann (2000) asserts that women are more likely than men to experience financial and relationship fallout after a heart attack and lack of resources to access health care and affordable medication.

Just how well cardiovascular disease is being addressed in the incarcerated woman is not readily identified. A focused plan to begin extracting demographics from penal systems and correlating it with corresponding health records may be a good start. Various judicial limitations, custodial rights over medical records, and the Health Insurance Portability and Accountability Act (HIPAA) create barriers to this endeavor. Lynn Smaha of the American Heart Association suggests that barriers to the quality of care exist on all fronts for women (Levine 2000). As a result, the evidence is clear that women are not being managed appropriately or aggressively enough to compensate for such a deadly disease.

Epidemiology

Holly Andersen from Cornell University states that the overall mortality rate from CVD is actually decreasing in the United States for both males and females, but at a slower rate for women (Ting, McLartey, and Andersen 1999). In 1998, the Centers for Disease Control found that women were less likely to receive preventive counseling for CVD or recommendations regarding modifiable risk factors. A national poll addressing cardiovascular disease showed that 61 percent of women saw breast cancer as their greatest health risk and only 7 percent perceived heart disease as the greatest risk. Fewer than 33 percent knew that heart disease was the leading cause of death in women. Fewer than 20 percent of women in all ethnic groups felt well informed about heart disease and fewer than 15 percent about stroke (McKeown 2000; Grayson 2002). Many doctors have not been trained to identify the danger signs of heart disease in women (Hoffmann 2000). White men over sixty years of age and elderly women are regarded as the typical victims. While men are at increased risk compared to women during their younger years, the risk equalizes for both sexes by the age of sixty-five (Ting, McLartey, and Andersen 1999). Women generally live longer than men and the assumption was that they died from heart disease because they were older. However, Ting, McLartey, and Andersen (1999) and Palkhivala (2001) found that women under the age of fifty who had heart attacks die two times as often as men of the same age.

Societal myths say that a woman is expected to experience adverse health outcomes merely due to incarceration. That this status is frequently coupled with low socioeconomic status and homelessness, themselves indicators of poor health, contributes to this myth. However, there is no literature to support the idea that incarceration alone directly leads to adverse outcomes. In fact, my experience reflects quite the contrary. I have learned that most of the patients receive better medical care while incarcerated and for many, the care received while incarcerated is the first and only encounter with any health care provider.

Clinical Presentation

Men and women are different at the macro and micro levels, with women having smaller arteries and hearts that beat faster, even during sleep. Heart size is considered in terms of heart mass per unit area. It is thought that the pacemaker's intrinsic rhythmicity in women's hearts is different, especially at the molecular level of the cardiac cell membranes. Men and women have different protein channels that regulate relaxation time (Legato, Lewis, and Oz 2000). The clinical significance of all these factors is germane to assessing the mechanisms of the female heart during rest, exercise, and imaging studies.

The 500,000 women who die each year from heart disease may have had signs and symptoms that were silent, unrecognized, or misinterpreted. Women are frequently misdiagnosed with acute indigestion, gallbladder disease, or anxiety attacks. This is usually due to the discomfort being localized to just under the breastbone. Twenty percent of women will not present with the classic "clenched fist" profiled chest pain. Instead, nausea may predominate with epigastric pain that is often referred to the back, fatigue, light-headedness, palpitations, or a profound sense of shortness of breath. Men commonly present with typical substernal chest pain or heavy pressure feeling with radiation into the arm (Legato, Lewis, and Oz 2000).

The routine clinical pathway of females entering correctional facilities begins at the point of intake into the facility with a medical screening that involves documenting a full set of vital signs, medical history, current medical problems, and medications. Complete honesty is not commonplace for the "criminal" population, nor do they make the best informants. Therefore, verification of this information via physician's office, pharmacist, direct visualization of prescription bottles, and request for previous health records is the next step. Data from surveying eighteen jails and one prison in five states of the southeast United States and consulting with the corporate medical director and associate corporate medical director of prisons for Prison Health Services revealed that the success rate for medication verification ranged from 75 percent to 90 percent for the jails (Prison Health Services, Inc., is the founder of the provate managed correctional health care field). The time frame required to confirm information ranged from ten minutes to thirty-six hours, with an average period of one hour. Factors contributing to success are patients having current prescriptions in hand; established relationships with local pharmacists, clinics, and hospitals; and access to prior medical records for repeat offenders. Common barriers to the verification process are inadequate information from the patient, out-of-state patients, and free indigent clinics that provide medication samples and are managed by multiple physicians.

It is customary to inform every incoming inmate about how to access medical services through a written sick call request or notification by an officer. Identified chronic care patients are automatically scheduled to see practitioners within a specified time of their admission for initial assessment and establishment of a treatment plan. In the jail setting, it is not uncommon to lose up to 40 percent of all intakes within ninety-six hours. Therefore, a significant number of patients never see a practitioner but may receive a few days of medication depending on their presenting diagnosis. As expected, such turnover in the prison setting does not exist. The rate of release in jails is a major hindrance to affecting change in the medical conditions of the incarcerated patient.

Risk Factors

Cardiovascular risk factors are universal for both sexes. They include family history, excessive caloric and alcohol intake, illicit drug use, hyperlipidemia, sedentary life style, and inadequate calcium intake, especially for the elderly and African Americans (JNC-V 1993). Those risk factors specifically affecting women include age, gender and ethnicity, postmenopausal status, and smoking and substance use (Hayes 2003; Ting, McLartey, and Andersen 1999).

Age
Forty years of age is the baseline at which heart disease begins to manifest. However, the Seventh Joint National Committee on Prevention, Detection, Evaluation, and Treatment of High Blood Pressure report indicates sixty-five years and greater for women. Age, whether alone or in conjunction with other risk factors, will automatically impose the need for treatment in some women. This is most evident when considering the latest hyperlipidemia guidelines (Warner 2003).

Gender and Ethnicity
African American women have a higher incidence and die from heart disease twice as often as white women (Peck 2000).

Postmenopausal Status

Although estrogen provides many protective properties for women's circulatory system, such as increased HDL and elasticity of vessels, decreased LDL and fibrinogen, and improved sugar levels, it remains to be irrefutably substantiated as an option for treatment and prevention of cardiovascular events (Grayson 2002). The latest studies recommend that menopausal women and those with primary heart disease should not go on hormone replacement therapy (Palkhivala 2001). There is no benefit and possibly an increased risk of heart attack within the first year of medication for women in this stage of life (Grayson 2002; Stephan 2000).

However, in the face of no definitive benefit, postmenopausal women are ten times more likely to die from heart disease than from cancer, presumably because of the loss of the aforementioned benefits of estrogen lead to plaque and blood clot formation and stroke (Grayson 2002; McKeown 2001). As reported in the February 5, 1992, issue of the *Journal of the American College of Cardiology,* less than 33 percent of women without CAD had low estrogen levels. The presence of other risk factors like diabetes and smoking may diminish any protective benefits from estrogen (Ting, McLartey, and Andersen 1999). For now, practitioners should evaluate each patient on a case-by-case basis and inform patients of the pros and cons related to hormone replacement therapy and management. The best thing a woman can do to improve her risk of heart disease is to manage her cardiovascular risk factors in the years preceding menopause. Good health during the pre- and perimenopausal years will reduce the need for later treatment. An ongoing federal study entitled "Women's Health Initiative" will hopefully shed more clarity on this issue upon its completion in 2005 (Contreras and Parra 2000). In my experience, hormone replacement therapy is managed on a case-by-case basis. Treatment is not abruptly interrupted in incarcerated women, when verification of prior hormone usage and compliance is established. However, the chronic management of menopausal women requires counseling and education to help determine whether continuation of estrogen and/or its initiation will be in the best interest of the patient.

Smoking and Substance Use

Smoking is the single most significant contributor and most preventable risk factor for heart disease in women, and other drugs also increase the risk. Nationwide, 21.5 million women smoke, 4.5 million are alcoholics, and 3.1 million regularly use illicit drugs, with cocaine accounting for over half of that number (Women and Addiction 1999). "For a given dose of cigarettes, women have a higher risk than men," and the increase in tobacco use among adolescent women will undermine every effort attempted to free them from any imposed health risks (Hayes 2003). Among twelve- to thirty-five-year-olds, females surpass males in the use of cigarettes, cocaine, and crack (Making the Link 1995). "Alcohol related problems are the third leading cause of death for women between 35–55" (Substance Abuse and the American Woman 1996). Advertisements and perceived elegance, liberation,

TABLE 16.1

Hypertension classification for 18 and older

Category	Systolic (mm Hg)	Diastolic (mm Hg)
Normal	Under 130	Under 85
High Normal	130–139	85–89
Stage I (Mild HTN)	140–159	90–99
Stage 2 (Moderate HTN)	160–179	100–109
Stage 3 (Severe HTN)	180–209	110–119
Stage 4 (Very Severe HTN)	210 and above	120 an above

Source: National Heart, Lung, and Blood Institute (NHLBI) and JNC-VI

and thinness are considered some of the attracting factors (Palkhivala 2001). Women become addicted and develop substance-abuse-related complications sooner than men (Oncology Committee 1999). Over 140,000 women die each year from diseases due to smoking. Benefits associated with this practice can only be identified when one practices complete abstinence. Tobacco cessation for two years brings a woman's health risk back to the level of the nonsmoker. If a person quits smoking before the age of fifty, they will reduce their risk of dying in the subsequent fifteen years by 50 percent, compared to those continuing to smoke (AHA 2001). Coronary artery disease, stroke, peripheral artery disease, exercise tolerance, and a plethora of other acute and chronic illnesses are positively impacted when a person quits smoking, and the benefits of quitting continue to increase with time.

TABLE 16.2

Classification of blood pressure for adults

Category	SBP mmHg		DBP mmHg
Normal	<120	and	<80
Pre-hypertension	120–139	or	80–89
Hypertension, Stage 1	140–159	or	90–99
Hypertension, Stage 2	>=160	or	>= 100

Source: JNC-VII

Many jails and prisons have banned smoking in their facilities by staff and inmates. Nicotine withdrawal programs are uncommon, however, and most facilities make the inmates go "cold turkey" if they are smokers. Medical requests for nicotine substitutes or other drugs touted for helping someone "kick the habit" are uncommon though many facilities will provide them upon request. Inmates appear to do fine without free access to tobacco products while incarcerated. Unfortunately, however, abstinence is not usually maintained once the inmate is released. Often, after not having smoked for a week or more, the first thing they desire to do is "light one up." This reoccurring cycle and the fact that studies support a true physical and psychological dependence raise the question of whether or not tobacco use is a choice.

Co-Morbidities and Target Organ Damage (TOD)

More often than not in cardiovascular disease, risk factors and co-morbidities are one in the same. The intimacy with which many of these illnesses are associated compounds their effect on one's health and collectively accelerates the development of target organ damage (TOD).

Hypertension (HTN)

Ninety to 95 percent of hypertension is of the essential type. The fact that men die of cardiovascular events more often than women has afforded us more relevant data related to women having more complications from hypertension. Hypertension is racial, class, and gender biased. African American women with lower socioeconomic status and less education are more likely to have hypertension than their white counterparts, in all age categories. Hypertension is increasing more in women compared to men and with a slower improving slope. The current criteria determining if one is hypertensive have dramatically changed since the Fifth Joint National Committee on Prevention, Detection, Evaluation, and Treatment of High Blood Pressure report in 1993. The new standards alone may negatively impact the population presently suffering from the commonly known "silent killer."

Information from the 1990 census, the U.S. Department of Health and Human Services' mid-course review in 1995, and the National Health and Nutrition Examination Survey III data (NHANES III) estimated that 50 million Americans have hypertension (National Center for Health Statistics [NCHS] 1995). In 1997, the National Heart, Lung, and Blood Institute estimated the number of Americans with hypertension at 60 million (JNC-VII 2003). There are approximately 2 million new cases of hypertension each year. Hypertension is the most frequent morbidity-related diagnosis physicians make in their offices. Of the 33 percent of U.S. western states' residents with HTN, 27 percent do not know they have it. Elevated systolic blood pressure (the top number in a blood pressure reading) poses a greater risk than high diastolic blood pressure (the bottom number), regardless of age. Hypertension is more prevalent in the elderly, with sixty years of age serving as the threshold. The latest Framingham Heart Study reported that normotensive patients at age fifty-five have a 90 percent lifetime risk of developing hypertension (JNC-VI 1997).

From young adulthood through middle age, high blood pressure is more common in men than women. However, blood pressure increases about two and a half times faster in women than men from ages twenty to sixty-five years and older. Among the elderly, 65 to 70 percent of hypertension is associated with only a high systolic blood pressure. Isolated systolic hypertension is more prevalent in women than men. The lower number, diastolic blood pressure, increases steadily until ages fifty to sixty and then levels or declines. African American women have a higher occurrence, earlier onset, longer duration, and higher rates of health complications and deaths related to hypertension than white women (Vasan et al. 2002). Common sequela from poorly managed hypertension leads to target organ damage (that is, cardiovascular disease, congestive heart failure, peripheral vascular disease [PVD], stroke, and renal disease). However, aggressive anti-hypertension management has been found to reduce the incidence of stroke by 30 to 40 percent, myocardial infarction 20 to 25 percent, and heart failure by greater than 50 percent (Gillum 1996).

The JNC-VII classification is based on two seated blood pressure readings during two separate office visits. There is a modification from the JNC-VI report regarding the addition of a "pre-hypertension" category and the merging of the later categories. However, the American Heart Association still considers 140/90 as the dividing line between normal and high blood pressure.

Obesity

The 1990 Department of Health and Human Services' dietary guidelines measures weight (overweight) in terms of body mass index (BMI), a calculated value that takes into account the person's weight and height. A value of 27.0 or greater is considered overweight, and obesity is classified as a BMI greater than 30.0. A BMI greater than 30 is associated with mortality rates from all causes of death 50 to 100 percent greater than those with BMI of 20 to 25. A drawback to using BMI alone is that muscular athletes may be declared overweight using this method because of their low percentages of body fat. Excess fat in the abdomen, out of proportion to total body fat, is an independent predictor of heart disease and morbidity. The accepted waist circumference for BMIs less than 35 are forty inches for men and thirty-five inches for women. Obesity is responsible for over 300,000 premature deaths and nearly $120 billion in associated costs. In April 2002, the IRS ruling 202-19 declared obesity to be a disease and therefore expenses to treat it tax deductible. Morbid obesity (BMI over 40) accounts for 5 percent of the adult population, and this is linked to increased risk and severity of cardiovascular disease. Adult-onset diabetes is reported to be twofold greater in the mildly obese and increased by fivefold in moderately obese and tenfold in severely obese persons.

Elevated triglycerides, stroke, and coronary artery disease commonly result from obesity as well (White and Tripuraneni 2003).

Recent review of the literature indicates that obesity is a significant risk factor for heart disease as well as a major player in a plethora of other illnesses; it is not merely a cosmetic issue but an epidemic in and of itself. Women, minorities, and those in lower socioeconomic classes are generally more overweight than their counterparts. The National Health and Nutrition Examination Surveys (NHANES) sampled 33,199 people and found that obesity increased from 14.5 percent in 1980 to 23 percent in 1994. Other publications for the same years indicated that approximately 25 percent of all adult women and 20 percent of adult men were clinically obese. Recent estimates are that 34 percent of Americans are overweight and 27 percent are obese. The main contributing factors are sedentary lifestyles, low physical activity, and unhealthy eating habits (White and Tripuraneni 2003).

Diabetes

Forty to seventy percent of adults with diabetes have hypertension. Diabetes develops two and a half times more often in those with hypertension. This combination of illnesses contributes to more cardiovascular events than either of them independently. The risk of stroke, heart attack, and renal disease are all accentuated. The blood pressure goal for this type of patient is now less than 130/80 (White and Sica 2002a). Obtaining this level significantly reduces the development of the aforementioned morbidities. The goal for blood sugar level is 100 to 110 mg instead of the historically acceptable 125 to 150, and hemoglobin A1c is targeted at 6 percent (White and Sica 2002b).

Coronary Artery Disease

Naturally, the prevention of heart attacks is the top priority in cardiac disease. Some studies show up to 50 percent of women presenting to the emergency room with typical anginal symptoms are not recognized as have significant coronary artery disease at all (JNC-VII 2003). The younger a woman is when she has a heart attack, the greater the chance of death, which, unfortunately, was probably not the heralding sign of her underlying disease (Ting, McLartey, and Andersen 1999). Women usually present with angina in some form or another, while men usually present with heart attacks (McKeown 2001).

In my personal experience as a physician working in a correctional setting, I have given orders to transport approximately five women to the emergency room for a cardiac evaluation. All of them were sent from a county jail and none from the female state prison that I periodically covered. They all complained primarily of chest pain with an assortment of other significant confounding variables. Not one spent the night in the hospital for observation, and every one that returned back to the infirmary, if not released from custody beforehand, was given a diagnosis unrelated to the heart, even if they had one or more risk factors.

Assessment and Treatment

The medical management for coronary artery disease (that is, beta-blockers, calcium channel blockers, nitroglycerine, lipid-lowering agents, aspirin and other platelet inhibitors) is well established. Benefits of therapies such as thrombolytic agents and emergent angioplasty may forever be lost if presenting angina is misdiagnosed in women. They are less likely to be referred to angiography and other diagnostic testing for risk stratification even though they have more bleeding complications and a 50 percent chance of dying during cardiac surgery. Instead, women are offered more conservative management. Once the diagnosis of myocardial infarction has been made, women and men are treated relatively equally, particularly when managed in tertiary centers. But the fact remains that there is a disparity in the aggressiveness with which physicians offer treatment for coronary disease in women.

The approach to managing hypertension in the jail setting is often inconsistent with the latest treatment recommendations. The patients are usually treated more aggressively in the jail setting because the usual short length of stay does not allow for the recommended monitoring and follow-up periods. An attempt to provide a patient with some medication while in jail is always a consideration, and at times patients are released with a limited amount of medication—usually three to five days—to last until they can see an outside provider. Once a patient is identified as having high blood pressure, physician orders are written to initiate treatment right away. For those patients who cannot provide a current list of medications and are clinically stable, a blood pressure protocol may be instituted to collect data prior to a practitioner's visit or the institution of an appropriate regimen. Some factors interfering with a practitioner's ability to implement the standard approach for high blood pressure treatment in jails are limited exposure to the patient and the unlikely opportunity for follow-up.

Incarcerated diabetics are handled in the same manner as hypertensives and maybe more aggressively. Identified diabetics, at the point of intake medical screening, begin to receive glucose finger sticks right away, followed by administration of regular insulin per site specific sliding scales. Juvenile-onset diabetics (insulin-dependent) and type II diabetics (insulin-independent) routinely undergo glucose finger sticks twice a day and those maintained only on oral agents, once a week. In my experience, this is one of the most difficult populations to treat. Noncompliance ranks relatively high in this group. Lack of insight about the disease, refusal to follow diet recommendations, free commissary access, the bargaining power of food among inmates, and high turnover are strong competitors.

Diet

The assortment of diets on the market has elicited more confusion than insight. The average person does not possess the wherewithal to comprehensively determine the best eating habit. Women have a unique challenge to maintain a total cholesterol level under 200mg/dl, triglycerides under 150 mg/dl, LDL under 100mg/dl, and HDL under 50mg/dl (Adult Treatment Panel III 2003). The NHANES III study found that HDL levels of 55 and greater provided excellent protection from heart disease. A total cholesterol to HDL ratio of 4 or greater is bad news. Endogenous estrogen contributes to high HDL levels in women. Keeping in mind that fish oil can hinder clotting mechanisms, the omega-3 fatty acids protect arteries, lower triglycerides, and improve glucose control in diabetics. One study demonstrated a reduction in arrhythmias, sudden death from arrhythmias, and repeat heart attacks with their use (Benjamin and Lebowitz 2000a).

Statins, the leading drugs for lowering LDL cholesterol, prevent the first heart attack in known coronary disease patients and stabilize vulnerable narrowing that may lead to acute coronary syndrome (Rosen 2001). Monosaturated fats lower and stabilize LDL, but trans fats should be avoided as much as possible. A simple shift from trans fats to polyunsaturated fats can drop a female's coronary heart disease risk by nearly 50 percent (Benjamin and Lebowitz 2000b). Oat bran and grains can be eaten in large amounts and will lower cholesterol dramatically. Soy products are known for reducing apolipoproteins, which have been identified as indicators for premature coronary atherosclerosis. Complex carbohydrates are better than the insulin surge caused by simple sugars because insulin causes truncal fat deposition and direct damage to artery linings.

Orders for diabetic and low salt–low cholesterol diets are routine in corrections facilities. Jails and prisons normally contract out their food services, and the incumbent health care provider has little to no involvement in menu selections. Early in my experience, I had reason to inquire about the specific foods offered to patients due to multiple complaints of either not receiving what they perceived to be correct or receiving insufficient amounts. This inquiry took place on several occasions, in particular when the vendor changed. I was always assured that each specialty diet met the minimal requirement of the community standard, but the only obligation that food services had to meet was the mandatory daily caloric amount. The combination of foods used to obtain the calorie count was at the discretion of the responsible food service provider. I never challenged this explanation, accepting that this was just the way it was. A cursory review of cardiovascular and diabetic diets currently in place at twenty jails in the region revealed no consistency. All listed specific caloric levels but varied in content.

Exercise

Anyone who elevates their heart rate to the recommended level (men: [220 – age] x 0.7; women: [226 – age] x 0.7) and sustains it for twenty to thirty minutes, several times a week, will reap cardiovascular benefit (Pulse Tronic 1999–2000). The goal is to reduce weight and body fat. The rate of loss should be one to two pounds per week and no more than 10 percent weight loss in six months. A loss of ten pounds affords a meaningful risk reduction in many diseases, that is, lowered blood pressure, reduced blood sugar, and improved lipid levels. Manson et al. (2002)

demonstrated that women over fifty who spend two and a half hours per week walking briskly can lower their risk of cardiovascular disease by 30 percent.

Institution of medication management is warranted when prevention, diet, and exercise fails to bring about desired end points. Slightly over half of those who know they are hypertensive are on medication. The financial burden to the United States is $37 billion for the management of high blood pressure and associated morbidities; $15 billion of that total are attributed to the cost of drugs. A single thiazide-type diuretic is the initial medication of choice for uncomplicated hypertension. However, given the presence of concurrent conditions, most patients will require at least two antihypertensives to reach the appropriate blood pressure goal. Initiating treatment with two drugs is particularly recommended when the patient presents with a blood pressure more than 20 mmHg above the recommended level. For renal disease, maximal management of co-morbidities is crucial. Diet and mineral and electrolyte control serve as the main therapy.

An opportunity to exercise is mandatory in correctional facilities. Patients are allowed to engage in some form of calisthenics three hours per week to one hour

TABLE 16.3
Lifestyle modification recommendations

Modification	Recommendation	Avg. Systolic Blood Pressure Reduction Range*
Weight reduction	Maintain normal body weight (BMI 18.5–24.9 Kg/m2)	5–20 mmHg/10 kg
DASH eating plan	Adopt a diet rich in fruits, vegetables and low fat dairy products with reduced content of saturated and total fat.	8–14 mm Hg
Dietary sodium reduction	Reduce dietary sodium intake to < 100mmol /d (2.4 g sodium or 6 g sodium chloride)	2–8 mm Hg
Aerobic physical activity	Regular aerobic physical activity (e.g., brisk walking) at least 30 minutes/ day, most days of the week	4–9 mm Hg
Moderation of alcohol consumption	Men: limit to <= 2 drinks/day**. Women and lighter weight persons: limit to <=1 drink/day**	2–4 mm Hg

* Effects are dose and time dependent.

** 1 drink = ½ oz or 15 ml ethanol (e.g., 12 oz beer, 5 oz wine, 1.5 oz 80-proof whiskey).

Adopted from JNC-VII

per day. This practice is strictly governed by custody with the rare exception of a medical need initiated by a physician's order to the client. In my opinion, the correctional setting is not conducive for establishing a formal exercise program for patients, given the multiple restrictions and stipulations required for safety and security.

Conclusion

The 1995 U.S. census showed patients with heart disease accounted for 12 percent of hospital admissions, with the average length of stay ranging from five to eight days (Nutritional Strategies 1996). Review of the literature indicates the overall cost of medical care for females is typically higher than males in the free world, and the same appears to be true for those who are incarcerated. In my experience, medication costs are 25 to 40 percent higher for women than men in jails and prisons. This suggests either access to care more frequently and/or more costly diagnoses. I found women to be less receptive to medical recommendations and more demanding of medical and correctional personnel time than men. Most of my encounters with the female population were for sick call problems related to gynecological, dermatological, or various muscular skeletal pains. I rarely saw females for primary cardiovascular problems. This could be a reflection of the lack of disease prevalence in the reported median age of incarcerated women (Hoffmann 2000). In a coed jail, my experience was limited to no more than five to ten identified females with hypertension and/or diabetes. I directly managed one woman with ESRD in five years. Just like in the community at large, noncompliance was the number one reason for treatment failure.

Hopefully, you have deduced that the presence of one manifestation of cardiovascular disease plays an intricate role in the next. Let's revisit the age-old myth that "women don't have cardiovascular disease." Today, if the clinical authority at any correctional facility practices medicine with this belief, a major opportunity to significantly impact the leading cause of death in women is lost. Meeting the unique health needs of such a small female population will certainly require some creativity and tenacity, but it is possible. The patient, client, nurses, and other clinical support staff depend on the medical director to possess cutting-edge medical knowledge to lead an anticipatory and proactive approach. Awareness ultimately reduces the risk of malpractice. There is clearly a demand to find the necessary resources to provide a more comprehensive approach to the management of cardiovascular disease in all women. Education should be the first priority. The better informed we are as clinicians, the better we are able to inform the patient, thus empowering them to help themselves. Ignorance is neither preventive nor defensible for the patient or practitioner.

Clinicians who are new at providing health care to incarcerated patients are usually a product of the local community and are predictably inclined to practice much as they would in their private practices. Once they are reasonably exposed to the specific nuances of correctional medicine, those who stay develop an appreciation for its professional and rewarding challenges. From a medical management and public health perspective, recidivism could work in our favor. Confinement is an isolated opportunity to offer education and treatment. Collaborative efforts between community and correctional practitioners could lead to improvement in sharing patients' information and the joint development of practice guidelines and formularies. This will help maintain continuity of care upon release. Disease management and drug treatments are constantly changing, and this phenomenon can afford dynamic interactions between professional colleagues from all arenas. Enhancing work relationships between penal institutions and public health agencies may assist in the development of more intracorrectional programs toward prevention, education, and screening in cardiovascular disease for women. "Women heart victims have no community support, no ribbon, no racc" (Hoffman 2000), but more research is being done on the effects of CVD in women and its associated morbidity and mortality. However, "knowing is not enough; we must apply. Willing is not enough; we must do" (Goethe in Institute of Medicine 1999, iii).

REFERENCES

Adult Treatment Panel III. 2003. National Cholesterol Education Program: *Third report of the expert panel on detection, evaluation and treatment of high blood cholesterol in adults.* WebMD.

American Heart Association (AHA). 2001. *2002 Heart and stroke statistical update.* Dallas: AHA.

Bell-Wilson, J. A. 2002. *Getting to the heart of cardiovascular disease in women.* San Diego, CA: IDEA Health and Fitness Source.

Benjamin, S., and N. Lebowitz. 2000a. *Nutritional supplements: Can they help with heart disease?* Her Health Forum, 2000.

Benjamin, S., and N. Lebowitz. 2000b. *Hearty meals: Dietary recommendations for heart disease.* Her Health Forum, 2000.

Centers for Disease Control and Prevention (CDC). 1998. Missed opportunities in the preventive counseling for cardiovascular disease: United States, 1995. *Morbidity and Mortality Weekly Report* 47: 91–95.

Contreras, I., and D. Parra. 2000. Estrogen replacement therapy and the prevention of coronary heart disease in postmenopausal women. *American Journal of Health-System Pharmacy* 57: 1963–71.

Gillum, R. F. 1996. Epidemiology of hypertension in African American women. *American Heart Journal* 131: 385–95.

Grayson, C. E. 2002. Women and heart disease. WebMD, Health.

Haran, C. 2003. *Heart disease in women. Her Health Forum,* 1999. Hosted by Paul J. Monitz, WCBS-TV.

Hayes, S. N. 2003. *Heart disease facts: What every woman should know.* Rochester, MN: Mayo Clinic Women's Heart Clinic.

Hoffmann, C. 2000. What you (and your doctor) don't know can kill you. WebMD, Medical News.

Institute of Medicine. 1999. *Crossing the Quality Chasm: A New Health System for the 21st Century.* Washington, DC: National Academies Press.

JNC-V. 1993. The fifth report of the Joint National Committee on Prevention, Detection, Evaluation, and Treatment of High Blood Pressure. *Archives of Internal Medicine* 153: 154–83.

JNC-VI. 1997. The sixth report of the Joint National Committee on Prevention, Detection, Evaluation, and Treatment of High Blood Pressure. *Archives of Internal Medicine* 157: 2413–46.

JNC-VII. 2003. The seventh report of the Joint National Committee on Prevention, Detection, Evaluation, and Treatment of High Blood Pressure. *Archives of Internal Medicine* 42: 1206.

Legato, M., B. Lewis, and M. Oz. 2000. Men's hearts, women's hearts: How are they different? Her Health Forum. Hosted by David R. Marks, MD, WNBC, New York.

Levine, J. 2000. Studies show treatment lacking in women with heart disease. WebMD, Medical News.

Making the link: Alcohol, tobacco, and other drugs and women's health. 1995. National Clearinghouse for Alcohol and Drug Information. Rockville: Center for Substance Abuse (CSAP).

Manson, J. E., P. Greenland, A. Z. LaCroix, M. L. Stefanick, C. P. Mouton, A. Oberman, M. G. Perri, D. S. Sheps, M. B. Pettinger, and D. S. Siscouick. 2002. Walking compared with vigorous exercise for the prevention of cardiovascular events in women. *New England Journal of Medicine* 347: 716–25.

McKeown, L. A. 2000. When it comes down to disease, women's fears are misdirected. WebMD, Medical News.

McKeown, L. A. 2001. Most women unaware heart disease is their no. 1 enemy. WebMD, Medical News.

National Center for Health Statistics (NCHS). 1995. Current estimates from the National Interview Survey. Hyattsville, MD: U.S. Department of Health and Human Services.

Nutritional strategies efficacious in the prevention or treatment of hypertension. 1996. Leawood, KS: American Academy of Family Physicians.

Oncology Committee. 1999. Oncology Committee 1998 Annual Report.

Palkhivala, A. 2001. Heart disease not just a guy thing. WebMD, Medical News.

Peck, P. 2000. Heart health of U.S. women alarmingly poor. WebMD.

Pulse Tronic heart rate monitor. 1999–2000. Maximum heart rate calculation methods. Millenitek.

Rosen, R. S. 2001. Preventing heart attacks with statins. *Her Health Forum.*

Stephan, M. 2000. Making sense of heart disease, Humana. WebMD Health.

Substance abuse and the American woman. 1996. The National Center on Addiction and Substance Abuse at Columbia University. Science Blog.

Ting, W., A. McLartey, and H. Andersen. 1999. Is heart disease in women on the rise? Her Health Forum. Hosted by: Paul J. Monitz, WCBS-TV.

Vasan, R. S., A. Beiser, S. Seshadri, M. G. Larson, W. B. Kannel, R. B. D'Agostino, and D. Levy. 2002. Residual lifetime risk for developing hypertension in middle-aged women and men: The Framingham Heart Study. *Journal of the American Medical Association* 287: 1003–10.

Warner, J. 2003. Women: Tend to your heart now, not later: Making changes before menopause lowers heart disease risk. WebMD, Medical News.

White, J. J., and R. Tripuraneni. 2003. Diagnosing and treating overweight and obese patients. *CME Resource.*

White, W. B., and D. Sica. 2002a. Understanding the link between hypertension and diabetes. *Her Health Forum*, 2002.

White, W. B., and D. Sica. 2002b. Hypertension and diabetes: Treatment goals. *Her Health Forum.*

Women and Addiction. 1999. New York State Office of Alcholism and Substance Abuse Services. OASIS Publication.

17

Asthma

NORMAN DEAN

The Expert Panel Report #2 defines asthma as a chronic inflammatory disorder of the airways (NIH 1997, 1999). In susceptible individuals, the inflammation causes recurrent episodes of wheezing, breathlessness, chest tightness, and cough. These episodes are usually associated with widespread but variable airflow obstruction that is often reversible either spontaneously or with treatment. The inflammation causes an increase in the asthmatic's bronchial hyperresponsiveness to a variety of stimuli.

Asthma prevalence, severity, and mortality are higher in females than males in the United States (CDC 1998, 2003; Tarwick, Holm, and Wirth 2001; Ford et al. 2001). The burden from asthma in the United States has increased over the past twenty years (CDC 2002b; CDC 2003; Fuhlbrigge et al. 2002). In 2001, 31 million people were diagnosed with asthma during their lifetimes; 20.3 million had asthma at the time of interview, that is, current prevalence. Twelve million asthmatics, 60 percent of those who had asthma at the time of the survey, had experienced an asthma attack in the previous year (CDC, NCHS 2003). Females had a 10 percent higher rate for lifetime asthma, a 30 percent higher rate of current asthma, and a 40 percent higher asthma attack prevalence than males (CDC, NCHS 2003). The CDC considers asthma attack prevalence to be an indicator of patients with suboptimal asthma control at risk for poor asthma outcome (CDC, NCHS 2002, 2003). African Americans had higher prevalence rates than whites and Hispanics (CDC, NCHS 2002, 2003).

The report cited atopy, the genetic predisposition for the development of an IgE mediated response to common airborne allergens, as the most important predisposing factor for developing asthma. Emphasis was placed on periodic monitoring of symptoms and using portable peak flow meters to assess lung function. Efforts to reduce factors that contribute to asthma severity were recommended, including avoidance of exposure to tobacco smoke and treatment of co-morbid diseases such as rhinitis. Severity classification was modified into mild intermittent and mild, moderate, and severe persistent asthma based on frequency of symptoms and lung function. Medications were classified into two types: long-term anti-inflammatory daily medications and quick relievers to address acute symptoms and exacerbations; examples include inhaled steroids for control of inflammation and inhaled short-acting beta 2 agents for symptom relief.

In the year 2000, 4,487 asthmatics died from the disease (CDC, NCHS 2003). Sixty-five percent of these deaths occurred in women. African American females had the highest age adjusted mortality rate due to asthma with 4.2 per 100,000 (NCHS 2002). In the year 2000, non-Hispanic African Americans had an asthma death rate over 200 percent higher than non-Hispanic whites and 160 percent higher than Hispanics (NCHS 2002).

Co-Morbidities with Asthma and Incarcerated Females

Co-morbidities frequently documented with asthma include allergic rhinitis, perennial rhinitis, sinusitis, and gastroesophageal reflux (Corren et al. 1999; Coyle et al. 2003; Crystal et al. 2002; Dean 2001; Ford et al. 2001; Frew 1997; Fuhlbrigge et al. 2002; Magnussen, Kanniess, and Richter 2000). Incarcerated females also have a high prevalence of co-morbid psychological disorders and addictions (Dean 2001; Dean, Sadat, Jackson, et al. 2001; Dean, Worf, Lewis, et al. 1999; Dean, Worf, Rider, et al. 2000; NCCHC 2001). Addictive behavior and psychological dysfunction has often led to their incarceration. Poverty, physical and sexual abuse, high-risk lifestyles, and increased susceptibility to dysfunctional and addictive behaviors characterize this population (NCCHC 2001). Genetic and hereditary predispositions have been documented for asthma (Batra et al. 2003), as well as psychological disorders and addictions (Becker et al. 2001; Breslau 1995). Genetics, environment, co-morbidities, gender, and ethnicity are all important variables impacting asthma prevalence and morbidity (Duffy, Mitchell, and Martin 1998; Ford et al. 2001; Lewis et al. 2002; Leynaert et al. 1997; Marsh, Neely, and Breazeale 1994; Meyers, Postma, and Panhuysen 1994; Postma et al. 2003).

Genetics and Environment in Asthma and Addictions

Asthma and Genetics

Genetic and hereditary predisposition to asthma has been documented by Marsh, Neely, and Breazeale (1994); Meyers, Postma, and Panhuysen (1994); Martinez, Salomon, and Holberg (1998); and Duffy, Mitchell, and Martin (1998). Cookson (2002) has recently described asthma as an epidemic due to a combination of strong genetic and environmental factors. In discussing asthma genetics, Cookson describes genome screens for linkages to traits underlying asthma with loci most often identified on chromosomes 5, 6, 12, and 13. Inhaled beta 2 adrenergic agents are the most commonly used medications for the treatment of asthma (Israel et al.

2000). Genetic polymorphisms of the beta 2 adrenergic receptor can affect the response to regular use of these agents (Israel et al. 2000; Lipworth et al. 2004; Taylor et al. 2000). Kauffmann et al. (2002) cite results of epidemiologic asthma and atopy studies, concluding that smoking tobacco is directly related to IgE levels and asthma severity. Additional genetic variables affecting asthma phenotype and presentation have been identified (Ulbrecht et al. 2000; Burchard, Silverman, et al. 1999). Genetic epidemiology is an area of vigorous interest and active research (Le Souef, Goldblatt, and Lynch 2000, Von Hertzen and Haahtela 2004).

Addiction and Genetics

Genetic factors involved in nicotine addiction are reviewed by Batra et al. (2003), with editorial comments by Wornsnop (2003). Batra and Wornsnop emphasize that the hereditability estimates for tobacco smoking addiction in twin studies have been comparable to hereditability estimates for asthma and alcoholism. The twin studies cited by Batra and Wornsnop document genetic influence on tobacco smoking initiation, persistence, and volume of cigarettes smoked both in males and females. Batra reviews the literature of genetic factors involved in nicotine addiction and cites the candidate genes involved in the metabolism of nicotine and dopamine.

Ethnic differences in nicotine metabolism have been identified (Carballo et al. 1998; Pérez-Stable et al. 1998). Wornsnop (2003) estimates that the majority of smokers in developed nations where smoking prevalence rates range from 20 to 30 percent are nicotine addicts. Batra et al. (2003) and Wornsnop (2003) emphasize the effects of nicotinic receptors in the brain and activation of the dopaminergic system releasing dopamine, believed to be important in reinforcing addictive behavior. Becker et al. (2001) describe that cocaine and metamphetamines act via dopamine release that they cited to be more pronounced in females. The results of nicotine in effecting dopamine release are similar to those of other addictive drugs and is an area that Batra recommends for future investigation. Gender differences in susceptibility to addictions noted by Becker et al. merit further study.

Female Sex Hormones and Their Affect on Asthma

Female sex hormones and their fluctuations play an important role in defining the clinical expression of asthma including exacerbations and severity (Chrousus 1995; Chrousus, Torpy, and Gold 1998; Skobeloff et al. 1992; Skobeloff et al. 1996). The increased asthma prevalence in females at puberty that persists throughout adulthood and then moderates at menopause illustrates the lifelong influence of progesterone, estrogen, luteinizing, and follicle-stimulating hormones. Postma, Boezen, and Watson (2003), Skobeloff et al. (1992, 1996), and Cydulka (1999) noted that hormonal changes unique to females are associated with prevalence, progression, and severity of asthma. Perimenstrual asthma exacerbations and asthma status during the stages of pregnancy and postpartum period are dramatic examples of fluctuations in female sex hormones and their effect on asthma control (Schatz, Harden, and Forsythe 1998; Shames et al. 1998; Skobeloff et al. 1992, 1996; Tan and Thompson 2000; Tan, McFarlane, and Lipworth 1999). The adverse effects in asthmatics of hormone replacement therapy during the postmenopausal period has been emphasized (Tan, McFarlane, and Lipworth 1997; Troisi et al. 1995).

Perimenstrual Exacerbations of Asthma

Perimenstrual asthma exacerbations were a dramatic example of the influence of female sex hormones and their impact on asthma that Dean, Sadat, and Nunnery et al. (2001) observed in an incarcerated population. Perimenstrual asthma exacerbations are well documented and are estimated to occur in 40 percent of asthmatic females (Eliasson, Scherzer, and DeGraff 1986; Benyon, Garbett, and Barnes 1988; Magnussen, Kanniess, and Richter 2001; Shames et al. 1998). The largest symptom and objective measurement changes occur during the late luteal phase just prior to menses (Tan, McFarlane, and Lipworth 1997; Postma, Boezen, and Watson 2003). Skobeloff et al. (1992, 1996) described the fourfold increase in asthma visits to the emergency room by females during the perimenstrual period and attributed this increase in severity of asthma to changes in estrogen and progesterone levels. Tan, McFarlane, and Lipworth (1997) cited the loss of normal beta 2 adrenoreceptor regulation and increased perimenstrual response to adenosine monophosphate in stable female asthmatics. Tan, McFarlane, and Lipworth also demonstrated that asthmatic patients receiving oral contraception had attenuated changes in airway reactivity that were attributed to suppression of the luteal phase rise in sex hormones. Vrieze, Postma, and Kertjeans (2003) and Martinez-Moragon et al. (2004) have emphasized the importance of the perimenstrual period in profiling high-risk and difficult-to-treat female asthmatics. Agarwal and Marshall (1999) present data that healthy women during the perimenstrual period had a shift in the type-1/type-2 cytokine balance toward a type-2 asthmatic cytokine balance. They used the ratio of interferon gamma to interluken 10 to reflect type-1 (TH1) and type-2 (TH2) cytokine balance. Agarwal and Marshall demonstrated that the interferon gamma to interluken 10 ratio decreased during the menstrual period, and they proposed that this cytokine change is clinically reflected in an increase in asthma severity.

Stress, the Immune System, and Asthma

Psychological stress has been evaluated as both an acute precipitant of asthma exacerbations as well as having a role in the development of severe asthma (Busse et al. 1995). Lui and colleagues (2002) demonstrated in college students that stress associated with final examinations can produce an increase in severity of response to antigen challenge. This effect was more pronounced in the subjects with asthma. Agarwal and Marshall (1998, 2001) have demonstrated that stress can affect the immune system by suppressing TH1 cytokines combating infection and enhancing TH2 cytokines associated with asthma and inflammation. Chrousus (1995) and colleagues (1998) investigated the interaction between the hypothalamic pituitary-adrenal axis and the female reproductive system. They described interactions between corticotropin-releasing hormones (CRH) and female reproductive hormones, and identified stress-related time periods when females would be more vulnerable to asthma exacerbations, steroid-resistant asthma, and autoimmune disease. McEwen and Stellar (1993) and McEwen (1998) developed the concept of chronic stress as allostatic load with the potential to negatively impact the immune system with increased risk for asthma and autoimmune disease. Ten Brinke and Ouwerkerk et al. (2001) reviewed the impact of psychological dysfunction in severe asthmatics with respect to health care use. Ten Brinke and his colleagues noted that severe asthmatics with documented psychological disorders had an increased odds ratio for emergency room visits, exacerbations of asthma, and hospitalizations compared to severe asthmatic patients without psychological disorders. Ten Brinke suggested that psychopathology in severe asthmatics is a risk factor for loss of asthma control and increased health resource use.

Incarceration Stressors for Asthmatic Females

Incarceration per se is a stressor, and the prison environment can augment stressors. Incarcerated asthmatic women experience the stress of separation from families that often include underage children. Pregnant females are subject to additional stressors. Dean (2001) noted that over 100 pregnant females entered his correctional facility annually. Dean, Sadat, Jackson, and Worf (2001) observed that 50 percent of these pregnant asthmatics continued to smoke tobacco during incarceration despite counseling regarding the adverse affects of nicotine. Non-smoking inmates including pregnant inmates were stressed by the exposure to secondhand smoke in the prison (Dean 2001, Dean et al. 2001). When pregnant inmates go into labor, they are transported by custody officers to a designated local hospital, and within twenty-four hours after an uncomplicated vaginal delivery the inmates are separated from their newborn child and transported back to the prison facility. The stress of the postpartum period for an incarcerated asthmatic contributes to exacerbations (Dean 2001; Dean et al. 2001). There is a need for both medical and mental health providers to coordinate and target therapeutic interventions for postpartum inmates.

An increase in bronchial reactivity has been documented in females compared to males and attributed primarily to increased sensitivity of females to tobacco smoke and the indoor allergens: dust mite, cockroach, and cat (Eggleston et al. 1998; Lewis et al. 2002; Leynaert et al. 1997). Maternal asthma history and tobacco smoking have been associated with an increase in the prevalence of asthma in children (Dezateaux et al. 1999; Gilliland et al. 2002; Hoo et al. 1998; Martinez, Cline, and Burrows 1992; Morkjaroenpong et al. 2003; Postma, Boezen, and Watson 2003).

Appropriate Diagnosis in Incarcerated Females: Vocal Cord Dysfunction

The incarcerated asthma population presents a challenge to health care providers. Patients enter the correctional system with undiagnosed asthma or inappropriately diagnosed asthma (NCCHC 2001). Vocal cord dysfunction is one of the most important underdiagnosed masqueraders of asthma (Newman, Mason, and Schmalling 1995). Wood and Milgrom (1996) and Brugman and Simons (1998) have reviewed the clinical spectrum of vocal cord dysfunction that results from the paradoxical closure of the vocal cords during inspiration resulting in wheezing and shortness of breath. All these studies documented that a significant percent of these patients do not have any associated asthma and are inappropriately treated with daily inhalers and high doses of oral prednisone. The reports by Hayes et al. (1993) and Maillard, Schweizer, Broccard, et al. (2002) vividly illustrate that patients with vocal cord dysfunction use an enormous amount of resources.

The study by Newman, Mason, and Schmalling (1995) reviewed all patients hospitalized at their institution in Denver between 1984 and 1991 in whom vocal cord dysfunction was diagnosed. All of these patients were referred for evaluation of refractory asthma. Ninety-five patients fulfilled the criteria for laryngoscopically proved vocal cord dysfunction. Of the ninety-five, forty-two (44 percent) had vocal cord dysfunction without asthma, and fifty-three (56 percent) had combined asthma and vocal cord dysfunction. Forty-one of the forty-two vocal cord dysfunction patients without asthma were females compared to thirty-nine females out of fifty-three patients with combined asthma and vocal cord dysfunction. Thirty-four of forty-two patients with pure vocal cord dysfunction were receiving prednisone and thirty-seven of fifty-three patients with vocal cord dysfunction and asthma received prednisone. The pure vocal cord dysfunction patients' visits to emergency rooms were significantly more numerous than the patients with vocal cord dysfunction and asthma. Twenty-five percent of the forty-two vocal cord dysfunction patients without asthma had been intubated. Nine of the forty-two patients with vocal cord dysfunction without asthma had prior psychiatric hospitalizations compared with one of the fifty-three patients with asthma.

The reviews of Newman, Mason, and Schmalling (1995), Wood and Milgrom (1996), and Brugman and Simons (1998) cite the gold standard of diagnosis for vocal cord dysfunction as laryngoscopy performed while the patient is experiencing symptoms. During the procedure, a photograph of the paradoxical adduction of the vocal cords during inspiration provides objective documentation of vocal cord dysfunction (Brugman and Simons 1998). Dean (2001) and Dean, Sadat, Jackson, and Worf (2001) used this type of documentation by consultants to identify and treat a patient without asthma who had been intubated prior to incarceration. Wood and Milgrom and Brugman and Simons cited use of pulmonary function tests with flow volume curves showing flattening of the inspiratory loops as providing data that suggest vocal cord dysfunction.

Vocal cord dysfunction is seen predominantly in females and is frequently associated with psychiatric disorders including depression, obsessive-compulsive disorder, and post-traumatic stress disorder. Many of these patients have a history of sexual or physical abuse, and their vocal cord dysfunction may represent a variation of conversion disorder (Newman, Mason, and Schmalling 1995; Brugman and Simons 1998; Wood and Milgrom 1996). Dean and colleagues (2001) identified three new cases of vocal cord dysfunction without asthma during an asthma intervention program in a prison facility. The discussion of vocal cord dysfunction at a National Correctional Health Care Conference (Dean 2001) indicated that this condition needs to be considered more often in the differential diagnosis in patients in correctional health facilities diagnosed with difficult-to-control asthma. The social and psychological problems of incarcerated females are similar to those identified in vocal cord dysfunction patients (Dean 2001; NCHC 2002).

Asthma Guidelines and the National Commission on Correctional Health Care

The National Commission on Correctional Health Care (NCCHC 2001) has provided a guideline for correctional facilities based on a modification of the National Institutes of Health (NIH) "Expert Panel Report #2: Guidelines for the Diagnosis and Management of Asthma" (National Institutes of Health 1997, 1999). The NCCHC guideline reinforces the concept of early diagnosis of asthma and staging of patients as to severity of disease. Treatment of patients with moderate and severe asthma with inhaled steroids is emphasized. The NCCHC advocates that on entry to a correctional institution, a detailed questionnaire be used that addresses asthma, age of onset, hospitalization, emergency room visits, type and frequency of asthma medication, and use of peak flow meters. The NCCHC cites the importance of clinical monitoring of patients with peak-flow-based action plans. The NCCHC also emphasizes monitoring the ratio of use of short-acting beta 2 agents, that is albuterol, to inhaled steroids. The importance of identifying and treating co-morbid problems is cited, including nicotine use, rhino-sinusitis, and gastroesophageal reflux (GERD). The targeting of patients with moderate and severe asthma is justified by NCCHC because the 10 to 15 percent of patients with moderate to severe asthma account for 80 percent of asthma-related health care costs (NCCHC 2001).

The North Carolina Correctional Institution for Women (NCCIW) Asthma Intervention Program

Initiation, Organization, and Implementation of Interventions

In February 1998, an asthma intervention program was initiated at the North Carolina Correctional Institution for Women, a facility housing 1,150 inmates. The intervention improved asthma control and provided insights into issues faced by female asthmatic inmates (Dean, Worf, Lewis et al. 1999; Dean, Worf, Rider et al. 2000; Dean, Sadat, Jackson et al. 2001; Dean, Sadat, Nunnery et al. 2001; Dean 2001).

Ninety-six patients aged eighteen to forty-six fulfilling the criteria of the Expert Panel Report #2 (NIH 1997, 1999) for persistent asthma were recruited into the asthma intervention clinic. Exclusion criteria included bronchitis, emphysema, immune collagen diseases, schizophrenia, and upper airway obstruction. These excluded patients that were treated and followed in the airway clinic or medical clinic. A weekly asthma intervention clinic was staffed by a physician and a pharmacist from February 1998 through July 2000. The physician and nursing personnel continued to manage the clinic through January 2001 with input from the pharmacy staff. Spirometry reversibility tests and total and specific IgE levels were recorded (Dean et al. 1999, 2000, 2001). Asthmatics with a history of rhinitis or sinusitis were issued an allergy diary. Patients were educated and trained in medication use, technical practice with inhalers, and in recording their asthma triggers and peak flows in symptom diaries. Timing of menstrual cycle was added to diary recordings. Patients were provided with action plans based on their personal best peak flow. Documented data included recordings from asthma and allergy diaries, exacerbations, medication use, spirometry, IgE, emergency room visits, and hospitalizations. Co-morbid allergic rhinitis, sinusitis, and GERD were identified and treated.

Patient Demographics, Co-morbidities, Intervention, and Treatment

The ninety-six patients included fifty-one (53 percent) African Americans, thirty-nine (41 percent) Caucasians, and six (6 percent) others. The ninety-six patients with persistent asthma accounted for 60 percent of the incarcerated asthmatics during the intervention period.

Thirty-five (36 percent) of the patients reported a history of childhood exposure to secondhand crack cocaine. Sixty-seven (70 percent) had a history of personal past cocaine use, and fifty-eight (60 percent) reported an exacerbation of their asthma after smoking crack cocaine. Sixty (63 percent) patients had a parent or sibling with asthma. During childhood, fifty-five (57 percent) were exposed to secondhand tobacco smoke in their home environment. Fifty (52 percent) were current tobacco smokers, and fifty-six (58 percent) were former tobacco smokers. Forty-eight (72 percent) of the sixty-seven patients who used crack cocaine had experimented previously with tobacco smoking. Twenty-four (25 percent) patients reported initial use of tobacco prior to age twelve. Fifty (52 percent) patients reported smoking tobacco and crack cocaine during at least one pregnancy. Concomitant with crack cocaine and tobacco use, forty-five (47 percent) patients abused alcohol, twenty (21 percent) had snorted heroin, and forty (42 percent) had used marijuana. Crack cocaine was the drug of choice for the majority (70 percent) of patients. Sixty-four (66 percent) patients reported childhood physical and sexual abuse. Seventy-three (76 percent) asthma patients had co-morbid allergic rhinitis with documented elevated total and specific IgE levels to allergens. Indoor allergens were the most prevalent, with dust mites the most common allergen. Thirty-eight (40 percent) had chronic sinusitis and fifty-three (55 percent) had GERD. The intervention clinic incorporated co-morbid disease therapy for rhinitis, sinusitis and GERD; previously, less than 40 percent received such therapy (Dean, Sadat, Jackson, and Worf 2001). Thirty-eight (40 percent) of the patients reported perimenstrual exacerbation of their asthma. Documentation by serial peak flows and symptom scores confirmed perimenstrual exacerbations of asthma. The patients with perimenstrual asthma exacerbations improved with either an increase in inhaled steroid dose or a burst of oral steroids. The addition of a leukotriene antagonist provided improvement in a subset of perimenstrual asthma exacerbation patients with co-morbid rhino-sinusitis (Dean, Sadat, Nunnery, et al. 2001).

Pregnant Asthmatics

Eight pregnant asthmatic patients with a prior history of asthma exacerbations during pregnancy had asthma exacerbations and received inhaled steroids (Dean et al. 2001; Dean 2001). Six of the eight pregnant patients had co-morbid exacerbations of allergic rhinitis and sinusitis. Five pregnant patients were followed in a high-risk obstetric clinic. The eight pregnant patients delivered at term, during incarceration, at a community hospital housing the high-risk obstetric clinic. Despite counseling, five of the pregnant patients continued to smoke tobacco throughout pregnancy (Dean 2001). Four of the pregnant patients admitted to using crack cocaine while pregnant prior to incarceration. Four patients had postpartum asthma exacerbations (Dean et al. 2001; Dean 2001). The stress of separation of the postpartum patients from their newborns was recognized. As cited previously, we appreciate a need for both medical and mental health providers to coordinate targeted monitoring of this population.

Identification of Asthma Triggers and Intervention Results

Identified as common lung irritants producing symptoms of asthma and rhino-sinusitis were cleaning solutions and tobacco smoke. Once triggers and irritants were identified, exposures were reduced by modifying work and housing assignments. Only six of the ninety-six patients had previously used a peak flow meter, and none had used an asthma action plan with peak flow documentation. Patients treated with inhaled steroids increased from eight to all ninety-six with persistent asthma. Comparing the year after the asthma intervention with the prior year, emergency room visits and hospitalizations decreased by more than 50 percent (Dean, Sadat, Jackson et al. 2001; Dean 2001). No mortalities related to asthma occurred during the intervention period (Dean Worf, Rider et al. 2000; Dean 2001).

Correctional Care Issues and Female Asthmatics

The majority of newly incarcerated asthmatic females have had poor access to medical care and have poor knowledge about asthma and treatment strategies (NCCHC 2001; Dean 2001). Incarceration can represent an opportunity for improved access to care and a window of opportunity to improve patients' knowledge and participation in their own therapy for asthma. Therapeutic interventions compatible with national and community standards can be introduced during the period of incarceration. However, incarceration can also present environmental exposures harmful to asthmatics; limited access to expensive, state-of-the-art medications essential for asthma control; and perpetuation of addictive behaviors. The genetic predisposition to addictions and asthma noted above increase an inmate's vulnerability to harmful environmental variables such as tobacco smoke. Tobacco smoke has been documented to impair an asthmatic patient's response to steroids in addition to having a direct negative impact on airway inflammation (Chauduri et al. 2003). Tobacco also stimulates the release of dopamine as does cocaine and amphetamines (Breslau 1995). A correctional system that opposes the introduction of smoking cessation programs, sells cigarettes to inmates, and does not facilitate smoke-free dorms and work areas is condoning the perpetuation of nicotine addiction. An environment that is favorable to nicotine addiction enables the perpetuation of addictive behaviors to substances of abuse (Breslau 1995; Johnson and Gerstein 1998; Batra et al. 2003).

Epidemic of Cigarette Smoking, Cocaine Abuse, and Asthma

The NCCIW intervention program highlighted the heavy use of nicotine and cocaine in our asthmatic females. The higher bronchial reactivity observed in women than men has been attributed to the increased sensitivity of females to active and passive cigarette smoke, as well as to indoor allergens (Lewis et al. 2002; Leynaert et al. 1997). The negative effect of cigarette smoke on lung growth (Gold et al. 1996) and lung function (Xu, Li, and Wang 1994) has also been documented. The role of cigarette smoke in steroid resistance has recently been reemphasized (Chaudhuri et al. 2003). Morkjaroenpong et al. (2003) examined the relationship between environmental tobacco smoke and asthmatic schoolchildren. Data were collected from 590 primary caregivers of children of whom 98 percent were African American. The child's mother was the caregiver 90 percent of the time. Smoking in the home was reported by 29.4 percent of primary caregivers. A dose response between severity of asthma and the amount of cigarettes smoked in the home was documented. Caregivers who smoked in the home had less education and were poorer than nonsmokers.

Ness et al. (1999) assessed tobacco use by urine cotinine levels and cocaine use by hair analysis among 970 pregnant women aged fourteen to forty who were seen at the emergency department of a Philadelphia teaching hospital. These women were African American and receiving public assistance. Among the 400 women with spontaneous abortions, evidence of tobacco and cocaine use was 35 percent and 29 percent, respectively, compared with 22 percent and 21 percent among the 570 women with ongoing pregnancies followed through twenty-two weeks of gestation. This data provides further evidence of the high prevalence of nicotine and cocaine addiction in our inner-city populations. Smoking tobacco and using cocaine was magnified in incarcerated asthmatic females (Dean et al. 1999, 2000, 2001). Slama (2000) cites cofactors including alcohol and cocaine associated with tobacco smoking in the United States, the United Kingdom, Sweden, and Australia, where there are strong demographic differences between smokers and nonsmokers. Slama observed that tobacco smokers are younger, poorer, less educated, and more likely to manifest unhealthy and risky behaviors. Breslau (1995) identified specific cofactors of tobacco smoking that included alcoholism, illicit drug use, major depression, anxiety, and other psychiatric disorders. Breslau identified cocaine and other illicit drug use as being four times more frequent among female smokers than female nonsmokers in the United States. Johnson and Gerstein (1998) emphasized that research continues to accumulate indicating that cigarette smoking and alcohol play an early role in the process leading to additional substance abuse.

Dean et al. (1999, 2000, 2001) described a history of crack cocaine, snorting heroin, and tobacco smoking in an incarcerated female population along with elevated IgE levels, rhino-sinusitis, and asthma. Crack cocaine abuse has been cited by Rome et al. (2000) as precipitating severe asthma exacerbations. De los Bueis et al. (2002) reported that inhaling cocaine with heroin provokes acute asthma episodes. Snorting heroin has recently been cited as causing acute asthma exacerbations (Krantz et al. 2003).

Co-Morbid Medical and Psychological Issues

The female asthmatic population observed at NCCIW reflects the negative impact of poverty, substance abuse, and history of physical and sexual abuse on subjects' health status and severity of asthma. Dean et al. (1999, 2000, 2001) noted that during the preincarceration period, the following were identified as contributing to the severity of asthma: misdiagnosis, undertreatment of asthma, lack of access to health care, and high exposure to tobacco smoke (58 percent) and crack cocaine (70 percent). Sixty percent of the incarcerated asthmatic females met the criteria for persistent asthma, and 40 percent had intermittent asthma during the intervention program (Dean 2001; NIH 1997, 1999). The severity of persistent asthma documented by Dean was approximately 40 percent moderate, 20 percent severe, and 40 percent mild persistent asthma. The report by Coyle et al. (2003) of asthma among inner-city adults noted severity of 4.8 percent mild intermittent, 33.6 percent mild persistent, 32.7 percent moderate persistent, and 28.9 percent severe persistent. The severity of asthma described by Coyle et al. for an inner-city population and Fuhlbrigge et al. (2002) was consistent with the predominant persistent asthma severity observed by Dean (2001) in an incarcerated female population. Perimenstrual asthma exacerbations (40 percent), and exacerbations in pregnant asthmatics and postpartum inmates were observed in the NCCIW population (Dean, Sadat, Nunnery et al. 2001).

The high prevalence of co-morbid medical and psychological disorders in incarcerated females needs to be identified and treated to maintain asthma control (Dean 2001). Rhinitis (76 percent), sinusitis (40 percent), and GERD (55 percent) were prevalent in the incarcerated female asthma patients (Dean et al. 1999, 2000, 2001). Patients with a history of tobacco smoking and crack cocaine use were noted to have elevated risks for these co-morbidities and for additional medical and psychological problems (Dean et al. 2000, 2001; Dean 2001). Co-morbid HIV in six patients with preexisting asthma resulted in exacerbations of asthma, and rhino-sinusitis further increased severity of the asthma in these patients. Asthma patients with HIV infection have a decrease in CD4 counts that correlates with an increase in IgE levels and clinical flare-ups of asthma and rhino-sinusitis (Rancinan et al. 1997, 1998).

Problems of Access, Affordability, and Availability of Care in Corrections

Gibson (1994) noted that the poor and poorly educated are more likely to come to medical attention late in their disease process. Gibson defined access to health care in terms of affordability, availability, accessibility, and accommodation.

Incarceration provides an opportunity for an increase in access to health care by removing the issue of a patient's ability to pay for services (that is, affordability). The majority of asthma patients seen in the NCCIW clinic did not have access to health care prior to incarceration (Dean et al. 1999, 2000, 2001; Dean 2001). Inhaled steroids to control inflammation and short-acting beta 2 agents for symptom relief are formulary medications in correctional facilities. Documentation of need can result in obtaining medications such as long-acting beta 2 agents and combinations of long-acting beta 2 agents with inhaled steroids and leukotriene antagonists. However, steroid-resistant patients with severe asthma could, because of cost restraints, be unlikely to be approved for more expensive and effective medications such as omalizumab (Busse et al. 2001; Corren et al. 2003). The availability of medical personnel and the accessibility or location of health services relative to the population are important correctional variables that are frequently subject to budget and security constraints.

Accommodation Access and Continuity of Care

The term accommodation used by Gibson (1994) refers to the relationship between clients and providers in terms of perception of a medical problem and response to the problem. The intervention program at NCCIW provided insights into practical problems impacting availability, accessibility, and accommodation in a correctional facility. Asthma clinics require a group of designated providers whose time is specifically dedicated to the clinic. A multidisciplinary team including physician, nursing, and pharmacy personnel should be assigned to implement the clinic's goal of teaching, training, and providing instructions in the use of

peak-flow-based action plans. Continuity in personnel assignments is often difficult to maintain in correctional facilities with high turnover of personnel and limited resources. Correctional providers need to be alert to the overdiagnosis as well
as the underdiagnosis of asthma. Knowledge of masqueraders of asthma is essential. Sick call nurses as well as custody officers need to be educated and sensitive to
the inmate's use of peak flow meters and the inmate's need to have a rescue inhaler in their possession. The ability of patients to keep on their person rescue
inhalers and peak flow meters may at times be in conflict with security considerations, especially when an inmate is placed in a disciplinary segregation unit.

Health Providers' Knowledge, Continuing Education, and Correctional Care Insight

Asthma patients who do not have contraindications need to be offered yearly in-
fluenza vaccinations. Pneumococcal vaccinations also should be available. Obstacles to optimizing availability, accommodation, and continuity of care in
correctional facilities are budgetary constraints and the high turnover of personnel. It is vital that the nursing and custody staff be aware of perimenstrual exacerbations of asthma as well as the significance of wheezing in a pregnant patient.
The increased severity of asthma in incarcerated females and the gender and sex
aspects that impact asthma need to be understood by correctional health care
providers. The well-documented role of female sex hormones, menstrual cycle,
pregnancy, postpartum period, and oral contraceptive pills in asthma morbidity
should be reviewed, understood, and continually updated by health providers
(Martinez-Moragon et al. 2004; Schatz, Harden, and Forsythe 1998; Skobeloff et al.
1992, 1996; Tan et al. 1997, 1999; Troisi et al. 1995). The cooperation of sick call
nurses and custody officers is needed to implement peak-flow-based action plans
and maintain the continuity of care. The consequences of an asthma patient not
receiving an inhaler refill in a timely manner needs to be emphasized and staff
needs to be responsive to this issue.

Staff also needs to be alert to patients who may overuse beta 2 adrenergic
inhalers. Providers should be familiar with the concept of beta 2 adrenoreceptor
downregulation and keep updated on publications addressing ethnic and gender
differences in response to these agents (Burchard et al. 2004; Israel et al. 2000;
Lipworth et al. 2004; Tan et al. 1997, 1999). Pharmacy monitoring of inhaler refill
requests is essential. Patients who share inhalers need to be identified and counseled. Patients who overuse nebulized treatments need to be reevaluated and
their medication profile reviewed. The health care provider's acumen in distinguishing patient abuse of an inhaler from deterioration of asthma control is important in correctional facilities. Patients who continue to purchase cigarettes
and smoke while using inhaled steroids and beta 2 adrenergic inhalers need to be
vigorously counseled by knowledgeable providers. The negative impact of first-
and secondhand smoke on steroid responsiveness should be familiar to providers
(Chaudhuri et al. 2003).

Inmates' Manipulation and Secondary Agendas

Patients may inappropriately try to use their diagnosis of asthma to avoid work assignments. However, the activity and physical exertion involved in a work assignment is often an activity that the patient may engage in when not incarcerated. A severe asthmatic should receive documented restrictions. Patients with mild asthma who are smoking and inappropriately requesting to be removed from work assignments are encountered in correctional facilities. Individuals claiming that they have exertional limitations in a job assignment are not uncommonly documented engaging in high levels of physical exertion such as basketball and volleyball, as well as smoking tobacco. Both clinical judgment and correctional care experience are needed to guide the health care provider in recommending appropriate housing and work assignments.

Correctional Problems, Accommodation, and Environmental Conditions

There are buildings in correctional facilities that have inadequate and/or poor ventilation systems. Air-conditioned dorms with adequate ventilation are not as available as dorms without these advantages. Cleaning dorm units with emphasis on impacting antigen levels is an important component of asthma management (Sporik et al. 1998). Dampness and increased levels of humidity provide a favorable setting for antigens (Arbes et al. 2003). Inmates involved in cleaning assignments should be educated and monitored to avoid high concentrations of bleach and cleaning solutions. Programs to reduce indoor allergen loads are feasible in correctional facilities.

Reception and dorm areas are challenged by a large influx of prisoners. Buildings with low outdoor ventilation rates increase the risk of transmission of viral respiratory infections that increase morbidity in patients with respiratory problems (Myatt, Johnston, Zhengfa, Wand et al. 2004). Environmental tobacco smoke is a major problem for many correctional facilities. Nonsmoking asthmatic patients along with other nonsmoking inmates request smoke-free dorms, or at least smoke-free areas within a dorm. Environmental tobacco smoke has been demonstrated to play a critical role in asthma exacerbations, morbidity, and mortality (Chen 1994; Cunningham et al. 1996; Ford et al. 2001; Fuhlbrigge et al. 2002; Gold et al. 1996; Morkjaroenpong et al. 2003; Schwartz, Timonnen, and Pekkanen 2000).

Tobacco Smoking and Addictions: Challenges for Correctional Facilities and Health Organizations

Asthma patients are employed in work assignments located in buildings that need to address smoking and smoke-free environments. Dining rooms and recreation buildings also need to address smoke-free environments. The sale of cigarettes by corrections-operated canteens to inmates maintains the cycle of addiction and presents medical problems for nonsmoking asthma patients. One may conclude that there are correctional systems that do not understand that nicotine is an addictive drug and is often a "gateway" drug for cocaine (Breslau 1995; Johnson and Gerstein 1998). The window of opportunity to intervene in addictions leading to incarceration is lost when basic scientific knowledge of dopamine release by nicotine as well as illicit drugs is either not understood or ignored by agencies "providing" alcohol and substance abuse programs. The ongoing smoking by patients with HIV/AIDS and cardiovascular disease, as well as airway disease, exacerbates the associated medical problems.

The tobacco obstacle is likely to persist in many correctional facilities, particularly in a political environment in states that favor selling cigarettes to inmates and exclude the introduction of smoking cessation programs. Waxman (2002) referred to Kluger's (1996) *Ashes to Ashes* in citing the awesome power of special interests to undermine efforts to decrease tobacco consumption. Society will have to pay the health and social costs of state government programs that support the use of a preventable variable (that is, tobacco) in the rising prevalence of asthma, cardiovascular disease, and cancer.

Feminization of Asthma and Chronic Obstructive Pulmonary Disease (COPD)

This chapter has discussed the epidemic of asthma and the increasing burden of asthma in the United States. The higher prevalence, morbidity, and mortality in females compared to males were discussed. We noted the history of heavy exposure to tobacco and crack cocaine in an incarcerated female population and the association with persistent moderate and severe asthma. It should be at least noted in this discussion of asthma that the latest American Thoracic Society and European Respiratory Society guidelines for diseases of airflow obstruction also cite the global epidemic of COPD (Celli et al. 2004). In the year 2000, more women (59,936) than men (59,118) died from COPD in the United States, and the trend is ongoing. Tobacco is the main risk factor for COPD, and the increasing morbidity and mortality for females compared to males has been attributed to the increase in cigarette smoking by women starting in the 1940s (CDC 2002a).

The prevalence and severity of asthma and COPD occurring globally as we enter the twenty-first century are likely to be magnified in the vulnerable incarcerated female population.

REFERENCES

Agarwal, S. K., and G. D. Marshall. 1998. Glucocorticoid-induced type 1/type 2 cytokine alterations in humans: A model for stress-related immune dysfunction. *Journal of Interferon and Cytokine Research* 18: 1050–68.
Agarwal, S. K., and G. D. Marshall. 1999. Perimenstrual alterations in type-1/type-2 cytokine balance of normal women. *Annals of Allergy, Asthma and Immunology* 83, no. 3: 222–28.
Agarwal, S. K., and G. D. Marshall. 2001. Review: Stress effects on immunity and its application to clinical immunology. *Clinical and Experimental Allergy* 31: 25–31.
Arbes, S. J., R. D. Cohn, M. Yin, M. L. Muilenberg, H. Burge, W. Friedman, and D. C. Zeld. 2003.

House dust mite allergen in U.S. beds: Results from the first national survey of lead and allergens in housing. *Journal Allergy and Clinical Immunology* III: 408–14.

Batra, V., A. Patkar, W. H. Berrettini, S. P. Weinstein, and F. T. Leone. 2003. The genetic determinants of smoking. *Chest* 123: 1730–39.

Becker, J. B., H. Molenda, and D. L. Hummer. 2001. Gender differences in behavioral responses to cocaine and metamphetamines. Implications for mechanisms mediating gender differences in drug abuse in the biological basis of cocaine addiction. Quinones–Jenab (ed.), *Annals of the New York Academy of Sciences* 937: 172–218.

Benyon, H. L., N. D. Garbett, and P. J. Barnes. 1988. Severe premenstrual exacerbations of asthma: Effect of intramuscular progesterone. *Lancet* 2: 370–71.

Breslau, N. 1995. Psychiatric co-morbidity of smoking and nicotine dependence. *Behavior General* 25: 95–101.

Brugman, S. M., and S. M. Simons. 1998. Vocal cord dysfunction–don't mistake it for asthma. *The Physician and Sports Medicine* 26, no. 5: 63–85.

Burchard, E. G., E. K. Silverman, L. J. Rosenwasser, L. Borish, C. Yandava, and A. Pillari. 1999. Association between a sequence variant in the IL –4 Gene Promoter and FeV1 in asthma. *American Journal of Respiratory and Critical Care Medicine* 160: 919–22.

Burchard, E. G., P. C. Avila, S. Nazario, J. Casal, A. Torres, J. R. Rodriguez-Santana, et al. 2004. Lower bronchodilator responsiveness in Puerto Rican than in Mexican subjects with asthma. *American Journal of Respiratory and Critical Care Medicine* 169: 386–92.

Busse, W. W., J. K. Kicolt–Glaser, C. Coe, R. J. Martin, S. T. Weiss, and S. R. Parker. 1995. Stress and asthma: NHLBI workshop summary. *American Journal of Respiratory and Critical Care Medicine* 151: 249–52.

Busse, W., J. Corren, B. J. Lanier, M. McAlary, A. Fowler-Taylor, D. G. Cioppa, et al. 2001. Omalizumab anti-IgE recombinant humanized monoclonal antibody, for the treatment of severe allergic asthma. *Journal of Allergy and Clinical Immunology* 108: 184–90.

Carballo, R. C., G. A. Giovino, T. F. Pechacek, M. S. Mowery, P. A. Richter, W. J. Strauss, et al. 1998. Racial and ethnic differences in serum cotinine levels of cigarette smokers. Third National Health and Nutrition Examination Survey, 1988–1991. *Journal of the American Medical Association* 280: 135–39.

Celli, B. R., W. MacNee, and ATS/ERS Taskforce. 2004. Standards for the diagnosis and treatment of patients with COPD: A summary of the ATS/ERS position paper. *European Respiratory Journal* 23: 932–46.

Centers for Disease Control and Prevention. 1998. Surveillance for Asthma: United States 1960–1995. *Morbidity and Mortality Weekly Report* 47, no. ss-1: 1–27.

Centers for Disease Control and Prevention (CDC). 2002a. Chronic Obstructive Pulmonary Disease Surveillance: United States 1971–2000. *Morbidity and Mortality Weekly Report* 51, no. ss–6.

Centers for Disease Control and Prevention (CDC). 2002b. Surveillance for Asthma, 1980–1999. *MMWR* 51, no. ss–1.

Centers for Disease Control and Prevention. 2003. National Center for Health Statistics. Asthma Prevalence, Health Care Use and Mortality 2000–2001. (*http://www.cdc.gov/chhs/hestats/asthma/asthma.htm*)

Chaudhuri, R., E. Livingston, A. D. McMahon, L. Thomson, W. Borland, and N. C. Thomson. 2003. Cigarette smoking impairs the therapeutic response to oral corticosteroids in chronic asthma. *American Journal of Respiratory and Critical Care Medicine* 168: 1308–11.

Chen, Y. 1994. Environmental tobacco smoke, low birth weight, and hospitalization for respiratory disease. *American Journal Respiratory Critical Care Medicine* 150: 54–58.

Chrousus, G. P. 1995. The hypothalamic–pituitary–adrenal axis and immune mediated inflammation. Seminars in medicine of the Beth Israel Hospital, Boston. *New England Journal of Medicine* 332: 1352–62.

Chrousus, G. P., D. J. Torpy, and P. W. Gold. 1998. Interactions between the hypothalamic-pituitary-adrenal axis and the female reproductive system: Clinical implications. [NIH Conference]. *Annals of Internal Medicine* 129: 229–40.

Cookson, W. 2002. Asthma genetics. *Chest* 121, no. 3 (suppl.): 7s–13s.

Corren, J., D. S. Pearlman, W. R. Lumry, and H. Nelson. 1999. Recent advances in the use of intranasal steroids in seasonal allergic rhinitis and sinusitis. *Clinician* 17, no. 5: 1–24.

Corren, J., T. Casale, Y. Deniz, and M. Ashby. 2003. Omalizumab, a recombinant humanized anti IgE antibody reduces asthma related emergency room visits and hospitalizations in patients with allergic asthma. *Journal of Allergy and Clinical Immunology* 111: 87–90.

Coyle, M. C., C. C. Aragaki, L. S. Hynan, R. S. Gruchalla, and D. A. Khan. 2003. Effectiveness of acute asthma care among inner-city adults. *Archives of Internal Medicine* 163: 1591–96.

Crystal, R., J. Peters, C. Neslusan, W. H. Crown, and A. Torres. 2002. Treating allergic rhinitis in patients with comorbid asthma: The risk of asthma-related hospitalizations and emergency department visits. *Journal of Allergy and Clinical Immunology* 109: 57–62.

Cunningham, J., G. T. O'Connor, D. W. Dockery, and F. Speizer. 1996. Environmental tobacco smoke, wheezing, and asthma in children in 24 communities. *American Journal of Respiratory and Critical Care Medicine* 153: 218–24.

Cydulka, R. K., C. L. Emerman, D. Schreiber, K. Molander, P. G. Woodruff, and C. A. Camargo. 1999. Acute asthma among pregnant women presenting to the emergency department. *American Journal of Respiratory and Critical Care Medicine* 160: 887–29.

de los Bueis, A. B., A. P. Vega, J. L. Ramos, J. A. Perez, R. A. Garcia, D. G. Jimenez, et al. 2002. Bronchial hyper reactivity in patients who inhale heroin mixed with cocaine vaporized on aluminum foil. *Chest* 121: 1223–30.

Dean, N. L. 2001. *An asthma intervention program with treatment of comorbid problems in an incarcerated female population.* Paper presented at the Clinical Updates in Correctional Health Care Conference of the National Commission on Correctional Health Care and Academy of Correctional Health Professionals, May 5–8, 2001. Las Vegas, Nevada.

Dean, N. L., A. Worf, T. Lewis, and R. Jackson. 1999. Results of an asthma intervention program in an incarcerated population. [Abstract]. *Chest* 116, no. 4: 273s–274s.

Dean, N. L., A. Worf, B. Rider, T. Rivers, and R. Jackson. 2000. A cost-effective asthma intervention program with improved asthma control in an incarcerated female population. [Abstract]. *Chest* 118, no. 4: 92s.

Dean, N. L., A. Sadat, R. Jackson, and A. Worf. 2001. A thirty-month intervention program targeting asthma and comorbid allergic rhinitis in incarcerated women [Abstract]. *Journal of Allergy and Clinical Immunology* 107, no. 2: s249.

Dean, N. L., A. Sadat, R. N. Nunnery, O. Umesi, and K. D. Harris. 2001. Montelukast provides superior efficacy for perimenstrual asthma exacerbations not controlled by inhaled steroids. [Abstract]. *Chest* 120, no. 4: 208s.

Dezateux, C., J. Stocks, I. Dundas, and M. E. Fletcher. 1999. Impaired airway function and wheezing in infancy – the influence of maternal smoking and a genetic predisposition to asthma. *American Journal of Respiratory Critical Care Medicine* 159: 403–10.

Duffy, D. L., C. A. Mitchell, and N. G. Martin. 1998. Genetic and environmental risk factors for asthma: A Cotwin-control study. *American Journal of Respiratory Critical Care* 57: 840–45.

Eggleston, P. A., D. Rosenstreich, H. Lynn, P. Gergen, D. Baker, M. Kattan, et al. 1998. Relationship of indoor allergen exposure to skin test sensitivity in inner city children with asthma. *Journal of Allergy and Clinical Immunology* 102: 563–79.

Eliasson, O., H. H. Scherzer, and A. C. DeGraff. 1986. Morbidity in asthma in relation to the menstrual cycle. *Journal of Allergy and Clinical Immunology* 77: 87–94.

Expert panel report (1997, 1999). Guidelines for the diagnosis and management of asthma (Report #2). National Institutes of Health.

Ford, J. G., I. H. Mayer, P. Sternfels, S. Findley, D. E. McLean, J. K. Fagan, L. Richardson. 2001.

Patterns and predictors of asthma-related emergency department use in Harlem. *Chest* 120: 1129–35.

Frew, A. J. 1997. The coexistence of rhinitis with asthma. Quaeritur: Focus VI. *European Respiratory Review* 7, no. 47: 283–307.

Fuhlbrigge, A. L., R. J. Adams, T. W. Guillbert, E. Grant, P. Lozano, S. Janson, F. Martinez, K. Weiss, and S. Weiss. 2002. The burden of asthma in the United States. *American Journal of Respiratory and Critical Care Medicine* 166: 1044–49.

Gibson, K. 1994. Respiratory disease in minorities: Issues of access, race and ethnicity. [Editorial]. *American Journal of Respiratory and Critical Care Medicine* 149: 570–71.

Gilliland, F. D., U. Yu-Fen, L. Dubeau, K. Berhane, E. Avol, R. McConnel, et al. 2002. Effects of glutathione S-Transferase M1, maternal smoking during pregnancy and environmental tobacco smoke on asthma and wheezing in children. *American Journal of Respiratory and Critical Care Medicine* 166: 457–63.

Gold, D. R., X. W. Wang, J. D. Wyp, F. E. Speizer, J. H. Ware, and D. W. Dockery. 1996. Effects of cigarette smoking on lung function in adolescent boys and girls. *New England Journal of Medicine* 335: 931–37.

Hayes, J. P., M. T. Nolan, N. Brennan, and M. X. FitzGerald. 1993. Three cases of paradoxical vocal cord adduction followed up over a 10-year period. *Chest* 104: 678–80.

Hoo, A.-F., M. Henschen, C. Dezateaux, K. Costeloe, and J. Stocks. 1998. Respiratory function among preterm infants whose mothers smoked during pregnancy. *American Journal of Respiratory and Critical Care Medicine* 158: 700–705.

Israel, E., J. M. Drazen, S. B. Liggett, H. A. Boushey, R. M. Cherniak, V. M. Chinchilli, D. M. Cooper, J. V. Fahy, J. E. Fish, J. G. Ford, M. Kraft, S. Kunselman, S. C. Lazarus, R. F. Lemanske, R. J. Martin, D. E. McLean, S. P. Peters, E. K. Silverman, C. A. Sorkness, S. J. Szefler, S. T. Weiss, and C. N. Yandava. 2000. The effect of polymorphisms of the beta 2 adrenergic receptor on the response to regular use of albuterol in asthma. *American Journal of Respiratory and Critical Care Medicine* 162: 75–80.

Johnson, R. A., and D. R. Gerstein. 1998. Initiation of use of alcohol, cigarettes, marijuana, cocaine, and other substances in United States cohorts. *Journal of Public Health* 88: 27–33.

Kauffmann, F., M.-H. Dixier, M.-P. Oryszczyn, N. LeMoval, V. Siroux, I. Annesi-Maessano, J. Bousquet, D. Charpin, J. Feingold, F. Gormand, A. Grimfeld, J. Hochez, M. Lathrop, R. Matran, F. Neukirch, E. Paty, I. Pin, and F. Demenais. 2002. Epidemiologic study of the genetics and environment of asthma, bronchial hyper responsiveness and atopy. *Chest* 121, no. 3 (supp.): 27s.

Kluger, R. 1996. *Ashes to Ashes: America's hundred-year cigarette war, the public health, and the unabashed triumph of Phillip Morris.* New York: Alfred A. Knopf.

Krantz, A. J., R. C. Hershow, N. Prachand, D. M. Hayden, C. Franklin, and O. Hryhorczuk. 2003. Heroin insufflation as a trigger for life-threatening asthma. *Chest* 123: 510–17.

Le Souef, P. N., J. Goldblatt, and N. R. Lynch. 2000. Hypothesis: Evolutionary adaptation of inflammatory immune responses in human beings. *Lancet* 356: 242–44.

Lewis, S. A., S. T. Weiss, T.A.E. Platts-Mills, H. Gurge, and D. R. Gold. 2002. The role of indoor allergen sensitization and exposure in causing morbidity in women with asthma. *American Journal of Respiratory and Critical Care Medicine* 165: 961–66.

Leynaert, B., J. Bousquet, C. Henry, R. Liard, and F. Neukirch. 1997. Is bronchial hyperresponsiveness more frequent in women than in men? *American Journal of Respiratory Critical Care Medicine* 156: 1413–20.

Lipworth, B. J., D. K. Lee, C. M. Bates, and C. M. Jackson. 2004. Cross-Tolerance to albuterol occurs independently of beta two adrenoreceptor genotype-16 in asthmatic patients receiving regular formoterol or salmeterol, (Abstract) *Journal of Allergy and Clinical Immunology* 113, no. 2: 35.

Lui, C. C., C. A. Swenson, E. A. Kelly, H. Kita, and W. W. Busse. 2002. School examinations enhance airway inflammation to antigen challenge. *American Journal of Respiratory and Critical Care* 165: 1062–67.

Maillard, I., U. Schweizer, A. Broccard, A. Duscher, L. Liaudet, and M.-D. Schaller. 2000. Use of botulism toxin A to avoid tracheal intubation or tracheostomy in severe paradoxical vocal cord movement. *Chest* 118: 874–76.

Magnussen, H., F. Kanniess, and K. Richter. 2000. Difficult or therapy-resistant asthma: Clinical phenotypes of near-fatal, fatal, premenstrual, and chronic fixed asthma. *European Respiratory Journal* 10, no. 69: 5–10.

Marsh, D. G., J. D. Neely, and D. R. Breazeale. 1994. Linkage analysis of IL-4 and other chromosome 5q31.1 markers and total serum immunoglobolin E concentrations. *Science* 264: 1152–56.

Martinez, F. D., M. Cline, and B. Burrows. 1992. Increased prevalence of asthma in children of smoking mothers. *Pediatrics* 89: 157–67.

Martinez-Moragon, E., V. Plaza, J. Serrano, C. Picado, J. B. Galdiz, A. Lopez-Vina, et al. 2004. Near fatal asthma related to menstruation. *Journal of Allergy and Clinical Immunology* 113: 242–44.

Martinez, F., S. Salomon, and C. Holberg. 1998. Linkage of circulating esinophils to markers on chromosome 5q. *American Journal of Respiratory Critical Care* 158: 1739–44.

McEwen, B. S. 1998. Protective and damaging effects of stress mediators. Seminars in medicine of the Beth Israel Deconess Medical Center. *New England Journal of Medicine* 338, no. 3: 171–79.

McEwen, B. S., and Stellar, E. 1993. Stress and the individual: Mechanisms leading to disease. *Archives of Internal Medicine* 153: 2093–2100.

Meyers, D. A., D. S. Postma, and C. I. Panhuysen. 1994. Evidence for locus regulating total serum IgE levels mapping to chromosome 5. *Genomics* 23: 464–70.

Morkjaroenpong, V., C. S. Rand, A. M. Butz, K. Huss, P. Eggleston, F. J. Malveaux, et al. 2003. Environmental tobacco smoke exposure and nocturnal symptoms among inner-city children with asthma. *Journal of Allergy and Clinical Immunology* 110: 147–53.

Myatt, T. A., S. L. Johnston, Z. Zhengfa, M. Wand, T. Kebadze, S. Rudnick, and D. Milton. 2004. Detection of airborne rhinovirus and its relation to outdoor air supply in office environments. *American Journal of Respiratory and Critical Care Medicine* 169: 1187–90.

National Center for Health Statistics. 2002. *Final Mortality Report 1999–2001*. http://www.cdc.gov/nchs/ (accessed June 5, 2004).

National Commission on Correctional Health Care (NCCHC). 2001. Clinical Guidelines for Correctional Facilities. Asthma Chronic Care. *Journal of Correctional Health Care* 8, no. 2: 97–107.

National Institutes of Health. 1997. *Expert panel report 2: Guidelines for the diagnosis and management of asthma* (NIH Publication No. 97-4051A). Washington, DC: U.S. Department of Health and Human Services.

National Institutes of Health. 1999. *Expert panel report 2: Guidelines for the diagnosis and management of asthma* (NIH Publication No. 98-4051). Washington, DC: U.S. Department of Health and Human Services.

Ness, R. B., J. A.Grisso, N. Hirschinger, N. Markovic, L. M. Shaw, N. L. Day, et al. 1999. Cocaine and tobacco use and the risk of spontaneous abortion. *New England Journal of Medicine* 340, no. 5: 333–39.

Newman, K. B., U. G. Mason, and K. B. Schmalling. 1995. Clinical features of vocal cord dysfunction. *American Journal of Respiratory Critical Care* 152: 1382–85.

Pérez-Stable, E., B. Herrera, P. Jocob, and N. L. Benowitz. 1998. Nicotine metabolism and intake in African American and white smokers. *Journal of the American Medical Association* 280: 152–56.

Postma, D. S., H. M. Boezen, and L. Watson. 2003. Differences between males and females in the natural history of asthma and COPD. In *Respiratory Diseases in Women,* vol. 8, Monograph 25, ed. S. Buist and C. E. Mapp. *European Respiratory Journal.* 50–73.

Rancinan, C., P. Monlat, G. Chene, F. Sailour, S. Guez, D. Lacoste, et al. 1997. Prevalence of allergic-type reactions during HIV infection course: A cross sectional study of 115 patients. *Review Medicine Internal* 18: 691–94.

Rancinan, C., P. Monlat, G. Chene, S. Guez, A. Baquey, A. Beylot, et al. 1998. IgE serum level: A prognostic marker for AIDS in HIV infected adults? *Journal of Allergy and Clinical Immunology* 102: 329–30.

Rome, L. A., M. L. Lippmann, W. C. Dalsey, P. Taggart, and S. Pomerantz. 2000. Prevalence of cocaine use and its impact on asthma exacerbation in an urban population. *Chest* 117: 1324–29.

Schatz, M., K. Harden, and A. Forsythe. 1998. The course of asthma during pregnancy, post partum and with successive pregnancies: A prospective analysis. *Journal of Allergy and Clinical Immunology* 81: 509–17.

Schwartz, J., K. L. Timonen, and J. Pekkanen. 2000. Respiratory effects of environmental tobacco smoke in a panel study of asthmatic and symptomatic children. *American Journal of Respiratory Critical Care Medicine* 161: 802–6.

Shames, R. S., D. C. Heilborn, S. L. Janson, J. I. Kishiyama, D. S. Au, and D. C. Adelman. 1998. Clinical differences among women with and without self-reported perimenstrual asthma. *Annals of Allergy, Asthma, and Immunology* 81: 65–72.

Skobeloff, E. M., W. H. Spivey, S. St. Clair, and J. J. Schoffstall. 1992. The influence of age and sex on asthma admissions. *Journal of American Medical Association* 268, no. 24: 3437–40.

Skobeloff, E. M., W. H. Spivey, R. Silverman, B. Eskin, F. Harchelroad, and T. V. Alessi. 1996. The effect of the menstrual cycle on asthma presentations in the emergency department. *Archives of Internal Medicine* 156: 1837–40.

Slama, K. 2000. How the evolution of smoking influences cofactors of smoking in active smoking. *Respiratory Epidemiology in Europe* 5, no. 15: 305–21.

Sporik, R., D. J. Hill, P. J. Thompson, G. A. Stewart, J. B. Carlin, T. M. Nolan, et al. 1998. The Melbourne House dust mite study: Long-term efficacy of house dust mite reduction strategies. *Journal of Allergy and Clinical Immunology* 101: 451–56.

Tan, K. S., L. C. McFarlane, and B. J. Lipworth. 1997. Modulation of airway reactivity and peak flow variability in asthmatics receiving the oral contraceptive pill. *American Journal of Respiratory Critical Care Medicine* 155: 1273–77.

Tan, K. S., L. C. McFarlane, and B. J. Lipworth. 1999. Loss of normal cyclic Beta 2 adrenoreceptor regulation and increased premenstrual responsiveness to adenosine monophosphate in stable female asthmatic patients. *Thorax* 52: 608–11.

Tan, K., and N. Thomson. 2000. Asthma in pregnancy. *American Journal of Medicine* 109: 727–33.

Tarwick, D. R., C. Holm, and J. Wirth. 2001. Influence of gender on rates of hospitalization, hospital course, and hyper-apnea in high-risk patients admitted for asthma. A 10-year retrospective study at Yale-New Haven Hospital. *Chest* 119: 115–19.

Taylor, D. B., J. M. Drazen, G. P. Herbison, C. N. Yandava, R. J. Hancox, and I. G. Town. 2000. Asthma exacerbations during long term beta agonist use: Influence of beta 2 adrenoreceptor polymorphism. *Thorax* 55: 762–77.

ten Brinke, A., M. E. Ouwerkerk, A. H. Zwinderman, P. Spinhoven, and E. Bel. 2001. Psychopathology in patients with severe asthma is associated with increased health care utilization. *American Journal of Respiratory and Critical Care Medicine* 163: 1093–96.

Troisi, R. J., F. E. Speizer, W. C. Willett, D. Trilhopoulos, and B. Rosner. 1995. Menopause, postmenopausal estrogen preparations, and the risk of adult onset asthma. *American Journal of Respiratory and Critical Care Medicine* 152: 1183–88.

Ulbrecht, M., M. T. Hergeth, M. Wjst, J. Heihrich, H. Bikeboller, H. E. Wichmann, and E. H.

Weiss. 2000. Association of beta 2 adrenoreceptor variants with bronchial responsiveness. *American Journal of Respiratory and Critical Care Medicine* 161: 469–74.

Von Hertzen, L. C., and T. Haahtela. 2004. Asthma and atopy: The price of affluence? *Allergy*
59: 124–37.

Vrieze, A., D. S. Postma, and H. A. Kertjens. 2003. Perimenstrual asthma: a syndrome without
known cause or cure. *Journal of Allergy and Clinical Immunology* 112: 271–82.

Waxman, H. A. 2002. Sounding board: The future of the global tobacco treaty negotiations.
New England Journal of Medicine 346: 936–38.

Wood, R. P., and H. Milgrom. 1996. Vocal cord dysfunction. *Journal of Allergy and Clinical Immunology* 98, no. 3: 481–85.

Wornsnop, C. W. 2003. Smoking: Not for anyone. [Editiorial]. *Chest* 123: 1338–40.

Xu, X., B. Li, and L. Wang. 1994. Gender difference in smoking effects on adult pulmonary
function. *European Respiratory Journal* 7: 477–83.

PART SIX

Social, Political, and Environmental Issues

18

Understanding the Parenting Rights of Incarcerated Women

SANDRA BARNHILL
TEMIKA WILLIAMS
I.RYTA

In this chapter we will present a general overview of the research that exists about incarcerated women. We will give a statistical profile of an incarcerated woman and discuss the most prevalent reasons behind her entry into the criminal justice system, namely violations of drug laws, defending herself and/or her children from an abuser, and charges related to mental illness. In light of the fact that up to 70 percent of women under correctional sanction have minor children, we will also examine the implications that a prison sentence has on her children and family members (Bureau of Justice Statistics 1999). Finally, we will offer recommendations and a call for action in order to improve outcomes for incarcerated women, their children, and family members who are adversely impacted by her imprisonment.

The most common issue an incarcerated woman is likely to face pertains to who will care for her children while she serves her sentence. She will likely find herself dealing with

- termination of her parental rights, often without due process of law;
- lack of knowledge regarding the procedure for appointing a temporary guardian of her children;
- uncertainty about how to maintain the parent-child relationship through visitation with her children at the prison;
- inadequate legal representation during criminal and child custody proceedings; and
- lack of knowledge regarding how to navigate the bureaucracy of the child welfare system when the state has assumed temporary custody of her children (based on the experience of Aid to Children of Imprisoned Mothers, Inc., or AIM).[1]

It is well settled that parenting is recognized as a fundamental right under the U.S. Constitution. This fundamental right cannot be taken away solely on the basis of a mother's incarceration. Imprisoned mothers are entitled to equal protection under the law in the same way as persons who are not under correctional supervision. In *Troxel vs. Granville,* Justice Sandra Day O'Conner, speaking for the Court, stated:

> The Fourteenth Amendment provides that no State shall "deprive any person of life, liberty, or property, without due process of law." We have long recognized that the Amendment's Due Process Clause includes a substantive component that "provides heightened protection against governmental interference with certain fundamental rights and liberty interests" and the liberty interest of parents in the care, custody, and control of their children . . . is perhaps the oldest of the fundamental liberty interests recognized by this Court. (527 U.S. 1069 [1999])

While society typically views a mother's separation from her children as a part of her punishment, this separation marks a critical time in which the mother-child bond must be maintained if there is to be any chance of successfully restoring the family unit after the mother is released. The location of women's prisons in rural areas often make them inaccessible for families with limited financial resources. For this reason, only 9 percent of women in state prisons are visited by their minor children (Van Wormer and Bartollas 2000). It is estimated that 85 percent of children in Georgia with imprisoned mothers live at least fifty miles away from the prison. Even a short distance is prohibitive for impoverished families without access to reliable transportation or the means to afford overnight accommodations when the prison is located in another city or state. Not surprisingly, an inmate mother's ability to sustain family ties, especially through visitation, may be the key factor in maintaining her self-esteem and giving her an incentive toward positive life changes that reduce recidivism.

Parenting from Prison

The most common legal issues of imprisoned women center on parenting from prison and the determination of who will care for their children while they serve their sentence. According to the statistics published by the National Women's Law Center, women prisoners who are mothers were almost always the primary caretakers of their children prior to arrest (Bloom and Steinhart 1993). This poses a significant problem in terms of maintaining family ties as most women's prisons are located long distances from the major urban areas where prisoners lived prior to incarceration—where their children continue to live, without their mothers. Unfortunately, many women take plea bargains without their defense attorneys fully exploring all possible defenses or informing them about the potential consequences of ending up with a conviction. Many women want and need to get their legal process over quickly, often due to concern for their children and the risk of job loss.

There are over 2 million children of incarcerated parents in the United States. Another 10 million children have parents who have been imprisoned at some time in their lives. Women currently in prison or jail are mothers to more than 250,000 children, the majority of whom are under eighteen years of age (Simmons 2000). The National Council on Crime and Delinquency estimates that a majority of children separated from their mother because of her incarceration subsequently live with their maternal grandmother. Only 17 percent of the children stay with their father. The remaining children live with other relatives, family, friends, or enter the child welfare system by way of foster care placement (Bureau of Justice Statistics 1999). Mothers in prison can literally lose their children in the foster care system as the child is shifted from family to family. The Federal Adoption and Safe Families Act of 1996 seeks permanent placement for children who are in foster care for long periods in order to achieve stability for children by making them eligible for adoption if they have been in state custody for fifteen or more months in any twenty-two-month period and the parents have not met their reunification goals to have custody returned from the state. When parental rights are terminated, the parent no longer has any right even to visit the child. Under the law, it will be as if the parent-child relationship never existed. All ties would be legally severed with the extended family as well.

A statistical overview conducted by the Child Welfare League of America revealed that an imprisoned mother's chief concern is who will care for her children (Seymour and Wright 2000). One in five children actually witnesses their mother's arrest. Because there are few, if any, law enforcement policies or protocols in place to ensure that children's needs are met, children are rarely treated as victims despite the fact that their mother's arrest is likely to be the latest of a long series of traumatic episodes. Children of incarcerated parents are at increased risk of anxiety, depression, aggression, truancy, attention disorders, and poor scholastic performance. According to the Center for Children of Incarcerated Parents, they are five times more likely than their peers to follow in their parents' footsteps of being arrested.

Many inmate mothers are under the misconception that they automatically lose their parental rights as a result of their incarceration, which is absolutely untrue. Their lack of knowledge about their rights and about the legal process can be used as a tool of intimidation. Although laws vary from state to state, there are general rights that an incarcerated mother has but may not be aware of if she does not have an attorney or other advocate for her legal rights. With some exceptions, an inmate mother has the right to

- have a say in decisions affecting the safety and well-being of her children;
- visitation with her children at the prison or jail;
- object to unreasonable goals set by the child welfare system in determining her readiness to regain custody of her children after release;
- have an attorney appointed by the court in all court proceedings regarding allegations of her children being deprived;

- be notified and transported to all court proceedings regarding allegations of her children being deprived; and
- present evidence in court to support her claim that it would be in her children's best interest to be reunified with her after her release from prison.

If a mother has been unable to arrange for care of her children shortly after her arrest, the state may intervene and initiate legal proceedings alleging that the children are deprived. In the case of a mother who is in prison, the deprivation will most likely be based on an alleged lack of parental supervision and care to ensure that the daily needs of the children are met. The name of the agency that brings such an action against an inmate mother varies from state to state; however, it is usually the Department of Human Services. In Georgia, the agency is the county office of the Department of Family and Children's Services (DFCS) under the oversight of the Department of Human Services. Deprivation matters are typically heard by a juvenile court judge. At the disposition phase of the case, DFCS is required to give preferential consideration to fit and willing relatives who would be a suitable placement for the children. If no relative is found, the children may be placed in foster care, which is a temporary living arrangement for children who are removed from the family home to be a dependent of the state.

While she serves her sentence, the biggest threat that an inmate mother faces with regard to her children is to lose her parental rights permanently, either to the state or the children's interim caregiver—usually the maternal grandmother. The longer her prison sentence, the greater the risk that an incarcerated mother's parental rights may be terminated by the court. The Federal Adoption and Safe Families Act of 1996 was enacted to decrease the likelihood that children would linger in foster care for years after being shuffled through multiple foster home placements. However, because the right to parent is fundamental, the state has a high burden of persuasion in order for the court to find that it is in the child's best interest for the mother's parental rights to be terminated. The standard is clear and convincing evidence. The many factors that the court considers include the length of a mother's prison sentence, history of alcohol or drug dependency, previous charges of abuse or neglect toward the children, and whether she is physically, mentally, and emotionally capable of caring for her children. In order to build her case for reunification with her children, an inmate mother will need to demonstrate to the court why it is in the best interest of her children to be reunified with her upon release. There are definitive steps she can take in order to fulfill her parenting role while in prison:

- maintain frequent contact with her children and the children's caregiver by writing and calling on a consistent basis;
- cooperate with the foster care case manager assigned to her children's case; request visitation with her children as much as possible—the foster care case manager can assist with visitation;

- participate in all groups, classes, and counseling programs offered at the prison to demonstrate self-help;
- keep track of all court proceedings involving deprivation and/or custody issues and request to be present for all hearings pertaining to her children; and
- communicate to the court how she plans to provide a stable home for her children upon release.

A common ethical issue that an incarcerated mother might face would be a conflict between her desire to be reunited with her children after release and the caregiver's desire to continue as the children's primary guardian. It is not uncommon for a mother to be faced with a custody battle with the maternal grandmother or other family member who has cared for her children during her incarceration. State laws generally recognize the importance of relationships between children and extended family members, particularly grandparents. It is not uncommon for a mother to find herself in an adversarial position with a state child welfare agency as well as with her own mother. What is in the child's best interest hangs in the balance as the competing interests of the three parties are sorted out by the court. In most states, the custody of a child cannot be given to someone who is not a biological parent unless it is determined by clear and convincing evidence that it would be in the child's best interest to live with the relative in question. The fitness of a parent may come into play, however, if DFCS or a grandparent caregiver introduces evidence of mental illness, drug and alcohol abuse, or risk of family violence—these are all factors that the court would consider under the best interest standard as they investigate the mother's capacity to provide a safe and stable home for her children.

The system in which an inmate mother is forced to navigate while working toward post release reunification with her children is best characterized as a "family separation paradigm." This paradigm begins at the sentencing phase when a mother is removed from the home and her children for a nonviolent offense that may be better rectified through an alternative to incarceration. Even when relatives step in to provide care, children may be separated from their siblings as child care arrangements are patched together, further exacerbating the trauma of separation. For children placed in foster care, what begins as an extended parent-child separation may become permanent as the confined mother struggles to meet the reunification requirements set forth by the state. A final illustration of the family separation paradigm is the failure to prepare women in prison for a self-sufficient, self-determined reentry into the community upon release. Recidivism and repeat family separation are more likely when women leave prison without having come to terms with such issues as substance abuse, domestic violence victimization, and childhood sexual abuse. All of these outcomes compromise their chances of resuming their role as the primary caregiver and provider for their children (Dressel, Porterfield, and Barnhill 1998).

Women in the Crossfire of Two Battlefronts:
The War on Drugs and Domestic Violence

By and large, incarcerated women are in prison for nonviolent offenses, usually related in some way to a violation of a drug law. Someone in the United States is arrested every twenty seconds and 117 people are locked up every day on a drug law offense. In 1998, the U.S. federal government spent over $16 billion on its "war on drugs"—that is, $508 per second (*Substance Abuse* 2001). In 2003, that expenditure was $19 billion (http://www.drugsense.org/wodclock.htm). Women currently serving time for drug offenses were often only couriers or "front" people. Many of these women were unknowingly exploited, coerced, or tricked into the drug trade. So-called drug mules are trapped by mandatory minimum sentence structures that were an outgrowth of the war on drugs.

Although men have historically been the subject of research on drug use, women in the United States have long been major consumers of both legal and illegal drugs. Many women's drug use stems from their need to self-medicate to deal with abuse and trauma in their lives. Because the use of illegal drugs violates societal expectations of women, their involvement in such an activity typically results in social isolation due to the negative stigma. Further, poor women who engage in street-level drug use and/or trafficking report a higher rate of criticism and loss of relationships (Inciardi, Lockwood, and Pottieger 1993). Despite the fact that drug dealing has been most commonly a male activity, women have become more involved in the trade as consumers following the introduction of crack cocaine.

The "war on drugs" declared under the administration of President Ronald Reagan in 1982 and the Anti Drug Abuse Acts of 1986 (21 USC §841) and 1988 (21 USC §844) are directly responsible for the subsequent exponential growth in the incarceration rate of female drug offenders (Bush-Baskette 2000). The incarceration of women for drug offenses was not common prior to the initiation of these drug policies, which focused policing tactics on both street-level drugs (such as crack, cocaine, and heroin) and street-level offenses (such as possession and trafficking). The combined effect is that women who use drugs in highly policed areas and those who have ties to a male drug trafficker comprise the majority of women who are incarcerated for criminal offenses (Van Wormer and Bartollas 2000). Most existing drug law policies often require the same punishment for persons who are accessories to a crime as those meted out to the primary perpetrator. Such policies are especially detrimental to women, who are rarely major drug dealers and are often drug users who commit crimes to support a habit for which they have not received any rehabilitative treatment (Van Wormer and Bartollas 2000).

Provisions written into the anti-drug acts include specific penalties linked to possession of small amounts of drugs as well as sanctions for conspiracy that are as severe as for committing the actual crime. While the 1986 anti-drug act provided mandatory minimum sentences for drug law violations linked to the amount of drugs involved, the 1988 act singled out crack from other forms of cocaine, doubling the mandatory penalties from ten to twenty years for an ongoing drug enterprise and a minimum five-year sentence for simple possession of more than 5 grams of crack. The implementation of mandatory minimum sentencing has had a major impact on the sentencing of women. The actual role the defendant played in the crime can no longer be considered during the sentencing phase. Also, family circumstances, such as the fact that the convicted offender happens to be a mother and primary caregiver to minor children will not be taken into consideration.

The primary goal of the war on drugs and anti-drug policies was to reduce the presence of drugs and drug use in American society. These laws and policies have failed miserably. It appears that the ends do not justify the means as billions of federal dollars are spent each year to combat a drug trade that continues to thrive. The largest outgrowth of the drug war has been to propel the United States into its current position of having the highest incarceration rate worldwide. As these drug policies pertain to women, an overwhelming majority of women serving time for drug offenses had little or no prior criminal record, did not commit violent crimes, and were rarely involved in dealing or possessing a substantial amount of drugs (Bush-Baskette 2000). The end result is indeed a harsh punishment—women serving time in prison as their children serve a sentence of their own.

Some battered women end up in the criminal justice system as defendants, often as a direct result of battering in their lives. For example, some women are forced to defend themselves and/or their children against their abusers' violence and are charged with homicide or assault. Others are forced into criminal activity by their abusers. Many women were using drugs as a way to cope with the trauma of physical and sexual abuse. Still others are unable to protect their children from their abuser's violence and are charged with the crime of "failure to protect." According to studies compiled by the National Clearinghouse for the Defense of Battered Women, a high percentage of battered women who kill their abusers are found guilty or pleaded guilty (Haley 1992). Despite the fact that a majority of these homicides occurred during an ongoing confrontation with the batterer, between 75 and 80 percent of them result in convictions or plea bargains.

Prisons and jails across the nation are filled with survivors of abuse. Women who were abused or neglected as children face a 77 percent higher chance of arrest than a comparison group of women who did not experience abuse or neglect (Bloom and Covington 1998). Once arrested, battered women face extremely difficult choices in the face of incomplete information and poor legal advice at each stage of the legal process. Generally, women are not properly warned about all of the potential long-term consequences of their imprisonment. A conviction or plea bargain that results in incarceration directly affects a woman's employment options, public benefits, housing, immigration status, and legal custody of her children.

Paula Dressel, sociologist and director of the planning, research, and development unit for the Annie E. Casey Foundation, contends that imprisonment, poverty, and racism have worked in concert to create the situation in which we find imprisoned women in the United States. When social assistance is not provided at a level that covers a family's basic needs, "some members of the population may be unable to conduct their lives within legitimate economic opportunity structures" (Dressel and Barnhill 1994). Thus, they turn to such economically motivated crimes as writing bad checks, obtaining public benefits by fraudulent means, drug trafficking, petty theft, and prostitution. The distorted popular image linking recipients of public benefits and crime perpetuate racist stereotypes that mobilize harsh public sentiment against people of color specifically and social assistance policies in general. Racism is implicated in the unequal opportunities in educational systems and labor markets that continue the cycle of poverty and disparately affect imprisoned women and their families (Porterfield, Dressel, and Barnhill 2000).

Recommendations for an Action Agenda

If women are to live healthy lives after release from prison, all of these issues must be addressed in some manner. To take on the issue of a woman's well-being means, by extension, to take responsibility for her children as well as other adults who may comprise her family unit. When a mother is arrested, her entire family is thrown into crisis. The most traumatized victims are often her children, who suffer in silence while separated from their mother. Children of imprisoned mothers tend to experience a wide range of psychological and emotional problems ranging from anxiety to guilt, shame, and fear. The children's problems frequently manifest themselves in behavioral acting out, poor academic achievement, truancy, involvement in gangs, abuse of drugs and alcohol, teen pregnancy, and juvenile delinquency (Gabel and Johnson 1995).

Correctional interventions do not effectively respond to the problems that women in the criminal justice system face. Even community-based correctional programs lack the gender-sensitive approach required of meaningful interventions. In order to lead a law-abiding life, a woman requires more than the typically punitive approach of correctional intervention. She needs the assistance of a large number of public systems such as financial assistance, employment, affordable housing, affordable child care options, public education, substance abuse treatment, and affordable health care for both physical and mental ailments. A woman's mental health may have legal implications should it be brought to the attention of child protective services as potential grounds to remove her children from the home, especially if she has an illness that leads to erratic behavior jeopardizing her welfare and that of her children. Women receiving treatment are more likely to be capable of maintaining their family (Barnhill 2002).

We make other recommendations stemming from our sixteen years of experience in providing direct service to children of incarcerated parents and their families. From the time of arrest and continuing through every stage of the legal process, all women should have access to a full spectrum of advocacy services, including competent legal counsel, support services within the correctional system, and community-based services that can assist women as they leave prison. Additional programming and transportation services are needed to ensure that imprisoned mothers are able to maintain relationships with their children. Programs might include overnight visitation for mothers and children as well as host facilities or families near the prisons where family members can stay while visiting an incarcerated mother.

It is essential that resources be made available to women reentering the community upon release from prison. Amy Hirsch, senior Soros Justice Fellow at the Center for Law and Social Policy (CLASP) offers the following recommendations:

- allow women access to subsistence benefits;
- increase outreach, remove barriers, and improve access to treatment;
- respond to violence against women and girls;
- increase the supply of safe, affordable housing; and
- assist women in getting education and job skills. (Hirsch 2002)

Additionally, the work of AIM confirms the importance of bridging the gap that exists between the child welfare and criminal justice systems in order to improve outcomes for imprisoned women on the inside and their children on the outside and to bridge the gap that often gets created between caregivers and imprisoned mothers.

We propose action steps that would introduce a "family success paradigm" in place of the current "family separation paradigm" referenced earlier. We can increase justice and legal fairness for imprisoned women by advocating on their behalf with the systems that have the power either to promote or prohibit justice. As community advocates, we can influence those systems by

- providing women in prison with information about what they can expect throughout the different phases of the criminal legal process;
- educating imprisoned women about their parental rights and helping them to explore community correction alternatives that would leave their families intact in lieu of traditional punitive measures;
- educating prison administrators about the gender-specific needs of women inmates;
- providing counseling and support groups for the three generations affected by a mother's incarceration: children, caregivers, and mothers themselves;
- challenging policy makers to examine the unintended results that drug laws have had on women as low-level participants in the drug trade;
- serving as mediators between imprisoned women and parties within the child welfare system and other government agencies;
- providing support for family cohesion during exit planning that includes a prerelease meeting involving the mother, children, and caregiver to discuss

such transition issues as a timeline in which the parental role will be transferred from the caregiver back to the mother; and

- collaborating with other community allies who have the best interests of imprisoned women and all women at heart.

To help women rebuild their lives and reclaim their families after prison, we must assist them in navigating the many public systems that affect their prospects for successful reentry. The most critical task of all, however, is to advocate for changes in these systems. Taking a systems advocacy approach would entail focusing less on the needs of individual incarcerated women and more on the various systems that have failed them. Such an approach targets those persons and agencies who make and enforce policies that impact incarcerated women.

NOTE

1. Since its inception in 1987, AIM, an Atlanta-based agency, has provided prison visitation, legal seminars, referrals to social services, and self-help publications to over 10,000 women, children, and caregivers. For more information about AIM, please visit the website www.takingaim.net.

REFERENCES

Barnhill, S. 2002. Residential and institutional services: Visitation and cohabitation strategies. In *Series on Women with Mental Illness and Co-occurring Disorders,* ed. S. Davidson and H. Hills. Delmar, NY: National GAINS Center.

Bloom, B., and S. Covington. 1998. Gender-specific programming for female offenders: What is it and why is it important? Paper presented at the Fiftieth Annual Meeting of the American Society of Criminology. Washington, DC.

Bloom, B , and D. Steinhart. 1992. *Why Punish the Children: A Reappraisal of the Children of Incarcerated Mothers in America.* San Francisco: National Council on Crime.

Bureau of Justice Statistics. 1999. Special Report: Women Offenders. NJC 175688.

Bush-Baskette, S. 2000. The war on drugs and the incarceration of mothers. *Journal of Drug Issues* 30: 919–28.

Dressel, P. L., and S. K. Barnhill. 1994. Reframing gerontological thought and practice: The case of grandmothers with daughters in prison. *Gerontologists* 34: 685–91.

Dressel, P., J. Porterfield, and S. Barnhill. 1998. The policy implications of putting more mothers behind bars. *Corrections Today* 60: 90–94.

Gabel, K., and D. Johnson. 1995. *Children of Incarcerated Parents.* New York: Lexington Books.

Haley, J. 1992. A study of women imprisoned for homicide. Georgia Department of Corrections (June): 15.

Hirsch, Amy. 2002. Every door closed: Facts about parents with criminal records. Philadelphia: Center for Law and Social Policy and Community Legal Services. http://www.clasp.org/publications/EDC_fact_sheets.pdf.

Inciardi, J. A., D. Lockwood, and A .E. Pottieger. 1993. *Women and Crack Cocaine.* New York: Macmillan.

Porterfield, J., P. Dressel, and S. Barnhill. 2000. The special situation of incarcerated parents. In *To grandmother's house we go and stay: Perspective on custodial grandparents,* ed C. Cox. New York: Springer.

Seymour, C., and L. Wright. 2000. *Working with children and families separated by incarceration: A handbook for child welfare agencies.* Washington, DC: CWLA Press.

Simmons, Charlene Wear. 2000. Children of incarcerated parents. *California Research Bureau* 7, no. 2 (March). http://www.library.ca.gov/crb/00/notes/v7n2.pdf.

Substance Abuse: The Nation's Number One Health Problem. 2001. Schneider Institute for Health Policy at Brandeis University and Robert Wood Johnson Foundation, Waltham, MA.

Troxel vs. Granville. 527 U.S. 1069 (1999).

Van Wormer, K., and C. Bartollas. 2000. *Women and the Criminal Justice System.* Boston: Allyn and Bacon.

19

Discharge Planning for Incarcerated Women

Linking Identified Needs with Community Support

AMY E. BOUTWELL
ALLISON KENDRICK
JOSIAH D. RICH

Incarceration offers a unique opportunity to identify and address the destabilizing stresses in an inmate's environment that led to her entry into the correctional system, and many women express interest in seizing this opportunity to make life changes. Structured support is critical in preventing released inmates from returning to poor health, unsafe living situations, and ongoing drug use that results in high rates of recidivism and a disproportionately high prevalence of HIV (Crosland, Poshkus, and Rich 2002; De Groot 2000). Integral to the lasting success of any progress made during the term of incarceration is the development and institution of a discharge plan to link the released inmate with needed community services in order to facilitate her stable and long-term transition into society. This chapter will review the physical, emotional, and social stressors faced by incarcerated women; discuss the role of screening for these problems during incarceration; describe four model discharge planning programs and highlight key elements of these programs; and conclude with recommendations for providing discharge planning to incarcerated women.

Identifying Needs

Incarcerated women are high-risk individuals who are traditionally underserved in their medical and social needs. They have higher rates of substance abuse, mental illness, and infection with HIV and other STDs than their nonincarcerated peers (Freudenberg 2001; Richie, Freudenberg, and Page 2001). A large proportion have experienced physical and/or sexual abuse (Conklin, Lincoln, and Flanigan 1998), and many report having sold or traded sex for drugs, money, housing, or security (De Groot 2000). During the first hours and days following release, women are highly vulnerable to relapse to drug use and/or criminal activity (Freudenberg 2001; Richie, Freudenberg, and Page 2001), reentering abusive relationships, returning to unstable living environments, and failing to address medical conditions.

Drug addiction is one of the greatest barriers to maintaining social stabilization and continuity of medical care for ex-offenders, and it is a pervasive problem; the increase in incarcerated women over the past two decades is largely attributable to an increase in drug-related arrests (De Groot 2000; Pelissier et al. 2003), and female inmates report higher rates of substance abuse than males (National Institute of Justice 2000). Drug addiction interferes with every aspect of the post-release transition into the community including housing, employment, and medication adherence. Many substance abusing female offenders face the added challenge of accessing substance abuse treatment while fulfilling child care responsibilities. Simple discharge referrals to residential or day programs without an understanding of the family obligations women face upon release are likely to fail.

Housing is another particular concern for women being released from incarceration. Not only are women less likely than men to have a family member or partner who is willing to provide housing (Rich et al. 2001), but incarcerated women often have histories of abusive and violent relationships, which make returning to the same environment both dangerous and unstable.

Role of Screening

Despite the high prevalence of physical, emotional, and social stressors in the lives of incarcerated women, screening for such problems occurs inconsistently throughout the correctional system (Ehrmann 2002). A national survey of women's jails reported that 72 percent screened women for substance abuse, 70 percent screened for mental illness, and 60 percent screened for health problems. However, fewer than 30 percent of jails screened for other significant challenges such as illiteracy, history of childhood sexual abuse, domestic violence, or parenting needs (Morash, Bynum, and Koons 1998). Failure to take advantage of the opportunity to screen these high-risk women for the conditions that directly influence their incarceration results in missed opportunities to identify the inmates who are most in need of discharge planning and linkage to community services.

In the institutions that do have screening programs in place, too often little is done with the information. For example, less than one-third of correctional facilities make appointments for inmates with identified medical or psychosocial needs when discharge is imminent (Hammett 2001; Hammett, Harmon, and Maruschack 1999). Furthermore, it is estimated that fewer than 10 percent of drug abusing women are offered substance abuse treatment while in jail or prison (Center on Addiction and Substance Abuse 1998). Many inmates receive diagnoses of physical or mental illness for the first time while in the correctional system. The failure to link them with medical, addiction, and/or psychosocial services in the community leaves them lacking the knowledge, skills, and support necessary to access the resources to manage their illness following release.

Model Discharge Planning Programs

Despite the fact that a lack of community-based transitional planning has been identified as a significant predictor of relapse to drug use and criminal activity among recently released inmates (Hammett, Gaiter, and Crawford 1998; Veysey et al. 1997), the majority of incarcerated individuals in this country are released into the community with nothing in place to help change the circumstances that led to their incarceration (Ehrmann 2002). However, the four model discharge planning programs described in this chapter serve as examples of how to provide inmates the linkage to medical and psychosocial services necessary to facilitate a healthy and stable reintegration into the community upon their release. Following a brief description of the key elements of each program, we will discuss the ways in which these programs successfully address critical issues for discharged inmates.

Hamden County Correctional Center

The Hamden County Correctional Center (HCCC) in Ludlow, Massachusetts, houses approximately 1,800 inmates from both jail and prison populations, roughly 8 percent of whom are women. The discharge planning program, initiated in 1992, is a collaborative effort between the HCCC, regional medical centers, and the Massachusetts Department of Health. Upon intake into the facility, the program begins with voluntary screening for substance abuse, high-risk sexual behavior, violence, HIV, tuberculosis, and hepatitis (Crosland, Poshkus, and Rich 2002). Inmates are then assigned to one of four community health centers according to their home zip codes. Medical teams from each of the four health centers provide services to inmates during their incarceration and following their release. Inmates receiving mental health services while incarcerated are linked to post-release psychological care via subcontracts with area community health centers and mental health clinics (Conklin, Lincoln, and Flanigan 1998). HIV-positive inmates are assigned a case manager who works with them to develop an individualized discharge plan addressing issues such as mental illness, vocational training, housing, family reintegration, and medical treatment. Expansion of this individual case management to include inmates with substance abuse problems is planned. Seriously and chronically ill inmates receive similar discharge planning from a full-time discharge nurse.

Health Link

Health Link is a collaboration between the New York City Department of Corrections, Hunter College, the Fortune Society, and local community organizations. The program is open to women in jail at the Rikers Island Correctional Facility. Entry into this voluntary program begins six weeks prior to discharge. Inmates receive access to education groups and are assigned to a case manager who is from a similar community and/or background as the inmate. The case manager works with the inmate to develop an individualized discharge plan, including links to community services for housing, employment, financial support, and substance abuse treatment. The case manager also provides follow-up support to the client for one year following release (Richie, Freudenberg, and Page 2001). In addition to direct case management, Health Link provides education about the needs of incarcerated women as well as technical assistance, training, and financial assistance to community service agencies and providers. Health Link has also organized a fifty-member community coordinating counsel in an effort to improve networking between service providers and is an active advocate for policy change.

Project Bridge

Project Bridge is a collaboration between the Rhode Island Department of Corrections, the Rhode Island Department of Health, and an academic medical center. Entry into the program begins when inmates are identified with HIV infection during routine intake screening. Medical services are provided to the inmates by a team of HIV specialist physicians during incarceration and following release. Thirty to ninety days prior to release, the inmate meets with both a social worker (who performs a detailed needs assessment for discharge planning) and an outreach worker (who is primarily responsible for facilitating access to services upon discharge). Case management services include primary medical care, gynecological care, enrollment in methadone programs, substance abuse counseling and referral, mental health care referral, and assistance with social services such as housing, entitlements, and nutrition services. Upon discharge, the remainder of the inmate's medications are issued to her, up to thirty days' worth. Following release, an outreach worker visits the ex-offender in the community within the first week of release and weekly for three months. Outreach workers follow up with clients if appointments are missed and can provide transportation assistance to and from appointments to help facilitate access to services. Case management services are provided for eighteen months following release (Rich et al. 2001).

Criminal Justice Initiative

The New York State Criminal Justice Initiative (CJI) is a collaboration of the New York Departments of Health and Corrections, the Division of Parole, and community-based organizations statewide. The CJI was established in 1996 to facilitate and coordinate HIV-related services across the state's seventy-one prisons (Klein et al. 2002). Prior to the establishment of the CJI, a discharge planner at a state facility would arrange for housing, care, and support services for an inmate who was to be released to a community up to 300 miles away. The CJI created a system by which community-based organizations from one part of the state regularly communicate and share discharge plans for an inmate to facilitate continuity and provision of services upon release, even across geographic distance. In addition, case managers communicate with parole officers both prior to release and in the community to coordinate services with the rehabilitative goals of the ex-offender. Inmates are informed about the HIV-related services provided by the CJI at intake, while incarcerated, and at release. Transitional planning services are offered in person at fifty-four of the seventy-one facilities, and via hotline services at all other facilities.

Characteristics of Successful Programs

These model programs demonstrate that it is possible to engage and retain ex-offenders in discharge planning and case management services to address the health and social needs of ex-offenders. The characteristics of these successful interventions include progressive leadership from the departments of corrections; screening for a wide range of medical, mental health, addiction, and social problems, including gender-specific problems (such as history of trauma, abusive relationships, child care responsibilities, housing problems, and economic disempowerment); provision of pre-release treatment and/or counseling with linkage to appropriate treatment post-release; engagement of the inmate in an individualized needs assessment and discharge planning process; collaboration between diverse institutions and providers (such as case managers and parole officers) to facilitate the successful linkage of identified needs with available services in the community; and access to immediate services and community-based advocates upon release to maximize resources available to support plans for change during the first days following release (see figure 19.1).

Results of Model Programs

Both the Hamden County and Project Bridge programs reported high rates of retention in their programs as well as high rates of follow-up at community-based medical appointments (Rich et al. 2001; Skolnick 1998). A critical component of the successful community follow-up of these programs is the establishment of consistent relationships with medical and case management providers during incarceration that continue after release. The trust established by providing care both behind prison walls and following release into the community allows the providers to build on long-standing relationships, encourage ex-offenders to maintain plans for change, or assist a client who is failing to keep scheduled appointments. Also essential for successful community follow-up is acknowledgment of the myriad competing issues women inmates face upon release and the adoption of a harm-reduction approach to relapse to substance abuse or high-risk behaviors (Rich et al. 2001).

In addition to improving access to medical and social services, several model programs have reported success in reducing rates of recidivism among program participants. Lower recidivism rates at three and twelve months following release

Screen at Intake	Address Gender-Specific Issues	Link to Services
• medical • mental health • addiction • social problems	• trauma • abusive relationships • child care responsibilities • housing problems • economic disempowerment	• pre- and postrelease treatment • pre- and postrelease counseling • individualized needs assessment • discharge planning • access to immediate services and community-based advocates

FIGURE 19.1.   Three key elements of successful correctional discharge planning programs

were reported among female ex-offenders who participated in a discharge planning program in Rhode Island (Vigilante et al. 1999), and decreased rates of recidivism were also associated with continuity of medical care by a single physician (Sheu et al. 2002). The Hamden County program reported similarly decreased rates of recidivism at two years following release among ex-offenders who received discharge planning (Skolnik 1998). Additionally, Health Link reported decreased recidivism among women who received comprehensive discharge planning and community-based case management services as compared to women who received jail-based services only (Richie, Freudenberg, and Page 2001).

Programs that successfully foster community reentry that achieves social stabilization and facilitates linkage to health care services are cost effective (Conklin, Lincoln, and Flanigan 1998; Klein et al. 2002; Rich et al. 2001). For example, the Criminal Justice Initiative demonstrated that the savings realized from identifying HIV-positive individuals in the correctional system balanced out the costs of operating all other aspects of a comprehensive discharge planning and community-based case management program. Hamden County and Project Bridge also reported that comprehensive medical services and discharge planning can be provided in a cost-effective manner. The benefits to society accrued by reducing recidivism rates are difficult to calculate and should be considered in any cost-benefit analyses of these programs.

Recommendations

Incarcerated women have disproportionately high rates of medical and social problems that not only affect their own well-being, but also the health, safety, and resources of the general population. The discharge planning programs described in this chapter work to increase ex-offender access to community-based care and

Establish multi-institutional partnerships	• Department of Correction • Community Based Organizations • Academic/Community Providers
Provide services during incarceration and following release by same providers when possible	• Physicians • Counselors • Outreach workers
Identify and address needs in a comprehensive manner with a gender specific focus	• Medical care • Mental health and addiction care • Social Services • Education • Relationships (partners and children) • Economic disempowerment
Community follow up	• Consistent outreach workers • Contact within 1 week of release • Follow up if missed appointments • Linkage to social services
Adopt a harm reduction approach	• Recognize addiction is chronic illness • Maintain contact and service if relapse

FIGURE 19.2. Establishing successful discharge planning programs

to decrease rates of recidivism. Key elements of successful model programs include the establishment of ongoing relationships with service providers prior to release and continuity of care with the same providers after release; comprehensive discharge planning and individualized case management; community follow-up with outreach workers who personally meet with ex-offenders and assist them in keeping appointments; and a harm reduction philosophy that acknowledges the likelihood of relapse to substance use (see figure 19.2).

Although the process of aligning and coordinating interests across organizations that have different interests is challenging and labor-intensive, promising models for such partnerships, such as those described in this chapter, exist. The programs discussed in this chapter outline the ways in which the interests of these different organizations can align to benefit individual and public health as well as public safety and effective resource use. The demonstrated benefits that can be achieved through these partnerships suggest that expanding these models is an important endeavor.

The evidence that the programs described in this chapter work to increase access to health care and decrease rates of recidivism for incarcerated women argues for uniformly instituted discharge planning for all prison inmates. More pilot programs are needed to build this body of evidence. Additionally, the facilities that are currently operating successful discharge planning programs should expand to other facilities and/or to broader inmate populations in order to demonstrate that discharge planning can succeed on a large scale. There are numerous challenges inherent in pursuing this research and expanding discharge planning services to inmates, notably securing adequate funding and political support for these initiatives. Continuing to generate evidence that these programs benefit both public health and public safety priorities will help policymakers view discharge planning as an important and effective part of successful community reintegration.

REFERENCES

Center on Addiction and Substance Abuse. 1998. *Behind bars: Substance abuse and American prison population.* New York: Center on Addiction and Substance Abuse.

Conklin, T. J., T. Lincoln, and T. P. Flanigan. 1998. A public health model to connect correctional health care with communities. *American Journal of Public Health* 88, no. 8: 1249–50.

Crosland, C., M. Poshkus, and J. D. Rich. 2002. Treating prisoners with HIV/AIDS: The importance of early identification, effective treatment, and community follow-up. *AIDS Clinical Care* 14, no. 8: 67–71.

De Groot, A. S. 2000. HIV infection among incarcerated women: Epidemic behind bars. *AIDS Reader* 10, no. 5: 287–95.

Ehrmann, T. 2002. Community-based organizations and HIV prevention for incarcerated populations: Three HIV prevention program models. *AIDS Education and Prevention* 14(B): 75–84.

Freudenberg, N. 2001. Jail, prisons, and the health of urban populations: A review of the impact of the correctional system on community health. *Journal of Urban Health* 78, no. 2: 214–35.

Hammett, T. M. 2001. Making the case for health interventions in correctional facilities. *Journal of Urban Health* 78, no. 2: 236–40.

Hammett, T. M., J. Gaiter, and C. Crawford. 1998. Reaching seriously at-risk populations: Health interventions in criminal justice settings. *Health Education and Behavior* 25: 99–120.

Hammett, T. M., R. Harmon, and L. U. Maruschack. 1999. *1996–97 update: HIV/AIDS, STDs, and TB in correctional facilities.* (NCJ Publication No. NCJ 176344). Washington, DC: National Institute of Justice.

Klein, S. J., D. A. O'Connell, B. S. Devore, L. N. Wright, and G. S. Birkhead. 2002. Building an HIV continuum for inmates: New York State's criminal justice initiative. *AIDS Education and Prevention* 14 (supplement B): 114–23.

Morash, M., T. S. Bynum, and B. A. Koons. 1998. Women offenders: Programming needs and promising approaches. (NCJ Publication No. 171668). Washington, DC: National Institute of Justice.

National Institute of Justice. 2000. Arrestee drug abuse monitoring program. *1999 annual report on drug use among adult and juvenile arrestees.* (NCJ Publication No. NCJ 181426.) Washington, DC: National Institute of Justice.

Pelissier, B. M., S. D. Camp, G. G. Gaes, W. G. Saylor, and W. Rhodes. 2003. Gender differences in outcomes from prison-based residential treatment. *Journal of Substance Abuse Treat-ment* 24: 149–60.

Rich, J. D., L. Holmes, C. Salas, G. Macalino, D. Davis, J. Ryczek, and T. Flanigan. 2001. Success-ful linkage of medical care and community services for HIV-positive offenders being released from prison. *Journal of Urban Health* 78, no. 2: 279–89.

Richie, B. E., N. Freudenberg, and J. Page. 2001. Reintegrating women leaving jail into urban communities: A description of a model program. *Journal of Urban Health* 78, no. 2: 290–303.

Sheu, M., J. Hogan, J. Allsworth, M. Stein, D. Vlahov, E. E. Schoenbaum, P. Schuman, L. Gardner, and T. Flanigan. 2002. Continuity of medical care and risk of incarceration in HIV-positive and high-risk HIV-negative women. *Journal of Women's Health* 11: 743–50.

Skolnick, A. A. 1998. Correctional and community health care collaborations. *Journal of the American Medical Association* 279: 98–99.

Veysey, B. M., H. Steadman, J. P. Morrissey, and M. Johnsen. 1997. In search of missing linkages: Continuity of care in U.S. jails. *Behavioral Sciences and the Law* 15: 383–97.

Vigilante, K. C., M. M. Flynn, P. C. Affleck, J. C. Stunkle, N. A. Merriman, T. P. Flanigan, J. A. Mitty, and J. D. Rich. 1999. Reduction in recidivism of incarcerated women through pri-mary care, peer counseling, and discharge planning. *Journal of Women's Health* 8: 409–15.

20

Illness among Women in Prison and Compassionate Release

CYNTHIA CHANDLER
JUDY GREENSPAN
JENNIFER ROTMAN

We are your sons and daughters, and as exasperated and dispirited as you may become, remember: We do not want to die. We do not want to die in here alone, and possibly under questionable circumstances. Help us, love us, teach us, and pray for us, please.

–Prisoner living with HIV/AIDS at the
California Medical Facility at Vacaville, 1992

For two decades, prisoner advocates have argued that prisoners incapacitated and disabled with serious illness should be granted early release to be cared for and to die with family and friends in their communities. This chapter presents an overview of compassionate release legislation, beginning with its history and a discussion of how women in prison are disproportionately in need of such policies, and ending with an argument for its expansion and the need to address women's health care concerns in our communities while challenging imprisonment.

History of Compassionate Release

The HIV/AIDS epidemic in prisons and jails in the mid-1980s served as the original catalyst for prisoners, legal advocates, family members, legislators, and correctional officials to raise the issue of early release for seriously ill and dying prisoners. All over the country, particularly in states with high HIV rates (for example, New York, New Jersey, Florida, and California), large numbers of people in prison were dying of HIV-related illnesses behind prison walls, alone and without access to approved or experimental drug therapy. It was clear that something had to be done.

At the California Medical Facility at Vacaville—where most male prisoners living with HIV/AIDS in California's prisons were housed in the 1980s and early 1990s—HIV peer educators and prisoner organizers kept a running list of the men who died from HIV/AIDS-related complications. Although no list was created regarding the number of women in prison dying in California prisons at that same time, prisoners report there were at least two deaths a month. Prisoners are 10 to 100 times more likely to be HIV positive than members of the general population (DeGroot, Hammett, and Scheib 1996), and the infection rate is higher among women in prison than men in prison (Hammett, Harmon, and Maruschak 1999).

While the HIV epidemic resulted in numerous premature deaths, family members throughout the country were being denied deathbed visits. There were countless stories of family members not being informed of their loved one's serious medical condition until after they had died, or of being stopped at prison gates because visiting hours were no longer in effect. Prisons were not set up to facilitate clearances for emergency visiting. Security kept getting in the way of end-of-life-reunification with family members and friends. One humane solution to ensure people would not die alone and their families would be allowed to reunite and heal was to develop a procedure for early release from prison for seriously and terminally ill people. This journey has by no means been a simple one.

"Compassionate release" is the term used to refer to early release from prison for dying prisoners (Greenspan 1996–97). It quickly became a rallying cry of those concerned about HIV/AIDS in prison. Early campaigns initiated by prisoner rights and AIDS activists included demonstrations and protests throughout the country. In the early days of the epidemic, there were no codified procedures for compassionate release. Rising to the challenge, innovative lawyers and community activists latched onto little-known mechanisms in state penal codes, often referred to as recall and resentencing laws (see, for example, California Penal Code §1170[d]), originally designed to reward prisoners who provided information leading to the arrest or prosecution of another, to win the release of prisoners dying from HIV/AIDS. Slowly, state legislatures began to officially codify the compassionate release process, clarifying the process. California did not codify its compassionate release statute until 1998, more than ten years into the HIV epidemic, and after numerous demonstrations and rallies at the state capital and outside of women's and men's prisons.

Contemporary Demands for Compassionate Release

With the advent of highly active anti-retroviral therapy, the death rate inside United States prisons from HIV-related illnesses has decreased. However, the need for compassionate release, particularly among women, has not diminished. Increasingly harsh criminal penalties combined with penal policies that imprison the sick and elderly have created medical and fiscal crises in our contemporary prison system.

Since 1980, the United States incarceration rate has skyrocketed, particularly among women. The United States has the highest imprisonment rate in the world (Lichtenstein and Kroll 1996)—beyond that of China and Russia—with women comprising the fastest growing prison and jail population (De Groot, Hammett, and Scheib 1996; Siegal 1998). The rate of imprisonment among women has tripled since 1980, more than double the rate for men (De Groot, Hammett, and Scheib 1996; Siegal 1998). This increased rate of imprisonment is not reflective of an increased rate of violent crime. Rather, this increase is directly related to racist, classist, and sexist penal policy. "This increased imprisonment is directly linked to an increased out-casting of poor communities of color. For example, studies indicate that women of color are 'over-arrested, over-indicted, under-defended, and over-sentenced' as compared to white women" (Kurshan 1996, 152). "For women in particular, increasing imprisonment is directly linked to an increased intolerance for and out-casting of poor communities of color through such policies [as the war on drugs, poverty, and mental illness]. Non-violent crimes, for which women are disproportionately imprisoned, are 'linked to persistent poverty and biased law enforcement practices in low income communities of color'" (Chandler 2003, 22).

Mass imprisonment has been accompanied by serious health epidemics among people in prison, particularly poor women of color. The same societal stigmas that render women of color and poor women of all races vulnerable to imprisonment also render them vulnerable to life-threatening illness. "Societal discrimination directly undermines and interferes with education, prevention, and care" (Chandler and Kingery 2002; Global AIDS Policy Coalition 1993). Typical of impoverished individuals and people of color, women in prison have very limited access to preventative health care in the United States (Smith and Dailard 1994). Therefore, they enter prison with disproportionate rates of serious and preventable illnesses, including HIV, hepatitis, and reproductive diseases and cancers. For example, hepatitis C (HCV) has reached epidemic rates in prisons throughout the United States (Associated Press 2001). California alone estimates that 40 percent of its prison population is infected, and the rate is thought to be higher among women in prison than men in prison (Chandler 2003). Sadly, as a direct result of the HCV epidemic and its disproportionate impact on imprisoned people, HIV is becoming again a strong cofactor of in-prison deaths as coinfection complicates treatment. Once imprisoned, women prisoners face multiple barriers to care and medical neglect, further complicating their already fragile medical condition (see, for example, Chandler 2003; Chandler, Patton, and Job 1999).

Mass imprisonment is also accompanied by a graying of the prison population, creating a crisis of immense proportions for this nation's prison system. As a result of harsher sentencing laws, including "three strikes" legislation and the refusal of many state prison systems to parole people convicted of murder, there is an ever-growing number of elderly and infirm people in prison. In 2002, there were nearly 121,000 prisoners in the United States who were fifty years of age or older (McMahon 2003). Because of the physically and mentally stressful nature of imprisonment in the United States, studies conclude that prisoners' physiological age is at least seven years older than their chronological one. A recent study in Florida estimates that a prisoner's physiological age is actually eleven and a half years older than his or her chronological age (Turley 2003). As the prison population rapidly ages, the cost to maintain prisoners increases.

Professor Jonathan Turley, founder of the Project on Older Prisoners at George Washington University in Washington, D.C., and others have determined that medical care for aging prisoners costs at least three times more than care for younger prisoners (2003). As prisoners age, chronic illnesses become life-threatening diseases, and frequent trips to outside hospitals are common (Warren 2002). A *Los Angeles Times* article on aging prisoners stated that at the California Institution for Women in Corona, a prison that holds a large number of life-term prisoners, "vans carrying sick convicts make 350 trips a month to outside hospitals—at $233 per trip just for the guards and gasoline" (Warren 2002).

Aging women prisoners present their own unique set of health challenges. Older women prisoners suffer increasing complications from menopause, hormone deficiencies, and breast, uterine, and ovarian cancer (Hammett, Harmon, and Maruschak 1999). Therefore, aging women prisoners require a level of care that is not readily available in any women's prison in this country.

The growing fiscal and human costs of incarcerating and treating terminally ill, aging, and physically incapacitated prisoners in the contemporary age of mass imprisonment necessitates a renewed approach toward developing a workable compassionate release process. Additionally, there is a strong need to challenge the systems of oppression that lie at the root of both mass imprisonment and life-threatening illness. In order to evaluate strategies for such action, it is first necessary to understand how compassionate release currently is implemented, its drawbacks, how the process could be improved, and its inherent limitations.

Overview of Current Statutes

The majority of states as well as the Federal Bureau of Prisons have a mechanism to provide for the release of terminally ill or incapacitated prisoners (Volunteers of America 2001; Hammett, Harmon, and Maruschak 1999). Although each state employs different procedures, there are four basic systems for compassionate release in the United States: medical parole, administrative release, executive clemency, and judicial proceedings (Russell 1994).

The most prevalent release procedure is medical parole. Medical parole is a special form of parole for prisoners that are permanently incapacitated or terminally ill and therefore pose no threat to society (see, for example, Connecticut Medical Parole 2003; Idaho Medical Parole 2003; Missouri Medical Parole 2003;

Ohio Medical Parole 2003; New York Medical Parole 2003). Physicians, prisoners, prison officials, or occasionally family members or interested third parties may initiate a request for medical parole (see, for example, Montana Medical Parole 2003; New Jersey Medical Parole 2003). The state's parole board considers applications for medical parole and typically requires a medical evaluation to determine the severity of the prisoner's illness (see, for example, New Jersey Medical Parole 2003). Medical parole provisions often require that the prisoner have a discharge plan, which identifies where she will go following her release (see, for example, Alaska Medical Parole 2003; Texas Medically Recommended Intensive Supervision 2003).

Nearly all states that have a medical parole statute limit eligibility for release based on a variety of factors, such as the type of crime committed (Chandler et al. 2003; see, for example, District of Columbia Medical Parole 2003) and the amount of the sentence already served (Russell 1994; see, for example, Oregon Adjusting Release Date 2003). A few states limit medical parole based on life expectancy (Chandler et al. 2003; see, for example, Nevada Residential Confinement 2003).

Unfortunately, most medical parole statutes do not include any provision to ensure expeditious processing of applications for humanitarian release (Russell 1994). The states that do have time limitations require that requests for medical parole be processed in thirty to sixty days (see, for example, California Compassionate Release Statute 2003; District of Columbia Medical Parole 2003), although the provisions do not provide enforcement mechanisms to ensure timely consideration.

Once medical parole is granted, it may be revoked based on improvement in the prisoner's condition or a violation of the conditions of parole (see, for example, Delaware Eligibility for Parole 2003; Florida Conditional Medical Release 2003).

Approximately nineteen states have implemented procedures to allow for administrative release, medical leave, or medical furlough based on humanitarian considerations (Hammett, Harmon, and Maruschak 1999; Russell 1994; see, for example, Arizona Medical Furlough 2003). Under these provisions, the director of the department of corrections may permit a terminally ill prisoner to be transferred to residential or community confinement for treatment in a hospice, hospital, or nursing home (see for example, Maine Supervised Community Confinement 2003; Nevada Residential Confinement 2003).

A number of states rely on executive clemency or commutation of the sentence in considering requests for compassionate release. Some states allow for a request directly to the governor, while others require application to the board of parole and pardons, which can then recommend release to the governor (Russell 1994).

In addition to statutory mechanisms for release, federal prisoners can move for a reduction in sentence pursuant to Federal Rule of Criminal Procedure 35(b). However, rule 35(b) motions are rarely granted (Russell 1994).

Recently, some state legislatures have passed new legislation (Maine Supervised Community Confinement 2003) or revised outmoded compassionate leave programs (California Department of Corrections 2003a; New York Medical Parole 2003). Nonetheless, there are still a number of states that have no statutory or regulatory provisions for compassionate release. However, prisoners can attempt to secure compassionate release through general parole provisions, general claims for executive clemency, and commutation of sentence through the administrative procedures of the department of corrections (Russell 1994).

Barriers to Compassionate Release

While the majority of jurisdictions have compassionate release legislation, in practice there are significant barriers to implementation, which greatly limit the use of such statutes and extends the suffering of prisoners and their families. For women, these barriers have a particularly racialized and gendered impact, resulting in the permanent fragmentation of families and communities of color.

To illustrate these barriers, we draw from our experience working with women prisoners in California. Through our organizations, California Prison Focus and Justice Now, we primarily work with women that have serious or terminal illnesses who are imprisoned at Valley State Prison for Women (VSPW) and the Central California Women's Facility (CCWF). Located across the street from one another in the small rural California town of Chowchilla, VSPW and CCWF are the world's two largest women's prisons, together confining approximately 7,000 women (California Department of Corrections 2003b). The information in this chapter is largely drawn from our experiences interviewing and advocating for hundreds of women at these two institutions. While this analysis is grounded in and shaped by the experience of women in these particular prisons, their experience is relevant to the broader concept of compassionate release nationally as the sheer size of these prisons, combined with California's political influence on other states' and countries' punishment policies (see Gilmore 1998–99), renders these prisons an appropriate focal point for review of the impact of compassionate release on women.

Political Agendas

The primary, and most insurmountable, barrier to the compassionate release of dying, elderly, and severely disabled prisoners is that their release is unnecessarily politicized. Fear of appearing soft on crime and/or a desire to impose an even greater punishment than the judicially imposed sentence plagues the process at all levels and ignores the actual risk posed by individuals.

Doctors are afraid to initiate releases for fear of reprisals from correctional staff; the women with whom we work report that some doctors have refused to initiate the process for patients they deem "unworthy" of release. Increasingly, women with whom we work are not even being told they are terminally ill—instead, they are being told that they are in remission or "it's all in your head" until they are within days or hours of death. Such misinformation denies women the basic dignity of being able to prepare for their deaths. As 80 percent of women in prison are mothers, this misinformation has a devastating impact on children and communities (particularly communities of color), denying them also the ability to find closure before their loved one dies, and resulting in complete fracturing of the family. For example, in 2002, Justice Now settled a lawsuit against the California Department of Corrections for the wrongful death of Rosemary Willeby as well as the negligent and intentional infliction of emotional distress on her son and her mother for not only failing to notify them when Willeby was dying, but deceiving the family by claiming she was well when she was dying and even sending written correspondence confirming that Willeby was receiving appropriate care at a time after her demise (*Willeby v. Terhune* 2001).

Even if a doctor initiates the process and applications make it to the next level, wardens and department of corrections officials are often worried about the longevity of their political appointments and appearing responsive to the putative threat to public safety from dying prisoners and are reluctant to approve releases. Caroline Parades, a sixty-five-year-old woman dying of stomach cancer with whom we worked, was serving a sentence for real estate fraud. Her release was denied even when she was completely bedridden and unable to tend to any of her basic needs because, it was argued, her crime was a "crime of the mind"; she might be able to reoffend. She died in prison. Another woman, Beverly Dias, dying of metastasized liver cancer and unable physically to do more than bathe and dress herself, was denied release because it was believed that she had the strength to use illegal drugs. She had served four years on a six-year sentence for possession of six grams of cocaine—she was not asking to be spared from a significant sentence. Moreover, during her imprisonment she completed several drug-treatment programs, and, should she manage to use illegal drugs, her compromised health would result in her imminent death.

Sentencing judges are so removed from the prison system that, in our experience, they do not believe prisoners are really dying. We worked with one woman whose judge repeatedly insisted that her health would be fine because state-of-the-art medical care would be provided to her at the California Medical Center in Vacaville, despite being shown evidence that that prison was a men's facility and it would be impossible for her to be transferred there. In jurisdictions where judges are elected, they too worry about appearing soft on crime (Turley 2003). A judge hearing the case of one woman we worked with voiced her opinion in open court that if the prisoner was going to die anyway, she should consider increasing the sentence rather than ordering release to buy her some "free tough on crime" points with little human sacrifice. Luckily, the California compassionate release law prevents judges from imposing penalties that are harsher than the original sentence (Cal. Pen. Code § 1170[e] 2003a).

As the "tough on crime" political climate has increased, compassionate releases have decreased over the last decade. Jonathan Turley of the Project on Older Prisoners notes that in 2001, only fifteen prisoners were granted compassionate release in California. He attributes this decrease to a complicated release procedure and the current political climate (Turley 2003). The California Department of Corrections' internal statistics reflect the dwindling number of compassionate releases in the state since peaking at only forty-one releases in 1995; only ten people in California prisons received compassionate release in 2003 (California Department of Corrections 2003a).

Some of the most blatant examples of politics trumping safety concerns within the context of compassionate release involve prisoners serving life terms for homicide charges. At the time of writing this piece, we have worked with two seriously ill women serving life terms for murders resulting from domestic violence. Claudia Reddy, dying of uterine cancer that metastasized to her lungs, remained on life support for over two months, shackled to her bed and watched over twenty-four hours per day by two armed guards earning double overtime, before she died without family by her side (Taylor 1997). The California Board of Prison Terms refused to even calendar discussion of her release at their monthly meetings. Pictures of her condition prior to death were used by Amnesty International as proof of medical neglect in United States women's prisons tantamount to international legal standards of torture (Amnesty International 1999). Reddy could not pose a threat to her community while she lay on life support, calling into question any objective basis upon which her release was denied.

Similarly, the release of Charisse Shumate was supported by two wardens, a litany of correctional staff, and hundreds of members of her community, when she succumbed to several life-threatening illnesses. Her son had not seen her since the day before she killed her abusive husband over ten years earlier because her family lacked the resources to bring him to see her. However, she died without seeing her son, who had grown into an adult while she was in prison, because the California Board of Prison Terms and Governor Gray Davis refused to act on her case. To avoid releasing her, the governor's aides spent the last weeks of Shumate's life debating whether they could legally force her to be confined to a locked mental hospital for the remainder of her life despite the fact she had no psychological disorder.

Narrow Scope

Political agendas have also detrimentally limited the scope of compassionate release legislation, rendering it nonfunctional. Because of prison and government officials' fears of appearing weak on crime, release (in practice) is rarely recommended when prisoners have more than just a few weeks or days of life remaining. As a result, many prisoners die before the process is completed or are too sick to be transported home when they are released. Their families are in turn denied the ability to reconnect with them.

Attempts to address the necessity for timely release have resulted in movements to expand the definition of who is medically qualified for compassionate release to the elderly, permanently incapacitated, and those within a year of death, as compared to six months to a few days. However, opposition to such proposals is aggressive and politically powerful, albeit logically weak.

For example, prior to codification of the California compassionate release law, we were able to win the release of prisoners in permanent vegetative states or those unable to access necessary life-saving treatment in prison but who were not yet within six months of death. Now we are constrained to only those within the six-month life-prognosis window. Arguably people who are permanently incapacitated or gravely ill would not pose a threat to society, yet there is no mechanism for their release. For example, one woman at Valley State Prison for Women was bitten by a tick while working in a prison orchard and contracted Lyme disease, causing her to become completely paralyzed except for half of her face. We could not win her compassionate release, and she remained in that condition for the duration of her sentence, at great taxpayer expense. Despite examples such as this, a 2003 bill proposed by California state senator Denise Moreno Ducheny that would have allowed for the medical parole to community medical facilities of the permanently incapacitated and those in a vegetative state was vetoed by Governor Gray Davis. In his veto message, Davis cited his disbelief that such releases were in the interest of public safety (Davis 2003).

Similarly, advocates for the elderly argue for the inclusion of elderly prisoners in state compassionate release laws. Recognizing that recidivism is generally the first excuse used to argue against the compassionate release of prisoners, Professor Jonathan Turley of the Project on Older Prisoners points out that the recidivism rate for prisoners older than fifty is less than half that of younger prisoners. In fact, as the prisoner ages, recidivism decreases (Turley 2003, 17). However, despite unopposed evidence that older prisoners present a low risk for recidivism, such legislative change has not been embraced nationally, and a compassionate release provision for elderly prisoners was specifically vetoed in Ducheny's 2003 bill in California (Ducheny 2003).

Absent Accountability and Due Process

Corrections and governmental agencies' political agendas would not create such a formidable barrier to compassionate release if the legislation itself were enforceable. However, there is virtually no governmental accountability or oversight surrounding compassionate release, leaving ample opportunity to sabotage the compassionate release process.

First, the application processes are extremely slow and difficult to satisfy. The application process can be so lengthy that prisoners die while they wait. Even in states like California, where there are time limitations on each tier of the process, the process still takes one to two months to complete (Chandler et al. 2003). Importantly, there is no way to enforce these time limits. In our experience, prison officials and the judiciary regularly choose to take longer periods of time than is allotted for each stage of the process or, in the case of the Board of Prison Terms, simply refuse to hear the petition. The only recourse a prisoner has in such a circumstance is to file a writ in court forcing the decision to be made. Even if a prisoner had the resources to employ this remedy, in all likelihood the prisoner would die before such litigation could be resolved. Even if it were resolved, the prisoner's release is likely to be rejected once the offending party's hand was forced.

Secondly, prisoners have few, if any, due process rights within the compassionate release process. The complicated nature of the process poses a significant barrier to release for prisoners who are physically and/or cognitively unable to advocate for themselves due to illness (Chandler et al. 2003). Prisoners are not entitled to an attorney, and most prison administrations refuse to communicate with prisoners' families surrounding prisoners' health care due to confidentiality concerns. Moreover, prisoners and their advocates have no right to view information used to evaluate their suitability for release, and they therefore have no means of correcting invalid information. Prisoners are left with no one to advocate for them when they are most vulnerable and with no knowledge of what information is being considered surrounding their release.

Women prisoners are disproportionately affected by this lack of due process. Because fewer women are in prison, economies of scale dictate that there are fewer women's prisons. Therefore, women in prison tend to be even more isolated from their communities and families while in prison than are men, and their families disproportionately lack funds to travel the significant distances to visit with them. For many women, the telephone is the only way they can communicate with their families, and when they are too ill to stand in line to make a collect call, their families and advocates no longer receive any information about the prisoner's health. This lack of involvement is used against women prisoners in compassionate release proceedings. It is assumed that the family does not have an interest in receiving their loved one home if they are not in contact with the administration. All too often, when we get involved in a case and contact family whom the department of corrections claims is disinterested, we find that they honestly had no idea how ill their loved one was.

Finally, the lack of accountability and procedural safeguards available to prisoners now is further threatened by the growing privatization of prisons and prison health care. Since the purpose of private prisons is to make a profit, there is every reason to believe that overall health care will not be adequate in these facilities. Invariably, these prisons will reduce staff and services in order to make money. There has already been a spate of incidents to prove this point. The Corrections

Corporation of America (CCA), the largest private prison operator in the country, has been hit with multiple lawsuits challenging the dangerous conditions and poor care provided in these for-profit prisons (Sentencing Project 2002). Navigating a compassionate release through a private prison would invariably be much more difficult.

Private prisons may reduce corrections costs, but they are less likely to be accountable to the policies and procedures of the state prison system. A recent study of CCA concluded that private prison operations provide substandard medical care, by "scrimping on medical care in order to reduce their operating costs" (Mattera, Khan, and Nathan 2003, 67). The study cited a case of a prisoner at a CCA prison who did not receive his prescription when he had only ten days left to serve on his sentence. The prisoner, who had a life-threatening breathing disorder, went into crisis and died as a result of this negligence. According to this study, medical care provided by a private prison is also not well supervised. In May 2002, a woman prisoner in an Oklahoma jail suffered a drug overdose and was hospitalized after hoarding her psychotropic medication. Prior to this incident, another prisoner committed suicide with similarly hoarded medications (Mattera, Khan, and Nathan 2003).

Overall, the influx of for-profit business into the prison industry will only add to the lack of accountability and political susceptibility of the compassionate release process. For women in prison, this will mean that more and more of them will die without reuniting with their families.

Model Release Policies

In light of the significant problems with the current compassionate release process, there is a great need for a more efficacious method of addressing the needs of the elderly and disabled in prison. The compassionate release process should ideally be a combined effort of medical and correctional staff. It should be viewed as a humane attempt to release dying, incapacitated, and low-risk prisoners who are no longer likely to reoffend back into the community. In order to succeed, it must be a practical and workable program that can be incorporated into the overall health care plan for prisoners. It should have a method for linking people in prison with housing and health care in their communities. It should not be a politically laden decision filtered by systems of retribution. It is difficult to imagine what such a model program would look like, as no policy in any jurisdiction has been aptly constructed and implemented. However, there are some important components that deserve mention.

For the terminally ill prisoner, the timing of the release and enforceable time limits throughout the procedure for determining release are essential. Given the pitfalls and delays in most current compassionate release processes, and the lack of accountability when government agencies shirk their duties to comply with time limits when they do exist, a terminally ill prisoner should be eligible to begin the process when he or she is within one year of death. The current six-month-to-death language in state statutes, combined with the timidity of medical staff to initiate the procedure and government agencies to review the request, often guarantee that the prisoner will be dead before the process is completed.

The physically incapacitated and the elderly also should be incorporated into the compassionate release plan. All elderly prisoners should be reviewed for early release when they reach the age of fifty-five. Priority should be given to those elderly prisoners who have been imprisoned in the prison system for long periods of time and have exhausted their minimum requirements for release. Physically or cognitively incapacitated prisoners should also be prioritized for release.

A successful compassionate release process requires a streamlined, minimalist approach that affords prisoners procedural protections that ensure they or an agent they specify has a right to access the information being evaluated and the ability to learn the status of the request throughout the process. It is a wonder that any compassionate releases are successfully completed in light of the cumbersome process and the lack of information currently afforded prisoners. For example, the California process requires the approval of prison medical staff, a correctional counselor, the warden, the director of the Department of Corrections, and the sentencing judge. The prisoner is not entitled to know where in the process the request is or what information is being considered. In the case of life-term prisoners or in states where medical parole is in effect, the parole board additionally has to weigh in on the early release.

The question remains how to minimize the steps for compassionate release and yet broaden the decision-making body. We argue that compassionate release must be a joint public health and correctional medical decision and that measures must be taken to encourage, not discourage, reluctant prison physicians to sign off on compassionate releases.

The statutory models for compassionate release developed to date usually involve medical parole or recall of sentence. The California experience, where the reluctance of the parole board and the governor to grant parole has made national news (ADAP Report 2001), shows how involvement of such purely political actors in the process creates additional barriers to the timely release of dying prisoners. Yet even without these actors, compassionate release processes have demonstrated their ineffectiveness and unenforceability. What is required now is a bold approach to this complex issue.

The American Bar Association (ABA) suggested that establishing a special public health–correctional interagency governmental mechanism to process compassionate releases might lead to more success than using traditional release mechanisms. Such a procedure would expedite and facilitate decision making regarding cases of severely ill prisoners (ABA 1996). The ABA postulates that the creation of a panel of public health professionals and prison doctors could more successfully determine compassionate release suitability. A representative of the department of corrections specializing in compassionate release issues would also be a member of this panel. Arguably, if the purpose of compassionate release is to release dying, incapacitated, and elderly prisoners who no longer pose a threat to public safety back to the community, then public health and custody officials should be able to jointly participate in the process.

Under the ABA's proposed model, once the panel has made the decision to support compassionate release, this information will be sent to the sentencing court for a recall of sentence or compassionate release hearing. The court will have ten days in which to hold the hearing and render its findings. Family members will be located and invited to testify at the hearing. Before granting release, the court must rule that (1) the prisoner is terminally ill and within one year of death; or (2) the prisoner is permanently and physically incapacitated; or (3) the prisoner is at least fifty-five years of age and parole eligible; and in all three criteria, must be found incapable of posing a danger to the community. Additionally, the joint panel will order the department of corrections to develop a suitable release plan within five days of the hearing. For life-term prisoners, the parole board will be asked to implement a workable parole plan. This release plan will be written up prior to the court hearing and forwarded to the hearing judge. The department of corrections will have forty-eight hours to release the prisoner following the court hearing.

There have been recent attempts to improve upon existing statutes. California state assemblywoman Carole Migden authored Assembly Bill 675 in 2001 in collaboration with our organizations to make the California compassionate release process user-friendlier to prisoners and their family members by reducing decision-making time, thus affording prisoners basic due process rights such as the right to appoint an agent and be informed of the process's status. The bill also attempted to extend medical criteria for release to include physically incapacitated prisoners (Migden 2001). While the bill had bipartisan support and was passed by both houses of the legislature, unfortunately it was vetoed by Governor Gray Davis as part of his "tough on crime" political platform. This veto highlights the political nature of compassionate release that is virtually unavoidable, and points to the need for other solutions for decarcerating ill prisoners who pose no threat to society.

Conclusion

In order for compassionate release policies to be successful in ameliorating the human and economic waste of mass imprisonment, they must be fully depoliticized and recognized as part of basic medical care services. However, if such a vision were to occur, it would require a radical challenge to our current punishment mindset that increasingly focuses on instilling maximum retribution upon many of the most vulnerable in our society. The real failing is not due to the inability to articulate a model compassionate release statute or to develop a system for its implementation but stems from our current reliance on prisons as a solution to our most intractable social problems (such as poverty, homelessness, addiction, and physical and mental illness). With fewer and fewer resources available in the outside free world to those in need, people are increasingly tracked into imprisonment.

Therefore, while it is essential to push for legislative reform aimed at releasing the incapacitated and elderly, it is also critical that we begin to challenge the systems of oppression that make those people targets for imprisonment in the first place. We must work to develop and fund community health care services and universal health care, increasing care options in our communities for all people, including those exiting prison. Moreover, we must work to prevent imprisonment of people with illnesses and other special needs by intervening and showing our community support for such people prior to their arrest.

Rebecca Langley, imprisoned in the Central California Women's Facility, stated, "A society is only as strong as its members, and ours is in the beginning of destroying itself. People are like links of a chain. When the chain becomes weak and is not repaired . . . it will just fall apart. When enough people are incarcerated, there will come social destruction" (Chandler and Kingery 2000).

REFERENCES

ADAP Report. 2001. *Corrections: Compassionate release for prisoners with AIDS* 9, no. 1: 21–24. Bethesda, MD: Paraxel.

American Bar Association. 1996. *Compassionate release of terminally ill prisoners: Draft report of the Compassionate Release Working Group.* Unpublished draft.

Alaska Medical Parole, Alaska Stat. § 33.16.085 (West, WESTLAW, through 2003 legislation).

Amnesty International. 1999. *United States of America: Breaking the chain: The human rights of women prisoners.* http://www.amnesty.org/ailib/intcam/women/booklet.html. (accessed December 29, 2003).

Associated Press. 2001. Hepatitis C spreads in U.S. prisons. *Arizona Daily Wildcat,* September 1. http://wildcat.arizona.edu/papers/95/12/05_4_m.html (accessed November 12, 2002).

Arizona Medical Furlough, Ariz. Rev. Stat. § 31-233 (West, WESTLAW, through 2003 legislation).

California Compassionate Release Statute, Cal. Penal Code § 1170(d) (West, WESTLAW, through 2003 legislation).

California Department of Corrections. 2003a. Penal Code Section 1170(d) and (e) Compassionate Release Cases Submitted for the Director of Corrections' Recommendation 1991 through 2003. On file with authors.

Chandler, C. 2003. Death and dying in America: The prison industrial complex's impact on women's health. *Berkeley Women's Law Journal* 18: 40–60.

Chandler, C., and K. Kingery. 2000. Yell real loud: HIV-positive women prisoners challenge constructions of justice. *Social Justice* 27, no. 3: 150–57.

Chandler, C., and K. Kingery. 2002. Speaking out against state violence: Activist HIV-positive women prisoners redefine social justice. In *Policing the national body: Race, gender, and criminalization,* ed. J. Silliman and A. Bhattacharjee. Cambridge: South End Press. 81–102.

Chandler, C., G. Patton, and J. Job. 1999. Community-based alternative sentences for HIV-positive women in the criminal justice system. *Berkeley Women's Law Journal* 14: 66–95.

Chandler, C., M. Rifkin, J. Rotman, and J. Walker. 2003. Prisons and jails. In *AIDS and the law,* ed. D. Webber. New York: Aspen Publishers. 419–84.

Connecticut Medical Parole, Conn. Gen. Stat. Ann. § 54-131a to 54-131g (West, WESTLAW, through 2003 legislation).

Davis, G. 2003. *Veto Message for SB 278.* E-mail to author, October 14.

DeGroot, A. S., T. M. Hammett, and R. G. Scheib. 1996. Barriers to care of HIV-infected inmates: A public health concern. *AIDS Reader* 6, no. 3: 78–87.

Delaware Eligibility for Parole, Del. Code. Ann. tit. 11 § 4346 (West, WESTLAW, through 2003 legislation).

District of Columbia Medical Parole, D.C. Code Ann. § 24-464 (West, WESTLAW, through 2003 legislation).

Ducheny, D. 2003. *Senate Bill 278; An act to amend Section 3041 of, and to add Section 2654 to, the Penal Code, relating to prisoners.* http://www.leginfo.ca.gov/pub/bill/sen/sb_0251–0300/sb_278_bill_20030911_enrolled.pdf (accessed June 23, 2004).

Florida Conditional Medical Release, Fla. Stat. Ann. § 947.149 (West, WESTLAW, through 2003 legislation).

Gilmore, R. W. 1998–99. Globalization and U.S. prison growth: From military Keynesianism to post-Keynesian militarism. *Race and Class* 40, no. 2/3: 171–87.

Global AIDS Policy Coalition. 1993. *Toward a new health strategy for AIDS: A report of the Global AIDS Policy Coalition.* Cambridge: Global AIDS Policy Coalition.

Greenspan, J. 1996–97. The fight for compassionate release in California. *North Coast XPress* 4, no. 4.

Hammett, T., P. Harmon, and L. Maruschak. 1999. *1996–1997 update: HIV/AIDS, STDs, and TB in correctional facilities.* Washington, DC: National Institute of Justice, CDC, Bureau of Justice Statistics. NCJ 176344.

Idaho Medical Parole, Idaho Code § 20-223(f) (West, WESTLAW, through 2003 legislation).

Kurshan, N. 1996. Behind the walls: The history and current reality of women's imprisonment. In *Criminal injustice: Confronting the prison crisis,* ed. E. Rosenblatt. Boston: South End Press. 136–64.

Lichtenstein, A. C., and M. A. Kroll. 1996. The fortress economy: The economic role of U.S. prison system. In *Criminal injustice: Confronting the prison crisis,* ed. E. Rosenblatt. Boston: South End Press. 16–39.

Maine Supervised Community Confinement, Me. Rev. Stat. Ann. tit. 34 § 3036-A (West, WESTLAW, through 2003 legislation).

Mattera, P., M. Khan, and S. Nathan. 2003. Corrections Corporation of America: A critical look at its first twenty years. Joint Project of Grassroots Leadership, the Corporate Research Project of Good Jobs First and Prison Privatisation Report International. http://www.grassrootsleadership.org/downloads/FINAL_cca.htm (accessed December 24, 2003).

McMahon, P. 2003. Aging inmates present prison crisis. *USA Today,* August 10, A3.

Migden, C. 2001. *Assembly Bill 675: An act to amend Section 1170 of the Penal Code, relating to sentencing.*

Missouri Medical Parole, Mo. Rev. Stat. § 791.235 (West, WESTLAW, through 2003 legislation).

Montana Medical Parole, Mont. Code. Ann. § 46-23-210 (West, WESTLAW, through 2003 legislation).

Nevada Residential Confinement, Nev. Rev. Stat. § 209.3925 (West, WESTLAW, through 2003 legislation).

New Jersey Medical Parole, N.J. Stat. Ann. § 30:4-123.51c (West, WESTLAW, through 2003 legislation).

New York Medical Parole, N.Y. Exec. Law § 259-r (West, WESTLAW, through 2003 legislation).

Ohio Medical Parole, Ohio Rev. Code Ann. § 547.20 (West, WESTLAW, through 2003 legislation).

Oregon Adjusting Release Date, Or. Rev. Stat. § 144.126 (West, WESTLAW, through 2003 legislation).

Prisoner living with HIV/AIDS at the California Medical Facility at Vacaville. 1992. Letter to Judy Greenspan, December 5.

Russell, M. 1994. Too little, too late, too slow: Compassionate release of terminally ill prisoners – Is the cure worse than the disease? *Widener Journal of Public Law* 3: 799.

Sentencing Project. 2002. *Prison Privatization and the Use of Incarceration.* http://www.sentencing project.org/pdfs/1053.pdf (accessed June 23, 2004).

Siegal, N. 1998. Women in prison: The number of women serving time behind bars has increased dramatically. Is this equality? *Ms. Magazine* (September/October): 65–72.

Smith, B. V., and C. Dailard. 1994. Female prisoners and AIDS: On the margins of public health and social justice. *AIDS and Public Policy Journal* 9, no. 2: 78–85.

Taylor, J. 1997. Dying inmate's family pleads for mercy. Mother makes last plea: Can't she die with us? *Fresno Bee,* A1. November 15.

Texas Medically Recommended Intensive Supervision, Tex. Gov't Code Ann. § 508.146 (West, WESTLAW, through 2003 legislation).

Turley, J. 2003. *California's aging prison population.* Statement before a Joint Hearing of the Senate Subcommittee on Aging and Long Term Care, Senate Committee on Public Safety, Senate Select Committee on the California Correctional System, Sacramento, CA, February 25th.

Volunteers of America. 2001. *Incarceration of the terminally ill: Current practices in the United States.* Alexandria, VA: GRACE Project.

Warren, J. 2002. The graying of the prisons; Incarceration: Longer terms and fewer paroles give the state a growing number of old inmates. Many are easy prey for fellow cons and a financial burden on the system. *Los Angeles Times,* A1, June 9th.

Willeby v. Terhune. 2001. No. Civ. S-00-2349 GEB GGH (E.D. Cal., signed Sept. 5, 2001).

Afterword

HENRIE TREADWELL

This book entitled *Health Issues among Incarcerated Women*, edited by Ronald L. Braithwaite, Kimberly Jacob Arriola, and Cassandra Newkirk, is a clarion call to all who work to eliminate gender bias, assure women's rights, support strong families, reduce health disparities, and champion social justice. The authors are to be commended for developing a comprehensive and informative compendium of gender health issues for incarcerated women. Racial and ethnic disparities are described in the first chapter. The reader is then taken on a journey that examines the issues of adolescents and adults. Age-related issues are just one valuable aspect of the book as the reader also examines the specific conditions ranging from interpersonal violence, infectious diseases, prenatal care, mental health, and substance abuse treatment to chronic diseases.

The stories of the women in the text are particularly illuminating. The plaintive voice of one woman is heartwrenching. In her words, "Being sick in prison is like being buried alive." This statement is a stirring indictment of the system that women must endure while incarcerated. But the trauma does not end there. There is palpable agony in the words of women as they describe their efforts to reunite with their children and families with no assistance from reentry or public social support systems. The reader must conclude that the system inside prison and the reentry systems are not geared towards individuals' rehabilitation, nor are they family centered. The reader must ask themselves how we, as a nation, have come to this place.

The authors dissect the complex, multisectoral issues that facilitate incarceration and illuminate the plethora of social and physical morbidities that exist and that are not addressed effectively by the prison primary health care system. Poignantly, there is an underlying theme of social distress that reappears in every chapter. The theme is woven around historical discrimination that women have faced in their struggle for equal access, equal pay, equal opportunity, and for honor and respect. Discrimination and lack of respect towards women continues to abide among the providers and administrators of correctional institutions and of the judicial branch. Data on race and color are also presented and the authors deal forthrightly with these additional factors. Disturbingly, we learn, African American women bear the double stigma of gender and color and are incarcerated at higher rates than others. The failure to learn from history and assure equal access and treatment, regardless of race and gender, is enormous. The authors show how women, who have endured and who have been historically most subjected to gender-based discrimination, are subjected to this discrimination in prison.

Throughout the pages of this richly textured volume, we are reminded of the special vulnerability of women, particularly poor women and women of color. Race, poverty, poor education, and socioeconomic condition continue to be strong predictors of who will find themselves in prison. Many of these women are vulnerable in a macho society that fails to curb abuse of women and acknowledge the sequellae of violence in sentencing and rehabilitation programs. Being subjected to harm and violence may begin or precipitate a faster descent into the abyss of criminal justice networks, family disruption, certain types of infectious diseases, and poor health that is not taken into account by the judiciary when women enter the system. We must wonder why the criminal justice system is blind to the violence of poverty and to the horrific price that we as a society pay when we simply incarcerate and do not rehabilitate the mind and the body. Mental and physical health are inextricably integrated except, apparently, in the lives of the women described in the text. The data and the voices bear out this conclusion. Sadly, generations are damaged when we fail to act with prudence and justice as the children of the women witness and endure the disparities of a flawed system.

Having read and been fully educated, we now must assess the implications for health policy researchers, social scientists, indeed for the academy at large. How can future research be shaped that factors in all the variables that cause poor health and subsequent limited lifetime achievement? The rising numbers of infectious diseases, the scores of women with a need for mental health services, and the other conditions described in the text are a drumbeat for change.

The authors have transcended the shackles of basic research to embed what we have seen as simply illness or morbidity within the legal, moral, social, and political factors that our society must address if we wish to rehabilitate individuals and reform family. After reading the book, we are left with the compelling need to act in defense of the human spirit and to save civil society. The clarion call issued by the authors with data and voices mandates a response. The art and craft of devising national dialogue that begins to see those incarcerated within the framework of civil society is the first step. Then, all of us, the academy, the health policy community, healthcare and social service providers, the economic development sector, students, and citizens must implement systems with scientific rigor amply modified with compassion to serve not only the women in our prisons but to serve ourselves, as well.

NOTES ON CONTRIBUTORS

KIMBERLY JACOB ARRIOLA is an assistant professor in the department of behavioral sciences and health education in the Rollins School of Public Health of Emory University. She has two lines of research, one focusing on black women's sexual risk behavior and the other on promoting organ and tissue donation in the black community.

KAREN Y. BAUCOM is board certified in OB-Gyn and is a former assistant professor in OBGYN at University of Kansas Medical Center. Currently in private practice, she is active in women's health issues and is an advocate for holistic approaches to menopausal and hormonal issues of women.

SHARON L. BAUCOM is the medical director for the department of public safety and correctional services for the state of Maryland. Her interests include the impact of corrections on the health of African American women.

SANDRA BARNHILL is a former defense attorney and is currently executive director/CEO of Aid to Children of Imprisoned Mothers, Inc. (AIM), a nonprofit community-based organization that assists inmate mothers, their children, and other family members in maintaining critically important family ties during the mother's incarceration.

AMY E. BOUTWELL is a resident in the primary care–internal medicine program at Massachusetts General Hospital, Boston, Massachusetts.

KISHA BRAITHWAITE is an assistant professor in the department of psychiatry at Morehouse School of Medicine (MSM), and psychologist with the Community Voices Program with the National Center for Primary Care at MSM. She recently completed a postdoctoral fellowship in the Bloomberg School of Public Health of Johns Hopkins University. Her work addresses mental health disparities in communities of color.

RONALD L. BRAITHWAITE is an educational psychologist by training. He is a professor in the department of community health and preventive medicine and in the department of family medicine at the Morehouse School of Medicine (MSM). He recently returned to MSM after twelve years at Emory University. He formerly served as a Soros Foundation senior justice fellow. His research involves studies of HIV/AIDS in prisons and jails, substance abuse prevention, health disparities, and community empowerment.

PAULA D. BROWN is currently employed by the Department of Public Safety and Correctional Services (DPSCS) and is a part of the Office of Inmate Health Services' team. She is the Special Projects Manager, and she performs compliance audits related to the DPSCS medical contract as well as many other duties.

JACKIE BUTLER is a professor emeritus in the department of psychiatry of the University of Cincinnati's College of Medicine and the CEO of the Crossroads Center, a behavioral health clinic. She is a licensed independent social worker, a licensed addiction's counselor, and a licensed forensic counselor.

CYNTHIA CHANDLER is a cofounder and codirector of Justice Now, a nonprofit organization based in Oakland, California, that provides direct legal services to women in prison in conjunction with organizing grassroots campaigns challenging the prison industrial complex.

JOHN CLARK is chief medical officer for the Los Angeles County Sheriff's Department. He received an MD from Meharry Medical College and an MPH in health services and hospital administration from the University of California–Los Angeles.

RHONDA C. CONERLY is a research assistant professor in the department of community health and preventive medicine at Morehouse School of Medicine. Her research interests include minority health and health disparities.

NORMAN DEAN is director of Airway Clinics at the 1,500-bed North Carolina Correctional Institution for Women. His specialty is internal and pulmonary medicine and he is a certified correctional health care provider. From 1972 to 1990, Dean was a clinical professor of medicine at Yale University School of Medicine.

ANNE S. DE GROOT is an associate professor in community health and medicine at Brown University, chief executive officer of EpiVax, Inc., and founder of GAIA Vaccine Foundation. Her research pertains to the development of vaccines for infectious diseases. She also provides medical services to those with communicable diseases at clinics and prisons.

MARGARET FARROW is studying sociology at Emory University. She is a research associate at Morehouse College's Public Health Sciences Institute.

RENATA FORTENBERRY finished an MPH at Emory University's Rollins School of

Public Health in May 2005. She plans to focus her career on mental health research and to obtain her Ph.D. in the next few years.

JUDY GREENSPAN is the chair of the HIV/Hepatitis C in Prison Committee of California Prison Focus. In 1997, as director of the HIV in Prison Project of Catholic Charities of the East Bay, she successfully coauthored and won passage of compassionate release legislation. Greenspan continues to fight for the human rights of California's most vulnerable prisoners.

DONNA L. HUBBARD is an ordained minister and director of the Women at the Well Center, which is a transitional home for formerly incarcerated women. She is a motivational speaker who talks of her experiences as a former addict and criminal offender.

I.RYTA was nurtured at the feet of Gabon' breadfruit tree. She has served as the research and community outreach coordinator at Spelman College's Sister's Chapel. Currently she is pursuing graduate studies at the Graduate Theological Union in Berkeley, California.

ALLISON KENDRICK is a resident in internal medicine at the Baylor College of Medicine.

SAUNDRA MAASS-ROBINSON is a psychiatrist in private practice in Atlanta, Georgia. Her practice focuses upon mood and anxiety disorders in children, adolescents, and women. She also provides psychiatric services to the Metro State Prison for women in Atlanta as well as consultant services in the field of forensic psychiatry.

GRACE E. MACALINO is affiliated with the Tufts New England Medical Center Institute for Clinical Research and Health Policy Studies. She is an infectious disease epidemiologist and her area of research includes HIV and other blood-borne pathogens among marginalized populations, including injection drug users and incarcerated populations.

SYLVIA McQUEEN is an internist who currently serves as the Southeast regional medical director for Prison Health Services, Inc. McQueen's correctional health care experience extends back to 1995 when she began as the site medical director for Davidson County Jail in Nashville, Tennessee.

RACHEL MADDOW is a consultant and advocate on the issue of HIV/AIDS and hepatitis in prisons. She has helped overturn discriminatory HIV/AIDS policies in several U.S. prison systems.

HAROLD W. MOUZON is the tuberculosis data manager for the Department of Public Safety and Correctional Services for the state of Maryland.

CASSANDRA F. NEWKIRK is a forensic psychiatrist completing her psychiatry training at Emory University. She has worked in various correctional settings as a staff psychiatrist and clinical as well as corrections administrator. She also serves as an expert witness in correctional litigation cases and has a special interest in the mental health issues of incarcerated women.

JOSIAH D. RICH is associate professor of medicine and community health at Brown Medical School and attending physician at the Miriam Hospital. He is a practicing internist and an infectious disease specialist. He provides medical care both at the Miriam Hospital Immunology Center and at the Rhode Island State Prison where he does infectious disease subspecialty care. He conducts research involving the treatment and prevention of HIV infection.

ALYSSA G. ROBILLARD is an assistant professor of health in African and African American studies at Arizona State University. Her interests include HIV prevention among adolescents and the achievement of health equity for minority populations.

JENNIFER ROTMAN is a partner at Immigrant Law Group, LLP, in Portland, Oregon. Her work includes litigation over the rights of detained immigrants. Rotman graduated from University of California–Berkeley School of Law, where she co-founded the Prisoner Action Coalition.

DAVID SATCHER is director of the National Center for Primary Care and interim president of the Morehouse School of Medicine. He is the sixteenth surgeon general of the United States and is a former director of the Centers for Disease Control and Prevention.

L. SHAKIYLA SMITH currently serves as a fellow in the division of violence prevention at the Centers for Disease Control and Prevention's National Center for Injury Prevention and Control. Through her work, she seeks to build livable, violence-free communities.

MICHELLE STAPLES-HORNE is the medical director for the Georgia Department of Juvenile Justice. Her clinical training is in pediatrics from Columbia University and preventive medicine at Morehouse School of Medicine. Her interests are in correctional medicine and public health.

BECKY L. STEPHENSON is a clinical assistant professor in the division of infectious dseases in the School of Medicine at University of North Carolina at Chapel Hill. Her works seeks to improve health care for vulnerable populations.

PAMELA EVERETT THOMPSON is a clinical psychologist with a faith-based private practice that offers individual, couples, and group therapy for adults as well as adolescent females in the custody of Georgia's department of child and family services. She recently completed four years of service, most recently as co-clinical director at Metro State Prison for Women in Atlanta.

HENRIE TREADWELL is the director of Community Voices at the National Center for Primary Care at the Morehouse School of Medicine. The program works to remediate health disparities for the uninsured, underinsured, and underserved and promotes excellence in primary health care, optimal health outcomes, and the elimination of health disparities.

CARMEN WARREN is a research associate with ORC Macro International, Inc. Her primary interests are minority health and the reduction of racial/ethnic health disparities.

SALLIE GLOVER WEBB is currently incarcerated in a Georgia State Prison and has served sixteen years of a thirty-year sentence at the time of this writing.

TEMIKA WILLIAMS is a child advocate attorney with the DeKalb County Child Advocacy Center where she represents children in abuse and neglect cases filed against parents by Georgia's Department of Family and Children's Services.

INDEX

substance abuse (*continued*)
incarceration, 20, 21–23, 38–39; factor for mood disorder, 95–96; higher rates for incarcerated women, 19; HIV/AIDS rates, 239–240; homelessness, 199; increased risk of HIV, 57, 75, 77; individual treatment plan, 81; in state and federal prisons, 8; intake screening, 182; mental health, 79; methadone withdrawal and pregnancy, 187; peer associations, 77; physical and sexual abuse, 56; prevalence rates, 125–127; programs, 29; prostitution, 21, 39, 199; psychiatric disorder, 55; risk behavior and implications for intervention, 140–161; self-medication, 24; sexual abuse and, 56; sexual activity, 77; sexual risk behavior, 146–153; theory-driven HIV/AOD intervention activities, 154; treatment of, 129–130, 129, 137; tuberculosis, 199–200; unemployment, 199; violence, 53–54, 126; women at risk for, 18. *See also specific substance abuses*
Substance Abuse and Mental Health Services Administration (SAMHSA), 144
substance use disorders: anxiety disorders, 114–115; behavioral health status and violence, 125–127; overview, 124–125; sentencing and role of drug courts, 127–130
suicide: challenges, 99–100; intake screening and risk for, 182; post-traumatic stress disorder, 119; prevention, 33; rates for incarcerated women, 19; rates for traumatized women, 13; relationship to child abuse, 51; traumatized women, 58
syphilis, 183

target organ damage (TOD) and cardiovascular disease, 267–269
terminally ill inmates, 329–330
Texas, 196, 197
theft. *See* property offenses
theory-driven HIV/AOD intervention activities, 154–157
thought disorders. *See* anxiety disorders
TOD. *See* target organ damage
Todaro v. Ward, 170
Torres v. Wisconsin Department of Health and Social Services, 25

tough on crime political agenda, 325–326, 331
transsexual/transgender issues, 188
trauma: adolescents, 71, 788; post-traumatic stress disorder, 116; substance, 126; theory, 58
Treatment Readiness Program, 135
trichomonas infection, 74
tricyclics, 105
Troxel vs. Granville, 300
trusting relationships, 119, 314
Truth, Sojourner, 129
TST. *See* tuberculin skin testing
tuberculin skin testing (TST), 201, 202–203, 203, 210
tuberculosis: abacillary TB, 208; American Thoracic CDC guidelines, 205–207; antimicrobial therapy, 201–202; Bacilus Calmette-Guerin vaccine, 203–204; case management, 212–214; coinfection (HIV/AIDS), 199–200; comeback bug, 194; compulsory incarceration for nonadherence, 216–217; contact investigation and contract tracing, 214–216; correction's ethnic minorities, 196; drugs and infection, 199; drug therapy, 208–209; factors for, 195; gender insensitivity and custody challenges, 197–199; global and national impact, 194–195; history, 200–202; HIV/AIDS, 194, 199–200; HIV/TB short-course therapy, 211; intake screening for, 183; isolation cell admissions, 211–212; isolation issues, 198–199; latent TB infection, 204–205; multiple-drug-resistant —, 200; overview, 193; poverty and gender, 195; pregnancy, 206, 210–211; prison overcrowding and race, 196–197; racial and ethnic disparity, 195–196; renal dialysis, 210; resistance to treatment, 197, 198, 200; signs and symptoms, 207; special clinical conditions, 209–211; sputum analysis and culture, 207–208; targeted testing, 214; targeted tuberculin skin testing, 202–203; testing for, 72, 202–203, 203, 214
Turley, Jonathan, 322, 326, 327

unemployment, 10, 199
United Nations Minimum Rules for the Treatment of Prisoners, 169